CW01590251

McGILL-QUEEN'S STUDIES IN THE HISTORY OF RELIGION

Volumes in this series have been supported by the Jackman Foundation of Toronto.

SERIES TWO In memory of George Rawlyk
Donald Harman Akenson, Editor

1 Marguerite Bourgeoys and Montreal, 1640–1665
Patricia Simpson

2 Aspects of the Canadian Evangelical Experience
Edited by G.A. Rawlyk

3 Infinity, Faith, and Time
Christian Humanism and Renaissance Literature
John Spencer Hill

4 The Contribution of Presbyterianism to the Maritime Provinces of Canada
Edited by Charles H.H. Scobie and G.A. Rawlyk

5 Labour, Love, and Prayer
Female Piety in Ulster Religious Literature, 1850–1914
Andrea Ebel Brozyna

6 The Waning of the Green
Catholics, the Irish, and Identity in Toronto, 1887–1922
Mark G. McGowan

7 Religion and Nationality in Western Ukraine
The Greek Catholic Church and the Ruthenian National Movement in Galicia, 1867–1900
John-Paul Himka

8 Good Citizens
British Missionaries and Imperial States, 1870–1918
James G. Greenlee and Charles M. Johnston

9 The Theology of the Oral Torah
Revealing the Justice of God
Jacob Neusner

10 Gentle Eminence
A Life of Cardinal Flahiff
P. Wallace Platt

11 Culture, Religion, and Demographic Behaviour
Catholics and Lutherans in Alsace, 1750–1870
Kevin McQuillan

12 Between Damnation and Starvation
Priests and Merchants in Newfoundland Politics, 1745–1855
John P. Greene

13 Martin Luther, German Saviour
German Evangelical Theological Factions and the Interpretation of Luther, 1917–1933
James M. Stayer

14 Modernity and the Dilemma of North American Anglican Identities, 1880–1950
William H. Katerberg

15 The Methodist Church on the Prairies, 1896–1914
George Emery

16 Christian Attitudes Towards the State of Israel
Paul Charles Merkley

17 A Social History of the Cloister
Daily Life in the Teaching Monasteries of the Old Regime
Elizabeth Rapley

18 Households of Faith
Family, Gender, and Community in Canada, 1760–1969
Edited by Nancy Christie

19 Blood Ground
Colonialism, Missions, and the Contest for Christianity in the Cape Colony and Britain, 1799–1853
Elizabeth Elbourne

20 A History of Canadian Catholics
Gallicanism, Romanism, and Canadianism
Terence J. Fay

21 The View from Rome
Archbishop Stagni's 1915 Reports on the Ontario Bilingual Schools Question
Edited and translated by John Zucchi

22 The Founding Moment
Church, Society, and the Construction of Trinity College
William Westfall

23 The Holocaust, Israel, and Canadian Protestant Churches
Haim Genizi

24 Governing Charities
Church and State in Toronto's Catholic Archdiocese, 1850–1950
Paula Maurutto

25 Anglicans and the Atlantic World
High Churchmen, Evangelicals, and the Quebec Connection
Richard W. Vaudry

26 Evangelicals and the Continental Divide
The Conservative Protestant Subculture in Canada and the United States
Sam Reimer

27 Christians in a Secular World
The Canadian Experience
Kurt Bowen

28 Anatomy of a Seance
A History of Spirit Communication in Central Canada
Stan McMullin

29 With Skilful Hand
The Story of King David
David T. Barnard

30 Faithful Intellect
Samuel S. Nelles and Victoria University
Neil Semple

31 W. Stanford Reid
An Evangelical Calvinist in the Academy
Donald MacLeod

32 A Long Eclipse
The Liberal Protestant Establishment and the Canadian University, 1920–1970
Catherine Gidney

33 Forkhill Protestants and Forkhill Catholics, 1787–1858
Kyla Madden

34 For Canada's Sake
Public Religion, Centennial Celebrations, and the Re-making of Canada in the 1960s
Gary R. Miedema

35 Revival in the City
The Impact of American Evangelists in Canada, 1884–1914
Eric R. Crouse

36 The Lord for the Body
Religion, Medicine, and Protestant Faith Healing in Canada, 1880–1930
James Opp

37 Six Hundred Years of Reform
Bishops and the French Church, 1190–1789
J. Michael Hayden and Malcolm R. Greenshields

38 The Missionary Oblate Sisters
Vision and Mission
Rosa Bruno-Jofré

39 Religion, Family, and Community in Victorian Canada
The Colbys of Carrollcroft
Marguerite Van Die

40 Michael Power
The Struggle to Build the Catholic Church on the Canadian Frontier
Mark G. McGowan

41 The Catholic Origins of Quebec's Quiet Revolution, 1931–1970
Michael Gauvreau

42 Marguerite Bourgeoys and the Congregation of Notre Dame, 1665–1700
Patricia Simpson

43 To Heal a Fractured World
The Ethics of Responsibility
Jonathan Sacks

44 Revivalists
Marketing the Gospel in English Canada, 1884–1957
Kevin Kee

45 The Churches and Social Order in Nineteenth- and Twentieth-Century Canada
Edited by Michael Gauvreau and Ollivier Hubert

46 Political Ecumenism
Catholics, Jews, and Protestants in de Gaulle's Free France, 1940–1945
Geoffrey Adams

SERIES ONE
G.A. Rawlyk, Editor

1 Small Differences
Irish Catholics and Irish Protestants, 1815–1922
An International Perspective
Donald Harman Akenson

2 Two Worlds
The Protestant Culture of Nineteenth-Century Ontario
William Westfall

3 An Evangelical Mind
Nathanael Burwash and the Methodist Tradition in Canada, 1839–1918
Marguerite Van Die

4 The Dévotes
Women and Church in Seventeenth-Century France
Elizabeth Rapley

5 The Evangelical Century
College and Creed in English Canada from the Great Revival to the Great Depression
Michael Gauvreau

6 The German Peasants' War and Anabaptist Community of Goods
James M. Stayer

7 A World Mission
Canadian Protestantism and the Quest for a New International Order, 1918–1939
Robert Wright

8 Serving the Present Age
Revivalism, Progressivism, and the Methodist Tradition in Canada
Phyllis D. Airhart

9 A Sensitive Independence
Canadian Methodist Women Missionaries in Canada and the Orient, 1881–1925
Rosemary R. Gagan

10 God's Peoples
Covenant and Land in South Africa, Israel, and Ulster
Donald Harman Akenson

11 Creed and Culture
The Place of English-Speaking Catholics in Canadian Society, 1750–1930
Edited by Terrence Murphy and Gerald Stortz

12 Piety and Nationalism
Lay Voluntary Associations and the Creation of an Irish-Catholic Community in Toronto, 1850–1895
Brian P. Clarke

13 Amazing Grace
Studies in Evangelicalism in Australia, Britain, Canada, and the United States
Edited by George Rawlyk and Mark A. Noll

14 Children of Peace
W. John McIntyre

15 A Solitary Pillar
Montreal's Anglican Church and the Quiet Revolution
Joan Marshall

16 Padres in No Man's Land
Canadian Chaplains and the Great War
Duff Crerar

17 Christian Ethics and Political Economy in North America
A Critical Analysis of U.S. and Canadian Approaches
P. Travis Kroeker

18 Pilgrims in Lotus Land
Conservative Protestantism in British Columbia, 1917–1981
Robert K. Burkinshaw

19 Through Sunshine and Shadow
The Woman's Christian Temperance Union, Evangelicalism, and Reform in Ontario, 1874–1930
Sharon Cook

20 Church, College, and Clergy
A History of Theological Education at Knox College, Toronto, 1844–1994
Brian J. Fraser

21 The Lord's Dominion
The History of Canadian Methodism
Neil Semple

22 A Full-Orbed Christianity
The Protestant Churches and Social Welfare in Canada, 1900–1940
Nancy Christie and Michael Gauvreau

23 Evangelism and Apostasy
The Evolution and Impact of Evangelicals in Modern Mexico
Kurt Bowen

24 The Chignecto Covenanters
A Regional History of Reformed Presbyterianism in New Brunswick and Nova Scotia, 1827–1905
Eldon Hay

25 Methodists and Women's Education in Ontario, 1836–1925
Johanne Selles

26 Puritanism and Historical Controversy
William Lamont

Political Ecumenism

Catholics, Jews, and Protestants in de Gaulle's Free France, 1940–1945

GEOFFREY ADAMS

McGill-Queen's University Press
Montreal & Kingston · London · Ithaca

© McGill-Queen's University Press 2006
ISBN-13: 978-0-7735-3076-8 ISBN-10: 0-7735-3076-2

Legal deposit fourth quarter 2006
Bibliothèque nationale du Québec

Printed in Canada on acid-free paper.

This book has been published with the help of a grant from the Canadian Federation for the Humanities and Social Sciences, through the Aid to Scholarly Publications Programme, using funds provided by the Social Sciences and Humanities Research Council of Canada.

McGill-Queen's University Press acknowledges the support of the Canada Council for the Arts for our publishing program. We also acknowledge the financial support of the Government of Canada through the Book Publishing Industry Development Program (BPIDP) for our publishing activities.

Library and Archives Canada Cataloguing in Publication

Adams, Geoffrey, 1926–
Political ecumenism : Catholics, Jews, and Protestants in de Gaulle's Free France, 1940–1945 / Geoffrey Adams.

(McGill-Queen's studies in the history of religion. Series two ; 46)
Includes bibliographical references and index.
ISBN-13: 978-0-7735-3076-8 ISBN-10: 0-7735-3076-2

1. Religion and politics – France – History – 20th century. 2. France – Politics and government – 1940–1945. I. Title. II. Series.

DC397.A33 2006 944.081'6 C2006-901781-6

Typeset in New Baskerville 10/13
by Infoscan Collette, Quebec City

Contents

Chronology of Events

1940

18 June	De Gaulle's appeal to the French over BBC; launching of La France libre
28 June	British government recognizes de Gaulle as "Chef des Français libres"
7 August	De Gaulle/Churchill accord regulates relations between Free French and UK
27 October	Conseil de défense de l'Empire created at Brazzaville in the Congo
24 December	British government recognizes the Conseil

1941

14 July	De Gaulle condemns St. Jean d'Acre armistice between Vichy and UK which ends Syrian conflict
24 September	Creation of Comité national français (CNF)

1942

1 January	Jean Moulin parachuted into France to coordinate internal and external resistance

9 July	USA recognizes CNF as "the symbol of French resistance to the Axis"
14 July	La France libre becomes La France combattante
8 November	Allied landings in French North Africa; Algiers Gaullists stage coup; Admiral Darlan orders resistance to Allies
9 November	General Giraud arrives in Algiers
13 November	Darlan recognized by USA as High Commissioner for North Africa; La France combattante rejects Darlan
7 December	Darlan assumes role of head of state in Algiers, creates a Conseil impérial
24 December	Darlan assassinated
26 December	Giraud becomes civilian and military commander-in-chief, North Africa

1943

15 May	The Conseil national de la Résistance (CNR) is founded inside France; de Gaulle is recognized as its leader
30 May	De Gaulle establishes headquarters in Algiers
3 June	Creation of the Comité français de libération nationale (CFLN) in Algiers with de Gaulle and Giraud as co-presidents
31 July	CFLN names de Gaulle sole president
26 August	UK, USA, and USSR offer limited recognition of CFLN
13 September	France combattante landing in Corsica
17 September	Formation of Assemblée consultative provisoire in Algiers

1944

1 February	Creation of Forces françaises de l'intérieur (FFI)
7 March	*Ordonnance* grants 60,000 Muslims French citizenship
21 April	CFLN *ordonnance* defines the organization of public authority as of Liberation
3 June	CFLN becomes the Gouvernement provisoire de la République française (GPRF) with de Gaulle as president
4 June	De Gaulle returns to London on eve of D-Day
6 June	D-Day
8–20 July	Allied governments recognize GPRF
14 June	De Gaulle installs first *Commissaire de la République* in Normandy

9 August	GPRF *ordonnance* restores republican legality on liberated French territory
25 August	Liberation of Paris
31 August	Transfer of GPRF to Paris
9 September	Formation of a Ministry of National Unanimity under de Gaulle
23 October	De jure recognition of GPRF by UK, USA, USSR
7 November	First session of Assemblée consultative provisoire
26 November	Founding convention of the Mouvement républicain populaire (MRP), Maurice Schumann president, Marc Sangnier honorary president

1945

22 February	*Ordonnance* establishes comités d'entreprises, confirmed by law on 16 May 1946
5 April	Pierre Mendès France resigns
7–9 May	Nazi Germany capitulates
8 May	Bloody revolt by Algerian nationalists at Sétif
21 October	Legislative elections
13 November	De Gaulle heads new government

1946

20 January	De Gaulle resigns
16 June	De Gaulle speaks at Bayeux on need for constitutional reform
23 October	Episcopate warns of new battle over *laïcité*

1947

7 April	Launching of the Rassemblement du peuple français (RPF)

Free French Leadership: A Politically Ecumenical Coalition

CATHOLICS

Georges Bidault
François Bloch-Laîné
Claude Bouchinet-Serreulles
René Capitant
Francis-Louis Closon
Geoffroy de Courcel
Charles de Gaulle
Elisabeth de Miribel
Christian Fouchet
Claude Hettier de Boislambert
Louis Joxe
Gaston Palewski
René Pleven
André Postel-Vinay
Maurice Schumann
Pierre Viénot
Simone Weil*

JEWS

José Aboulker and the Jewish Gaullists of Algiers
Raymond Aubrac
Marcel Bleustein-Blanchet
Georges Boris
René Cassin
Jean-Louis Crémieux-Brilhac
René Mayer
Pierre Mendès France
Jean Pierre-Bloch
André Weil-Curiel
André Wormser

---

* See chapter 11 for an analysis of Weil's non-sacramental links to Catholicism.

PROTESTANTS

Lucie Aubrac
Jean-Marc Boegner
François Coulet
Maurice Couve de Murville
Pierre Denis ("Rauzan")
André Diethelm
Albert Guigui
Pierre Lefranc
René Massigli
André Philip
Jacques Soustelle
Louis Vallon

Free French Organization at the End of 1943

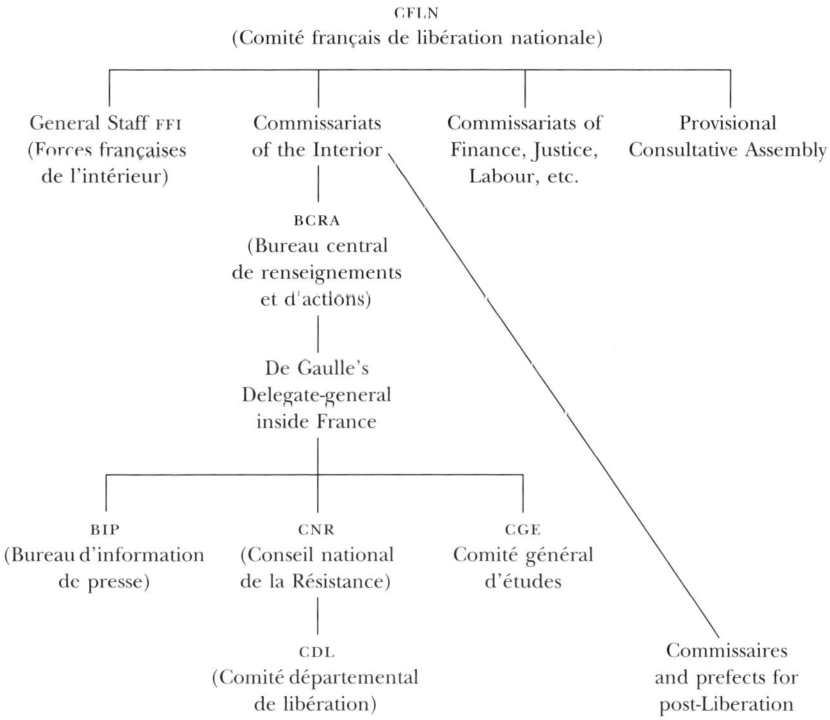

Abbreviations

AMGOT	Allied Military Government for Occupied Territories
AN	Archives nationales
BCRA	Bureau central de renseignements et d'action
CAS	Comité d'action socialiste
CFLN	Comité français de la libération nationale
CFTC	Confédération française des travailleurs chrétiens
CGE	Comité général d'études
CGT	Confédération générale du travail
CNF	Comité national français
CNR	Conseil national de la Résistance
CRIF	Conseil représentatif des institutions juives
DGSS	Direction générale des services spéciaux (Alger)
FFI	Forces françaises de l'intérieur
FNSP	Fondation nationale des sciences politiques
GPRF	Gouvernement provisoire de la République française
HSI	Haute société israëlite
HSP	Haute société Protestante
MLN	Mouvement de la libération nationale
MRP	Mouvement républicain populaire
MUR	Mouvements unis de Résistance
PCF	Parti communiste français
PDP	Parti démocrate populaire
PS	Parti socialiste

SFIO	Parti socialiste français (Section française de l'Internationale ouvrière)
STO	Service du travail obligatoire
UDSR	Union démocratique et socialiste de la Résistance
UGIF	Union générale des israélites de France

Acknowledgments

While this study was still at the conceptual stage, the author was fortunate enough to receive both encouragement and friendly admonition from a number of established scholars. Jean-Louis Crémieux-Brilhac, whose masterful account of La France libre is enriched by vivid memories of his own experience as a Jewish recruit to the Gaullist cause in wartime, found the perspective of my research unconventional but well worth pursuing. Professor Jacques Poujol, who has written extensively about the French Protestant minority in the modern era, offered invaluable guidance, not only as to the project's overall design but in terms of particular leads to follow. Professor René Remond, whose many studies of French Catholicism since the Revolution have become standard reference works, saw in my proposal a reflection of his own interest in the coming together of the Two Frances, Catholic and republican, through their shared struggle against fascism. Professor Michel Meslin of the Sorbonne warmly encouraged both my proposal and its particular approach and recommended a number of key figures to interview.

As it turned out, the timing of this research project was very fortunate. By 2000, a generation after de Gaulle's death, nearly all his wartime colleagues had either published an account of their involvement in La France libre or confided their personal papers to public archives. Several of the general's wartime collaborators were still alive during the early stages of this investigation and were kind enough to share their memories of the Free French epic during what were (from the writer's point of view at least) rewarding interviews. Jean-Marc Boegner, *ambassadeur de France,* one of de Gaulle's intimates after the war; Maurice Couve de Murville, future diplomat and prime minister, who joined the Gaullist camp in Algiers; Pierre Lefranc, the Protestant law student who organized the first Free French demonstration inside France in November 1940; and Maurice Schumann, broadcaster of the Free French gospel over the BBC during the war, all conveyed, each in his own way, the politically ecumenical spirit which had animated the Gaullist struggle against Vichy and the Nazis.

Nowhere in my pursuit of primary sources, unpublished theses, or personal contacts, was this researcher given a warmer welcome or more effective guidance than at the Fondation nationale des sciences politiques. The Foundation's chief archivist, Odile Gaultier-Voituriez, matched generous interest in my investigation with vital information about key persons to meet and documentation to track down. Catherine Trouiller, chief archivist at the Institut Charles de Gaulle, pointed me toward works in progress close to my own research and facilitated meetings with their authors. Agnès Callu, in charge of many of the twentieth-century holdings at the Archives nationales, guided me toward relevant holdings in the public domain and indicated to whom I should turn to consult papers still kept from unauthorized access.

At the Quai d'Orsay, Monique Constant introduced me to diplomatic papers from the improvised "Foreign Affairs" branch of Free France. Raphaële Ulrich-Pier very kindly shared with me some of her ongoing research on the Protestant diplomat René Massigli. Christine Lévisse-Touzé of the Musée Jean-Moulin et de la Résistance helped me understand the labyrinthine politics of French North Africa in the 1940s. Karen Taïeb of the Centre de documentation juive contemporaine very kindly forwarded photocopies of unpublished letters written by Jewish participants in the November 1942 insurrection of Gaullists in Algiers. Mme Marie-Louise Gaultier-Voituriez graciously made available a series of primary and secondary documents concerning Marc Sangnier, a seminal figure in the adaptation of French Catholic thinkers to republican and democratic thought.

Jean-Paul Coupal, while engaged in his own multi-volume historiographical research and publication, took time out to read the text at an early stage and urged a number of excisions and elaborations, all of which were gratefully adopted, allowing me to produce what I believe is a more coherent and persuasive argument. My friend Neville Saulter, an accomplished translator with a fine feeling for nuance in both English and French and a keen eye for clarity of expression, helped me find more felicitous turns of phrase or clearer renderings of one language into the other.

Members of Scholars' Circle, a congenial group of colleagues at Concordia University who meet once a month to share and critique works-in-progress, offered warm support for this project from the outset. Two of them in particular, former students of mine, gave me precious personal encouragement. Robert Calderisi, who won a Rhodes Scholarship in 1968, went on to pursue a distinguished career with the World Bank and has published a book on the challenges facing sub-saharan Africa and the means of resolving them; Abigail Sibley, who obtained a doctorate in history at McGill University, taught in the Humanities Department of Dawson College before retiring to demonstrate her gifts as an artist. Both convinced me to make a number of changes in the form and the content of what follows.

I owe a great deal to the staff of Concordia University Interlibrary Loans Department, and in particular to Ursula Hakien, Wendy Knechtel, and Paule Taschereau, for their invaluable help in negotiating the transfer to Montreal of monographs from a wide variety of sources in Canada, the United States, and France.

I am especially obliged to Philip Cercone, senior editor of McGill-Queen's University Press, who offered his support for my manuscript from the beginning; to Joan McGilvray, coordinating editor who guided and reassured me through the steps leading from submission to publication; and to Kate Merriman, a perfectionist with a scholarly interest in ecumenical dialogue, who did her best to correct and enhance my style and thereby to make my argument as coherent as I could wish it to be.

In the end, it must be said, none were more directly or personally involved in bringing this project to fruition than Catherine Bergeron, Nevena Jerić, Crystal Leger, and Louise McDuff, who took on the tedious task of transforming my scrappy typescript into elegantly formatted text. For their patience, good humour, and deft execution, I am truly grateful.

For whatever flaws in style, errors in fact, or questionable argumentation may remain in what follows, I am of course solely and entirely responsible.

Soupault, lead cartoonist for the weekly *Au Pilori*, portrays Léon Blum, his Popular Front colleagues, and media supporters as part of a Judeo-Masonic cabal that has put the French state in grave peril and makes clear that their root-and-branch removal is essential. A few years later Vichy propagandists, using equally brutal imagery, would help incite the arrest, deportation, even the death of Jews and Freemasons. (Courtesy Roger-Viollet, Paris)

The platform party at the founding convention of the Mouvement républicain populaire held in Paris, November 1944. At the microphone is Maurice Schumann, leader of the new formation. To his left is Marc Sangnier, founding father of French Christian Democracy, who had just been named président d'honneur of the MRP. (Courtesy Roger-Viollet, Paris)

Elisabeth de Miribel typed de Gaulle's famous 18 June 1940 speech to the French people over the BBC, then spent three years championing the Free French cause across Canada before moving to Algiers. (Photo by Karsh, courtesy Portrait Gallery of Canada)

René Mayer, grandson of the Chief Rabbi of Paris, a senior public servant in the interwar years, remained in France until the German occupation of Vichy territory in November 1942 when he escaped to Algiers to serve as CFLN commissioner of the merchant marine and of communications. (Courtesy Roger-Viollet, Paris)

Professor René Cassin provided a juridical framework for Free France, championed republican values within the Gaullist camp, and, at the war's end, demanded that collaborators be appropriately punished. (Courtesy Roger-Viollet, Paris)

The left-wing ethnologist Jacques Soustelle joined Free France in the fall of 1940 and served as propagandist, counter-intelligence organizer, and, occasionally, as speech-writer for de Gaulle. (Courtesy Roger-Viollet, Paris)

Medical student José Aboulker led the predominantly Jewish insurrection against Vichy forces in Algiers timed to coincide with Operation "Torch", the Anglo-American landings in North Africa on 7/8 November 1942. (Courtesy Mémorial de la Shoah/CDJC)

Socialist deputy and law professor André Philip arrived in London in July 1942 and was immediately named commissioner of the interior, in which role he served as a vital link to the Resistance. In November 1943, de Gaulle put him in charge of relations with the fledgling Provisional Consultative Assembly established in Algiers. (Author's photo)

Pierre Mendès France in his Air Force uniform poses with a group of comrades in front of the Free French banner. Mendès flew on a number of bombing missions over France in the summer and fall of 1943. (Courtesy Michel Mendès France)

Members of the "French Committee of National Liberation" as constituted in Algiers in November 1943 under the presidency of General de Gaulle. This same body, somewhat modified by "cabinet shuffles," designated itself as the Provisional Government of the French Republic on 3 June 1944, three days before D-Day. (Courtesy Roger-Viollet, Paris)

President de Gaulle of the CFLN and his finance minister Pierre Mendès France, Algiers, Fall 1943. In the post-war era, de Gaulle led a rassemblement on the Right while Mendès become an icon of the Left. (Photo courtesy Michel Mendès France)

"Ecumenical" diplomacy in the post-war world: The Protestant Maurice Couve de Murville and the Catholic Georges Bidault represent France at an international conference. (Courtesy Roger-Viollet, Paris)

POLITICAL ECUMENISM

INTRODUCTION

The Free French Challenge: Reuniting the Two Frances

It has been rightly noted that men of all backgrounds, believers and unbelievers, Jews and Christians, met and came to know one another in the ranks of the Resistance. Rationalists and Catholics, whose rivalry has filled the history of modern France, found an underlying kinship of inspiration during this experience. Barriers between them fell away and eyes were opened.

Raymond Aron, *De l'Armistice à l'insurrection nationale, Introduction* (1945)

When, on 18 June 1940, in the aftermath of France's defeat and the assumption of power by Marshal Philippe Pétain, Charles de Gaulle appealed to his fellow citizens over the BBC to join him in continuing the fight against Nazi Germany, he initiated a process that would reunite the Two Frances (revolutionary and counter-revolutionary) which had been in open or covert conflict since 1789. And, when men and women of France's "three religious families," Jews and Protestants as well as Catholics, who had been involved in this conflict, joined him to fight under a banner on which the Cross of Lorraine was superimposed on the republican tricolour, they helped create, in real as well as symbolic form, the "political ecumenism" which has characterized French public life ever since.

No attempt will be made in what follows to argue that the Catholics, Jews, and Protestants who joined Free France were proponents of interconfessional communion: their ecumenism was strictly political; their motivation in joining de Gaulle, while strengthened in many cases by religious conviction, was primarily an act of patriotic republican commitment. There is, nevertheless, a suggestive parallel between the wartime rally of men and women from France's three religious families and the movement launched in 1909 to bring Christians of different confessions to reach greater mutual understanding. As of the 1930s, the concrete expression of this ecumenical movement, the World Council of Churches, established itself at Geneva under the presidency of William Temple, Archbishop of Canterbury. Its vice-president, Pastor Marc Boegner, head of the French Protestant Federation, remained in France during the Occupation. All of Boegner's sons served the Free French cause.

The Protestant concept of ecumenism aimed at bringing all Christians together across confessional lines, an approach explicitly condemned by Pius XI in the encyclical *Mortalium Animos* (1928). Catholic officialdom was prepared for dialogue, but only with Anglicans and Orthodox Christians. On the other hand, at a lower level, French Catholics and Protestants joined in discussing the problems facing the Jews of Europe, in sharing space in the review *Esprit* founded by the Catholic Emmanuel Mounier, in forming a radical organization called Terre Nouvelle during the Popular Front designed to marry Christian faith and Marxist thought, and in shared Biblical exegesis.[1]

The terms "Catholic," "Jew," and "Protestant" will be used here in their broad sociological or cultural sense to include not only *pratiquants,* men and women who adhered to the practices of their faith as well as to its creed, but also *croyants,* who retained their religious convictions but paid little or no attention to ritual observances, and *détachés,* who kept no formal link to their ancestral belief but were, at least in all cases that concern us here, appreciative of its influence in their lives.

Catholics, whether nominal or practicing, were an overwhelming majority in Vichy as well as in German-occupied France and were an influential minority in Free France and the internal resistance.[2] Men and women of faith on both sides of the wartime divide invoked papal encyclicals, the directives of the Catholic hierarchy, as well as the reflections of contemporary theologians, to justify their actions and to inspire the faithful. What is noteworthy here is the degree to which, in both camps, lay Catholics rather than clerics articulated a vision of socio-economic as well as political regeneration following the defeat, thus heralding what some have called the "Great Return" of the Catholic majority to the centre stage from which it had been ejected two generations earlier. Partisans of Free France were inspired by the martyrdom of Navy Lieutenant Honoré d'Étienne d'Orves, executed in June 1941 following his arrest as a Gaullist agent; Catholic supporters of Vichy saw in the execution of Propaganda Minister Philippe Henriot by the Resistance grounds for a much-publicized memorial mass in Notre Dame Cathedral in June 1944.

It is worth noting that, unlike their colleagues from other confessions, the Catholics who played key roles in the Free French organization were, with very few exceptions, devoutly practising members of the Roman communion. Indeed, some were remarkable for the intense quality of their spiritual life, including Captain (and future general) Philippe Leclerc de Hautecloque; Georges Thierry d'Argenlieu, an ex-Carmelite monk who had joined the navy in 1939; Maurice Schumann, a convert from Judaism who was chief spokesperson for Free France over the BBC; Simone Weil, also Jewish in background, a near-convert, whose search for martyrdom in the fight against fascism made her seem saintly to many; and most members of de Gaulle's inner circle.

Catholic Gaullists belonged to a generation during which, for many at least, their faith and French nationalism, whether in Free France or at Vichy, became intimately associated. The general himself, as his close collaborator the Protestant Couve de Murville once observed, was inspired by "la religion de la patrie," a conjoined passion which led to his being satirized by his "Anglo-Saxon" allies as a self-styled modern-day Joan of Arc and abandoned as the war ended by Catholic colleagues with a more pan-European perspective.

Members of the tiny Jewish minority (1 per cent at most of the population) who joined Free France, with the exception of René Mayer, an orthodox Jew, had few or no formal links to the religion of their ancestors. Emancipated by the Revolution, which in their view transformed France into the "New Jerusalem," French Jews had been enjoined by Napolean to forego any thought of constituting themselves a separate nation within the state.

Some Jews, like the Rothschilds, remained orthodox; others devised a reformed version of their faith and practice, modifying the design of their synagogues and the dress and function of their rabbis. Many became "detached" from their religious background, adopting a purely secular outlook, entering the worlds of commerce and finance, the professions and politics.[3] It is worth noting, however, that even the most evidently secular and assimilated Jews, including premiers Léon Blum and the wartime Gaullist Pierre Mendès France, were circumcised and had Bar Mitzvahs. Whatever their attempt at accommodating the mainstream, however, as Alfred Dreyfus in 1894, Blum in 1936, and Mendès France in 1954, discovered they were not only defined as Jews but often excited a virulent anti-Semitism.[4]

A small but significant number of Jews fulfilled the hope expressed by their would-be emancipator, the abbé Grégoire, in 1787, that, escaping from the isolation and discrimination they faced under the ancien régime, they would be converted to the Roman communion, and thus become fully assimilated.[5] Gaston Palewski and Maurice Schumann, both converts to Catholicism, occupied key positions in the Free French camp. Simone

Weil, a brilliant intellectual who repudiated her Jewish inheritance and hovered throughout her adult life on the verge of conversion, played a fascinating if marginal role in La France libre.

Except for the converts Palewski and Schumann, most Jews who joined de Gaulle encountered prejudice in the Free French camp. Fortunately, the general sheltered them from active discrimination. The Jews who stayed in Vichy or in occupied France faced not only prejudice but the prospect of extermination. One of the long-term by-products of this grim fate, however, was the creation in 1943 of the Conseil représentatif des institutions juives (CRIF), the first all-encompassing grouping of the French Jewish community which defined Jews, secular or religious, as having a common identity, a form of collective differentiation. In the postwar period, in line with this new, more comprehensive categorization, many Jews decided to shed the traditional label "Français israëlites" for the more assertive "Juif français."

The Reformed who found themselves in the Gaullist camp belonged to a Protestant tradition which regarded personal reading of the scriptures or the inspiration of one's conscience as valid avenues to spiritual truth and saw the pastor as primus inter pares within the congregation. As a result, versions of the faith among the Reformed have over the centuries sometimes verged on Socinianism, deism, or even Free Thought.[6]

A spirited, sometimes eccentric, individualism was, inevitably, one of the chief characteristics of men and women who depended so much on personal inspiration. During the first half of the twentieth century, André Gide, the product of an austere Calvinist upbringing, who repudiated his faith early in life, damned the family as an institution, openly adopted a homosexual lifestyle, and flirted briefly with Communism, was seen by many as representing Protestant individualism run amok.

The Protestant political analyst André Siegfried, conceding that his co-religionists had a potentially anarchist and subversive temperament, also noted that their minority status (never more than 2 per cent of the population in the modern period) forced them on the defensive in a self-consciously Catholic nation. This insecurity brought the Reformed to turn to France's Protestant neighbours, not only for spiritual comfort but for financial connections which would enhance their wealth and influence throughout Europe. What resulted, Siegfried notes, was a cosmopolitanism which French Catholics rarely developed.[7] As it turned out, the anglophilia of de Gaulle's Protestant companions in Free France (most notably René Massigli and André Philip) made them natural (if not necessarily effective) interlocutors with the "Anglo-Saxons" whom the general neither liked nor trusted.

The structure of the Reformed church, based on a sharing of power between laity and pastorate from the presbytery at the congregational level to the national synod, provided what can be seen as a model of democratic governance. Whether or not they were natural democrats, the Reformed, especially in the south of France, had long been rebels against priestly as well as monarchical tyranny, most notably in the age of Louis XIV. Protestant maquisards, underground fighters against Vichy and the Germans, often modelled themselves after the camisards, Huguenots who rose up in 1702 against Louis XIV and the local clergy to defend their freedom of worship. Throughout the Third Republic, a majority of the Protestant vote went to parties of the Left (Radicals, Socialists, or Communists) in part at least because of their militant anticlericalism.

A clear recollection of past persecutions helped shape the collective memory of the Reformed, even among those who had drifted away from the faith. Protestant dignitaries still gather once a year at the Musée du Désert in the Gard department to commemorate the heroism of their ancestors who gathered to worship publicly during the century when their faith was proscribed (1685–1787). Patrick Cabanel notes that Gaston Doumergue, twice premier of France, long after he had ceased to be a *pratiquant*, went on this annual pilgrimage after learning that he was mortally ill and opted for a funeral in the Reformed rite.[8]

Lifestyle is often seen as a reflection of the Protestant character. In the Reformed establishment (bankers, magistrates, upper civil servants and the like) probity, integrity, and *pudeur*, sometimes even standoffishness, are qualities both admired and deplored. The government functionary Maurice Couve de Murville clearly possessed these qualities, which helped endear him to de Gaulle. By contrast, Protestants of the Huguenot tradition, concentrated in the rural Midi, invested with an *esprit d'indépendance*, proud of their role as armed fighters for freedom of conscience, were represented in the Free French camp by Jacques Soustelle.

The alliance of devout but ecumenically minded Catholics with Jews and Protestants of less evident religious faith but clear attachment to their cultural roots provided Free France with a powerful moral and political bond. The relatively small number of civilian recruits to Free France made it possible for the writer to trace their individual political and spiritual itinerary before and after 1940 and to examine at some length their particular contribution to the common struggle against Vichy and the

Third Reich.[9] While the focus of this study is on the political ecumenism of the external resistance led by Free France, it should be noted that interconfessional collaboration also occurred in the internal resistance which, by May 1943, had placed itself under de Gaulle's overall command.[10]

Although both de Gaulle and Pétain scorned the Third Republic and held its leaders in contempt, their own rival claims to lead France in 1940 were based on personal links to the moribund regime.[11] In fact, however, both derived their political and, more important, their moral authority, not from the Third Republic, but from the diametrically opposed versions of France's destiny that had been formulated during the revolutionary crisis of the 1790s and restated, with variations, in the following century and a half.

On one side of this ideological divide between the Two Frances stood militant defenders of the hegemonic power of the Catholic church who argued (as some still do) that, as of AD 495, when Clovis, king of the Franks, converted to the orthodox Catholic as opposed to the Arian version of Christianity, he committed all of France definitively to the Roman communion.[12] Devotion to Church and crown were henceforth conjoined and heresy equated with subversion. The Catholic sacraments, administered at birth, marriage, and just before death, were also titles of citizenship and inheritance, signs of membership in the same secular as well as spiritual communion.

That, throughout the centuries that followed Clovis's conversion, entire regions of France or whole social classes seemed indifferent to Mother Church in no way discouraged those who clung to the myth that France was by God's design *toute-catholique*. While sociologists of religion have tried to establish an objective evaluation of Catholic faith and practice,[13] the myth that France remains bound to the Roman communion surfaced as recently as January 1995, when François Mitterrand, the socialist former president of the Fifth Republic, was given a Catholic burial; one zealous commentator insisted that the ceremony reflected the reintroduction of Catholicism as France's official state religion![14]

The preservation of France's spiritual unity, formalized by Louis XIV when he issued the Revocation of the Edict of Nantes in 1685, became increasingly problematic during the eighteenth century and, in 1787, influenced in part by Enlightenment thought, Louis XVI issued a limited bill of rights to the Reformed[15] and mandated one of his ministers, the liberal Chrétien de Lamoignon de Malesherbes, to prepare a brief on the advisability of releasing the tiny (45,000) Jewish minority from isolation and discrimination. Malesherbes's reflections were paralleled by a public debate on the pros and cons of Jewish emancipation.[16] Together, these two initiatives in favour of religious minorities made on the eve of the Revolution opened the way to the recognition by the crown of religious pluralism.

The king's implicit acceptance of confessional diversity was given formal expression in the early stages of the Revolution when the Reformed pastor turned deputy Rabaut-Saint-Étienne, backed in ecumenical mode by the liberal Archbishop Champion de Cicé, persuaded the assembly to pass the Declaration of the Rights of Man and of the Citizen which granted each of the king's subjects freedom of expression, including in matters of religion, provided that its manifestation did not trouble public order.[17] A concrete bill of rights was granted the Protestant minority (defined as "non-Catholic") in March 1791; French Jews had to wait until September of that year to gain the same freedom.

In parallel but contradictory fashion, the legislators of the revolutionary decade tried to establish a single national church attuned to the new order. The most ambitious and in the end the most divisive of these, the Civil Constitution of the Clergy (1790), aimed at creating a regenerate, all-inclusive church, adhering to traditional Catholic doctrine but governed from below, inverting the Roman hierarchical pyramid and vesting spiritual power in the local priest, who was to be elected by the entire parish (non-Catholics included), paid by the state, and committed by oath to the new secular order.

In vowing to abide by the Civil Constitution, roughly half the Catholic clergy, led by the abbé Henri Grégoire, who had championed the emancipation of blacks as well as Jews before 1789, accepted the state's redefinition of their role and status and, by implication at least, endorsed the Revolution in its totality.[18] Elected bishop of Blois in February 1791 and welcoming the proclamation of the Republic in September 1792, Grégoire remained equally devoted to the Republic and to his liberal view of Catholicism until his death in 1831. During the bicentennial celebrations of the Revolution in 1989, thanks in large measure to an initiative by the Catholic and socialist president of the Republic, François Mitterrand, Grégoire's ashes were transferred to the Panthéon (the shrine of republican heroes), a gesture designed to symbolize the coming together of the Two Frances after two centuries of latent or open conflict.

Refractory clergy, those who refused to accept the Civil Constitution, helped provide an ideological base for counter-revolution. Catholic laypeople as well as clergy who perished at the hands of revolutionaries in the civil war of the mid-1790s offered to posterity what was seen as martyrdom in a holy cause.[19]

During and after the 1790s, counter-revolutionary propagandists, including the vicomte Louis de Bonald and Joseph de Maistre, offered an intellectually coherent (if improbable) analysis of the causes of the Revolution and proposed measures by which France might restore the spiritual and political unity of the ancien régime. The Revolution, they argued, together with all the violence, chaos, and civil war it engendered, had been sent by God as a scourge to chastise the French for their apostasy during the Enlightenment; a coalition of subversive minorities, led by Protestants, Jansenists, philosophers, and Freemasons, had taken advantage of this spiritual lapse to plot the overthrow of both throne and altar;[19] the appropriate response to this tragedy was a collective act of expiation and a reconsecration to Christ and his church; finally, a purge or repression of the minorities responsible for overthrowing France's God-given political and spiritual order was both just and appropriate.

The "Plot thesis" resurfaced (with variations) following France's defeat by a Prussian-led German coalition in 1870, in the wake of which Jews were added to the list of those conspiring against the national interest. At the turn of the century, Charles Maurras formulated a comprehensive indictment against four categories of alleged subversives – Jews, Protestants, Freemasons, and *métèques* (a catchall term meant to identify ethnic minorities living in but inherently not part of *le pays réel*) – who had managed to seize control of the legal apparatus of the state, *le pays légal*.[21]

Three opportunities for realizing the kind of counter-revolution dreamed of by conservative pamphleteers occurred between Napoleon's defeat at Waterloo and the Battle of France in 1940. The Bourbon restoration of 1814–30, the "Moral Order" established by conservative monarchists between 1871 and 1875, and the creation of *L'État français* at Vichy in July 1940, were all accompanied by efforts to restore the primacy, if not the hegemony, of the Catholic Church and by the search for a monarch or, after the 1880s, when the plausibility of finding a suitable princely candidate seemed remote, by a military figure of appropriate piety, and by attacks on "alien" minorities held to be responsible for the nation's moral, political, and military collapse. A fourth possibility for monarchical restoration, however fanciful, arose in November 1942 when Henri, comte de Paris, presumptive heir to the throne, arrived in Algiers following the Anglo-American landings on the North African coast and was rumoured to be involved in the assassination of Pétain's deputy, Admiral Darlan, with a view to advancing his own claim to power.[22]

The struggle among Catholics between adherents to and opponents of the Civil Constitution left both factions exhausted and did nothing to advance the cause of religious liberty. Subsequent attempts to legislate into being a nation-wide church based on the ideas of the eighteenth-century philosophes and aimed at inculcating a sense of civic responsibility and republican devotion had little resonance in the public at large.[23]

Legislative efforts to found a new national church having failed, revolutionary France under the rule of the Convention decreed the outright separation of church and state on 21 February 1795. The primary aim of this legislation, the text of which was drawn up, in politically ecumenical mode, by the Protestant François Boissy d'Anglas, with the support of the abbé Grégoire and the atheist Joseph Cambon, was to end any residual pretension of the Catholic Church to be the official faith of the French. Grégoire pointed out, rather extravagantly, that the best means of achieving this end was to promote religious pluralism to the limit, for instance, by encouraging the nation's tiny Muslim and Hindu minorities to practice their faith openly!

The slow recovery of France's three religious families from the trials, divisions, and legislative contradictions of the revolutionary decade had begun when Napoleon Bonaparte staged his coup d'état in November 1799. Within the next few years, through a mix of forceful diplomacy and administrative fiat, Bonaparte established a precedent-setting basis for the legalization of religious pluralism, completing the work begun under Louis XVI.

In a concordat signed with Pius VI in 1801, the general-turned-First Consul conceded that the Catholic Church, representing the faith of the majority, deserved a privileged (but no longer exclusive) status within the state. Then, through the Organic Articles (1802), he established a system of church governance under state supervision for both the Reformed and Lutheran minorities. Finally, in 1806 and 1808, Emperor Napoleon issued regulations governing the Jewish minority, mandating the creation of consistories for those who wished to retain and practice their faith, while obligating all French Jews to forego any thought of retaining a sense of separate identity and insisting that they integrate into the national culture.

During the two generations between the fall of Napoleon and the confirmation of the Third Republic in 1875, France's three religious families lived in relatively peaceful coexistence. True, the Bourbon Restoration brought a renewed bond between the Catholic Church and the state and a "White Terror" descended on Protestants in the south of France, led by Catholic neighbours who correctly saw the Huguenots as, in the main, partisans of the Revolution. On the other hand, the arrival of Louis-Philippe d'Orléans on the throne in 1830 was accompanied by anti-Catholic rioting;

the new king chose the Reformed historian François Guizot as his prime minister in 1840; and the liberal philosophy articulated by the Protestants Benjamin Constant and Mme de Staël (constitutional monarchy, laissez-faire capitalism, unrestricted freedom of expression, and avoidance of any concern with the social question) became the prevailing ideology of the new bourgeoisie, many of them Jewish or Protestant, whose financial power would became disproportionately large by mid-century.

During the so-called Golden Age of French Protestantism (1830–80), the wealthiest banking families with links to the Reformed faith (Hottinguer, Vernes, Mallet, Schlumberger, Neuflize, and Mirabaud) became known as the Haute société Protestante (HSP). However indispensable its contribution to France's overall growth, the HSP became the object of vitriolic attack by reactionary polemicists who saw Protestant financial power as divorced from the national interest. Charles Maurras in the pages of *L'Action française* denounced the HSP for having at one and the same time a cosmopolitan outlook and a determination to dominate French domestic politics.[24]

The Haute société israëlite (HSI), the complement of the HSP, was made up of a small group of Jewish financiers whose fortunes developed following the Revolution. Some were conservative in their outlook, like the Rothschilds who adjusted to the many shifts in regime after 1815 while retaining a close link to their ancestral faith. Others, known as "banquiers nouveaux," financed railway and canal building, helping to lay the foundations of France's rapid industrialization. Typical of this group were the Péreire brothers, Isaac and Émile, who helped launch the Crédit Mobilier, and Achille Fould, a convert to Protestantism and minister to Napoleon III in the 1860s. Some of these families sought full assimilation through conversion or inter-confessional marriage.[25]

By the late 1840s, the Orleanist regime, during which both Jews and Protestants had found new freedom and prosperity, was in crisis. A series of political scandals, protests against the highly restricted franchise, a seemingly passive foreign policy, and the demands of the new industrial working class helped engender a spontaneous rising against the government in February 1848. Catholic as well as Jewish and Protestant involvement in this insurrection turned it into a precocious example of inter-confessional collaboration. The commitment of a number of Catholic leaders to this insurrection was due in part to the editors and contributors to the newspaper *L'Avenir* (1830–31), among them Henri de Lacordaire and Félicité de Lamennais, who proposed a reconciliation between Church and Revolution based on a corporate rather than purely individualist reading of the revolutionary principle of liberty. This broader vision implied freedom of the press, support for the *écoles libres* (church-funded private schools, mostly Catholic, sanctioned by law since 1833), freedom for monastic orders, banned since the Revolution, as well as for workers' associations, and finally, freedom for Europe's "captive nations," Catholic Italy, Ireland, and Poland.

The first months (February–June 1848) of the Second Republic witnessed a remarkable display of this "political ecumenism." In the evening of 24 February, Archbishop d'Affre of Paris went to the City Hall to offer his support to the new government; and, on 12 March, Pius IX, in a brief delivered by his nuncio in the capital, congratulated the triumphant republicans for the respect they had shown the Church and its clergy. Rejoicing in the rebirth of the republican ethos, the Grand Rabbi of France marched through Paris in the company of Catholic priests and Protestant pastors under a banner bearing the inscription *Union des Cultes. Fraternité universelle,* while Catholic and Reformed clergy joined in planting "Trees of Liberty" in the city's many squares. Two Jews, the lawyer Adolphe Crémieux and the banker Michel Goudchaux, made history as the first of their faith to become government ministers. Catholics of radically different outlook, including the liberal Charles, comte de Montalembert, the Christian democrat Henri Lacordaire, and the Christian socialist Philippe Buchez, hailed the fall of Louis-Philippe, while the abbé Godard, in *Les principes de 1789 et la doctrine catholique,* proclaimed the sovereignty of the people to be perfectly compatible with Christ's teachings.[26]

During these weeks of interconfessional harmony, members of France's religious communities supported decrees abolishing the nation's royal houses, invited their followers to join together in asking for divine blessing on the new regime, and added the socialist principle of the right to work to the revolutionary mantra Liberty, Equality, Fraternity. The *quarante-huitard* mentality which inspired these commitments remained part of the collective memory of republicans for generations. It might even be argued that the "spirit of '48" inspired a number of early Gaullists such as the Catholics Maurice Schumann and Louis Closon.

The election of Louis-Napoleon Bonaparte as president of the Republic in December 1848 and his subsequent rule as Napoleon III (1852–70) were accompanied by a relative stability in the relationship among France's three religious communities.[27] The dialectical struggle between the Two Frances, however, resurfaced with new intensity following the defeat of Napoleon III's armies by a Prussian-led coalition in the late summer of 1870. On 4 September, the people of Paris rose up to proclaim what would become the Third Republic, and a Provisional Government of National Defence was set up to sustain the war effort. Although the capital was besieged the following week, the new government fought on until 28 January 1871 when it sued Bismarck for an armistice. When a National Assembly was elected on 8 February to ratify the armistice and the pursuit of peace, the result was an outright triumph for deputies animated by a counter-revolutionary mentality, who championed not only capitulation to the new Germany but monarchical restoration and social conservatism.

The socially reactionary and defeatist mood in the Assembly helped to provoke the Paris Commune of March 1871, an insurrection led by men and women of mixed revolutionary inspiration (Jacobin, Marxist, and anarchist), none of whom can be seen to have represented any of France's three religious traditions.[28] The repression of the Commune during "Bloody Week" in May 1871 was paralleled by the killing of the archbishop of Paris, an act cited by conservatives as signalling the triumph of barbarism within the gates. In the aftermath of this brief but brutal civil conflict, moderate republicans, many of them Protestant or philo-Protestant, presented themselves as defenders of the social order against *communard* nihilism on the one hand and stultifying counter-revolutionary reaction on the other, both of which can be seen as caricatural representations of the Two Frances. Meanwhile, on 5 July 1871, the best-placed pretender to the throne, Henri, comte de Chambord, had subverted any chance of a monarchical restoration by issuing a manifesto in which he asserted his intention to rule by divine right and repudiated the tricolour, thereby refusing a symbolic reunion between the Two Frances.

The Third Republic, which found its constitutional formulation only in 1875, was dominated (except for its first half-decade) by men who had little or no connection to Catholicism, the faith of the overwhelming majority of their fellow-citizens. The definitive consolidation of the regime came in 1879 with the premiership of a Protestant, William Henry Waddington, five of whose cabinet colleagues were also his co-religionists at a time when Protestants were, at most, 2 per cent of the population.[29] In the generations which followed, until the collapse of the regime, very few key government portfolios were held by practicing Catholics. Instead, Freemasons, Freethinkers, Protestants, and Jews, together with a few nominal Catholics, dominated French political life for the next sixty years.[30]

This disconnect between the mindset of the political elite and that of the population at large was the product of two complementary phenomena: the alienation from the regime of many Catholics, including members of the clergy, aristocracy, and in certain areas, the peasantry, as well as of influential Catholic thinkers such as Louis Veuillot and Charles

Maurras; and the resolve of Republican politicians to pursue radical policies of secularization in key areas of French civic life where the Catholic Church had played a dominant role.

During a ten-year period beginning in 1877, when the ministry was either dominated or heavily influenced by Protestants (William Waddington, Charles de Freycinet, and the philo-Protestant Jules Ferry), the government passed a series of laws which radically advanced the cause of *laïcité,* a neologism as of 1871 which was to become something of a shibboleth in republican circles.

The Protestant historian and sociologist Jean Baubérot describes *laïcité,* or *laïcisation* (roughly translatable as secularism or secularization) as the process by which political, juridical, educational, and medical life were legislatively detached from organized religion and, more particularly, from clerical influence and control. Baubérot notes that, while Protestants were allied during the secularizing campaign with militant unbelievers who saw *laïcité* as a far more radical process by which *all* religious influences were to be removed from the public sphere, most Protestant leaders saw themselves as honest brokers between the Two Frances, determined to preserve the greatest possible religious freedom and to avoid gratuitously provocative assaults on the nation's predominantly Catholic population.[31]

Claude Nicolet, student and celebrant of the most intransigent form of *laïcité,* sees among his modern heroes men such as Léon Gambetta and Emile Combes[32] who waged unremitting war against die-hard champions of Catholic reaction such as Pius IX and Pius X. The historian of radicalism insists upon the "irréductible dualité" of post-revolutionary French ideology and, writing in 1982, in the aftermath of the electoral victory of the Left in 1981, exhorts his fellow-believers to remain "unitary and discriminatory" and never to reach a compromise with *cléricaux,* that is, with any group influenced by religious thought, including those Catholics who formally accept the republican regime.[33]

The Catholic sociologist Émile Poulat sees the campaign for *laïcité* as an integral aspect of liberalism, a corrupted form of the revolutionary ideal of *Liberté,* which had promoted absolute individual freedoms, however contradictory and conflicting, within a totally secularized society in which there was neither any unifying faith nor any recognition of vital corporate freedoms. The revolutionary ideal of *Fraternité,* on the other hand, reflected the centuries-old Christian (and, more particularly, Catholic) pursuit of social harmony, rooted in the need to guarantee the corporate foundations of society (the family, religious orders, and trade unions) following the Revolution, which had left the individual and the state as the only legal entities.[34] Writing in 1997, Poulat argues that the dialectical struggle between Liberty and Fraternity had ended, partly as a result of the Two Frances coming together in and after World War II when Catholics joined lay champions of the secular Republic in endorsing *laïcité* in the constitutions of the Fourth and Fifth Republics, laying the groundwork for "a new civility" in their relationship.[35]

The centrepiece of the program of *laïcité* is associated with Education Minister Jules Ferry, who in the early 1880s guided through the French parliament what leaders of the First Republic had only sketched out by creating a national system of free, compulsory, and laic education at the primary school level. Teachers in this system would undergo training at normal schools created by a trio of Protestant educators and lawmakers (Jules Steeg, Ferdinand Buisson, and Jean Pécaut). The curriculum of this pedagogical revolution was rooted in what has been described as a diluted form of Protestantism – a belief in the divine worth of the individual, an invocation of private conscience as a key inspiration for action, an encouragement of private prayer, and the suggestion that good works may be rewarded after death.[36]

During this same period of *laïcisation,* crucifixes were removed from courtrooms, as were oaths before God; limits were placed on the role played by priests in hospitals and charitable institutions; and seminarians were no longer exempted from military service. Divorce, which had been permitted by law in 1793 and then forbidden in 1818, was re-legitimized as a result of a bill introduced in 1884 by the Jew (and Freemason) Alfred Naquet; and a form of civic baptism at local town halls was made available in 1878.

This ambitious, largely Protestant-inspired effort to transform the nation's collective mentality was no doubt bound to fail. In any event, by the end of the 1880s, the champions of this initial version of *laïcité* in the classroom had been challenged by intellectuals such as the historian Alphonse Aulard, the sociologist Émile Durkheim, and the positivist Émile Littré, who saw all forms of religion as intellectually stultifying and politically reactionary and thus wished them purged from the classroom. Thus was born what traditional Catholics denounced as *L'école sans Dieu,* a source of renewed division between the Two Frances.[37]

Catholics were divided in their response to this assault on the place of their Church in national life. Led by the count Albert de Mun, some favoured the creation of a purely Catholic political party to fight for Christian values inside the parliamentary system. However, the failure of the nobleman's campaign for seats in the 1885 elections, together with a virtual veto on his tactics imposed by the pragmatic Pope Leo XIII (1878–1903), ended the experiment.

In the pope's view, the increasing political weakness of Catholic influence in France, too often tied to the now clearly hopeless monarchist cause, together with the continuing intensity of the government's campaign of *laïcité,* forced the Church to consider whether it might not be better served by seeking an accommodation with the Republic.

To open the way to what would be called the Ralliement, Leo XIII turned in the end to Cardinal Lavigerie of Algiers whose views were similar to his own and whose leadership in the campaign to abolish slavery in Africa had made him a popular national personality. As a result, following a series of discreet meetings with key members of the government in Paris, Lavigerie travelled to Rome in October 1890 where he and His Holiness engaged in a subtle verbal battle about which of them should make the proposed overture to the Republic. In the end, under pressure from the pope, the cardinal agreed to take the lead, seizing the opportunity offered by a visit of the French Mediterranean fleet to Algiers the following month to launch his political trial balloon. At a 12 November dinner in honour of the fleet's officers, in the presence of civic as well as ecclesiastical dignitaries, Lavigerie offered what would be called the "Toast of Algiers," proposing that "an unqualified commitment (*une adhésion sans arrière-pensée*) " should be given the existing government which "in no way violates the principles necessary to the life of a civilized and Christian nation."[38]

Although Cardinal Lavigerie's attempt to reconcile the Two Frances was soon subverted, most notably by the confessionally divisive impact of the Dreyfus Affair, it was paralleled by other, less dramatic, but in the long term more significant, efforts to bring Catholics into the republican mainstream. The most enduring of these efforts was launched by a devout layman, Marc Sangnier, who tried to convert a whole generation of French youth to the view that Christianity and democracy were synonymous.[39] The movement he founded (Le Sillon) to promote this position posed a direct challenge to the Vatican. The radical Catholic further alienated Rome by creating Le Grand Sillon in 1907 in an effort to persuade Protestants and unbelievers to join his campaign for social and political democracy. Sangnier's radicalism was condemned by the *intégriste* pope Pius X in 1910. The rebel yielded; but, after serving in World War I, he was elected to the Chamber of Deputies as a reform-minded Catholic in 1924 and helped found the Parti démocrate populaire. His spiritual heirs (Maurice Schumann most significantly) were among de Gaulle's companions in London and Algiers.

The feeling of alienation from the Republic among Catholics which Cardinal Lavigerie and Marc Sangnier had tried to attenuate was accompanied during the late nineteenth century by rising popular anger at the disproportionate wealth and power of Protestant and Jewish banking houses. In response to Christian as well as socialist criticism of contemporary capitalism, which Jewish and Protestant financiers were often seen to epitomize, Leo XIII published a seminal encyclical (*Rerum Novarum*) on the social question on 15 May 1891. Noting the mass misery created by accelerating industrialization and the disappearance of the guilds which had offered artisans protection against exploitation during the ancien régime, the pope by implication endorsed the formation of trade unions. At the same time, Leo XIII denounced contemporary socialism on the ground that it threatened the natural right to private property and promoted class warfare, and condemned modern capitalism because it encouraged heartless competition. His Holiness pointed to the role the state must play in promoting social harmony by ensuring fair wages and decent working conditions. Many of de Gaulle's supporters during the war (some of whom banded together as *gaullistes de gauche* after the Liberation) took their inspiration in large measure from *Rerum Novarum.*

While Leo XIII was promoting a radical shift in Catholic political and social policy, key figures in the French Reformed community came together in 1887 to found Christianisme social, a movement with its own newspaper. The champions of "Social Christianity," like the pope, rejected the capitalist notion of "economic man," urged cooperation in place of competition, and pressed for personal as well as communal regeneration through the application of the social Gospel.[40] The influence of Christianisme social was felt in Free France through such personalities as the Socialist André Philip.

While attacks on capitalism by Catholic and Protestant thinkers were rooted in religious conviction and aimed at the reform of the existing order, Jewish critics of the socio-economic system came from intellectuals with a secular outlook such as Léon Blum, the journalist Bernard Lazare, and the sociologist Lucien Lévy-Bruhl and were more frequently socialist than reformist in outlook. Following World War I, Blum, a fully assimilated upper-middle class Jew, became leader of the Socialist Party, Section française de l'Internationale ouvrière (SFIO). Several of his close associates joined de Gaulle in London; the confidence Blum placed in them and in their devotion to the general allowed them to serve as effective intermediaries between the key figure in French socialism and the leader of Free France.

In a society already troubled by resentment at the disproportionate power of Protestant and Jewish banks, the conviction of the Jewish artillery captain Alfred Dreyfus in 1894 on a treason charge produced an atmosphere of virtual civil war. It is worth noting, however, that the campaign to revise the guilty verdict brought together a remarkably ecumenical group, including not only Jews (the writer Bernard Lazare who had penned an essay on anti-Jewish sentiment, *L'Antisémitisme,* in the year in which Dreyfus was arrested, the radical politician Joseph Reinach, and the young writer Marcel Proust[41] and Protestants (Senator Charles-Auguste Scheurer-Kestner from the "lost province" of Alsace where the Dreyfus family had lived until 1870s, the Paris lawyer Louis Leblois, and the eminent historian Gabriel Monod), but Catholics as well, including Lieutenant-General Georges Picquart who uncovered evidence pointing to the real culprit (Major Charles Ferdinand Esterhazy); Fernand de Rodays, the editor of *Le Figaro,* who opened the pages of his paper to the revisionist polemic of Emile Zola; and the poet Charles Péguy.

In the end, the forces ranged against Dreyfus were just as strong as his champions. They included the mass-circulation Catholic press, notably *La Croix,* salons hosted by prominent Catholic women, members of the French Academy, and a league of influential Catholic intellectuals (including Léon Daudet, Paul Déroulède, and Jules Lemaître). Together, these forces were more than enough to leave the impression that Catholic France was convinced of Dreyfus's guilt – or willing to sacrifice him even if he were proven innocent![42]

Between the Republican electoral victory of 1898 which helped set the stage for the vindication of Dreyfus and the 1905 legislation which severed the links between church and state, the liberal Catholic historian Anatole Leroy-Beaulieu made a passionate but vain appeal for an end to the destructive inter-confessional battles which the Dreyfus Affair had reactivated. In *Les Doctrines de haine, L'antisémitisme, l'antiprotestantisme, l'anticléricalisme* (1902), Leroy-Beaulieu denounced what he saw as three reciprocally stimulated prejudices which were seriously threatening France's stability. Each antipathy had its source in religious, racial, economic, and political paranoia. The anti-Semite saw the Jew as a racial alien living among Aryans, a rootless cosmopolitan linked to external, anti-national forces. The anti-Protestant saw French devotees of the Reformed faith as more attached to their co-religionists in London, Geneva, and Amsterdam than to their compatriots in Paris. The anticlerical saw the ultramontanist tendency which made some Catholics turn to the Vatican for inspiration.[43]

Anti-Catholic feeling was certainly a factor in the realization in 1905 of what many champions of *laïcité* saw as their ultimate goal – the severing of all ties linking church and state. The principle of separation had also been endorsed at a national synod of the Reformed in 1872. Finally, it was backed by a minority of Catholics who, like Lamennais in the 1830s, believed that their Church's spiritual purpose would be better served if the generous, but sometimes heavy, hand of the state were removed.[44] Such a measure in its most extreme form, sometimes referred to as *laïcité de combat,* had been urged since the 1860s by members of what became the Radical party. It was supported in the early 1900s by key Socialists such as Aristide Briand, Jean Jaurès, and Francis de Pressensé, a pastor's son, all of whom felt that its enactment would stop the Radicals from prolonging the campaign for *laïcité* to deflect attention from the social question.

The first years of the twentieth century turned out to be a propitious time for the unilateral abrogation of the Republic's official relations with France's ecclesiastical organizations and especially with the Catholic religious establishment. Whether justly or not, the Catholic clergy were seen to have supported the charge of treason levelled against Dreyfus. At the same time, diplomatic relations between France and the Vatican, already tense because of the friendly relations the Quai d'Orsay had established after 1870 with newly united Italy (whose territory included the former Papal States), had worsened following disputes over French episcopal appointments and other matters, leading to a formal rupture in 1904.

The final, relatively moderate, text of the Separation law was drawn up in large measure by Louis Méjean, son of a Reformed pastor, with the aid of Paul Grünebaum-Ballin, a Jewish member of the Conseil d'État.[45] Passed on 9 December 1905, the legislation declared that, while French citizens remained free to worship (or not) as they saw fit, henceforth all religious organizations were divorced from the state and from public funding. The most provocative element in the legislation, Article IV, stipulated that the property of such organizations was to be administered by associations cultuelles (church administration organizations), whose members would be elected by laypeople chosen by the appropriate confessional group.

The declaration that ecclesiastical property was now subject to government inspection and control was followed by the inventorying of France's churches and their assets by state functionaries, beginning in January 1906, often provoking Catholic rioting. In *La grande pitié de France* (1906), the Catholic novelist and sometime political candidate Maurice Barrès denounced this intrusive action as a violation of sacred space by bureaucrats who respected neither faith nor tradition.

At the beginning of February 1906, Pius X condemned the Separation law in the bull *Vehementer Nos*. As His Holiness saw it, the prestige of the Holy See was compromised by legislation about which it had had no say; the precedent set by France might be followed by other predominantly Catholic states; and the creation of associations dominated by the laity posed a direct threat to the Church's hierarchy.

When, in 1908, the chief organ of Maurassian propaganda, *L'Action française*, edited by the brilliant journalist Léon Daudet, became a daily newspaper distributed by militant volunteers known as Camelots du roi, the campaign of denunciation against allegedly anti-national minorities reached a very wide readership, including members of the aristocracy, the professions, law and medical students, as well as shopkeepers and other petit-bourgeois. Rarely, since the polemical fury of counter-revolutionary pamphleteers of the 1790s, had the dialectical opposition between the Two Frances been given a more explicit and politically charged definition.

CHAPTER ONE

1905–1940: A Generation United in War, Divided in Peace

During 1906, when French Catholics were beginning to absorb the shock created by the Separation law, the nation's attention was drawn toward the serious external threat posed by Germany, which was openly challenging France's increasing influence in Morocco. Since their humiliating defeat in 1870, the French had been debating whether to challenge Germany directly on the Rhine, in an effort to regain domination of the Continent, or to compensate for their losses in Europe by expanding their colonial holdings in Asia and North Africa. The appointment in 1912 of General (future Marshal) Hubert Lyautey as *commissaire-résident général* in Morocco provided champions of both views with a timely hero. A Catholic by conviction, a monarchist by inclination, and an aristocrat by temperament, Lyautey governed the protectorate brilliantly, leaving in place the established order and respecting the Muslim faith in a precociously ecumenical spirit. Gathering around him a team of young, gifted, and mostly Catholic lieutenants – including two future *gaullistes,* Pierre Viénot and Gaston Palewski – the general prepared the way for Morocco's modernization while supervising the training of regiments of indigenous troops who would play a vital role in World War I. The Two Frances, republican and counter-revolutionary, found in Lyautey's imperial career a glorious example of "the civilizing mission" Jules Ferry had assigned France in the 1880s, which the Right had then disdained and now saluted.

The opening of World War I, during which Lyautey served as war minister in 1916, provided an opportunity for a fuller reconciliation between the Two Frances, at least ephemerally. On 4 August 1914, in the Chamber of Deputies, the Socialist and atheist deputy Édouard Vaillant, a veteran of the Paris Commune, crossed the floor to embrace the Catholic comte de Mun, who had been among those urging military repression of the 1871 insurrection. This gesture was followed a year later, in October 1915, by the appointment of the Catholic Denys Cochin as *ministre d'État* in the *Union sacrée* government, which brought together nearly all the component elements of French political life until November 1917, when the virulently anti-clerical Georges Clemenceau became prime minister.[1]

While France's political elites were concerting their energies to promote the Sacred Union, special masses were being said all over the nation for those heading to the front. On 13 September 1914, a procession paraded through Notre-Dame-de-Paris with relics of patron saints Geneviève and Denis and images of the soon-to-be-sainted Joan of Arc. Ironically, parish priests, compelled by what was intended as an anticlerical law of 1889 to serve in the military, won hearts by risking their lives on the battlefield. Committees to support those adversely affected by the war were brought together in a number of cities, in some cases, as at Nancy, including Jews and Protestants as well as Catholics. Mgr Baudrillart, rector of the Institut Catholique in Paris and future *pétainiste,* was invited to take charge of propaganda from France abroad through a Comité catholique de propagande à l'étranger; the Catholic poet Paul Claudel accepted a similar commission vis-à-vis neutral states.

Maurice Barrès, who had rationalized the condemnation of Dreyfus, was so moved after reading scores of letters and diaries written by soldiers of all faiths that he published in April 1917 *Les diverses Familles spirituelles de la France.* Much of the text is a series of dithyrambic salutes to *poilus* and their chaplains, Jewish and Protestant as well as Catholic, many of whom had already died in battle.[2]

The "communion of the trenches" helped prepare the way for a de facto second Ralliement after the war. The canonization of Joan of Arc in Rome on 16 May 1920, in the presence of a large contingent of French political dignitaries, symbolized a new-found mutual respect between the Catholic Church and the Republic. A year later, diplomatic relations between the Vatican and the Quai d'Orsay, ruptured in 1904, were restored. Pius XI (1922–39) did his best to promote this new accommodation, naming to the cardinalate men who would help end old rancours. In December 1926, in a ruling that seemed to confirm the second Ralliement, the pope placed a number of Maurras's works on the Index, on the ground that their author (who was in fact agnostic) had argued for the primacy of political over spiritual values.

The Separation law of 1905 is seen by many scholars as having, paradoxically, stimulated a remarkable resurgence in French Catholicism that lasted through the first half of the twentieth century.[3] The culmination of this revival, at the popular level, came during the 1940s with a renewed devotion to the Virgin Mary.[4] At a more sophisticated level, it was reflected in the powerful influence exercised by French Catholic theologians in the radical transformation of the Church's teachings which led up to Vatican II. Étienne Fouilloux has even observed that, in the decades leading up to the crisis of 1940, French Catholicism produced two gifted but ideologically opposite elites, one of which would serve Vichy while the other contributed invaluable cadres to the internal resistance as well as to Free France.[5] At the inter-confessional level, during this period, Jacques Le Goff and René Rémond note that the Dominican Yves Congar and a priest from Lyon, the abbé Paul Couturier, created an ecumenical prayer for Christians across denominational lines; a dialogue was opened with French Jews through the Amitié judéo-chrétienne; and Professor Louis Massignon founded the Cercles islamo-chrétiens to encourage spiritual exchanges with the world of Islam.

The intellectual brilliance of Catholic lay writers during these decades reached a nationwide, even an international, audience. Charles Péguy, who died in battle toward the beginning of World War I, helped inspire a generation of French youth to see spiritual devotion and republican faith as part of the same mystique. The novelists François Mauriac and Georges Bernanos, who revealed the anguish of troubled believers in their novels, spoke out about fascist tyranny in the public forum; both men were Gaullist *sympathisants* during the war.

The philosopher Jacques Maritain and his Russian-Jewish wife Raissa were converts to Catholicism, thanks in large part to the proselytizing efforts of the writer Léon Bloy, whose *Le Salut par les juifs* (1892) was widely read. Maritain helped set the basis for a new humanist and ecumenically inspired Catholicism in the 1930s and, while rejecting an offer by de Gaulle that he join the Free French wartime administration, played a key role at the war's end by serving as French ambassador to the Vatican. Maurice Schumann, a Jewish convert to Catholicism, was a gifted journalist who did his best to warn of the fascist threat during the 1930s. Simone Weil, a near-convert to Catholicism, spent her brief adulthood (including the last months of her life in London with the Free French) trying to sacrifice herself for the republican cause. A number of Dominican priests and the lay Catholic Stanislas Fumet edited periodicals in which progressive Catholic voices warned against the spiritual threat posed by fascism.

On the social front, meanwhile, lay Catholics, inspired by Leo XIII's *Rerum Novarum*, created a series of associations aimed at infusing Christian principles of social justice into Catholic industrial, agricultural, and student life.[6] The cadres formed by these associations played a key role during *les années noires* (the years between defeat and Liberation), some by trying to implement Leo XIII's directives in Vichy France, others by acting as liaison between the internal resistance and Free French headquarters in London.

Not surprisingly, the rift between Catholics who embraced the revolutionary ethos and those who repudiated it was reflected in their political choices during the interwar years. Those who abominated the Third Republic read Charles Maurras's *Action française*.[7] Indeed, anyone who takes Henri Amouroux's provocative thesis that there were 40,000,000 *pétainistes* in France between 1940 and 1941 (that is, that the entire population succumbed to the crypto-fascism of *L'État français*) might conclude that Catholic France in those years accepted without reservation the Maurrassian world-view.[8]

In fact, conservative Catholics participated actively in parliamentary politics. After the war many of them voted for the Fédération républicaine, founded in 1903 and led by a practicing Catholic, Auguste Isaac, who was a minister in the Bloc national government elected in 1919.[9] Louis Marin, an equally devout Catholic who succeeded Isaac, steered the Federation in an increasingly clerical and nationalist direction. Despite his ultraconservative outlook, Marin defended the Reynaud government to the end in June 1940 and, three years later, joined de Gaulle in Algiers, where he was the most right-wing voice in the Free French coalition.

As of 1925, the Fédération républicaine was given lobbying support by General Édouard de Castelnau who created the Fédération nationale catholique (FNC) to fight against the leftist and militantly anticlerical Cartel des Gauches, which had been elected the year before. Two of Castelnau's Catholic lieutenants later held influential portfolios at Vichy: the anti-Semite Xavier Vallat was put in charge of Jewish affairs while Philippe Henriot acted as chief radio propagandist for the regime, engaging in vigorous combat over the airwaves with Maurice Schumann, de Gaulle's spokesperson in daily BBC broadcasts beamed at France.

By contrast with their more influential conservative rivals, two small parties, neither of which defined itself in confessional terms but both of which were inspired by Marc Sangnier, emerged in the interwar period, one of them on the centre-right of the political spectrum, the other on the centre-left.[10] The Parti démocrate populaire (PDP), launched in November 1924, favoured the coming together of workers and bosses in a corporatist system; it supported conciliation in the debate between public schools and *écoles libres;* and it worked toward Franco-German rapprochement.[11] Jeune République (JR), a party with a more leftist orientation, sometimes referred to as the *frère ennemi* of the PDP, was led by Sangnier until 1932, when the passionately internationalist Catholic layman left the party to devote himself exclusively to Franco-German reconciliation.

Jeune République, which backed the Popular Front, elected four deputies in 1936, including Philippe Serre, who became a devotee of de Gaulle and a keen supporter of the colonel's program of military reform. The PDP, twelve of whose candidates won election, presented a number of well-known candidates, including two key contributors to the Catholic newspaper *L'Aube.* Georges Bidault, a professor at the Lycée Louis-le-Grand in Paris and future chief lieutenant of de Gaulle in the internal resistance, made clear his commitment to democratic and republican values during the campaign. His editor-in-chief at *L'Aube,* Francisque Gay, who also became a *résistant* inside France, ran against opposition from the local clergy who backed a candidate endorsed by the FNC.[12] Another gifted Catholic intellectual, Emmanuel Mounier, founder of Personalism, a movement aimed at the simultaneous realization of individual spiritual fulfillment and a new social harmony, was an initial supporter of the Popular Front but later grew disenchanted with it.[13]

The electoral options made by Catholic voters in 1936 prefigure the choices they would make in 1940. A minority, including the deputies elected under the JR banner, not only backed the Popular Front; they voted against awarding plenipotentiary power to Pétain four years later; and many joined the resistance in London or at home. The vast majority, including most PDP members, welcomed, or at least accepted, Pétain.[14]

Unlike the Catholic majority, France's Protestants had quickly complied with the Separation law of 1905, creating two *associations cultuelles* to represent separately the orthodox and liberal elements in the Reformed communion. Then, in October 1909, to forestall further fracturing of their minority status, the Reformed joined other, smaller, Protestant denominations in the Fédération Protestante de France (FPF). The Federation was led from the beginning by Pastor Marc Boegner, a charismatic but at the same time pragmatic personality, who became the dominant figure in French Protestantism over the next half-century and a vital force in the world-wide ecumenical movement.[15] The major theological and moral influence on French Protestantism during this same period was the Swiss Karl Barth (1886–1968), who admonished his fellow-Christians to remember that God's realm and the secular world were absolutely distinct and that, as a result, any efforts to redeem society here on earth, whether based on the cult of race or of class, were tragically misplaced and bound to fail.

Following World War I,[16] France's Protestants were no longer seen by their critics to be acting collectively to further their own interests or to be subverting those of the majority.[17] In fact, the Bolshevik Revolution and the emergence of the Parti communiste français (PCF) in 1920, together with a sense of outrage at what was seen to be a radical moral as well as spiritual decline among their co-religionists, led some Reformed leaders to create a precedent-setting Protestant right-wing movement.[18] At the other end of the ideological spectrum, the partisans of Christianisme social, a radical organization founded by Pastor Tommy Fallot in 1887 and committed to the replacement of capitalism by a "Third Way," urged both individual and social regeneration through cooperation rather than competition and adopted a policy of integral pacifism in the interwar period.[19] Equally resolute in the pursuit of peace was the Mouvement international pour la réconciliation (MIR), led by Henri Roser, a Jewish convert to Protestantism.

Between 1919 and 1940, the Reformed were, by contrast with the period 1879–1914, only intermittently present in government, nearly always representing the Radical Party. Gaston Doumergue, who had served as foreign minister at the beginning of World War I, was called back from retirement in February 1934 to rescue France from what seemed like imminent civil war following right-wing riots in Paris on the 6th of the month. Two years later, three other Protestant (and more leftish) members of the Radical Party – Paul Bastid and Marc Rucard (who both later joined the internal resistance), as well as Jean Zay[20] – served in the Popular Front administration of the Socialist Léon Blum. André Philip, the only practicing Christian of any prominence in the Socialist camp in those days, piloted the forty-hour week, a key element in the government's reform agenda, through the Chamber of Deputies.[21]

Given the wide ideological division within French Protestantism between the two wars, it is not surprising that even the high point of the appeasement policy, the Munich settlement of 1938, failed to bring about a unanimous resolve to fight fascism. While Protestants rallied when the call to arms against Nazi Germany came in September 1939, they appear by and large to have become, less than a year later, in July 1940, like the rest of France, *très largement maréchaliste*.[22]

The passage of the Separation law came at a time when the Jewish minority began to see itself as finally accepted into the national community.[23] To comply with the new legislation, religious Jews created a Consistoire central israélite de France which, from the beginning, stuck strictly to matters ecclesiastical, entrusting the defence of Jewish civil rights to the republican establishment. To reinforce this general sense of confidence, however, a number of prominent Jews joined the Ligue des Droits de l'Homme, founded during the battle to rehabilitate Alfred Dreyfus.[24]

The vindication of Captain Dreyfus in 1906 had produced a tremendous euphoria in the Jewish community. Eight years later, with the election of the distinguished Jewish philosopher Henri Bergson to the Académie française, the sense of integration and acceptance reached a new height. Patriotic participation in World War I was recognized even by ethnic nationalists such as Barrès.[25] Béatrice Phillipe insists that the process of Jewish assimilation was never so far advanced as during the years between 1906 and the end of World War I.[26]

Serious problems both within and outside their community, however, radically transformed the optimistic outlook of French Jews as the war ended. New waves of Jewish immigrants, from central and eastern Europe as well as from Algeria (some 150,000 in all), created resentment and alarm in the Franco-Jewish establishment and helped excite a virulent new strain of anti-Semitism in society at large. The newcomers, often devout Hassidim, speaking Yiddish and living in ghetto-like isolation where they worked as artisans or craftsmen, had little contact with the well-entrenched Jewish bourgeoisie. To make matters worse, they often brought with them a radical political perspective (Zionist, anarchist, or revolutionary socialist), which alarmed their assimilated cousins.

Prejudice against the new immigrants on the part of fellow-Jews was hurtful enough. Vicious assaults by fascistic intellectuals such as Drieu La Rochelle, Ferdinand Céline, and Robert Brasillach, who charged that the newcomers posed a heightened threat to France's already compromised "racial purity," were more dangerous because of the wide audience they reached. This anti-Semitic propaganda, together with a general xenophobia that intensified as unemployment grew in the early 1930s, brought the government to limit immigration in 1934–35 and again in 1937–38.

Deep rifts within the Jewish community over immigration and other issues were already apparent when Hitler came to power in 1933. A year later, on 6 February 1934, a putsch against the regime by right-wing crowds in Paris created a sense of alarm among all defenders of the Republic. Surprisingly, however, the Jewish response to the 6 February rising seemed ambivalent at best. The Central Consistory even flirted with the Right in an effort to reassert its patriotic credentials; some conservative Jews formed a Union patriotique des Français Israélites which, among other initiatives, lobbied against further immigration.[27]

In the short term at least, a few militant Jews opposed these attempts to conciliate the forces of reaction. Bernard Lecache, for one, the son of East European immigrants, founded the Ligue internationale contre l'antisémitisme (LICA) in 1928. More significantly, Jewish Radicals, Socialists, and Communists helped to create the leftist political coalition which brought the Popular Front to power in June 1936.

That the leader of the Popular Front was the brilliant Jewish intellectual and socialist politician Léon Blum brought French anti-Semitism to a new level of intensity. Anticipating this development, the nationalist Jew Edmond Bloch indicated his bitter opposition to Blum's assumption of the premiership as did the Radical deputy and practicing Jew René Mayer, who joined de Gaulle in Algiers in 1943.[28] Sharing this nervous concern, the Central Consistory signalled to Blum during the spring election its desire that, if elected, he not take over the government. When, following his electoral victory, Blum faced the Chamber of Deputies on 6 June 1936, the openly racist Xavier Vallat expressed his outrage that "this ancient Gallo-Roman country will be governed by a Jew."[29]

Blum's reform agenda, which was backed, as we have seen, by some Catholic as well as Protestant deputies, created panic within the French bourgeoisie; his downfall and replacement in April 1938 by Édouard Daladier reflected (among other things) the need to arrest what was seen as a threat to the established order. The drift to the Right in 1938 included not only the Munich agreement, the crowning moment of the appeasement policy, but the rounding up of Spanish Republican refugees as well as German Jews fleeing west after Kristallnacht.[30] In these increasingly disturbing circumstances, some French Jews seriously considered a "Return to the Ghetto."

The military and political collapse of 1940 found French Jews both divided and dispirited. Key leaders of the Jewish community were naïve enough to believe that the Vichy regime would guarantee their rights, as had been the case with all administrations since the Revolution. Ironically, this trust and the resultant political passivity may have helped shield the Jews of France from the far more grim fate visited upon their Central and East European cousins. In any event, the small band of Jews who joined Free France or the internal resistance or who, like Blum and Mandel, defied the new regime, stand out all the more for their devotion to democratic and republican values, which the vast majority of their co-religionists were either unwilling or unable to manifest.[31]

In the four years between the triumph of Blum and of the Popular Front and the creation of the État français presided over by the nominally Catholic Phillipe Pétain in July 1940, the 150-year-old battle between secular republicanism and the revolutionary inheritance on the one hand and religious reaction and political counter-revolution on the other reached a new climax. Blum and his colleagues saw themselves as heirs to the First Republic and did their best to transform the revolutionary shibboleths of Liberty, Equality, and Fraternity into reality by legislating paid holidays and collective bargaining rights for workers and a radical change in imperial-colonial relationships. In July 1940, Pétain, whose proto-fascist supporter Maurras had hailed France's defeat as a "divine surprise," headed a regime which not only concocted its own counter-revolutionary slogan ("Travail, Patrie, Famille") but did its best, with the support of a spiritually sclerotic and politically reactionary episcopate, to eliminate or at least disenfranchise minorities (most notably Jews and Freemasons) whose freedom had been won during the Revolution.

Ironically, on 19 May, two months before Pétain's accession to power, just as the government of Paul Reynaud, who had replaced Daladier as premier in March, began to disintegrate and de Gaulle's tank corps was in retreat after a brilliant breakthrough near Laon, the entire cabinet had joined the premier at a special high mass in Notre Dame Cathedral, thus bringing the Republican establishment and that of the French Catholic Church together to pray for the nation's survival. Most of the prime minister's colleagues were Freethinkers, devoid of any religious faith; a few were well-known Freemasons; one, Georges Mandel, was a non-practicing Jew.

During the service, relics of Saint Denis and Saint Geneviève, patron saints of France and of Paris, were carried in solemn procession toward the altar where Mgr Beaussant asked for God's intercession in their name: "Come, saints of France, expel the enemy attacking this nation which belongs to Christ and wishes to remain in Christ." Following this invocation, the assembled throng joined in singing the Marseillaise, the revolutionary anthem of Republican France.

By their participation in this incongruous mix of Catholic and Republican rites, Reynaud and his ministers were in their own pathetic way reciprocating the commitment of the Church to the Republic made by Cardinal Lavigerie in 1890. As the celebrated historian of the Third Republic, Jacques Chastenet, has wryly noted, the crowd milling around the cathedral portals must have concluded from the goings on inside that something was gravely amiss![32]

A month later, following the French defeat, Charles de Gaulle's dramatic appeal to his fellow-citizens to join him in the battle against Vichy and the Third Reich initiated the process through which the reconciliation between the Two Frances, sought by Cardinal Lavigerie half a century earlier, would in fact be completed. This was the real "divine surprise" of June 1940.[33]

CHAPTER TWO

Charles de Gaulle: Devout Catholic, Pragmatic Republican, Political Ecumenist

While his chief biographers point to the mix of qualities which, against all odds, helped de Gaulle become the saviour of his nation's honour in 1940, none of them would maintain that the general was a plausible champion of France's republican or democratic tradition.[1] In any event, those republican patriots ready to continue the battle against fascism following France's defeat in 1940 would normally have looked for leadership from among the agnostics, Jews, Protestants, and Freemasons who had governed the Third Republic since 1879. As it turned out, such a potential leader existed in the person of the Jew Georges Mandel, born Louis Rothschild, who had changed his name to avoid its politically compromising association with the great banking family.[2]

Mandel was a moderate member of the Radical Socialist party who had been a close collaborator of "The Tiger," Georges Clemenceau, during World War One. During the thirties he had spoken out with vigour against the rising peril of fascism at home and abroad and he was known to Churchill and General Edward Spears, whom the British prime minister had chosen as his liaison with Premier Reynaud.

On 16 June 1940, Spears had sought Mandel out, urging the interior minister to fly to England. Mandel declined, pointing out that his departure during the crisis would be denounced as cowardice, if not treason, and that his Jewish background made him doubly susceptible to such a charge. The next day, the newly named premier, Philippe Pétain, ordered Mandel arrested on a trumped-up charge of plotting a putsch. On 18 June,

Britain's Minister of Colonies, Lord Lloyd, renewed the invitation to Mandel to move to London and was again turned down.

After rejecting flight to Britain, Mandel decided, like several other leading parliamentarians, to take ship to North Africa where the battle might be pursued on sovereign French territory. Arriving in Casablanca on 24 June, he quickly discovered that there was no will to fight among the French military elites in the Maghreb and the reactionary European settler community. After listening to Britain's Lord of the Admiralty, Duff Cooper, then in Morocco, Mandel reversed himself and opted to go to England. However, before he could act on this impulse, he was put under house arrest.[3]

Before leaving France, Mandel had on 13 June asked to see Under-Secretary of State for War Charles de Gaulle who, sensing that the government was about to yield to the group of defeatists in the ministry, was then on the point of submitting his own resignation. Mandel urged him to retain his official status. "Think only of what should be done for France and how, should circumstances change, your present function might facilitate things," the interior minister argued. As de Gaulle notes in his memoirs,[4] "I must admit that this argument convinced me to wait before resigning. It is perhaps that reasoning which, concretely speaking, set the stage for what I was about to do." In fact, de Gaulle's decision not to cut his link to the duly elected government allowed him to arrive in London with sufficient credentials to make a case for Free France as the trustee of the republican tradition. Ironically, the Jew Mandel had thus become the "inspired mentor" of the devout Catholic who was about to champion the cause the agnostic Paul Reynaud had abandoned when he ceded power to Pétain.

In the call to arms to his compatriots, which he issued over the BBC on 18 June 1940, de Gaulle said nothing about his Catholic background or his republican commitment. After noting that France's military leaders had taken over the government and sued for a cease-fire, the general insisted that the nation had been defeated only because of the enemy's superior tactics. Our use of these same tactics, he added, together with the vast resources of the French empire, Britain's imperial power and her control of the high seas, and the endless industrial power of the United States would lead inevitably to the enemy's defeat in what was clearly a world-wide conflict. If France wished to participate in the peace which followed, she must now fight on. De Gaulle ended with an appeal to all French soldiers, wherever they might be, to join him in London. One way or another, the flame of French resistance must not be allowed to die.[5]

The reticence the general continued to show about his political outlook during his early months in London was based on two considerations: he could not afford to alienate the officers who rallied to him at this stage, many of whom despised the republican regime which had gone down to defeat; and he had to take into account Vichy propaganda, which tried to convince the French that Gaullists were in the pocket of the same "subversive" minorities which had dominated the nation during the Popular Front.

To make up for de Gaulle's ideological discretion, several of his early recruits (the Jews Georges Boris and René Cassin, the *catholique d'origine* but agnostic Henry Hauck, the leftist deputy and Foreign Legion Captain, Pierre-Olivier Lapie, and the Catholic convert Maurice Schumann in particular) managed to give the Free French cause an articulately republican expression. And, as the war intensified and the internal resistance, including its militant Catholic component, joined in the struggle against fascism, de Gaulle came more and more clearly to incarnate the spirit of the Two Frances as they fought together for a rejuvenated republican regime in which the Catholic majority could at last fully participate.

The young general who persuaded Churchill to recognize in him the leader of the Free French was a Roman Catholic in the fullest and deepest sense.[6] Baptized a day after his birth on 23 November 1890 in the Église Saint-André in Lille and married to Yvonne Vendroux in Notre-Dame-de-Calais on 7 April 1921, Charles de Gaulle received the last rites from the abbé Jaugey, the village priest of Colombey-les-Deux-Églises, on 9 November 1970, holding the rosary given him by Pope Paul VI.

Family influence conditioned the young Charles to express more than formal respect for the sacraments of the Church. His mother was extremely pious, associating deep religious belief with faith in the monarchy and a yearning for its restoration. Charles's father, less fervent, nevertheless ended up a sincere believer. A Catholic education complemented the influence of family environment. Charles attended Saint Thomas, a private school run by the Frères des Écoles chrétiennes, beginning in 1896, then the Jesuit College of the Immaculate Conception in the rue de Vaugirard until the Society of Jesus was expelled, when he transferred to Belgium to continue his studies under their auspices, then, finally, the prestigious College Stanislas in 1908.

Military training followed at Saint-Cyr where many of de Gaulle's comrades were, like himself, practising Catholics. His great height and aloof presence earned him the nickname *Le Connétable*[7] during his brief stint as a corporal. The term, used by commanders of the army in the middle ages, stayed with him for many years.

The education which de Gaulle received from the Jesuits helped turn him into a Christian humanist, as familiar with Cicero as with Corneille, with Marcus Aurelius as much as with St. Augustine. Yet in terms of spiritual outlook the future leader of Free France turned out to have a rather Jansenist cast of mind. The fundamentally pessimistic view of human nature, the belief that only God's grace gratuitously given could redeem even the most fervent believer, had been transmitted through St. Augustine to the Dutch theologian Jansenius in the seventeenth century and thence to French writers such as Blaise Pascal. Jansenism had been a powerful influence in the lives of members of the French aristocracy and upper middle class between the mid-seventeenth century and the Revolution. Practitioners of this variant on Christian life had cultivated a rich inner spirituality while leading an austere, self-disciplined public life.[8] De Gaulle's attraction to the Jansenist world-view is reflected in the walking tour of the Jansenist ruins at Port-Royal-des-Champs, west of Paris, which he took with his wife in the summer of 1945 during which he recounted to her the life and works of Pascal and Mère Angélique, a key figure in the Jansenist movement during the reign of Louis XIV.[9]

Something about the nature of de Gaulle's demeanour, his all too evident contempt for most of his followers, his disdain for money, and his extreme *pudeur* (none of his fellow-recruits in the army ever saw him in the showers) all in the end added to the mystique which surrounded de Gaulle while making intimate friendships rare. One of the few to achieve that intimacy was Maurice Couve de Murville, as austere a Calvinist as the general was a Catholic.

While de Gaulle's personal spirituality may be seen as Jansenist in style, his tendency to associate Catholic devotion with fervid French nationalism situates him squarely within the Gallican tradition, that is, the belief that the French church occupied a privileged and quasi-autonomous place inside the Roman communion and in the overall evolution of Western Christendom.

Not surprisingly, given this outlook, de Gaulle as leader of La France libre followed with close attention the wartime behaviour of the French clergy, more particularly that of the Catholic hierarchy, which was by and large favourably disposed to the Vichy regime and its reactionary policies, including its overt anti-Semitism. In these circumstances, the courageous resistance to the État français offered by a few members of the upper clergy, most notably Archbishop Saliège of Toulouse, attracted the general's attention. What resulted was a secret correspondence between the two men, including a letter of 27 May 1942 in which de Gaulle expressed his concern at the apparent collusion between the episcopate and Vichy which, in his view, might seriously jeopardize the long-term influence of the church in French public life.[10] Further admonitions followed and at the Liberation the general, in consultation with Rome, secured the resignation of seven of the most notoriously reactionary bishops.[11] Critical surveillance of the ecclesiastical hierarchy was matched by a favourable response from de Gaulle and his colleagues to the appearance of the underground Christian resistance paper *Témoignage chrétien* and to the presence of a number of influential lay Catholics, including the journalist Francisque Gay, the history professor Georges Bidault, and the law professor Pierre-Henri Teitgen, in the underground opposition to Vichy.

To sustain and enrich his faith, de Gaulle maintained a close contact with the leading figures in contemporary French Catholic thought.[12] At least as significant as any of these writers in the repertoire of intellectual references to which the mature de Gaulle turned were the texts of a group of turn-of-the-century Catholic social critics, including Pope Leo XIII. As a result, the general was familiar with both Social Christianity and Christian Democracy. His father had introduced him to the writings of the marquis de La Tour du Pin and he knew about Sangnier and Le Sillon, the organ of Christian Democracy. The influence of both the conservative and the progressive expressions of Catholic social thought remained with him throughout his life. In a remarkable speech delivered at Oxford on 25 November 1941, de Gaulle pointed the way toward a middle course between capitalism and socialism in which all social classes might fulfill their full potential.[13] The outline of the general's post-war battle to promote *participation,* the full involvement of workers in the management of capitalist enterprise, is clearly foreshadowed in this speech.

A sophisticated lay Catholic with a broad interest in contemporary thought, Charles de Gaulle was at the same time a devoted *pratiquant:* regular attendance at mass was an integral part of his spiritual life. In 1934, when de Gaulle and his wife purchased La Boisserie, a modest property in the village of Colombey-les-Deux-Églises (a town not far from Joan of Arc's birthplace at Domrémy), they went on the first Sunday to mass at the local church, a Romanesque structure built in the thirteenth century. Their son Philippe describes his parents' regular attendance at Notre-Dame-des-Champs when they were in Paris during this period:

> My parents appreciated religious services most when they were conducted attentively and piously without any ostentation and strictly in accord with canon law, whether it was the poetic sobriety of the low mass or the fuller, more public expression of high mass, accompanied by the solemn splendor of organ music and the singing of Gregorian chants ... From priests, for whom they had the deepest

respect (except for minor criticisms), they expected to find officiants of the sacraments and the sole dispensers of the Gospel. They had no interest in sophisticated exegesis, especially by the lay critics from whom one hears so much these days.[14]

While in London, the de Gaulles took communion together out of the public view in the small chapel of St. Mary's. The general studiously avoided showing up at Notre-Dame-de-France in the British capital, whose congregation was notoriously *pétainiste,* reflecting the way in which he associated religious faith and patriotic devotion.

The journalist Jean Marin, who observed de Gaulle at close range during his sojourn in London, gives us an intimate glimpse into his spiritual life in exile:

Without a personal confessor, de Gaulle often sought the services of French-speaking clerics whom he ran across in the capital. He had a rosary but had not brought with him in the single suitcase with which he arrived in England either a prayer-book or a copy of *The Imitation of Jesus Christ.* English nuns offered him missals but they were not needed since he always prayed without reading the text, standing up, listening attentively to the Epistle and the Gospel.[15]

In London, Algiers, and later, back in France, de Gaulle did everything possible to avoid letting his acts of religious devotion signal support for a special relationship between church and state. The Catholic novelist Mauriac observes: "Never has a secular or Freemasonic French president been more scrupulous about not interfering or exercising any spiritual or confessional pressure than this Catholic general."[16] His most effective means of achieving this – not to take communion in public in a setting where it might cause a stir – was subverted only once, by his wife, during a state visit to the Soviet Union in 1966.[17]

If de Gaulle took great pains to avoid having his participation in the sacraments interpreted as having any political significance, he was equally cautious about identifying himself as Catholic when making political statements. There were, however, some exceptions. As Jean Lacouture has pointed out, early in his role as leader of the Free French, the general, queried by the British press, declared, "I am a Free Frenchman, I believe in God and in the future of my country."[18] Even more explicitly, in a 1 August 1940 radio appeal to Canadians of French extraction, he linked his cause to that of his faith, inciting them to do the same: "I feel no embarrassment in addressing you because I wish to speak of France and I know that no one in the world can understand the French fact better than French-Canadians. I will not spell out for you our various military, moral, and national errors. The soldier, the Catholic, the Frenchman who is speaking to you knows and acknowledges them."[19]

If the Catholic faith of Charles de Gaulle was obvious in June 1940, it was not flaunted. The general's republican convictions were similarly hidden from view during the early stages of La France libre. The young Charles had been witness to the divisiveness within the republican regime which accompanied and followed the Dreyfus Affair and came to regard with equal contempt *dreyfusards* and *antidreyfusards,* whom he described as "two packs of dogs," ready to tear the state to shreds with their partisan fury.[20] The purge of army officers who had spoken out against the French artillery captain, or who were openly anti-republican, and the separation of church and state which followed the triumph of a militantly republican coalition in the 1898 elections, exposed the rift between the Two Frances, Catholic and republican, which had been in conflict, latent or overt, since 1792.

It was in the aftermath of these punitive actions against the church and the army that Charles Maurras launched *L'Action française* to promote the monarchist cause and to denigrate the republic and its leadership. Charles de Gaulle became to a larger or lesser degree a *maurrassien* over the better part of the next three decades. At the same time, he was moved by the lyrical portrait of Joan of Arc traced by the poet and essayist Charles Péguy, who presented the Maid of Orleans not only as Catholic saint and patriotic hero but as proto-republican,[21] renewing the mystical bond between people and nation which St. Joan had so thrillingly incarnated. In the end, Charles de Gaulle made it his life's work to bring these conflicting visions together. As orchestrator and architect (with his collaborator Michel Debré, a Jewish convert to Catholicism) of the Fifth Republic, he invented a system in which the president, chosen by the whole people, assumes much of the prestige and power of a monarch while the legislative assembly, also rooted in popular sovereignty, keeps (in theory at least) the power from below achieved in the 1790s.

Heroic combat in World War I brought de Gaulle wounds and decorations, promotion to captain's rank, and capture by the Germans. The latter experience helped inspire de Gaulle's first book, *La Discorde chez l'ennemi,* published by Berger-Levrault in 1924, in which the young captain argues that the German defeat was based on two factors: a failure of the national will and the recklessly irresponsible initiatives taken by military and naval leaders in defiance of their nominally superior civilian superiors, a lesson the resolutely anti-Bonapartist leader of Free France took to heart.

Much of de Gaulle's time in the interwar decades was spent as a military historian and instructor. Between 1932 and 1937 he served as a member of the Secrétariat général de la Défense nationale, a body of experts who advised the prime minister on the best means of preparing the nation for war. His *Vers l'armée de métier*, published in monograph form in November 1934, put the case for the creation of special tank divisions supported by air wings to serve France in the event the highly mechanized war the lieutenant-colonel anticipated became a reality.

As was intended, the book attracted the attention of a number of parliamentarians. De Gaulle's friend, the young lawyer Jean Auburtin, made sure the government's finance critic Paul Reynaud got a specially dedicated copy. Reynaud was sufficiently impressed to agree to meet the colonel on 5 December. In the end, the meeting took place in the presence of a third party, Gaston Palewski, a convert to Catholicism of Polish Jewish background, who had served under Lyautey in Morocco and was now part of Reynaud's staff. Following this first successful contact, Palewski agreed to help the young officer draw up a brief detailing his proposals for military reform, and de Gaulle wrote a series of letters to Reynaud stressing the need for political action to implement the desired changes in the nation's military establishment.

On 14 March 1935, while de Gaulle listened from the visitors' gallery, Reynaud made an impassioned appeal to his colleagues in the Chamber of Deputies in favour of the ideas expressed in *Vers l'armée de métier*. Lacouture suggests that this close rapport with one of the leading figures in the French parliament helped eradicate the last vestiges of Maurrassian ideology in the patriotic young officer:

> In sum, having long since ceased to be a monarchist – if in fact he had ever been such beyond his adolescent years – he openly declared his republicanism. To join a government of the Third Republic – even if it was the last and weakest – was an honour for him and throughout the crisis of 1940 he would be the closest ally of those who championed the Jacobin spirit ... against the military elite for whom defeat was all the less distressing since it could be presented as a product of the democratic regime.[22]

In May 1936, with the triumph of the Popular Front, the balance of parliamentary politics shifted sharply to the left. Undeterred by this ideological reorientation, de Gaulle managed to arrange a meeting with Premier Léon Blum on 14 October 1936. Blum showed real interest in the lieutenant's thoughts on tactics and strategy but insisted that France's existing military posture,. while limited in terms of launching an aggressive war, was adequate in terms of any enemy assault. In the immediate aftermath of the meeting, the results were of course disheartening to de Gaulle. In the longer term, however, each man recognized the leadership qualities of the other, and Blum's favourable impression, reinforced by that of those of his socialist associates who joined de Gaulle in London, many of whom were Jewish, like himself, resulted in a clear endorsement of the general's republican credentials from the leader of the SFIO, then under house arrest in Vichy France.

What turned out to be the last chance for the adoption of a Gaullist strategy by the Chamber of Deputies came on 27 January 1937, when Reynaud tried in vain to put the case for the lieutenant-colonel's ideas before his colleagues. Full colonel as of December 1937, Charles de Gaulle had a special opportunity to put his military reflections before the French public in the fall of 1938. The Catholic writer Daniel-Rops, an editor at the Plon publishing house, who had been asked to launch a series of essays dealing with contemporary issues, turned to the colonel for a contribution. The result was *La France et son armée,* which appeared on 27 September 1938.[23] The text is a critical analysis of relations between France and her army from the ancien régime to the 1930s in a continuum in which political and military leaders are singled out for praise or censure according to their perception of how military resources might best serve the nation's interest. Particular plaudits are awarded to two republican heroes – Lazare Carnot, orchestrator of the mass mobilization decreed by the First French Republic, and Léon Gambetta, who marshalled the human and material resources of France at the beginning of the Third Republic – as well as to heroic figures from the monarchist era such as Marshal Louvois, who masterminded Louis XIV's strategy.[24]

On 2 September 1939, Colonel de Gaulle was put in charge of an armoured tank corps covering Alsace, where he waited out the phoney winter war of 1939–40. He welcomed the cabinet shuffle of March 1940, which brought his patron Reynaud to the premiership. On the eve of the German blitzkrieg in the spring of 1940, he took command of the Fourth Armoured Regiment and convincingly demonstrated the use of tightly concentrated tank formations by cutting through German lines near Laon in mid-May. A week later, on 23 May, de Gaulle was named general *à titre temporaire,* and on 1 June the premier appointed him undersecretary of state for war. A bare two weeks later, bitterly frustrated by the capitulation of Reynaud to the defeatist forces in the cabinet, he thought of resigning, then flew off to London to launch his defiant appeal to his fellow-citizens over the BBC on 18 June.

A Catholic who had committed himself to the Republic in the years preceding World War II, Charles de Gaulle might well have responded to the challenge facing him in 1940 as the leader of an essentially Christian crusade. Indeed, there were times when this impression was created both by the general and by some of his intimates. But the appeal which de Gaulle issued to his compatriots on 18 June was clearly inclusive, and Jews as well as Protestants responded to it as eagerly as Catholics. What resulted over the next four years was an exercise in ecumenical politics, often tense but ultimately successful. De Gaulle's attitude toward both Jews and Protestants, based no doubt in part on his indifference to their religious background and his willingness to take their patriotic devotion as sufficient ground for membership in La France libre, made this precedent-setting exercise a success both in the short and the long term.

At the time of de Gaulle's birth, the Jewish question had become a major issue in French politics. The future leader of Free France was still a child when the guilt or innocence of Captain Alfred Dreyfus on a charge of treason became a matter of public debate and animated dinner-table conversation. Charles's father, while devoted to those twin pillars of conservative faith, the army and the church, came nevertheless to believe in the Jewish captain's innocence; and, as he reflected on the case years later, his son agreed. De Gaulle's wartime collaborator Maurice Schumann, with whom he talked about the case at length, concludes that de Gaulle became a *dreyfusiste,* that is, a supporter of the captain's personal integrity and patriotism, without becoming a *dreyfusard* or public partisan of the officer's cause.[25]

As we have seen, the young de Gaulle, like many in his generation, read the works of Charles Maurras; but, whatever else he may have absorbed from reading the right-wing polemicist (from whom he would in any event be estranged by the mid-1930s), the future leader of Free France never developed a generalized antipathy toward French Jews. The general's attitude toward them, like his attitude toward other minorities, depended to a large extent on their identification with the nation. Favourably disposed if they were integrated or even better, assimilated, he could be unsympathetic if they remained self-consciously apart from the dominant culture. His attitude toward non-French Jews, especially when they stood out as a ghettoized minority inside a well-defined national culture, could be essentially negative.

It is clear from his own on-the-spot observations, while in post-war Poland as part of a French military expedition to help defend the reborn nation against the Red Army, that de Gaulle felt a certain revulsion in the presence of eastern European Jews. To begin with, the Polish officers he encountered in mess halls were bound to sound off about the "world-Jewish conspiracy" emanating from Moscow and abetted by rootless Jewish intellectuals such as Trotsky. In letters to his mother, de Gaulle expressed his sympathy for the Polish masses who were being exploited by an unnamed parasitical minority, in all likelihood a coded reference to the Jews. And in the account of his Polish experience which he published in the 1 November 1920 issue of the *Revue de Paris*, he was more specific: great distress was being felt by the old Polish elite, but theatres were full of a very Jewish display of elegance (*pleins d'élégances bien israélites*). In similar vein, the future leader of Free France described the attitude of arrogant polyglot men who were flaunting new wealth obtained through trafficking in currency fluctuations.

Such disdain is, however, balanced on occasion by compassion. In one passage, de Gaulle describes "the constant swarming about of Polish Jews crowded together, trying hard to trade in something in spite of the gibes and brutality to which they have so long been subjected, living in permanent insecurity and terror, feeling in their inner hearts an equal detestation for Budenny's Cossacks and Polish Uhlans."[26]

In a final, equally compassionate passage from this same account, de Gaulle tells of arriving at a small Polish town where the Bolsheviks had established a soviet with the help of local Jews. After repossessing the town, Polish soldiers had set upon these Jews without pity, carrying off many men for summary execution. The women, after wailing in grief, had hastened to bury their dead in conformity with Jewish tradition.[27]

The occasional lapses into anti-Jewish prejudice to which de Gaulle succumbed while serving in Poland after World War I are nowhere to be found in the young officer's relations with French Jews in the interwar years. Following the death in 1932 of his father, who had played a key role in his intellectual and moral formation, Charles de Gaulle found a new mentor in Colonel Émile Mayer, a brilliant, fully assimilated Jewish artillery officer.[28] Born in 1851 in Nancy to parents of modest means, Mayer attended the École polytechnique in Paris but, once in the army, found his promotion blocked after he openly expressed doubts about the treason charge levelled against Captain Alfred Dreyfus. He was rescued from oblivion, then promoted to lieutenant-colonel, by Georges Picquart, the Catholic officer who had uncovered the real culprit in the Dreyfus case. Already in his mid-sixties in 1914, Mayer commanded the western defences of Paris during World War I.

For five years beginning in 1932, de Gaulle (who had been in correspondence with Mayer since 1925) became a regular participant in a small group of the older man's intimates, who met every Sunday morning in the apartment of Mayer's son-in-law Paul Grünebaum-Ballin (who had written the articles of the 1905 Separation law dealing with Jewish religious organizations) to discuss matters military. Grünebaum-Ballin arranged the 14 October 1936 meeting between de Gaulle and Léon Blum, at which the author of *Vers l'armée de métier* tried to persuade the prime minister of the need to shift France's military strategy. Georges Boris, a close advisor to Blum (and after 1940 one of de Gaulle's most valued Jewish counsellors) published Mayer's last articles endorsing the Gaullist doctrine concerning modern tank warfare in the socialist *La Lumière,* which he edited. When Mayer died in 1938, Charles de Gaulle made a very rare display of personal grief.

In the immediate circumstances of 18 June 1940, as de Gaulle issued his appeal over the BBC to his compatriots asking them to join him in the fight against Vichy and the Nazis, he was ready to welcome those French Jews who heeded his call to arms. Given the relatively meagre response which his appeal evoked in the overall population, it is worth noting the proportionately large number of Jews, all of them *assimilés* and most of them sympathetic to the Popular Front, who showed up in London. That these *juifs assimilés,* despite the prejudice which they encountered in the British capital, were able to serve the cause of Free France is due in no small measure to the willingness of Charles de Gaulle to rise above whatever vestigial anti-Jewish feelings he may have retained from his milieu or his military experience and to his determination to deal with the intolerance of his overtly racist subordinates in London.

The Jews who rallied to de Gaulle were drawn to La France libre by patriotic feeling and by a strong commitment to the republican and democratic cause. Like most of their Catholic and Protestant colleagues in London, however, none of them focused in 1940 on the wartime fate of European Jews. The threat to the Continent's Jews and the urgent need to guarantee that Jewish refugees fleeing Hitler's Germany would find asylum in Palestine was, nevertheless, brought to the attention of de Gaulle soon after his arrival in London. Two organizations with agents in the British capital – the World Jewish Congress (WJC) and the Jewish Agency for Palestine (JAP) – both pressed *Le Connétable* for support.[29]

Created in the 1930s to mobilize world opinion against the rising tide of European anti-Semitism, the WJC had originally been based in Paris. Following the French collapse, the Congress moved its headquarters to

New York, where it was directed by Dr. Stephen Wise. A London chapter, headed by Dr. Maurice Perlzweig, was assigned the responsibility of reporting on the fate of Europe's Jews. Perlzweig was vigorously seconded in this mission by Albert Cohen, a Cypriot-born Jew who had spent the interwar years in Paris where he edited *La France juive* and in Geneva where he served on the staff of the International Labour Organization. At the beginning of the war, Cohen had tried unsuccessfully to get the French government to raise a legion made up of foreign-born Jews ready to join in the battle against fascism. Fleeing France just before the Armistice, he arrived in London on 20 June just three days before the promulgation of the first Vichy legislation restricting Jews' rights.

Also in the British capital in the spring of 1940 was the president of the World Zionist Organization, Chaim Weizmann, who had in addition become ex officio head of the Jewish Agency for Palestine. The Agency had been created in 1929 to oversee the fulfillment of the promise contained in the Balfour Declaration of 1917 that a Jewish homeland would be established in Palestine. As it turned out, Weizmann recruited as counsel the same Albert Cohen who was to lobby the Free French on behalf of the WJC.

It was Dr. Perlzweig, however, who made the first move. Soon after the Churchill government's recognition of de Gaulle as leader of the Free French, the London agent of the WJC assured the general that his cause had the support of the Jewish people as well. De Gaulle (whose political orientation was a matter of some concern to Perlzweig) promised the Jewish leader that Free France would work for the full restoration of Jewish rights. Soon afterward, the British section of the WJC decided to establish formal contact with La France libre and appointed Cohen to serve as liaison.

Beginning in mid-July, Cohen met a number of key Gaullist personalities, including René Pleven and Pierre-Olivier Lapie, who were at that point responsible for the embryonic foreign relations of La France libre. Subsequently, having heard rumours that de Gaulle was an anti-Semite, Cohen went to see the Jewish jurist René Cassin, an early recruit to Free France, who assured him that the general's principles in matters racial were liberal.[30]

On 9 August, the former editor of *La France juive* was received by de Gaulle at Carlton Gardens, where he put the case for reciprocal recognition and support. The general followed up this discussion with a letter to Cohen on 22 August, in which he relayed his awareness of the historically tragic role played by Europe's Jews as scapegoats during times of crisis and vowed that at the end of the war France would restore the civil liberties taken from the Jews by Vichy and make restitution for any material losses they might incur as a result of that regime's racist legislation. The leader of Free France backed up this pledge in a letter to Dr. Wise of the WJC on November 11:

> Be assured that, since we repudiate everything which has been perpetrated through treachery in France since 23 June, the cruel decrees directed against French Jews can and will have no validity for La France libre. These measures are no less a blow to the honour of France than they are an injustice to her Jewish citizens … When our victory is achieved not only will all the wrongs be righted but France will again resume her traditional place as the champion of freedom and justice for all men, regardless of race or creed, in a new Europe.[31]

An opportunity to redeem this pledge to rescind Vichy's anti-Jewish legislation as well as to express (if only ephemerally) Free French support for the Zionist cause came in the late spring of 1941. The threat of a generalized Arab revolt fomented by Nazi propaganda and beginning in Iraq, coupled with renewed pressure on Egypt and the Suez Canal by General Rommel, led Churchill to endorse a pre-emptive strike against the Syrian capital Damascus, where French forces loyal to Vichy were solidly implanted. Jewish volunteers moving up from Palestine would also be engaged. On 15 May, the British prime minister wrote to de Gaulle urging that Free French troops join the operation. Lacouture describes what he conjectures was the general's perspective at this critical juncture in the war:

> One cannot call it as pro-Zionist as that of the United Kingdom was pro-Arab … But for a variety of reasons which include de Gaulle's fascination with Utopian dreamers such as those living in the early kibbutzim, his sense of obligation to respond to Vichy's *Statut des Juifs*, the suspicion which he felt towards Arab nationalism and the Anglophobia which kept welling up inside him, the general sensed that all these considerations would come together on the ground as Gaullist troops and Jewish combatants rose up together against Nazism.[32]

In 1968, during a conversation with Jean-Jacques Servan-Schreiber, de Gaulle, who had been charged with making anti-Semitic remarks following Israel's triumph in the Six Days' War, recalled the fraternal combat of 1941: "So they say I'm perhaps not a friend of Israel? In that regard, I still recall Palestine in 1941. The young Jews were marvellous! They fought side by side with us while the Arabs, to be quite frank, were on the other side."[33]

The joint military operation began on 8 June. Jewish settlers in Palestine shouted encouragement to units of La France libre as they passed. However, the message delivered by the man in charge of Free French forces, General Georges Catroux, a disciple of Marshal Lyautey who knew the Muslim world intimately, was that of Arab liberation and an end to the mandate awarded France over Syria and Lebanon in 1920 by the League of Nations.

The war, which pitted Gaullist soldiers against men devoted to Pétain, lasted only two weeks. Damascus was captured on 21 June, and an armistice signed at St. Jean d'Acre, without the participation of Free French authorities, allowed forces loyal to Pétain to be repatriated. On 21 July, less than a month later, representatives of the World Jewish Congress in New York challenged René Pleven (who happened to be in Manhattan at the time) to live up to the Gaullist pledge that Vichy's anti-Jewish laws would be rescinded in the newly liberated territory. This challenge was met soon enough: on 5 August, Dr. Wise and his colleagues were assured that these laws were now null and void. Wise was told the Free French apply only legislation enacted before 18 June 1940, together with the subsequent ordinances of La France libre.[34] De Gaulle himself reiterated this assurance in a letter to the World Jewish Congress on 4 October, the 150th anniversary of the emancipation of French Jews in the early stages of the French Revolution.[35]

No concrete follow-up to de Gaulle's earlier expression of interest in the Zionist cause was forthcoming, however, partly because Catroux, in whom the general had entrusted his Middle East policy, remained determinedly pro-Arab and partly because the Foreign Office had made it abundantly clear that Free France had no business speaking out on matters related to the administration of the British mandate in Palestine.

As we shall see, de Gaulle and his colleagues would have a second opportunity to establish their credibility vis-à-vis French and the world Jewish community following the Allied landings in North Africa in November 1942, when the restoration of Jewish rights there which Vichy had abrogated became a pressing issue.[36] In any event, whatever its validity, the charge that the general was at heart an anti-Semite would resurface after the war.[37]

While de Gaulle had Jewish friends and associates both before and during the war, his familiarity with French Protestant society was clearly limited. He had no close friends in either the Reformed or the Lutheran communities and makes no reference to Protestants or to their role in the nation's civic life in his prewar writings. As leader of La France libre, however, de Gaulle welcomed a number of Protestant supporters, some of whom (including the Socialist André Philip) were publicly identified with the Reformed communion. The general must surely have known that the *inspecteur des finances*, Maurice Couve de Murville, and the diplomats François Coulet and René Massigli were members of the Reformed church. And Jacques Soustelle, while detached from the Calvinist faith of his childhood, regularly and openly celebrated his Huguenot ancestry.

The eminent Protestant jurist and academic Jacques Robert, noting the absence of references to members of his communion in de Gaulle's writings and speeches, argues that the general, who surely knew the contribution the Protestant minority had made to France over the centuries, was bound to be drawn to Protestants (and they to him) because of a number of traits recommending them to the service of La France libre. These included

> A certain rigor in their outward appearance; a proper restraint in their choice of words; intellectual, moral and financial integrity, based no doubt on a more direct familiarity with God; a welcoming attitude towards others, notably the oppressed and excluded, nurtured through a lengthy tradition of persecution; a devotion to public life; and an indispensable aptitude for state service.[38]

Le Connétable may well have ignored the religious background of some of his Protestant supporters. He certainly came nevertheless to know one key figure in the French Protestant community living in London, whose presence played a vital role in the spiritual life of practicing members of the Reformed communion who joined Free France. Pastor Frank Christol had since 1928 been in charge of the congregation of the Huguenot church in Soho Square, which had served Protestants fleeing French religious persecution since the sixteenth century. As soon as he was made aware of de Gaulle's arrival in London, he decided, with the backing of his presbytery, to join the Free French movement and to serve as chaplain if such a role were offered.

When Christol showed up at Carlton Gardens, however, he was told by a Catholic chaplain who happened to be present that volunteering for such a position was pointless since there were no Protestants in the ranks of La France libre! Fortunately, the tone changed dramatically when de Gaulle met Christol on 27 December 1940 and accepted the pastor's offer. It was not, however, until May 1941 that Christol was appointed chaplain to the Free French armed forces with the rank of captain. One of the pastor's sons, Jean-Claude, was killed fighting with the *maquis* in June 1944. A second son, Jacques, fought under General Leclerc in North

Africa, while a third spent many months as a prisoner of war. Pastor Christol and de Gaulle became regular correspondents throughout and after the conflict.

Discretion within Free France about the religious background of one's colleagues was echoed by the rare references made to Protestants in de Gaulle's public utterances during the war. On 23 June 1942, in a speech made in Edinburgh, the general referred to the historic military and political ties that had bound France and Scotland together beginning in the Middle Ages, noting, "In our age-old alliance, there was not only a common policy, intermarriage and military collaboration ... There were also a thousand profound links binding souls and minds together ... And how could we not acknowledge what is so intimately shared by the Church of Scotland and the doctrine of Calvin?"[39]

Again, on the eve of Armistice Day 1942, de Gaulle, by referring specifically to the temples in which the Reformed worshipped, invited Protestants as well as Catholics to demonstrate their faith in France in their public as well as private prayers: "French men and women! On 11 November ... you will be gathered together either in your churches or temples, at work or at home. Together you will offer up your prayers and your thoughts to France."[40]

Finally, toward the end of the war, *Le Connétable* wrote to the president of the synodal committee of the Reformed churches in Strasbourg:

> During the bitter years, through which we have just lived, neither the Christians of Alsace nor French Protestantism in general have lost sight of the true interest to be found in the sacred service of the fatherland. On many occasions, courageous voices among them have been raised up to proclaim this. Such an attitude is in conformity with the noble spirit of independence, resistance to oppression and fidelity to the flag which inspires your church's tradition.[41]

Jews and Protestants, whatever prejudice they may have aroused among the reactionary military men who joined de Gaulle in London, suffered no personal discrimination at the hands of the general. A still greater test of de Gaulle's (and Free France's) capacity for ecumenical accommodationcame with the liberation of French North Africa by Allied troops beginning in November 1942. The transfer of what had by then become "Fighting France" to Algiers brought with it (after a good deal of delay) the restoration of Jewish rights which Vichy had abrogated. It also brought Gaullists to confront pressing demands by the Muslim majority in the Maghreb, some of whom favoured full integration. As will be noted in

Chapter 14, the failure of General de Gaulle and his colleagues to satisfy these demands and the resultant nationalist riots beginning at Sétif in May 1945 marked the limits of Gaullist ecumenical outreach.

Catholic by deep conviction, respectful of the Republic because, as much as the monarchy, its leaders had effectively defended the nation in times of crisis, ecumenical in outlook because he judged the men and women who rallied to his cause not on the basis of their religious confession but on their patriotic devotion, Charles de Gaulle offered the Two Frances, Catholic and republican, a vision they could share.

CHAPTER THREE

The General's Inner Circle: Christian and Republican

To the great distress of *Le Connétable,* his 18 June appeal for support was, with a few exceptions, greeted with silence by France's military, political, socio-economic, and religious elites. The most logical political allies in the struggle against fascism (Paul Reynaud, Léon Blum, and Georges Mandel) opted, for different reasons, to stay in France. With the exception of Admiral Émile Muselier and four-star General Georges Catroux, dismissed from his post as Governor-General of Indo-China by Vichy, none of the nation's military chiefs were willing to join de Gaulle in rebelling against Marshal Pétain, nor did any of the administrators of France's vast colonial empire offer their support. Upper-level civil servants were almost unanimous in shifting their allegiance to the État français. Apart from one or two courageous personalities such as Cardinal Saliège of Toulouse, the Catholic hierarchy was either pro-Vichy or at best ideologically neutral. Pastor Marc Boegner, head of the French Protestant Federation, a friend of Pétain, chose to stay with his flock the better to protect them from whatever the new regime might decree. The spiritual leaders of France's Jews, quickly put on the defensive by Vichy's anti-Semitic legislation but trusting nevertheless in Pétain's benevolence, were in no mood to react with vigour. Some leading intellectuals (Raymond Aron in London, Jacques Maritain and Georges Bernanos in the Americas) offered conditional support to La France libre, but only François Mauriac, living out the Occupation near Bordeaux, can be thought of as a true believer.

The deep frustration which de Gaulle felt at the feeble response to his 18 June appeal and at the sometimes rather mediocre quality of those who joined his movement was substantially attenuated by the presence around him in London of an inner circle of supporters, most of them devoutly Catholic like himself, tolerant of (or indifferent to) the religious background of recruits to Free France, and prepared to work for the restoration of a republican and democratic regime when Liberation came. This inner circle included the Catholics Claude Bouchinet-Serreulles, Geoffroy de Courcel, Claude Hettier de Boislambert, Elisabeth de Miribel, René Pleven, and Gaston Palewski, many of whom came as close as was possible to intimate friendship with de Gaulle, and the Protestant François Coulet who would become a lifetime friend.

These young Gaullists gave the Free French cause much of its early mystique. They were eager to engage in front-line action as evangelists for the cause in Canada, Africa, and the Levant. Most were both anglophile and bilingual, ready to do their best to improve the often tense relations between La France libre and Great Britain. Their moral integrity and their courage (paralleled by that of their Christian colleagues in the internal resistance) helped to secure Catholics the *droit de cité* they had been denied since the consolidation of the Third Republic and to erase the stain left by their lay as well as ecclesiastical contemporaries who had trafficked with Vichy and the Nazis.

The first of these close companions, Geoffroy de Courcel, could be described as a "prehistoric" Gaullist.[1] When the twenty-seven-year-old cavalry lieutenant, on leave from Beirut, had shown up at the War Ministry in the rue Saint Dominique on June 6 still wearing his uniform, Pierre de Leusse, a family friend, told him that he was ideally suited to become aide-de-camp to General de Gaulle, who had just been named undersecretary for war. An hour later, eager to accept the post, Courcel was introduced to the general. The conversation between *Le Connétable* and his new-found aide-de-camp was brief and to the point. The following day, Courcel took up his new responsibilities. Then, on June 8, de Gaulle informed him that they were both on their way to London!

Courcel had an aristocrat's bearing. De Gaulle's counter-intelligence chief, André Dewavrin, describes him as having a small skull dominated by a hawk-like nose atop a tall slim body. Like his friend Claude Bouchinet, he had been a student at the Collège Stanislas where most students were Catholic. Courcel's faith was particularly fervent, however, which led him to request special permission to seek confession off the school premises.[2]

The deeply personal piety which Courcel had demonstrated at Stanislas remained with him for life. Like de Gaulle, the aide-de-camp was a *pratiquant*, a regular participant in the Eucharist. In the eulogy which she gave following Courcel's death, his friend, the writer Françoise Parturier, remarked how significant the presence of this spiritually charged companion must have been for de Gaulle during the stressful and sometimes tragic moments of exile in London and Algiers: "I am certain that de Gaulle, while in London, abandoned by all the dignitaries, aristocrats and members of France's grande bourgeoisie, found comfort and hope in the presence beside him of this young ambassador's secretary, Saumur horseman and graduate of Stanislas who had left everything behind – his chateau and his fortune – for an uncertain adventure, for France, for honour and for freedom."[3]

Courcel's spiritual fervour, linked as it was to his love of country, matched that of his friend Elisabeth de Miribel, to whom he wrote on 17 August 1940 putting the blame for France's shameful defeat on the Catholic Right.[4]

Following in the tradition of his grandfather Alphonse, who had been France's ambassador to Britain between 1894 and 1898, Courcel passed the entrance exams which paved the way for him to pursue a career at the Quai d'Orsay in 1937. He was shortly thereafter posted to Warsaw to serve as secretary to the French ambassador.

Inevitably, from the moment the idealistic young Catholic joined de Gaulle's staff, he was made aware of the frantic discussions under way in the Reynaud cabinet, where the premier's mistress Hélène de Portes was doing her best to undermine the influence of those willing to remain at war. Utterly disheartened, Courcel submitted a letter of resignation on 14 June to Reynaud, who assured him that the government was about to move to Algiers where it would regroup. Two days later, Courcel was en route to London with de Gaulle, taking with him the 100,000 francs Reynaud had given him to underwrite the general's trip.

In the British capital, Courcel joined Jean Monnet, chairman of the Franco-British War Supply Board, and his deputy René Pleven, to discuss a radical new element in an already dramatic situation – Winston Churchill's offer to the government of France that the two nations sustain their battle against Hitler by merging their vast empires.

When the prime minister's proposal failed to win over the French ministry and news of Pétain's request for an armistice reached London on 17 June, Courcel urged de Gaulle to formulate a prompt response. The result was the critically important 18 June appeal by the general to the people of France over the BBC.

The text of de Gaulle's speech having been formulated, Courcel turned to his friend Elisabeth de Miribel to type it out. Mlle de Miribel had a pedigree any French reactionary might envy.[5] A great-granddaughter on her mother's side of Marshal MacMahon, president of the Republic in the early 1870s who served as surrogate for the monarchist cause, she was descended on her father's side from General de Miribel, named by Prime Minister Gambetta to be the army's chief of staff. As an adult, Elisabeth counted among her cousins Henri, comte de Paris, the leading pretender to the throne.

Elisabeth grew up on the Miribel estate where politics was too vulgar a topic for dinner-table discussion, but she realized as she matured that her milieu was as conservative politically as it was in matters of religion. Negative evidence for this became clear when military advancement for men on both sides of the family was blocked following the Dreyfus Affair, when Minister of War General L.J.N. André, with the help of his Masonic aide-de-camp, did his best to purge the army of suspected enemies of the Republic and to promote those faithful to the regime.

To the great distress of her parents, Elisabeth showed an interest early in life in the problems experienced by abnormal children, and studied with the Swiss Jean Piaget, a contemporary expert in child psychology, a field of endeavour then thought to be entirely unsuitable for someone nurtured in the Catholic faith. Elisabeth came to see this wilfulness over a career choice as an effective preparation for her role as political rebel in 1940.

On the day war was declared, 3 September 1939, Elisabeth de Miribel, then aged twenty-four, signed on as a translator and editor at the French Ministry of Foreign Affairs. She was soon assigned to work in London under the writer and diplomat Paul Morand, who was in charge of French liaison with the British in establishing an economic blockade of Nazi Germany. When Geoffroy de Courcel, an old family friend, phoned asking if she would lend the fledgling Free French organization a hand, Elisabeth showed up the same day. Her first impression of de Gaulle was of a very tall man in battle dress, long legs cased in leather leggings. Invited to share a cup of tea, the newcomer, who had turned up hoping to hear of a new Miracle on the Marne, was thunderstruck when de Gaulle instead predicted Reynaud's resignation and Weygand's agreement to sue for peace. In turn, she told the general that her colleagues in the Morand mission talked only of going home to France as soon as possible. For her part, Elisabeth indicated a desire to visit wounded French soldiers in British hospitals, to which de Gaulle nodded encouragement.

It was while on one of these hospital visits the next day that Mlle de Miribel heard of Pétain's speech suing for an armistice. On the verge of tears, she fought off despair. When Courcel called again, this time to ask for secretarial help, she went to Seamore Square at once to find Courcel and de Gaulle on the point of leaving for lunch with Alfred Duff Cooper, Britain's information minister, who sanctioned the general's history-making speech over the BBC that evening. At about 4 p.m., de Gaulle returned and Elisabeth set to work, stabbing at the typewriter with two fingers. The general took the text to Broadcast House without proofreading.

The next day, 19 June, Free France moved to St. Stephen's House on the Embankment, where the staff occupied a dreary, unfurnished apartment. Elisabeth continued her amateur secretarial work for some six weeks. Then, in August, she was given what seemed a more promising as well as a more challenging assignment – the promotion of the Free French cause in Canada, where the francophone community (including some 20,000 French citizens) was seen to be a logical source of support.

In fact de Gaulle's emissary soon discovered that Pétain was the object of a cult in French-speaking Quebec. Priests relayed to her the refrain of France's Cardinal Gerlier: "Pétain is France and France is Pétain." And the French consul in Montreal, to whom she had to turn for a renewal of her passport, told her, "Your ancestor Marshal MacMahon would turn over in his grave at the idea that you are serving the Judeo-communist-gaullist cause."[6]

In the summer of 1943, following the transfer of Gaullist headquarters from London to Algiers, Elisabeth de Miribel responded to a call from Henri Bonnet, in charge of the information services of the CFLN, and left for North Africa.

The peripatetic evangelizing of Elisabeth de Miribel on behalf of Free France was no doubt far more rewarding to the cause (and to herself) than the ad hoc secretarial work she had done at Gaullist headquarters in London. Even that mundane activity, however, had been of considerable help. On her very first day at Seamore House, while de Gaulle and Courcel were discussing the general's proposed speech over the BBC, she had welcomed into the ranks Claude Hettier de Boislambert, who later boasted that he was the first man in uniform to join La France libre.

The Catholic Claude Hettier de Boislambert was born in 1908 in the Normandy department of Calvados.[7] On his father's side, he belonged to a family of wealthy landowners with ties to the city of Caen; his mother belonged to the Norman nobility. In middle age, Boislambert remembered that, when his mother took him to mass in Caen, his paternal grandfather (who was of the Reformed faith), joined them in what may be seen as an act of precocious ecumenism. His English governess meanwhile prepared him for what in wartime would be a critically useful bilingualism.

Formal education for Boislambert began at eight, when he was sent to Saint-Louis-de-Gonzague school to be taught by priests. Training at the Collège de Normandie came next, followed by studies at École libre des sciences politiques ("Sciences-Po") and the acquisition of a law degree from the University of Paris. The young nobleman then joined a cavalry regiment as sublieutenant. By 1940, he had attained the rank of captain.

Mobilized in 1939, Captain Boislambert became a liaison officer with the British Expeditionary Force in the spring of 1940. On 28 May, he met *Le Connétable* on the front line near the town of Laon and was able to participate in the remarkable tank assault, led by the author of *L'armée de métier*, which broke through German lines. Shortly afterward, following the collapse of the French army in the field and the abdication of Reynaud in favour of Pétain, he resolved to continue the battle and boarded ship at Brest in defiance of the new government's ruling that such an act constituted desertion.

Reaching Falmouth on the morning of 18 June, Boislambert showed up at Gaullist headquarters that same afternoon. He then met de Gaulle for the second time and was immediately named deputy director of the minuscule cabinet.

Soon after his arrival in London, Boislambert was engaged in one of the earliest and most remarkable of Free France's wartime exploits – the securing for the cause of vast stretches of France's African empire. Eager to establish a Free French presence on sovereign French soil, *Le Connétable* on August 6 issued an insurrectionary appeal to all of France's overseas populations, aimed especially at European settler communities but implicitly including native peoples. Then, backing this appeal with concrete action, he dispatched to French Equatorial Africa a small band of his earliest partisans, including René Pleven. Pleven was a member of the Franco-British Coordinating Committee set up in September 1939 to oversee joint wartime purchasing and chaired by Jean Monnet, an experienced businessman who had been involved in similar Allied planning during World War I.[8]

Born in 1901 to middle-class Breton parents, Pleven attended a public lycée, then studied at the Institut catholique in Paris before obtaining a law degree in 1930.[9] The young Pleven showed a keen interest in the progressive views of the Catholic lay radical Marc Sangnier; he read Sangnier's newspaper *Jeune République* and befriended Georges Bidault, who became one of the leaders of the internal Catholic resistance. This liberal Catholic outlook came naturally: René's father, Jules Pleven, was as committed a republican as he was a Catholic; he had kept Dreyfus company during the artillery captain's final trial at Rennes in 1906; and he subscribed to the Christian democratic newspaper *L'Aube*.

After obtaining his law degree, Pleven worked at the ministry of finance before winning a research bursary which took him to London, where he met leading figures in the British and American business community and made enough money to become financially independent. In October 1939, when the French government appointed the cognac producer Jean Monnet to be co-president of the committee set up to coordinate British and French wartime purchasing, Monnet named Pleven, whom he had come to know and respect, as his deputy. Pleven had met *Le Connétable* years earlier in 1921. When the two men came together again, Monnet (who witnessed the scene) noted not only that the two men were both strikingly tall but that an immediate sympathy seemed to extend from one to the other.[10]

On 19 June, Pleven joined Monnet on an eleventh-hour mission to Bordeaux to meet France's new foreign minister, Paul Baudouin. Not only was the mission fruitless, Pleven also learned from the Socialist leader Léon Blum that, whatever lay ahead, he was unwilling to quit French soil. Monnet's deputy returned to Britain ready to consider the possibility of helping to constitute a truncated version of the French republic in the United Kingdom which would stay loyal to the wartime alliance against fascism. A chance meeting in the streets of London with a group of fishermen from his native Brittany, who had made their way to Britain in response to de Gaulle's 18 June appeal, convinced Pleven to show up at St. Stephen's House late in June. He soon found himself engaged with the Jewish jurist René Cassin and the Protestant financier Pierre Denis in negotiating with Churchill's special emissary, General Edward Spears, the critical accord of 7 August between His Majesty's government and Free France. On 6 August, as these deliberations were reaching their happy conclusion, he left London for Africa with Hettier de Boislambert.

Soon after their arrival in what was then Britain's Gold Coast, Pleven, Boislambert, and their small band of would-be liberators set out on what became a stunningly swift series of victories. In three days, beginning on 26 August, they liberated Chad, Cameroon, and the Congo, persuading the local colonial leadership to embrace Free France. A subsequent effort to capture Dakar, the capital of Senegal, led by de Gaulle and backed by the British, ended in utter failure in the face of a stubborn defence of the city by its *pétainiste* commander, General Pierre Boisson. Among others captured during this fratricidal conflict (which de Gaulle as well as Churchill had been determined to avoid) was *Le Connétable*'s loyal lieutenant Boislambert.

Flown to France early in 1941, Boislambert, still ill from wounds suffered at Dakar, was taken to a military hospital at Clermont-Ferrand, where he learned that the Jewish parliamentarian Pierre Mendès France was a fellow prisoner. Tried on five separate charges in June 1941, Boislambert was condemned to death before having this grim sentence commuted by Pétain. Throughout his ordeal, the hospital chaplain provided solace to the dedicated Gaullist, and every Sunday Boislambert joined other prisoners walking in silent single file to mass after which they were again locked up in tiny wooden cells. Then, following transfer to another prison, he managed to escape and was shortly afterward lifted out of France by a British plane. When he showed up again at Carlton Gardens, de Gaulle embraced him with tears in his eyes, a most unusual expression of affection in someone so notoriously aloof.

The Catholic personalities who had joined Boislambert and Pleven in capturing much of French Equatorial Africa for the Gaullist cause tended no doubt naturally enough to see their effort as part of a Christian crusade. This notion was expressed with great vigour by General Edgar de Larminat, chosen by de Gaulle to be the territory's high commissioner. In a memorandum to Pleven, dated 24 April 1941, Larminat made this view quite explicit: "Greco-Roman civilization, Christianized, ordered and refined over the ages and only after many struggles, must now stabilize and then save the world. Since we are traditionally the best champions of this civilization, we cannot fail it now!"[11]

Larminat added that de Gaulle, in choosing the Cross of Lorraine as a symbol of battle against the neo-paganism of the swastika's twisted cross, had identified himself not only as a soldier and a Frenchman, but as a Catholic, and had thereby given new expression to the virile faith of the Crusaders, speaking of France in mystical rather than simply patriotic terms, echoing the warrior poetry of the medieval chansons de geste. The general went on to observe (perceptibly enough) that France had been undergoing spiritual renewal over the last generation, but that any true rebirth of faith could not occur inside a church which was, as under the Vichy regime, subject to the domination of a purely pagan Germany.

Pleven, who had been named secretary-general of French Equatorial Africa in the summer of 1940, offered his own variant on the high commissioner's view in a speech at Caxton Hall in London on 15 April 1941: "Some people criticize our organization as made up of left-over activists from the

Popular Front while others charge that we are basically fascist in outlook. We are in fact neither of the left or right; instead we seek a *rassemblement.*"

Pleven's use of a term that de Gaulle would later adopt is in itself interesting. The devout Gaullist goes on to say, perhaps making the best of Free France's failure to attract major political figures,

> We are not looking for personalities that are too clearly marked one way or another because that way we would be playing our adversaries' game. Our ideological baggage is light, made up of a few basic principles – democratic responsibility, human dignity, the rights of the individual and of the people. At the same time, we intend to maintain the "spiritual patriotism" which has for 2000 years been shared by all civilized peoples and which is called Christianity.

To clarify himself, Pleven explained that he had not meant to use the Christian reference in the confessional sense but rather to define "A certain spiritual outlook, a disposition of the soul which implies tolerance, liberalism, humanitarianism, philanthropy, fraternity and socialism and, transcending all of these, a love of one's neighbour, that supreme divine and human law which is the common denominator of all the world's great philosophical and religious teachings."[12]

Returning to London after helping General Larminat administer French Equatorial Africa, Pleven became a key aide to de Gaulle in London and then in Algiers until the Liberation. His colleagues recognized his administrative qualities from the beginning. Claude Bouchinet calls him "the only man of value" in the early days of La France libre, more flexible and more intelligent than his associates.[13] Jacques Soustelle describes Pleven as "very Celtic in character, at once calm and sensitive (*pathétique*), well suited to deal with the Anglo-Saxons." Soustelle adds that Monnet's former deputy easily established a sense of trust and confidence at Carlton Gardens. "Go and see Pleven! Submit that idea to Pleven!" became a regular refrain at headquarters because de Gaulle's deputy had shown both courage and administrative skill during his African sojourn.[14]

With the creation on 24 September 1941 of the Comité national français (CNF), Pleven was named commissaire à l'Économie, aux Finances et aux Colonies, an appointment which resulted in his becoming something of a "prime minister" under de Gaulle's de facto presidency. When de Gaulle and a few intimates left the British capital for Algiers at the end of May 1943, Pleven stayed behind again as vice-president of the CNF in case the transfer to North Africa did not succeed. Later, when he joined his colleagues in Algiers, he devoted himself primarily to France's colonies and their future. In the end, however, Pleven always played the role of faithful lieutenant rather than potential successor because he lacked the charismatic power to hold together the highly diverse elements inside the Gaullist camp.

The band of young Catholic lieutenants who surrounded de Gaulle in his first few weeks in London was reinforced in late July 1940 by the arrival of yet another devout member of the Roman communion, who was ready not only to serve the general but to press for his fuller commitment to liberal and democratic principles. Claude Bouchinet, who was in almost daily contact with *Le Connétable* between his arrival and the end of 1942, was born in 1912.[15] He describes his childhood as happy, privileged, and devoutly Catholic. When his father was wounded in battle in 1915, he learned later, his mother travelled to Lourdes to offer thanks to Bernadette Soubirous, the young peasant woman whose visions of the Virgin Mary in Napoleon III's France were at the origin of a popular cult and pilgrimage. After the war, Claude's father edited a review for the Catholic publishing house Plon.

After passing entrance exams to the diplomatic service, Bouchinet was named attaché to the commercial branch of the French embassy in Berlin. He saw the French ambassador to Germany, André François-Poncet, as "the living but unhappily misleading image of a powerful, self-assured France."[16] Like his British counterparts in the German capital, he was alarmed at the piteous state in which the democratic nations found themselves as a result of the appeasement they had shown toward Nazi Germany since 1933. Called up as a reserve lieutenant in 1939, Bouchinet was infuriated by "the aging, potbellied generals" he encountered in the field. Assigned as liaison officer with units of the British Expeditionary Force stationed at Arras, he first heard of Charles de Gaulle during the night of 18–19 May when the newly promoted general made his victorious tank assault through German lines near Laon.

Inspired by *l'idée de la France* (Bouchinet's own term but one that de Gaulle would independently use), the young lieutenant felt conscience-bound to continue the combat against fascism. When he learned that a number of French parliamentarians were planning to board ship at Bordeaux in order to continue the fight from North Africa, he and his wife Janine headed to the port. On the quays crowded with men and women who had fled from the advancing German forces, no one talked to the new arrivals about de Gaulle's 18 June appeal over the BBC which the couple only learned about through reading an obscure paragraph in the local newspaper, *La petite Gironde*.

When the *Massilia* put down anchor in Casablanca on 24 June, the contingent of parliamentarians was not allowed to disembark, in line with a decision by the Pétain government. Bouchinet and his wife faced no such ban, however, and were given a warm reception by Morocco's governor-general, Charles Noguès, and his wife, who were both old friends. De Gaulle had counted on Noguès to join him in refusing to accept the Armistice and, immediately following his arrival in Morocco, Bouchinet felt similarly optimistic about the governor's intentions, even enrolling in a regiment of Spahis whose officers believed Pétain was merely stalling for time and would soon resume the combat against Hitler. In the end, however, the authorities made clear their pro-Vichy stance and forbade all French nationals from leaving the territory.

Their illusions shattered, the Bouchinets determined to make their way to London, a decision that was reinforced when they ran into the Jew Jacques Bingen (future delegate-general of de Gaulle inside France) and his wife who were similarly inclined. In the end, the two men donned Polish uniforms and, with their wives, boarded a Polish ship heading for Britain on 2 July. The next day brought the grim news of the British attack on the French fleet anchored off the Algerian coast at Mers-el-Kébir. "Despite our anglophilia," Bouchinet notes, "we felt that dirty business as a supreme outrage."[17] When, during the voyage, the captain of the ship announced that General de Gaulle was to speak over the BBC, passengers and crew gathered around the ship's radio. Although heavy static prevented him from hearing more than a few scattered phrases, Bouchinet was struck by the general's tone, so impressed that he imagined the general surrounded by a substantial and distinguished retinue!

Arriving in Liverpool on 16 July, Bouchinet turned up in London four days later. Introduced to de Gaulle by Geoffroy de Courcel (who had been his schoolmate at Stanislas), the new arrival had a brief exchange with *Le Connétable*. Impressed rather than put off by the general's terse manner, the new recruit was delighted to be selected as de Gaulle's aide-de-camp.

Comfortably settled in fashionable Eaton Square (where he and his wife would entertained over the next few months), the newly appointed aide-de-camp turned up on 26 July at Carlton Gardens, where he shared an office with Courcel next to a room occupied by de Gaulle. Over the next two and a half years his relationship with de Gaulle was at once courteous and distant.[18]

Agreeing with de Gaulle that the failure to recruit more qualified supporters posed major problems, Bouchinet at one point suggested that the general turn to progressive elements among the French exiles in the

United States such as the philosopher Jacques Maritain. When de Gaulle frowned at this proposal, his aide-de-camp took the liberty of reading a recent letter from the Catholic philosopher calling on the leader of Free France to issue a new Declaration of Rights committing himself to guarantee that, following the liberation, fundamental liberties would be guaranteed. Maritain was in fact challenging de Gaulle to bridge the ideological divide created in 1789: "The immense responsibility which Providence has committed into your hands is to reconcile … as a result of this unanticipated conjunction of events … our two traditions of spiritual fidelity and temporal emancipation, the tradition of Saint Louis and that born with the Declaration of Rights (of 1789)."[19]

Having listened to Bouchinet, the general burst out: "But he's asking me to make a public profession of Catholic faith!" When his aide-de-camp tried to explain that this had clearly not been Maritain's intention, the general declared that he had in effect satisfied the philosopher's demand in speeches already delivered at the Albert Hall and elsewhere. Bouchinet ended this tense exchange by pointing out that the people of France, who might soon entrust their political destiny to him, had a right to know at once whether de Gaulle's intention was to establish a democratic regime after the war or to create a system based on his personal authority alone.

It had taken all of Bouchinet's nerve and energy to challenge de Gaulle in this manner, and he left the general's country property exhausted and dispirited. The conviction that his remarks had come directly from his conscience gave him some comfort. He found greater solace back in London when, after hearing a church choir intoning evensong, he went inside, knelt, and let the rich music of the organ drown out the stress and tension of the day just passed.[20]

In fact, despite this open challenge to de Gaulle, Bouchinet never doubted that, however diffident the general might be about making public professions of democratic faith, he would turn out to be, not a Bonaparte, but a French Washington, ready to yield up power to the people in whose name he had launched his 18 June appeal. Similarly, the trust *Le Connétable* placed in his aide-de-camp was unconditional. In the end, however, none of his assigned responsibilities satisfied the captain's urge to get involved directly in combat against the enemy. During de Gaulle's periodic absences from London, he took parachute training near Manchester, then at a special camp at Camberley. After much pleading, the general finally released his aide in the spring of 1943, and on 22 May he was dropped from the sky near Chateau-Thierry with a mandate to help coordinate the resistance movements in the north of France.

Less openly but just as strongly as in his comments to de Gaulle, Bouchinet felt a deepening concern at the failure of the Holy See to speak out against fascist atrocities as the war intensified. In the Easter Sunday (5 April) 1942 entry in his journal, imagining himself in the role of a journalist facing Pius XII at a press conference, he posed the question, "What is the Vatican waiting for?" What was the Holy Father prepared to do, he expanded, in the face of racial persecution and indiscriminate warfare? Staying neutral or intervening to save an occasional Jew or gypsy was in the end pointless, he went on, before concluding, "What is needed is to stir up a groundswell of outrage which will carry the day with millions of the faithful and in the end galvanize the whole world."[21]

Perhaps even closer to de Gaulle than Bouchinet in the struggle to make Free France an effective instrument of national redemption was Gaston Palewski, who had become, in fact, something of a *gaulliste avant l'heure* at their first meeting in Reynaud's office in December 1934.[22]

Born in Paris on 20 March 1901, Palewski was descended from Polish and Romanian Jews who had come to France in the nineteenth century and, in the ultimate act of assimilation, had converted to Catholicism. Beginning his education at the Collège Rollin before World War I, the young Gaston displayed a precocious intellectual as well as physical versatility, studying languages, history, and geography as well as enjoying sports and expressing an interest in the new world of aeroplanes. These and other interests were developed later at the lycée Henri IV, "Sciences-Po," the Sorbonne, the École du Louvre (where his fascination with the arts groomed him to be a fastidious connaisseur), and Oxford where he cultivated an interest in the English novel of manners (his own sophistication made him the model for a character in a number of novels by Nancy Mitford). This sophistication did not always impress, however. His colleague Bouchinet dismissed Palewski as superficial, more given to witty salon conversation then to serious political reflection.[23]

Reaching conscript age after World War I, Palewski asked to do his military service in Morocco, where he arrived early in 1925 just as a revolt by the nationalist Abdel-Krim was threatening the French protectorate. The young soldier brought with him a letter of recommendation to the territory's resident general, Marshal Lyautey. Immersing himself in the intricacies of local politics, Palewski soon became one of the marshal's entourage, ending up as a key advisor on civil affairs in the territory and a friend to members of a new generation of Muslim students.

Several members of the Lyautey team he had worked with in Morocco joined Palewski in Paris later to help with preparations for the Colonial

Exposition of 1931, which he was assigned to supervise as *chef de cabinet* of the brilliant colonial minister Paul Reynaud. Palewski remained with Reynaud throughout the 1930s whether the gifted parliamentarian was in government or in opposition. Something of an epiphany occurred on that day in December 1934 when he sat in on a meeting between Reynaud, then finance critic of the government, and Colonel de Gaulle who had come to argue the case for the ideas set forth in *Vers l'armée de métier.* As Palewski later recalled, "That half-day was to be decisive for me because I told myself at the time that from then on, whatever influence I might have had at that time in the Republic would be put at the service of Colonel de Gaulle's ideas."[24]

When Reynaud rejoined the government in April 1938, first as justice minister, then, following Munich, as finance minister, Palewski formed part of a group which argued against appeasement and for military preparedness (among other things, he helped to assure the continuing flow of military supplies to the Spanish Republicans).

As relations within the government of Premier Édouard Daladier became increasingly tense, Palewski tendered his resignation and rejoined his combat unit, the 34th Bomber Squadron of the Air Force. Stationed in Morocco at the time of the Armistice and learning of de Gaulle's 18 June call to arms, Palewski went to see Resident-general Noguès hoping to hear that the struggle would be continued. Although any such hope was dashed following the tragic confrontation between the British and French fleets at Mers-el-Kébir, Palewski, undeterred, obtained permission to travel to Tangiers and made his way thence to London.

Arriving in London in late October 1940, Palewski found a warm welcome with friends in Upper Grosvenor Street, where Bouchinet soon paid him a call. After learning that de Gaulle was absent on the Dakar expedition, the newcomer decided not to show up at Carlton Gardens until the man whose military insights and leadership qualities had so overwhelmed him six years earlier returned. When *Le Connétable* got back from the Dakar fiasco on 23 November, Palewski, who describes himself as "the first Gaullist, since I had committed myself to the general even before 18 June," met the general and after a brief exchange was put in charge of Free France's "Political Affairs." This catchall assignment included the analysis of news coming out of France and of attitudes toward La France libre in other countries, the development of a more formal administrative apparatus at Carlton Gardens, as well as the supervision of the equivalent of France's traditional counter-intelligence agency, the 2ième Bureau, which was being organized by André Dewavrin, an army captain who had reached

London following the evacuation of Allied forces from Narvik in Norway in the spring of 1940.

While Palewski was willing enough to take on these administrative responsibilities, he longed to play a more active role in the battle against Vichy and the Nazis. Consequently, when the experienced diplomat Maurice Dejean showed up in London, Palewski urged de Gaulle to let the new arrival take over the "Political Affairs" portfolio and release him to take part in the ongoing liberation of France's African empire. As a result, in February 1941, Palewski was put in charge of civil and military operations in those parts of France's East African sphere of influence that were still under the sway of Vichy. Before departing on this mission, Palewski insisted that two chaplains accompany him. One of them, Père Fouquier, turned out to be an invaluable collaborator.[25]

Palewski's mission in East Africa ended in November 1942 when he was recalled to London by de Gaulle, who was looking for a sure and trusted hand to administer the increasingly complex problems facing what had become Fighting France in July. As the private secretary and confidant of the general from 1 October 1942, he helped prepare the agenda of the Comité national and did much to smooth over relations with the British, which went through periods of severe crisis.

Following the American landings in North Africa in November 1942, Palewski used his close friendship with Admiral Harold Stark, Roosevelt's special emissary in London, to help avert what might well have turned into an open break between de Gaulle and the "Anglo-Saxons." He flew to Algiers with the general on 28 May 1943, determined to help limit the influence there of the American-backed General Henri Giraud, an ultra-conservative *ex-vichyssois* who had agreed to share power with *Le Connétable.*

As close to de Gaulle as Palewski, or any of the young Catholics in his wartime entourage, was the Protestant François Coulet who joined his staff in the spring of 1941.[26] Coulet, who had been making radio broadcasts for Free France in Haifa since October 1940, came to the general's attention through Geoffroy de Courcel during a tour in the Levant. Courcel was at this point anxious to leave the relatively sheltered life he had led at the general's side in favour of action in the field and saw Coulet as a promising successor. After making the Protestant ex-diplomat his deputy and testing his qualifications, Courcel urged the general to consider Coulet as his aide.[27]

François Coulet was born on 16 January 1906 into an upper-middle-class Protestant family in Montpellier; his father Jules was rector of the city's prestigious university. François's studies began at the École alsacienne in Paris (founded following the loss of Alsace and Lorraine to Germany in 1870), then at lycées at Grenoble, Montpellier, and at Louis-le-Grand in Paris. His university-level education led to a *licence* in both law and letters at the University of Montpellier and a diploma from "Sciences-Po" in Paris (where, he remembered years later, the cynical opportunist Talleyrand had been presented as a model for the Republic's future ambassadors). The future Gaullist described himself at this stage in his life as "bourgeois in terms of milieu, politically liberal in outlook, an academic by training and an uncomfortable unbeliever who ended up being a conformist." Bouchinet describes him as "a rigid Protestant" who brought a stern sense of public service to the Free French organization.[28]

After training for the diplomatic service, Coulet began his career as third secretary to the French embassy in Moscow in 1936. It was during the Popular Front that he helped arrange the transit through France of Russian soldiers on their way to help the Spanish Republicans. Munich had a traumatizing effect on Coulet: from September 1938 on, he began to distance himself from the instructions forwarded to the embassy from a government which he felt was betraying the national interest.

Back in Paris on a visit, he was disgusted by the anglophobe and pro-Italian sentiment expressed by his superiors at the Quai d'Orsay. Only one figure stood out in the dismal array of defeatists – his fellow-Protestant René Massigli whom he met for the first time just as the experienced diplomat, who had denounced the Munich accord, was about to leave Paris to serve as ambassador to Turkey, a clear demotion.

Between 1939 and 1941, while serving as first secretary to the French embassy in Helsinki, Coulet was briefly attracted to the Oxford Movement, which aimed at reconciling the Church of England with Rome and restoring the liturgy and ritual of the pre-Reformation Church. It was obviously a time of personal trial and anguish, made increasingly difficult first by the Soviet assault on Finland, then even more traumatizing by the rapid defeat of France in the spring of 1940. Although, like the overwhelming majority of his fellow citizens, Coulet did not hear de Gaulle's call to arms from London on 18 June, he learned of it later and was much moved, imagining from afar that "it would logically draw all Frenchmen who had the good fortune to be free along the path of what now became an obvious, easily followed, sense of duty."[29]

During the anguishing months which followed France's capitulation and especially after 18 July when he was dismissed for disloyalty to the Vichy regime, Coulet travelled all over eastern Europe, the Middle East, and Africa looking in vain for signs that de Gaulle's call to arms had evoked a response. He ended up helping to organize radio propaganda for France libre in the Levant, where Courcel had found him in April 1941.

To prepare him for his new role, Courcel made sure that Coulet was invited to a 7 April 1941 dinner for de Gaulle offered by the British High Commissioner in Palestine and Transjordan, Sir Harold MacMichael. Not surprisingly, the atmosphere during the meal was rather gloomy, given the tense relations between the British and the Free French over control of Syria and Lebanon. When the time came for coffee, de Gaulle asked if he might be allowed to leave the party to have a private chat with Coulet in his room. The result, for the Protestant diplomat at least, was the intoxicating beginning of what turned into a lifelong devotion to the general and to his vision of France's destiny in the world.

Invited to sit down as soon as he entered de Gaulle's room, Coulet listened for more than an hour as the general, pacing up and down, recapitulated the calamitous events of 1940 (including the Dakar fiasco) and then talked of the means of transcending defeat and moving on to national redemption, beginning with a reassertion of French power and prestige in the outposts of empire.

"Is this at last the great man, pure and simple?" Coulet wrote in his diary after this first encounter. Years later, the Protestant Gaullist recalled that in de Gaulle he had instantly recognized "a true phenomenon of nature, a man who never perspired even in the tropics, a leader to whom it would be impossible not to tell the truth, a figure with whom there was no comparison in the military, political and diplomatic worlds."[30]

The cashiered diplomat accompanied the general throughout the Middle East and Africa during the spring and summer of 1941, then returned with him to London at the end of August when he was formally made aide-de-camp to de Gaulle and later his *chef de cabinet.* At Free French headquarters in Carlton Gardens, the ex-diplomat made a determined effort to avoid the potential manœuvring and squabbling which plagued the government-in-exile. Coulet had been bitterly disillusioned by the radical decline in the standards governing French public life since the heyday of the Third Republic, when men such as William Waddington and Charles de Freycinet, Protestants like himself, had governed the nation. Interestingly enough in this regard, as one of the general's most intimate counsellors, Coulet discovered that the general, with whom he regularly shared the evening meal, was in the habit of reading Calvin's *Institutes* before retiring![31]

Daily contact with de Gaulle brought Coulet to witness the general's frequent outbursts of rage and frustration at what he saw to be the treacherous dealings of the "Anglo-Saxons." Like others who made the move to

Algiers with the general in 1943, he deeply resented what he saw as the duplicitous behaviour of the Anglo-Americans in North Africa and the intrigues of the Vichyite elements who still held office in the liberated parts of the territory. Fortunately, from Coulet's point of view, these unsettling influences were to some extent balanced by the resolute patriotism of three key members of the Comité français de libération nationale: the Protestants André Diethelm and André Philip and the Jew René Cassin.

Coulet recalled years later that, in their private conversations, he and the general frequently talked about the Dreyfus Affair. Despite his conservative background and the ideology which he had endorsed during his youth, de Gaulle revealed that he had always believed in the Jewish officer's innocence. Coulet responded with a family anecdote dating back to 1894 during the trial, which ended in the Jewish artillery captain's condemnation for treason. His grandfather had been a close friend of General Paul Darras who presided over the captain's degradation in the courtyard of the Invalides in 1894. That same evening, Darras had confessed to Coulet's grandparent the deep shame he had felt in inflicting this most humiliating of military punishments on an innocent man.[32]

Like his predecessor Geoffroy de Courcel, Coulet in time grew tired of the tensions and intrigues inside the Gaullist camp and longed to commit himself to battle. With de Gaulle's blessing, he took up parachute training in the United Kingdom and, after Fighting France moved to Algiers in May 1943, he was given the chance to show his military as well as administrative skills in the liberation of Corsica. At the Liberation, as we shall see, he would play a key role in establishing Gaullist authority in Normandy.

The small band of men and women who formed de Gaulle's inner circle in wartime came either from the French aristocracy or from the upper middle class. This background of privilege and poise no doubt made it easier for them to achieve as close a relationship as was possible with the austere and aloof leader of Free France and to help sustain him in what was (at least from his point of view) a lonely combat for the nation's salvation.

All the members of this group were also, like de Gaulle, devout Christians who saw the battle against fascism in spiritual as much as in political terms. If they had been appalled at the appeasement policy of the Republican elites in the 1930s and at the defeatism of the agnostic government which so readily yielded power to Pétain in June 1940, they were no less contemptuous of the conforming Christians at Vichy who justified collaboration with the atheists in Berlin.

All these early Gaullists were eager for front-line combat, frustrated by the necessary but tedious staff-work at Carlton Gardens. All were anglophile, eager to establish the warm personal friendships with their British partners which de Gaulle would never even attempt. In wartime, they formed a resolutely Christian guard of honour inside the Free French camp. When peace came, all would be prepared to make a precedent-setting Christian contribution to the restoration and revitalization of Republican life.

CHAPTER FOUR

René Cassin: Jewish Champion of Gaullist Legitimacy

Interestingly enough, one of the first well-known personalities to show up at Free French headquarters was René Cassin, a Jew. Cassin was a law professor at the University of Paris who brought to the cause a rich experience of public service in Geneva as well as France. His arrival and the warm welcome he received from de Gaulle established the general's indifference to the religious or ethnic background of would-be recruits and his clear willingness to override the evident anti-Semitism in his military entourage. As a jurist, Cassin would develop a persuasive case for the political legitimacy of La France libre. As a republican, he would help invest Free France with liberal structures and democratic values.

Born in 1887 in Bayonne, René Cassin moved to Nice with his parents four years later. His mother was pious, his father an anticlerical, free thinking, republican. One of the greatest influences in the young boy's childhood was Dr. Ducelliez, a Protestant army doctor, who was forced into exile in Tunisia after indicting the city's water company for refusing to acknowledge its responsibility for transmitting the croup germ to the local population. The incident occurred in the aftermath of the Dreyfus affair, and Cassin *père* took the occasion to remark to René, "See! You don't have to be Jewish to be persecuted!"[1] Cassin never forgot that prejudice was a universal plague which needed to be fought on all fronts.

His Alsatian uncle, Rabbi Honel Meiss, gave what turned out to be gratuitous instruction in the Jewish faith to Cassin in preparation for his bar mitzvah. Years later, reflecting on the process of assimilation which conditioned his own falling away from Jewish religious tradition and practice, Cassin observed, "At that time, French Jews had already been dejudaicized. They were taught little about their faith which of course facilitated their spiritual detachment. I was emancipated very rapidly, despite the pressure created by the religious practices my mother continued to observe."[2]

While in Aix-en-Provence to attend the city's lycée, Cassin befriended a number of young priests from a nearby seminary who belonged to Le Sillon, the organization founded by Marc Sangnier, who urged not only acceptance of the Republic by his fellow believers but the promotion of radical social and economic reform. The two men met on at least one occasion. At one point Cassin tells us that he was sufficiently impressed by Sangnier to consider conversion, but the problem of Christ's divinity stood in the way.

The comparative study of religion, which Cassin had already made at this early stage in his life, had persuaded him that, while each faith saw itself as absolute, all took on a quite relative aspect when viewed from outside. Cassin concluded, "Humanity is clearly religious by nature. Although, in my own case, I have never experienced any kind of religious anxiety, I continue to feel a great spiritual curiosity. But I retain a purely secular perspective."[3]

Following his lycée experience, Cassin began his military service in 1906. In the army, he tells us, Jews had to outperform others to succeed at a time when Alfred Dreyfus had just been exonerated after years of struggling to redeem his reputation. Had the ordeal of the Jewish officer not been so present in his own mind, Cassin reports, he would have considered a military career.

After the army, Cassin studied both law and history at the University of Aix-en-Provence before moving to Paris. In the capital he began a lifelong friendship with a distinguished Protestant jurist, Professor René Massigli. At the same time, the overwhelming support for the ideas of Maurras in the student world of the Left Bank discouraged him, as did the condemnation of Sangnier and Le Sillon by Pius X in 1910.

Called up at the beginning of World War I, Corporal Cassin was happy to observe that old prejudices between partisans of *laïcité* and champions of Maurassian nationalism disappeared in the trenches, where mutual affection and respect was the rule. Badly wounded in October 1914 in the battle for St.-Mihiel, Cassin was visited by the village priest, whom he received with courtesy and who assured him that the prayers he was making were ecumenically inspired!

After the war, Cassin taught law at the University of Lille while organizing a French and then a Europe-wide veterans' federation designed to bring relief to those who had been traumatized by the conflict. In 1924, he was chosen to join the French delegation to the League of Nations; in Geneva he came to know Anthony Eden and Edvard Beneš, future colleagues in exile in London. Between 1929 and 1939, Professor Cassin held the chair of civil law at the University of Paris where his students included Pierre de Gaulle, the future general's brother, and Geoffroy de Courcel, the general's aide-de-camp in 1940.

As a non-religious Jew with a reverential feeling for the Revolution of 1789, Cassin was drawn to the Alliance israëlite universelle (AIU), founded in 1860 by seven prominent French Jews to propagate the values of French civilization world-wide, with a special focus on the Mediterranean basin. During a trip to Palestine in 1930, he visited schools founded by the Alliance as well as colonies established by Zionist pioneers.

In politics, the agnostic professor was drawn to the secular liberalism of the Radical Socialist party and to two of its key personalities, Aristide Briand and Georges Mandel.[4] After the 6 February 1934 right-wing street riots in Paris, he joined the Comité d'action antifasciste et de vigilance, a key rallying point for anti-fascist liberals and leftists. Cassin reacted to the increasingly violent manifestations of Nazi anti-Semitism by expressing open pride in his Jewish origins: "I would have been the lowest of the low," he wrote years later, "if during this period of prolonged suffering, I had pretended to hide my background which for centuries had tied my family to France."[5]

With the outbreak of war, Cassin asked to serve under the eminent playwright Jean Giraudoux, *commissaire à l'Information*, in effect propaganda minister. Put in charge of documentation, he was rarely consulted. In April 1940, he published an article analyzing the subversion of the idea of popular sovereignty by contemporary irrational ideologies, including Pangermanism, whose nefarious influence he traced back to the German philosopher Fichte. Cassin's own wholehearted determination to combat such ideologies both as a Jew and as a Frenchman was made clear in a piece written for the *Cahiers* of the AIU years later: "For those of us who were French, as for those of us who were also Jewish, the war immediately became a war over human rights because not only were combatants involved; innocents as well were condemned to death by Hitler's will on the sole basis of their birth."[6]

To a passionate patriot like Cassin, the rout of France's armies in the field in the spring of 1940 was disheartening enough; but it was only after listening to Marshal Philippe Pétain's 17 June speech suing for peace that he decided to leave France. The law professor did not learn of de Gaulle's 18 June radio appeal over the BBC until the morning after it was broadcast as he was heading south to the Spanish border. At 3:30 in the morning, stopping his car as it reached the bifurcation point where the roads to Bordeaux and Toulouse fork, Cassin looked out the window, thinking of the nearby Jewish cemetery where his maternal ancestors lay buried.

Once home, Cassin informed his wife that he was heading to London to obey de Gaulle's call to arms. The couple drove to St. Jean de Luz where they boarded a Polish ship destined for Britain. On board Cassin met the brilliant philosopher and sociologist Raymond Aron, a secular Jew like himself, who wrote in support of La France libre while in exile but did not become a Gaullist until after the war. On their arrival in England, the professor and his wife passed through the usual interrogation procedures with ease once it was made known that they had come to know Anthony Eden in Geneva.

Cassin arrived at St. Stephen's House, the temporary headquarters of La France libre, on the morning of 28 June.[7] He had never met de Gaulle but had read *Vers l'Armée de métier* and, as a law professor, he had come to know two of the general's most intimate advisers: Pierre de Gaulle had been a student in the Paris law faculty; the general's aide-de-camp, Geoffroy de Courcel, had written a thesis there about his grandfather's diplomatic experience in Berlin during the Gambetta ministry. As it turned out, both men had testified to Cassin's character on the eve of his arrival.

De Gaulle greeted the newcomer with a courteous "Monsieur le professeur!" in a tone at once ceremonious and warm. The jurist replied with a cautionary statement about his Jewish background, surmising that this might make him an undesirable recruit. Unperturbed, *Le Connétable* offered an account of his own family's contribution to French public life. Put at ease, Cassin went on to express his long-term admiration for the Catholic republican Marc Sangnier and Le Sillon.

Mutual confidence having been established, de Gaulle offered an account of his experience to date in London, including the news that Churchill had just the day before recognized him as "Chef des Français libres." The general then challenged the professor to transform what had been a purely verbal recognition into a formal bilateral treaty. In effect, Cassin thought to himself, such an alliance would under the circumstances be a treaty between a sovereign state and a single man! There were no doubt recent precedents for such an arrangements – His Majesty's government had signed accords with the Czech Edvard Beneš and the Pole

Wladyslaw Sikorski – but these men were heads of government, forced out of office but nevertheless enjoying a status which no military personality, however outstanding, could be seen to possess.

When Cassin voiced some of these reservations, de Gaulle was unperturbed. *"Nous sommes la France!"* he thundered in one of those Nietzschean pronouncements that came to him spontaneously throughout his career. Thrilled by the general's sally, Cassin felt an instant empathy with his new-found leader. "What I can assert," he wrote in his war memoirs, "is that, thanks to the sheer willpower of two of her sons, France was truly present in that small room, furnished as it was with nothing more than a simple desk and three chairs."[8] The jurist's biographer adds, "Did not these two men after all represent a perfect synthesis of the very different forces which have shaped and molded modern France?"

Cassin's legal background no doubt prepared him well enough for the role he had been assigned, but he soon concluded that the immediate task ahead was more political than juridical. Before signing any diplomatic agreement, the British needed to be persuaded that the small band of Gaullist troops then in the United Kingdom represented the real France, which, by the 28 March 1940 agreement between the two Allies, precluded either from signing a separate peace, an agreement Pétain had clearly violated by seeking an armistice and then a separate understanding with Hitler.

To inform himself about the best case that might be made for a bilateral treaty, Cassin took note of everything dealing with French-British relations he could lay his hands on, including the text of a speech by Churchill in the House of Commons pledging to defend France's *grandeur* and *indépendance*. In addition, he canvassed the views of French troops based in England and drew up a list of French assets in the United Kingdom, clearly a potential bargaining chip in any negotiations. To anticipate any suggestion the British might make that early recruits to Free France were simply refugees who might better serve the cause in British uniforms, he suggested that any putative agreement include a clause stipulating that La France libre undertake to defend Great Britain, making the relationship a mutually binding pact between two psychologically equal forces. Among other documents, Cassin reviewed the pact signed between France and the Czech government in exile according to which Czech units continuing to fight after the fall of their country were to be commanded by their own officers speaking their own language under overall French command and operating with French financial credit.

On 30 June, Cassin returned to St. Stephen's House with a first draft for de Gaulle's consideration. During this second encounter, the general's counsellor felt impelled to ask quite bluntly whether the presence of a Jew in the Free French camp might jeopardize the cause. Reassured that the question of his religious origin was irrelevant and that the general would give the draft his full attention, Cassin turned to reflect on issues still needing clarification: whether Free French troops would serve under a distinctive flag, with their own officers speaking their own language and governed by their own rules of discipline and command structure and, just as important, how to avoid any suggestion of their being seen as mercenaries. The financing of the Free French military must be based, not on grants, but on loans to be reimbursed.

On 1 July, Cassin showed up again at Gaullist headquarters to discover that de Gaulle had made only minor modifications to his original text which was then forwarded to Churchill's right-hand man, Major Desmond Morton. After a brief delay made necessary by news of the July 4 attack by British ships on the French fleet at Mers-el-Kébir, Morton responded with a counter-proposal, suggesting that an exchange of letters between the British prime minister and de Gaulle, rather than a formal treaty, should suffice to meet the needs of La France libre.

Before considering any response to this seemingly less formal guarantee of British support, Cassin sought counsel with three other recent recruits to the Free French cause – the ambitious but gifted Admiral Émile Muselier, the Protestant banking expert Pierre Denis, and the Catholic René Pleven, Jean Monnet's former deputy. One of the results of their shared reflections was an insistence that, in the text of any exchange of letters, there should be a clause guaranteeing that Free French forces never be used in combat against troops loyal to Vichy. The possibility that a binding agreement with Britain might lead to internecine fighting was clearly something to be avoided at all costs.

On 30 July, the Foreign Office came up with yet another variant on a possible accord, going far toward the satisfaction of Free French requests. All French warships already committed to Admiral Muselier would be left under his command. General de Gaulle would be allowed to organize Free France troops on British soil, including the recruitment of French soldiers already in the United Kingdom or yet to arrive. Funding for the Forces françaises libres would be based on loans extended by the Bank of England, which Free France would settle at the war's end.

On 5 August, at the decisive final meeting attended by de Gaulle, Cassin, and Pierre-Olivier Lapie (the Socialist deputy for Nancy who had recently arrived in London), the British prime minister intervened decisively in favour of the text Cassin had worked so hard to refine.

Two days later, on 7 August, letters of exchange, which included a key phrase indicating that de Gaulle was recognized by Britain as "the supreme commander of all French volunteer forces" (by implication including members of the internal as well as external resistance), were signed by the British prime minister and the French general.[9]

Thanks in large measure to René Cassin's persistence and his jurist's appreciation of the extremely tenuous legal position of La France libre, the letters exchanged between Churchill and de Gaulle (and ratified by the House of Commons on 20 August) allowed Free France to play an autonomous role in the struggle against Vichy and the Third Reich. The credit extended to *Le Connétable* and his colleagues by the Bank of England ended in June 1943, when La France libre (transformed into La France combattante in July 1942) moved to sovereign French territory in Algeria. The military arrangements which had been arrived at released Gaullist recruits to do heroic battle in Africa, the Middle East, and in the liberation of continental Europe.

For better (and sometimes for worse), the political aspects of the 7 August accords depended in the end on the perennially difficult personal relations between the two chief signatories. Both were impetuous by nature as well as hypersensitive about their nations' conflicting interests in various parts of the world. As the war progressed, the British prime minister's increasing reliance on the bitterly anti-Gaullist Roosevelt led to the exclusion of de Gaulle from overall strategic planning, most notably before the liberation of French North Africa in November 1942 and in the weeks before D-Day. Despite these frustrations, the exchange of letters rescued Free France from political limbo and laid the foundations for France's substantial participation in her own psychological as well as political liberation.

If, during his first assignment for de Gaulle, Professor Cassin had found it difficult to fashion a legal case for La France libre, he had been able on the other hand to develop a powerful indictment of the Vichy regime. From the moment the government of Pétain had accepted the terms of the 22 June armistice with Nazi Germany, Cassin argued, it had subjected itself to foreign control and was thus no longer able to speak to France's true interests. And by ceding Alsace and Lorraine to a foreign state, Pétain's administration had violated the 1875 constitution, which forbade the cession of any part of the national territory without the express consent of the Chamber of Deputies. In fact, this single act constituted a coup d'état.[10]

Equally unconstitutional, according to Cassin, was the 20 July vote awarding special powers to Pétain which had been made by a truncated and therefore illegal representation of the National Assembly. President Albert Lebrun, an indispensable participant in the constitutional process, had not at that point resigned and could only be replaced by a duly constituted conclave of senators and deputies. Instead, in clear violation of an 1894 statute, a rump Assembly had given Pétain what amounted to monarchical powers. Under these circumstances, the people of France were no longer obligated to obey the so-called Vichy Government.[11]

As Jean-Luc Barré has noted, the support given Cassin by de Gaulle in the development of his case for Free France's legitimacy testifies to the general's conviction that the Republic, whatever its flaws, represented the continuity of the French state in the modern age. Evidence for this sharing of republican convictions was discovered by Barré in an *argumentaire* or brief drawn up by Cassin and vetted by de Gaulle found in the general's private papers. The case is made in this brief that, by violating the 1875 constitution which required that any constitutional revision needed the consent of both Senate and Chamber of Deputies as well as by obviating a law of 1884 which proclaimed that the republican constitution was not subject to revision, Vichy no longer exercised any legal authority over French citizens beyond its reach.[12]

Cassin's legal briefs for Free France became far more plausible as troops loyal to de Gaulle liberated four of France's sub-Saharan colonies in the summer of 1940. By an *ordonnance* (edict) issued from Brazzaville *en terre française* on 27 October 1940, the general created a Conseil de l'Empire. This Council was made up of the four governors of the newly freed territories, three military figures, together with three Gaullist notables, including Cassin. Professor Cassin, its only civilian member, was made permanent secretary of the Council; but, nervous about the anti-Semitic tendencies of many of his new colleagues, he insisted that de Gaulle obtain their explicit consent before he agreed to assume the post. The text of the edict made explicit Cassin's view of the Vichy regime: "There is no longer a French government properly speaking. In effect, the organism sitting at Vichy and which pretends to call itself a government is unconstitutional and subject to the invader."[13]

Repudiating Vichy, the Council arrogated to itself competence to pursue the war to liberate France as well as the authority to deal with foreign states.

A fuller rationale for the creation of the Conseil was published on 16 November in what became known as the Brazzaville Manifesto. In the course of his research in London, Cassin had uncovered a legal precedent for the bold initiatives taken by Free France since 18 June. In an *ordonnance* of 15 February 1872, usually referred to as the Treveneuc law, the fledgling

Third Republic had stipulated that, in extraordinary circumstances, subordinate political bodies such as the nation's *conseils généraux* (more or less representative bodies sitting in various parts of France's empire) could (and by implication should) assume provisional power to defend the Republic. Guided by this handy precedent, the leader of the Free French solemnly pledged that the Conseil would function in conformity with the 1875 constitution and that he would give a full account of its acts as soon as a properly constituted National Assembly could be convened.

The creation of the Council gave La France libre the beginnings of a more formally structured executive although, given de Gaulle's presidential rather than prime ministerial style, there was no cabinet solidarity, a republican principle Cassin lobbied for. Whatever its limitations, the new body led to a more assertive defence of French national interests. In reaction to the Vichy government's surrender of control over French Indo-China to Japan, the Council issued a declaration promising that Free France would defend "the integrity of all French territories around the world."[14] In addition, it began to act in concert with other exiled governments then in London, sending Cassin to the first meeting of the Interallied Conference on 12 June 1941. Following the Nazi assault on the Soviet Union shortly afterwards the jurist went to see Stalin's ambassador to the United Kingdom, Ivan Maisky, whom he knew from his days in Geneva.

While engaged in developing a legal case for La France libre, the Radical Socialist Cassin had felt a continuing concern about the organization's commitment to the republican ethos. It was true, of course, that Charles de Gaulle had a direct if tenuous link to the last government of the Third Republic:[15] he had been named under-secretary of war by Paul Reynaud on the eve of the debacle. However, during the months that followed his insurrectionary appeal of 18 June, *Le Connétable* had made no categorical profession of republican devotion; and many of those who rallied to his banner in the early days not only abominated the Third Republic but blamed their nation's defeat on the influence of the revolutionary tradition from which republicans derived their inspiration.[16]

One way in which Cassin was able to celebrate the Republic and the values it had inherited from the 1789 revolution was as editor of the *Journal officiel*, a task assigned him by de Gaulle at the beginning of 1941. The *Journal*, with the tricolour on its front page, published all edicts, decrees, and military orders emanating from La France libre, following traditional republican procedure.

Between June and September 1941, in de Gaulle's absence, Cassin took over the chairing of the Conseil. But, while the professor was a competent jurist, he was not suited by temperament to administer and, after this experience, *Le Connétable* never again entrusted Cassin with the same level of responsibility.

A further formalization of Free France's political structure came with the creation on 24 September 1941 of the Comité national français (CNF), an eight-member body made up of *commissaires* (commissioners) overseeing separate departments, which took unto itself both legislative and executive responsibility. Cassin had hoped to be named to the Labour portfolio in the new body, but was given Justice and Public Education instead. He saw both "bitterness and ingratitude" in this decision by de Gaulle to demote him to a secondary role.[17]

The democrat in Cassin worried throughout these months that the structure of La France libre remained essentially autocratic, lacking the counterweight of an independent assembly where public policy could be openly debated and executive authority subjected to critical scrutiny. In this regard, he managed to insert in the constitution of the new body a clause guaranteeing the convocation, as soon as circumstances allowed, of a consultative assembly based on the largest possible expression of the national will. This pledge was finally respected on 17 September 1943 when de Gaulle, by then in Algiers, called for convocation of an Assemblée consultative provisoire in the North African capital.

On 15 December 1941, again in response to Cassin's concerns, the CNF created a Commission de legislation auprès du Commissariat national à la Justice et à l'Instruction publique, in effect giving the resolutely democratic jurist the power to review the Committee's ordinances and decrees to ensure their conformity to republican tradition and usage.

De Gaulle meanwhile was clearly interested in guiding post-war France toward the acceptance of a strong executive. At one point during their London sojourn, he asked Cassin to enquire into the way the American presidency functioned; but when he learned that anyone seeking to become the chief executive of the United States had first to be selected by a vast convention and that the president did not have the power to dissolve the legislative branch, he lost all interest.[18]

Cassin used every available opportunity to promote the republican cause at home as well as in London. Speaking to his compatriots inside France over the BBC on 9 July 1942, he urged them to demonstrate their devotion to the Republic on Bastille Day by sporting red, white, and blue colours and singing the Marseillaise.

Among others left behind in London to maintain a Free French presence in the British capital when de Gaulle left for Algiers in May 1943, Cassin was given no portfolio on the CFLN but managed to keep a watching brief on developments in North Africa. The republican in him was wary from the beginning about any accommodation with General Henri Giraud, the conservative (and racist) officer whom the United States was backing in Algeria. Like other Gaullists, Cassin was distressed at the refusal of the American government to accept Free France as a democratic ally. In an attempt to influence opinion in the United States, the professor began by making clear in an interview given to the New York Herald Tribune on 8 January 1943, that from 11 July 1940 onward, following Pétain's illegal assumption of the title "Head of the French State," the republican constitution of 1875 had been consistently violated. As a result, he argued, the French people were no more obligated to obey Vichy than the Czechs to follow the collaboratory Hacha or the Norwegians to heed Vidkun Quisling. "There is in fact," he declared "only one legitimacy, that of the Republic and its laws. Following the principle set forth by our great revolution of 1789, sovereignty is vested exclusively in the nation. It is untransferable and imprescriptible." Cassin reminded the American correspondent that the Provisional Government of General Trochu, which emerged from a popular uprising in Paris following France's defeat at the hands of Germany on 4 September 1870, had been recognized just three days later by Washington, even though it had not been possible to summon a National Assembly until the following January.[19]

In a brief submitted to de Gaulle on 23 February, the professor specifically warned against any compromise with those who had been associated with the "pseudo-government" of Vichy. All the legislation which had emanated from L'État français, so much of which had been inspired by Nazi or fascist philosophy, should be considered null and void, he argued. Only when the French people were again free to exercise their sovereign rights should the nation's statutes be subject to modification.[20]

Fortunately from Cassin's point of view, the Machiavellian in de Gaulle which had brought him to accept a temporary deal with the reactionary Giraud in Algeria would bring him after forty days of co-presidency to displace his rival from power. Thus was founded what Jean Lacouture calls "*L'État gaulliste.*"[21]

Cassin signed an accord with the British which expressly identified the union, under the general's command, of the Free French Forces in the United Kingdom and the armed resistance inside France as the "Armies of the French Republic." Reflecting on the steps made since his first meeting with de Gaulle, he declared on 29 June 1943, "The profound truth contained in our founding myth has now been affirmed. Thanks to the joining together of France's resistance forces, those inside the nation as well as those outside, the myth has become a reality."[22]

From his first meeting with de Gaulle at St. Stephen's House on 28 June 1940, Professor Cassin's efforts to give Free France both constitutional credibility and a sound republican orientation had been tireless. In his memoirs, the Jewish jurist quite properly boasts of his success in both these efforts: "I can lay claim with great pride to the role I played in the progressive democratization of our various wartime institutions, in the restoration of republican liberties in every territory we liberated from Vichy control, in the creation of the Constituent Assembly as well as in the organization of the people's resistance inside France."[23]

De Gaulle, always chary of praise for his collaborators, endorsed this self-appraisal unreservedly: "Professor Cassin was my invaluable collaborator in the preparation of all the acts and documents on which were based, starting from nothing, our entire internal and external structure."[24]

While he remained in the British capital, Cassin experienced a series of radical mood swings, partly as a result of his decision to be self-effacing, partly because of pressures brought to bear on him by groups eager to exploit or to denounce his Jewish background. As he put it in a 1961 interview, de Gaulle's legal counsellor deliberately refused all special titles and honours during his sojourn in London "in order not to confer a too visible importance on an associate of Jewish background."[25] That Cassin's support staff (including Professor André Gros and Maître Simon as well as his assistant Berthe Levy) were also Jewish clearly added to the hostility he encountered among some of de Gaulle's military associates.

Toward the end of 1941, the law professor learned that someone had complained to the Catholic René Pleven about the excessive number of Jews at Gaullist headquarters, naming Cassin and his team explicitly. When the complainant went on to say that working around so many Jews affected his job performance, Pleven had replied with a curt, "Well, then, I'm quite happy to accept your resignation!" and the matter had been settled, but not without leaving a painful memory.[26]

That this "ecumenical" outlook in the end prevailed among Free France's political leaders, Cassin makes clear in his memoirs. The charge so often leveled against de Gaulle that he remained a Maurrassian at heart, that is, that he considered Jews as outside the nation, was false, the professor insists: "I must point out that, during that grim period of intolerance, General de Gaulle offered constant proof of his serenity and loftiness of view. Not only did he accept the commitment to Free France of foreign as well as native-born Jews, he declared publicly that in his opinion all French citizens who chose to participate in the liberation of France were equal."[27]

If his Jewish background brought Cassin a number of slights, some perceived, some very real, it also brought a series of flattering solicitations. Early in his stay in the British capital, the jurist, whose leftist sympathies were well known, was approached by a group of predominantly Jewish but anti-Gaullist French socialists who grouped themselves under the banner of Jean Jaurès. Cassin was utterly unimpressed by their arguments.[28] London-based Zionists meanwhile tried to gain his support for the creation of an exclusively Jewish army contingent with a view to exploiting its putative wartime exploits as a bargaining chip for the negotiation of a separate Jewish state at the war's end. Sensitive to the existence of a strong anti-Semitic current inside La France libre as well as in the "Anglo-Saxon" world, Cassin demurred, worried that any such purely Jewish mobilization might be more harmful than helpful. At the same time, Cassin felt it only reasonable that, at a time when Jews were being forced out of Europe, they ought to be guaranteed a secure life somewhere else.[29]

During Passover 1941, Cassin, who spoke frequently over the BBC to his fellow-citizens, addressed himself specifically to the "Israëlites de France." The jurist made clear from the beginning that he was neither a rabbi nor a chaplain in the Free French forces, nor for that matter a faithful follower of Jewish rites. He simply wished to express a deeply felt sense of solidarity with men and women of Jewish faith living under fascist tyranny. Cassin's central aim in this talk was to emphasize his conviction that the principles of toleration and equality enunciated in the Great Revolution remained in the hearts and minds of his fellow-citizens despite the racist propaganda to which they were being subjected. He reminded his listeners of the celebrated gesture of the Jewish chaplain, Bloch, who lost his life during the First World War ensuring that his colleague, a dying Catholic chaplain, receive the last rites in the Roman communion.

The current persecution of Jews in France, Cassin insisted, was not the product of popular feeling but of orchestrated manipulation. The jurist's view was that of an *assimilé* unable to believe that the heirs to 1789 were capable of complicity in a genocide. "It is in vain," he insisted, "that they (the Vichy government) are trying so hard to destroy the union among the spiritual families of France, that most precious source of her strength."[30]

The same confidence in the basically ecumenical outlook of France's spiritual leaders appears in Cassin's posthumous tribute to Cardinal Jean Verdier (1864–1940), which appeared in *Volontaire pour la cité chrétienne,* a monthly paper edited in wartime London by two prominent Catholic Gaullists, François-Louis Closon and Maurice Schumann. Cassin speaks of Verdier as a consistent defender of human rights in the 1930s. During the Ethiopian conflict, the cardinal had preached the unity of all humankind in the name of a church that was "The Internationale of Love"; during the Popular Front, he had championed the Declaration of the Rights of Man and had urged conciliation over the divisive school issue; at a eucharistic conference in Algiers in 1937, Verdier had been warmly received by men and women of all races and religions; he had vigorously condemned anti-Jewish persecution in pre-war Germany. After informing his readers that he had last talked to Verdier in November 1939 during a meeting of the *Secours national*, a civilian volunteer agency organized to back the war effort, Cassin concluded, "If this distinguished *Defensor civitatis* is no longer alive to protect without distinction all the inhabitants of Paris – Catholics, Jews or Communists – against monstrous executions and deportations, at least his example remains."[31]

A third effort to win Professor Cassin away from his loyalty to the Gaullist cause during his stay in London originated with Admiral Émile Muselier, one of the few high-ranking military figures to have rallied to de Gaulle from the beginning. In an effort to enrol Cassin in a September 1941 plot to supplant the leader of Free France, the admiral suggested that he was well placed to deflect the anti-Semitic feelings that the Jewish professor's presence would clearly evoke among the predominantly Catholic sailors under his command. This would-be guarantee, coming from a man Cassin describes as "a grandson of a Jew who calls himself a democrat," disgusted the professor, who told Muselier that he would gladly trust his fate to Breton sailors without any such intercession.[32]

Cassin's refusal to be deflected from the central purpose of La France libre was admirable. On the other hand, his avoidance of involvement in high-level policy decisions, where he would encounter men who clearly resented his Jewish background and his support of the Popular Front, led, understandably, to a growing sense of marginalization.[33] Cassin confided this feeling to the journal he kept during his time in London, in which he noted on 23 December 1940 that, while destiny had seemingly shaped him to contribute to an exalted enterprise, he felt more and more impotent.[34] While greeting Jacques Soustelle in January 1941, he worried aloud that he was being thought of back in Paris intellectual circles as no more than a token representative of the Popular Front in the Gaullist camp.

Part of Cassin's sense of isolation came from the absence in London of men of similar political sensibility. Thinking back during the early 1960s on his Free French experience, Cassin notes that there were only three other "men of the Left" in London – Pierre-Olivier Lapie, Georges Boris, and Henry Hauck. Thanks to pressure from right-wing army men, the left-wing Catholic Pierre Cot, whom Cassin had come to know during the Popular Front, had been turned away from La France libre and had gone to New York instead. More than anyone else, the professor missed the presence of the Radical Socialist leader Édouard Herriot, who would have made a difference had he chosen to leave France.[35]

Even after moving to Algiers in the summer of 1943, Cassin found no relief from this overwhelming depression. On 25 September, the professor confided to his diary that he was aging too fast, without close friends, unable to communicate with younger people and having neither children nor a body of work on which to base a lasting reputation. The cumulative effect of all this was "an appalling solitude" from which he thought he might never recover.[36] Yet, however despondent he might feel, Professor Cassin would have new challenges to face in multi-ethnic North Africa, which served in 1943 as the base for the renaissance of republican institutions and, ultimately, the liberation of France.

CHAPTER FIVE

Maurice Schumann: The Catholic Voice of La France libre

J'appartiens à une famille politique dont la raison d'être est de lutter contre la cassure de la France. Marc Sangnier a, dès le début du siècle, c'est-à-dire à une époque où ce langage était inintelligible à la plupart des citoyens, appris à déceler les artifices et les périls que comporte l'affrontement des deux blocs.

Maurice Schumann, 22 November 1962

Of all those who transmitted the Free French message of defiance, resistance, and hope to those living in Vichy France or in the German-occupied zone, none was more eloquent than the journalist-turned-broadcaster Maurice Schumann. Schumann was born in Paris on 10 April 1911 to upper-middle-class Jewish parents who were so thoroughly assimilated that they felt only the most nominal link to their ancestral faith.[1] Schumann *père* was a successful corset manufacturer; like his wife, he was devoted to the Republic and to the memory of the Revolution which had given it birth. Patriotism came naturally in this environment: Schumann tells us that his first clear memory of the wider world was of the victory parade down the Champs Élysées on Bastille Day, 1919.

The gravitational pull toward the deep Catholic faith of Schumann's mature years began as early as primary school where one of his teachers, Mlle Limandon, made him "a virtual Christian and Catholic." A series of spiritually charged encounters completed the process of his conversion. While attending the Lycée Jeanson-de-Sailly in Paris, the adolescent Schumann was encouraged in his religious quest by the school chaplain, the abbé Bottinelli, a *sillonniste* whose faith, like that of Marc Sangnier, was inextricably linked to a longing for social justice. Further guidance toward acceptance of Catholic doctrine was offered by Father Brodeur, an Oratorian who taught at the Collège Gerson.

While preparing entrance exams for the École normale, Schumann paid a visit to the headquarters of the Jeune République movement, on the

Boulevard Raspail, where he was greeted by Sangnier's secretary, the brilliant but non-conformist Catholic historian Henri Guillemin. In the end, a serious illness that prevented the would-be *normalien* from writing the prerequisite exam led Schumann to engage in a close exploration of the Christian mysteries. Following his convalescence, the putative Catholic enrolled at the University of Paris where he completed a *licence* in philosophy.

At this point in his spiritual journey, intellectual curiosity led Schumann to fall under the influence of two contemporary writers who would give his intuitive Catholicism a solid intellectual grounding. Henri Bergson, Jewish in background like himself, whom Schumann describes as "on the threshold of conversion"[2] at the end of his life, helped wean the philosophy student away from the positivist world-view that was still fashionable in Parisian academic circles. The author of *The Two Sources of Morality and Religion* even convinced Schumann that three of the icons of modern thought – Darwin, Marx, and Freud – were, respectively, the inspiration for twentieth-century racism, tyranny, and dehumanization.

Just as significant an influence in Schumann's intellectual and spiritual evolution was Charles Péguy, the poet and essayist from Orléans, whose conversion from agnostic humanism to Catholicism (partly due to Bergson) was a turning point in a brilliant career. Péguy was a non-conformist proselyte, a rare Catholic *dreyfusard* as well as a militant republican. As we have seen, he was also the first to fashion the myth of Joan of Arc as simultaneously Catholic saint, proto-Republican hero, and precocious nationalist, a myth Schumann endorsed with rapturous enthusiasm and exploited in his wartime broadcasts.[3]

Schumann's youthful religious quest was paralleled by an attraction to leftist political movements. His first such involvement was with the Ligue d'Action universitaire républicaine et socialiste (LAURS), a student association whose president was his future colleague in La France libre, Pierre Mendès France. At the same time Schumann was developing a friendship with the Socialist leader Léon Blum, with whom he shared not only a passion for greater social justice but for literature and the arts. Under Blum's influence and that of the then left-wing student leader (and future Gaullist) Georges Pompidou, Schumann joined the Jeunesses socialistes in the late 1920s. Both these student organizations, like their parent bodies, were notoriously anticlerical, creating a frustrating disjunction between Schumann's nascent Catholicism and his earnest desire to campaign for greater social justice.

When, at nineteen years of age, Schumann met Marc Sangnier, he experienced the life-changing epiphany which allowed him to see his spiritual quest and his search for social justice as one and the same pursuit.

Schumann was not unfamiliar with Sangnier's movement. Years earlier, when he was just thirteen, strolling with his brother near the family property on the Place Victor Hugo, Maurice had run into a gang of Camelots du Roi, street vendors for the right-wing *Action française*, who were attacking a youth selling copies of Sangnier's *La Jeune République*. The Schumann brothers sent the bullies packing and, as a result of the encounter, the young Maurice became a subscriber to the liberal Catholic weekly.

Schumann's first personal encounter with Sangnier came on Armistice Day 1930 during a public debate in the Salle des Sociétés savantes. Prompted to speak at the end of the discussion, Schumann argued passionately for the abrogation of laws banning Catholic religious orders from France and was so impressed by Sangnier's supportive response that he decided on the spot to become a follower. This was the deciding moment for the nineteen-year old. Thanks to Sangnier, "Christian democracy" was henceforth the guiding principle of his life and thought.

Although Schumann, as a result of this spiritually electrifying meeting with Sangnier, would henceforth see himself as a committed Catholic and although he joined La Jeune République in 1935 to bring his religious and political convictions into harmony, he did not yet take the formal step of seeking baptism in the Roman communion. This decision was based (in part at least) on a felt need to express solidarity with European Jews at a time of rising anti-Semitism.[4] In fact, Schumann was not baptized until the spring of 1942 in Birmingham, when the sacrament was administered by one of his earlier mentors, Father Brodeur, who had joined La France libre.

Sangnier's influence on Schumann not only led him to join La Jeune République, but also helped prepare him to consult the progressive Dominican Fathers who became a regular source of inspiration for the young philosophy student. Later in life, Schumann came to appreciate the role played by the Dominicans as well as by Sangnier in preparing a whole generation of Catholic intellectuals to win for their co-religionists the *droit de cité* which they had so long been denied. Schumann himself was of course an excellent example of this tutoring, as were Georges Bidault, Pierre-Henri Teitgen, and François de Menthon, all of whom would be actively involved in the internal resistance.[5]

Spiritually anchored and politically oriented following his encounter with Marc Sangnier, Schumann chose journalism as a career. Between 1930 and 1933, he worked in London as foreign affairs reporter for the Havas News Agency while contributing a number of articles on European political developments to the Dominican periodicals *La Vie intellectuelle* and *Sept*.

Schumann's focus on the deteriorating political situation inside France and throughout Europe intensified following his return to Paris. The political and diplomatic crises of the 1930s bitterly divided French Catholics, exposing what would become a widening rift between the minority who became *gaullistes* and the vast majority who turned *pétainistes* after 1940.[6]

Catholic participation in the Rassemblement populaire, a broad coalition of liberals and leftists brought together in advance of the spring 1936 election by the Socialist (and Jewish) Léon Blum, clearly exposed this division. Jeune République, the progressive Catholic party to which Schumann had committed himself in 1935, fielded a number of candidates for the Rassemblement, four of whom were elected. (All four, it is worth noting, were among the eighty deputies who voted to deny plenipotentiary power to Pétain on 10 July 1940).

Meditating on the involvement of Catholics in the ongoing election campaign and on the larger issue of the political orientation of the French Catholic community, the Dominican publishers of *La Vie intellectuelle* provoked the readers of the 10 March 1936 issue with the editorial query, "Dieu est-il à droite?" Answering their own rhetorical question in the negative, they at the same time urged against the formation of a specifically Catholic party, whatever its ideological orientation. Five weeks later, in a 17 April radio broadcast clearly inspired by the Dominicans' reflections, the Communist leader Maurice Thorez offered "an outstretched hand (*la main tendue*)" to Christian voters, asking them to help elect a Blum government.

Inspired by a parallel interest in the formation of a broad anti-fascist coalition, Schumann (using the nom de plume Maurice Jacques) wrote to Blum in January 1937, asking the Socialist leader what he thought of Catholic teachings on the social issue. Blum's reply, published in the 19 February 1937 issue of the Dominican review *Sept*, created an enormous stir: "Would it be so difficult to draw from the encyclicals which the Holy See devoted to social problems a half century ago similar formulae to those which the Popular Front is trying to transform into republican law? I don't hesitate, then, to reply that I believe collaboration to be possible and, given that it is possible, surely French Catholics would agree that it is desirable?"[7]

The shock created by Blum's response to Schumann among readers of *Sept* was so great that Pius XI (who had helped launch the periodical in the first place!) ordered the publisher to suspend operations in August 1937. In the end, happily for Schumann as well as for his friend Stanislas Fumet, the paper's first lay editor, *Sept* re-emerged that same year under a new masthead, *Temps présent*.

The Spanish Civil War, which erupted in the early months of the Blum administration, led a significant number of Catholic intellectuals to commit themselves to the republican and democratic values which the French and Spanish left held in common. The December 1936 "Déclaration des intellectuels républicains au sujet des événements d'Espagne," signed by (among others) Marc Sangnier, called upon the French government to come to the aid of the beleaguered Spanish Republic.[8] An even more remarkable expression of Catholic anti-fascism came with the denunciation of the assault on Spain's Basque minority by Franco's army and air force. Published in *L'Aube* on 8 May 1937 under the heading "Pour le peuple basque," the indictment was signed by Schumann's colleagues François Mauriac, Stanislas Fumet, Francisque Gay, Georges Bidault, Gabriel Marcel, Jacques Maritain, and Emmanuel Mounier, among others.[9]

Schumann's continuing commitment to the anti-fascist struggle at home and abroad was made clear in his editorials for *Temps présent.* It is worth noting here not only that Charles de Gaulle was an early subscriber (#7) to the new paper but that, on 14 June, when the editorial staff had relocated at Nantes, he joined Les Amis du *Temps présent* to show solidarity with a publication with a Catholic and republican outlook. The colonel had become increasingly sympathetic to the ideas of Marc Sangnier at this point and had even considered joining La Jeune République. After the war, de Gaulle went out of his way to receive the founder of Le Sillon and to assure him that he had "always belonged to (Sangnier's) spiritual family."[10]

In its first (5 November 1937) issue, *Temps présent* struck a defiant tone, remarking with pride on the controversy engendered by its predecessor, *Sept,* and promising more of the same, noting that it was appearing without clerical patronage in the tradition of the radical Catholics who supported the 1848 revolution. Positioning itself outside and above political parties, the new weekly numbered among its contributors an extraordinary roster of contemporary French Catholic intellectuals including Georges Bernanos, Charles du Bos, Claude Bourdet, Daniel-Rops, Henri Guillemin, Jacques Madaule, Gabriel Marcel, Jacques Maritain, Louis Massignon, François Mauriac, and Emmanuel Mounier. Using the nom de plume André Sidobre, Schumann wrote a regular Page One column for the paper dealing with the diplomatic scene.

The overriding focus of Schumann's analysis in these articles is the threat posed to Europe's peace and stability by what he calls *germanisme* (he avoids reference to the Nazis in large measure because he sees Hitler's aggressions as an extension of Kaiser Wilhelm II's imperialist strategy).[11] Pius XI, author of the 1937 encyclical *Mit brennender Sorge* ("With the

Deepest Feeling"), is given a special accolade for responding to the menace of Nazi anti-Semitism by offering not only a reproach to Hitler but also a spiritual alternative. On a visit to Vienna following the Anschluss of 1938, Schumann finds "a cadaver without a tomb" and notes prophetically that Austria's two main political parties (Social Christians and Social Democrats) will end up finding reconciliation "in concentration camps, prisons or cemeteries."[12]

As Schumann sees it, the last best hope for Europe as the diplomatic situation deteriorates in the late 1930s is the consolidation of the Entente Cordiale; but following the Munich agreement (which he blames essentially on a pusillanimous Chamberlain), the Catholic journalist describes the world as divided between the Pax Germanica in the West and the Pax Japonica in the East. The Ribbentrop-Molotov Pact of August 1939 is scathingly denounced. In his last articles for *Temps présent,* Schumann takes heart in the thought that, because the totalitarian states have rejected outright the most generous concessions of the democracies, "the nobility of our cause has never been more apparent." Victory will come, he assures his readers, when the German people come to realize that their leaders have mobilized the whole civilized world against them.[13]

The Catholic intellectuals who, like Schumann, had warned against the perils of fascism from the outset, had to wait through the dreary season of the Phoney War and the military disaster of the spring of 1940 before the call to redemption came. Meanwhile, as though to give heart to Catholic reactionaries, Pius XII, who had been elected to the papacy in March, lifted the interdict on the Action française on 10 July 1939. It might be noted that, a year earlier, Charles Maurras had been received into that sanctuary of literary and political conservatism, the Académie française.

Significantly for the existential choice which Schumann would make in June 1940, he had become familiar with Colonel de Gaulle's military writings by the late 1930s thanks to friends who shared both his progressive Catholic outlook and his concern about the deteriorating diplomatic situation in Europe.[14] The editorialist for *Temps présent* first heard about the young colonel from a fellow-member of Jeune République, André Lecomte, who went on to publish a series of articles analyzing de Gaulle's strategic ideas in *L'Aube,* a paper to which the colonel was himself an occasional contributor. Schumann was also aware that Philippe Serre, one of the deputies elected under the Jeune République banner in 1936, had defended the officer's concepts of tank warfare in the Chamber of Deputies. Finally, the lawyer Jean Auburtin, who had read *L'armée de métier* on the advice of Colonel Mayer and then introduced its author to Paul

Reynaud, spoke about de Gaulle's radical views of modern warfare at a meeting of Jeune République attended by Schumann.

Inspired by these favourable reports of de Gaulle's writings, Schumann made himself familiar with *L'armée de métier* and, last but not least for the combat ahead, he had a fleeting encounter with the young officer while paying a visit to his friend Henri Petiot. Petiot was, like Schumann, a Jewish convert to Catholicism who had adopted the pen name Daniel-Rops and was in the process of editing de Gaulle's *La France et son armée*, which would appear in 1938 as one of a series of book-length essays published by Plon under the rubric *Présences*.

Schumann enlisted in the army at the beginning of World War II and, during the grim days leading up to the French collapse, served as liaison officer with the British Expeditionary Force. Captured during the Nazi blitzkrieg, he made a quick escape, then, on 18 June, found his way to Bordeaux where the government of Paul Reynaud was quartered. Stopping to dine at a wayside inn at Niort, he counted it "a providential blessing" that he arrived in time to hear de Gaulle's speech over the radio. He and his host, a bemedalled veteran of World War I, listened enthralled to "this first message of action, sacrifice and hope." Years later, Schumann reflected that de Gaulle had clearly delivered the speech "with head held high."[15] Forty-five years later, he remarked, "18 June was the act of a man both penniless and weaponless. It offers proof that the spiritual values which made all of us commit ourselves to public life are in the end like the sword of the spirit spoken of in Scripture."[16]

The journalist-turned-soldier decided at once that he must join La France libre. On his way to a safe port of exit, he stopped over at Bordeaux to call on two old friends – Daniel-Rops and François Mauriac – who gave him a letter of introduction to de Gaulle. Both approved his decision to join the general.

On 21 June, Schumann left Saint Jean-de-Luz on a ship bound for England. The chaplain on board, an Irishman, said mass in the hold, which communicants somewhat melodramatically dubbed "The Catacombs." As they passed the Breton coast, the putative Gaullist gazed across to the shore where British troops were re-embarking for home. In that moment he experienced an epiphany. Listening over the waves to what sounded like a solemn but serene musical harmony, like the chant of departed souls, Schumann felt purged of all fear of death, confident that he would someday be greeted by those who had already passed from the earth.

Arriving in London on 28 June, Schumann went directly to the French embassy, where every effort was made to discourage him from contacting de Gaulle. A visit to his old office at the Havas Agency was equally disheartening. His colleague, the Protestant newsman Paul Bret, a resolute anti-fascist who nevertheless harboured deep reservations about de Gaulle, insisted that the general was the champion of a hopeless cause, entirely isolated and alone. "But that's just his strength! (C'est sa force!)" Schumann responded. The would-be Gaullist ended up two days later at St. Stephen's House, where he was greeted in a tiny, rather lugubrious apartment overlooking the Thames.

After welcoming Schumann, the general launched into a prophetic recapitulation of the global conflict ahead, anticipating the RAF triumph in the Battle of Britain, Hitler's attack on the Soviet Union, the commitment of Japan to war and its inevitable corollary, the entry of the United States on the Allied side. What was vital in the immediate circumstances, de Gaulle insisted, was that more than a handful of French volunteers be induced to join him. In this regard, the leader of Free France went on, Schumann might perform two key services: he might induce a more favourable attitude toward La France libre among his many British friends, including Anthony Eden; and he might use his considerable literary skills to rally more of his compatriots to the cause. Startled but excited, Schumann gave a tentatively favourable response.

Before committing himself, Schumann decided to consult his old friend, the francophile writer Raymond Mortimer, who had been hired to help organize the BBC's wartime propaganda.[17] As it turned out, the immediate circumstances of the 3 July meeting between the two old friends – the British attack on the French fleet at Mers-el-Kébir – were enough to dishearten the most zealous advocate of Franco-British amity. In the face of this disastrous news, Mortimer's advice to Schumann was blunt: his colleague must not hide the facts; he must somehow justify this murderous assault by men still formally allied to France.

In the end, the text Schumann penned was read over the BBC by Michel Saint-Denis, a prominent French actor/director who had adopted the nom de plume "Jacques Duchesne" after a prominent propagandist of the 1790s. It placed the entire responsibility for the Mers-el-Kébir tragedy on Nazi Germany, which clearly intended sooner or later to acquire France's fighting ships and had obviously put irresistible pressure on Vichy to make sure that Somerville's ultimatum was rejected.

No doubt Schumann's text had little impact inside France, where anglophobia was on the rise following the debacle. But it brought a rare compliment from de Gaulle ("C'est très bien! Continuez!"). More significantly in the long term, it resulted in Schumann's becoming for the next four years (18 July 1940–30 May 1944), the official porte-parole of Free France over the BBC. When he was in London, the general, who broadcast in person on special occasions, met Schumann daily to go over the text the Catholic journalist intended to deliver. But there was virtually no editing or censoring: Schumann was given what amounted to carte blanche.

Two of Schumann's closest collaborators in his role as spokesperson for Free France over the airwaves were the ethnographer Jacques Soustelle, of Huguenot background, in whom he discerned a natural gift for propaganda (and with whom he shared his London flat), and Georges Boris, a close confidant of Léon Blum and a key figure in the development of overall Free French political strategy.

Schumann followed a routine religiously over the next four years. He spent the day at Free French headquarters, then headed for the BBC where he appeared before the microphone wearing his officer's uniform with the badge "France" on his shoulder. His daily visits to St. Stephen's House and then Carlton Gardens brought the journalist-turned-propagandist into contact with a Frenchwoman, Lucie Daniel, who had been living in London when the war began and who volunteered to join de Gaulle after hearing his 18 June speech. Mlle Daniel, who was fluently bilingual, served the cause in a variety of ways, as switchboard operator, receptionist, and translator, before working for the Protestant Pierre Denis in the finance department, then as personnel manager. She and Schumann fell in love in London, but did not marry until after the Liberation in Paris.

Radio contact with France was of course subject to the good graces of the government-controlled BBC, and there were times when differences between de Gaulle and Churchill brought one party to boycott – or the other to censor – Free French broadcasts. As of 19 June, France's ambassador to the United Kingdom had secured a fifteen-minute time slot for use by the BBC's Radiodiffusion française; on 1 July, this was extended to a half hour (8:30–9:00 p.m.) to be called "Ici la France." Jacques Duchesne, who was friendly toward La France libre without ever becoming a member, took over this program on Bastille Day.

The close association between Duchesne and the BBC had thus already been established when de Gaulle on 17 July named Schumann his *chargé de liaison* with the British broadcaster. "L'émission de La France libre" was launched the following day. The first five minutes of this program, titled "Honneur et patrie," the only strictly Gaullist BBC broadcast, offered Schumann and other Free French spokespeople a splendid opportunity to inspire their compatriots to believe in an Allied victory and to encourage acts of patriotic resistance inside France.[18]

While Schumann's listeners across the Channel in France were very few in the summer of 1940, Jean-Louis Crémieux-Brilhac estimates that by the spring of 1941 some 300,000 of his fellow-citizens were tuning in to his five-minute BBC talks. A year later, as many as ten times that number are thought to have joined the audience.

Some idea of the effect Schumann had on his wartime audience may be gathered from the impact he had on René Cerf-Ferrière, a Young Turk among the interwar Radical Socialists who had, by 1942, become a leading member of the underground group Combat. The voice of Free France over the BBC often brought the Jewish resistance fighter to tears, not simply because of the inspirational text but also because of the way Schumann used his voice as a musical instrument. The result was not so much in the manner of a Lulli or a Mozart, Cerf-Ferrière tells us, but far richer, in the mode of a Berlioz or a Wagner. "Listening to him while I was in the vast prison that France had become," Cerf-Ferrière remembered years later, "I couldn't help thinking of the *Symphonie Fantastique* or the overture to the *Walkyrie*! I imagined a broad-shouldered figure, a bit on the corpulent side, with the profile of a Siegfried."

When the resistance fighter met Schumann for the first time, in London on 16 October 1943, he was astonished to find that "the grave, harmonious, magnificent voice" he had listened to with such intense emotion belonged to a tall, frail, slightly stooped man who seemed lost inside his lieutenant's uniform. The oval face, the abundant hair, the lips folding open in a welcoming smile made the visitor conjure up "an image not of Wagner but of Chénier, Musset or Lamartine, not at all of Wotan or Siegfried."[19]

Crémieux-Brilhac adds to our appreciation of the broadcaster's impact, describing the rich variations of tone and style ("in turn exalted, sarcastic and vengeful") with which Schumann "sang the praises of heroes, bore witness to the sacrifice of martyrs and scourged traitors."[20]

From the outset, Schumann's voice in these radio broadcasts was explicitly, even passionately, Catholic. The tone came naturally of course: de Gaulle's spokesperson had the fervour, the sense of exaltation, which the convert so often feels. More significantly, Schumann felt impelled to counter Vichy propaganda, which resonated with Catholic religiosity and which blamed the debacle of 1940 on the Jews, Freemasons, and agnostics who were seen to have subverted the national interest during the Popular Front and who were now pictured as the dominant element in La France libre. Champions of the État français presented the defeat not simply as divine retribution for France's abandonment of Christ, but as an opportunity for collective expiation and, ultimately, redemption. Under these circumstances, Schumann knew that it was critically important to identify Free France with Christian leadership and values.

Schumann's perspective as a champion of "Catholicisme social" is apparent from his earliest broadcasts. On 17 August 1940, addressing himself over the airwaves to his old friend Mauriac, he recalls the conversation the two men had in Bordeaux two months earlier. Mauriac, the broadcaster reminds his listeners, had tried his best during the 1930s to warn his compatriots against the betrayal of France by financial oligarchs who regularly invoked liberty as their inspiration but made sure that freedom remained a pure abstraction for the dispossessed. Let us at least learn from the nation's present plight so that we can make a clean break with the past and rediscover the true nature of liberty, he urged. Schumann adds that this rediscovery might well lie with the young generation of French farmers and workers who have "replanted the cross" in our factories and fields, a clear reference to the Confédération française des travailleurs chrétiens (CFTC) and the Jeunesse agricole catholique (JAC).

Schumann addresses Mauriac in this radio talk as a sacrificial figure who had stayed in France to bear graphic witness to the transforming faith through which all of France would ultimately be redeemed. Somewhat grandiloquently, he even declares, "Just as certain Italian masters offer us a dramatically foreshortened image of the crucified Christ, you symbolize for us France crucified."

More than three years after this extravagant tribute, on 28 November 1943, Schumann read to his listeners a passage from *Le Cahier noir*, a powerful resistance tract written by Mauriac under the pseudonym "Forez," and distributed clandestinely. In this passage, "Forez" defines Christians as "men and women who seek God above all else and find Him among those who suffer persecution for justice's sake, whether they be Christians or pagans, communists or Jews, because among all of these, the resemblance to Christ is in direct relationship to the indignities which they endure."

While Mauriac was a living mentor to Schumann, Péguy, with his vision of a France simultaneously Catholic and republican, remained a constant source of inspiration. On 16 June 1942, after hailing the part played by Free French troops at the battle of Bir-Hakeim in Egypt, Schumann called to mind Péguy's tribute to the soldiers of "L'An II" (1793, Year Two of the French Republic), assuring his listeners that descendants of these valiant defenders of the Revolution were coming to London from all over the empire as well as from France.

De Gaulle as well as Schumann used the BBC on a number of occasions to urge his compatriots to demonstrate resistance to Vichy and the Nazis in non-violent but manifestly Christian fashion. At Christmastime 1940, the general asked the people of France to signal this resistance by staying indoors for a one-hour period. Schumann (who could not know how little this appeal had been heeded) nevertheless on New Year's Day 1941 saluted those who had joined in "this mute struggle" in which they had been "united in the same silence." "March onward!" he intoned. "The plebiscite is over!" adding, "Listen well! France's guardian angel has resumed her flight!" an obvious reference to Joan of Arc.

Invocations to Saint Joan were natural enough coming from a man who had been stirred by Péguy's lyrical celebrations of the young native of Lorraine. On 9 May 1943, as Allied armies marched triumphantly through North Africa, Schumann reminded his listeners of the role the teenage martyr had played in rescuing France from foreign oppression. Her courage and sacrifice were the perfect inspiration for today's freedom fighters.

Exhortations to prayer were a constant in Schumann's radio talks. On 23 March 1941, after noting that entreaties to the Almighty throughout Britain had preceded the "miraculous deliverance" of the Anglo-French army at Dunkirk, the Catholic broadcaster told his audience that the United Kingdom was again about to engage in a nationwide day of supplication to end wartime suffering. The leader of the Free French, in an ecumenical order of the day, had urged "all members of La France libre, each according to their conscience, to join in this pious display of patriotic fervour."

The general's directive had appeared in *Glaive de l'Esprit,* a French-language Christian journal published in London. Asked by the paper's correspondent what he thought of the attitude of French Catholics during the conflict, the general had replied defiantly (if inaccurately), "I can affirm from clear knowledge of the facts that the clergy as a whole support resistance to the enemy. There is not a single house of worship in which daily prayers are not offered for an Allied victory. French priests are fully aware of the threat posed to the cross of Christ by the swastika."

It might be true, de Gaulle conceded, that some representatives of the priesthood had let themselves be misled by the so-called policy of national recovery (*redressement*) propagated by Vichy; but there were many Catholic chaplains in the Free French forces, and England's Cardinal Hinsley had been right to declare "that the spirit of St. Joan of Arc was still alive and will prevail." Schumann followed this quote from the general with the observation that, while all French citizens, whatever their origin or religious conviction, had their place in La France libre, Catholics had a special place of honour simply because "we Catholics are cast in the image of France."

Given the allegations made by Vichy propagandists that Free France was a hotbed of godlessness, Schumann took every opportunity to stress the prominent role played by devout Catholics in de Gaulle's entourage. When the journalist first met Captain (and future general) Philippe Leclerc de Hautecloque in London in July 1940, he was overwhelmed, he told his listeners on 1 September 1944. This was clearly a man driven by an inner spiritual compulsion, "suffused with sacramental nourishment (*ruisselant de nourriture sacramentale*)." Schumann was equally excited as he announced in September 1940 the arrival at Gaullist headquarters of Georges Thierry d'Argenlieu, who had entered the Carmelite (White Friars) order in 1920 and become a provincial but who, out of patriotic duty, had enlisted in the navy in 1939 and captained a corvette. Schumann noted that d'Argenlieu (who would serve La France libre as a chaplain and then as High Commissioner in the Pacific) had detected the nihilistic potential in Hitler from the very beginning by contrast with those professedly pious folk, blind to the fascist peril, who had invoked Christian values to justify capitulation in 1940. Finally, on 17 September, de Gaulle's porte-parole hailed the arrival of General Georges Catroux, who brought to the Free French cause the spiritual as well as military inheritance of Marshal Henri Lyautey, a symbol both of France's imperial greatness and her generous ecumenical outreach to the Muslim world.

Catholic faith and national patriotism were always closely linked in Schumann's mind. Nowhere did this symbiotic relationship surface more dramatically than in the "Lost Provinces" of Alsace and Lorraine, which had been forcibly integrated into the Third Reich following France's defeat. Schumann saw these territories as suffering a double martyrdom – military occupation and spiritual persecution – under Nazi control. The Cross of Lorraine which Free France had adopted as its emblem was thus the perfect symbol for a crusade which aimed at moral as well as military redemption. In his radio address of 11 May 1941, Schumann reminded his listeners that in 1873, two years after France had ceded the two provinces to Germany, patriots had planted the Cross of Lorraine bearing the inscription "Ce n'est pas pour toujours" on a site near Nancy (*La Colline inspirée*) made famous by the nationalist writer Maurice Barrès. Tomorrow, Schumann declared, on Saint Joan's birthday, some of you who gather around that cross will renew the original pledge in silent prayer. And Saint Joan will surely reply, "No! It will not be forever!"

Strasbourg, the centre of Alsatian religious and civic life, was the focus of several of Schumann's radio talks. On 20 October 1940, Schumann denounced the closing of the city's cathedral to Catholic worshippers and the abduction of local children for re-education in the Third Reich. It was clear from these actions, the broadcaster stressed, that the resolve of the racist ideologue Alfred Rosenberg to liquidate Catholicism was being ruthlessly pursued.

On 5 March 1942, Schumann voiced his outrage at the expulsion of native Alsace-Lorrainers from their homes and their condemnation to forced labour in the Third Reich while their farms were occupied by German settlers. In the same month, as the bitterness and suffering of those living under Vichy and the Nazis intensified, he talked not only of the misery being endured in the "Lost Provinces" but more broadly of *La grande pitié de la France*, whose people, like the early Christian martyrs, were "suffering without a murmur and bleeding without fear."

Suffering was of course often associated with expiation in Catholic theology, and apologists for Vichy often argued that France's physical and spiritual agony in 1940 would, if instructively understood, help atone for the sins of the corrupt Third Republic. If exercises in redemption through self-conscious suffering were aimed at softening German hearts, Schumann warned on 1 October 1941, those advocating such masochistic activities should study developments in Italy, where nothing but bitterness had followed that nation's passive surrender to fascist ideology and where people were impatiently waiting for a chance to rise against Mussolini.

While Italy was beginning in the fall of 1941 to demonstrate the tragic consequences of succumbing to fascism, Norway, by the following spring, was illustrating the power of Christian resistance to the same vile teaching. On 12 April 1942, Schumann, in full ecumenical mode, told his audience about the collective resignation of the Norwegian clergy in protest against the policies of Vidkun Quisling and the Nazis. The Lutheran pastorate had thus become their nation's leaders in "the spiritual battle against Evil and Untruth." No doubt the Norwegian church would pay a high price for these acts of defiance; hostages would surely be taken and would just as clearly become martyrs; but this suffering would also just as surely help achieve their people's deliverance. Schumann added pointedly that, if Quisling had been unable to mask the truth from the Norwegian church, how could Vichy possibly keep on hiding it from the church in France? Finally, Schumann noted, while Norway's spiritual leaders were showing their people the way to redemption, some 1,200,000 Germans had at Easter made their "first communion" in a Nazi rite that was an unmistakably blasphemous parody of the Eucharist.

Some Catholic prelates, at least, were prepared to follow the lead of their Norwegian confreres, as Schumann reported on 2 August 1942.

Cardinal Van Roey, primate of the Belgian church, had declared before his nation's Ligue des Femmes chrétiennes that "the Catholic ethic does not recognize race but applies to all people," while Cardinal Saliège of Toulouse had urged those in his diocese to pray for French workers who were being arbitrarily deported to Germany and chastised "the well-to-do who look the other way" in the face of this and other current abuses.

As of the spring of 1943, when the tide of war began to turn against the Axis, Schumann's references to the religious forces supporting fascist regimes took on an increasingly bitter and sarcastic tone. On 23 May 1943, as Allied troops continued their assault on the Italian peninsula, he asked his "right-thinking (*bien-pensant*)" fellow citizens mockingly how they would be feeling if the Christian culture they so cherished had not been defended by Mussolini. Had not Il Duce, in defence of Christian civilization, ordered the use of mustard-gas on unarmed Ethiopians? Had he not also chosen Good Friday to launch an attack on Albania?

It was clear, Schumann went on, that Italian fascism was approaching its death-agony. The railway coach which had carried Mussolini in triumph to Rome in 1922 was doubtless being prepared for a rapid exit from the city. Indeed, the broadcaster admonished, it was high time for all Catholics, including the clergy, to reflect on the harsh but salutary lessons which fascism in its last stages was teaching us. The Reichskommissar of the Netherlands had acknowledged that both the Reformed and Catholic churches in Holland had learned their lesson and were leading the battle against the persecution of Jews, against forced labour, and against the murder of innocent hostages.

On the eve of the Normandy landings, the Gaullist broadcaster shifted to triumphant mode, celebrating the impending victory of faith over tyranny and of the French nation over all those forces which had divided it since Hitler's rise: "Thus, the myths of class and race, running counter to the historic and human truth of the nation, are finally shattered; false gods and idols are smashed. Now – let both pastors and their flocks fully understand it! – comes the hour of the Christian!"

In a pre-recorded 9 June 1944 broadcast, Schumann told his listeners that he had extracted a solemn promise from de Gaulle during their first meeting: in exchange for taking on the role of spokesperson for the general over the BBC, he would be granted permission to serve in uniform again when the time to liberate France arrived. *Le Connétable* lived up to the bargain. On D-Day, Schumann was parachuted into Normandy with the Allied landing forces.

Schumann showed his journalist's skills in reporting from the field as he followed French forces from Normandy to the Rhine. In Bayeux on 9 June, he reported, the Cross of Lorraine was displayed everywhere, and he was delighted to have seen on the ground an illustration of the fraternal solidarity he and de Gaulle had been preaching. One of the canons of Bayeux Cathedral had embraced a notorious local anticlerical as both men waited to put on the uniform of La France combattante! When de Gaulle arrived in Bayeux on 14 June, it was Schumann who introduced him with the words "Honneur et patrie! Voici le général de Gaulle!"

Incorporated into the 2eme DB (Second Armoured Division), Schumann acted as liaison with the internal Resistance (Forces Françaises de l'Intérieur) as the armies of liberation advanced. Weeks later, he participated in mop-up operations during the liberation of Paris as part of an armoured assault group that broke through to the strategic Place de la Concorde on 25 August. To celebrate this triumph, he joined his old mentor Marc Sangnier, racing across Paris in a Jeep to the Vélodrome d'Hiver, the classic pre-war site of political rallies, where the founder of Le Sillon was to speak.[21]

Toward the end of the battle to liberate French territory, on 4 December 1944, Schumann told his audience of the rapture he left when he first glimpsed Strasbourg Cathedral against the background of the Vosges mountains. The Crusaders must surely have felt the same ecstatic joy when they sighted the Holy Land! The end of four and a half years of tyranny was nigh: the idol of death which the Nazis had erected inside the cathedral would soon be gone. French troops were about to restore Strasbourg to the nation and the city's chief shrine to God!

If Schumann's passionately Catholic perspective was evident throughout his four years of broadcasting over the BBC, his republican devotion was equally manifest. Typical was a radio talk on 5 September 1941, when he spoke of the 4 September 1870 popular rising in Paris which brought the Third Republic into being. The voice of Free France drew a clear parallel between the insurgency of 1870 led by Léon Gambetta against the capitulationist Emperor Napoleon III and the Gaullist call to arms of 18 June against the defeatist Pétain. At the beginning of both challenges, the cause had seemed hopeless; but in each case, the republican uprising which had emerged from the pride of a few had "won the respect of the nations and forged the spirit of revenge."

At no time more eloquently than on the eve of May Day 1942 did Schumann invite his listeners to make a display of their republican devotion and their unity in the struggle for a regenerate France. De Gaulle, he informed his audience, was calling on all those on the home front to join their working-class compatriots on 1 May in a silent march past local statues of the Republic, or in front of city halls on the eve of the annual proletarian holiday. This would be a reciprocatory gesture toward French workers who had participated in the celebration of Joan of Arc's birthday in 1941. Schumann waxed rhapsodical at this prospect of the Two Frances sharing each other's most meaningful festivities. "Old divisions have melted away in the crucible of shared suffering," he declared. Workers who had lost everything under fascism were expecting that liberation would bring with it social and economic emancipation. They must not be deceived: a bill of rights for the working class would be embedded in the constitution of the Fourth Republic. "Beneath the ashes of the duplicitous defeat and treason (of 1940)," he trumpeted, "the brazier of a new French Revolution is smouldering!"

Following the recognition of de Gaulle's leadership by the internal resistance and the transformation of La France combattante into the Gouvernement provisoire de la République française (GPRF) in Algiers in 1943, Schumann talked increasingly of the coming together of all the constituent elements of French public life across the great divide left by the Revolution. In his 25 May 1943 radio talk, the broadcaster even reported favourably on the 24 January handshake between de Gaulle and the conservative (and racist) General Giraud, a gesture which his colleague René Cassin found highly offensive. Then, as though to conciliate those of his listeners who might have found this call for an all-embracing *rassemblement* distasteful, Schumann recited a litany of names from the French past – in fact a dialectical mix of symbolic figures separately revered by the Two Frances, all of whom (Joan of Arc, Cardinal Richelieu, Napoléon, Charles Péguy, Marshal Foch, and Georges Clemenceau) were worthy of a niche in the national Pantheon. This fusion of allegiances, he pursued, had in fact already been achieved by Free France, which had rallied to its banner communists and royalists, socialists and republicans, democrats and Catholics, all of them serving under the Cross of Lorraine.

Schumann conveyed this same feeling of ecumenical hope to his listeners following two trips to the Mahgreb with de Gaulle, one in the spring of 1943 and another in November. Everywhere the general spoke, his spokesperson reported in an 8 May 1944 broadcast, he was rapturously greeted by crowds of Muslims as well as European settlers.

As his socialist colleagues Georges Boris and André Philip, in collaboration with the internal resistance, started working on drafts for post-war social and economic reform, Schumann's radio scripts took on a more radical tone. On 30 July 1943, the voice of Free France suggested that its leaders should take inspiration from the *levée en masse* of 1793. And on Armistice Day that same year, Schumann cited another revolutionary precedent, arguing that the creation of a new Committee of Public Safety might be the best means of assuring that truly national interests be given priority over the preoccupations of caste and class.

Early in 1944, Schumann relayed news to the homeland of the arrival in Algiers of men and women chosen from the internal resistance to be delegates to the proto-parliament in exile, the Assemblé consultative provisoire. On 3 March 1944, he hailed the arrival in North Africa of the Jewish resistance fighter Raymond Aubrac, who had just left "le front des Martyrs." Two weeks later, on 24 March, he reported with particular enthusiasm the presence in Algiers of Aubrac's Protestant wife Lucie, whose heroic actions against Vichy and the Gestapo had already turned her into something of a legend.

On 24 May, just two weeks before D-Day, Schumann reported to his audience inside France that the GPRF, heir to La France libre, had indeed come to represent "all the political and spiritual families of the nation." Political ecumenism had become a reality. Catholic republicans like himself were ready to join men and women of all faiths in the liberation, and then in the revolutionary transformation, of the nation.

CHAPTER SIX

Ecumenical Money-Managers: Pierre Denis, André Diethelm, André Postel-Vinay, Maurice Couve de Murville, and Pierre Mendès France

The long-term financing of Free France seemed highly problematic in the early summer of 1940. Unlike other Allied forces then in Great Britain – the Dutch, the Czechs, and the Poles, for instance – de Gaulle's organization began with only the most tenuous political legitimacy, and that status was put in jeopardy when Pétain's État français charged *Le Connétable* with treason. The obvious solution to this dilemma would have been for de Gaulle to allow his supporters to become part of Britain's armed forces, in effect turning them into mercenaries. The pride of the general and that of his devoted band of partisans precluded such an option. What remained was to improvise an arrangement which would allow for the funding of La France libre by the British Treasury based on a clear understanding that credit was being extended to a quasi-sovereign entity and that it would be repaid as soon as circumstances allowed.

To make this unusual bilateral arrangement work required ingenuity on both sides, as well as a high degree of financial competence and integrity on the part of de Gaulle's agents. As it turned out, a truly ecumenical series of gifted financial administrators (the Protestants Pierre Denis, André Diethelm, and Maurice Couve de Murville, the Catholic André Postel-Vinay, and the nominally Jewish Pierre Mendès France) would together meet this very special challenge.

Pierre Denis, who was to be chief financial officer of Free France, took immense pride in his Protestant origins and in "the spirit of unbridled freedom handed down by the Cévenol rebels which flowed like a strong current into the great stream of French national consciousness."[1] This pride was reinforced by memories of his family's contribution to the nation since the Revolution. Pierre's grandfather had served in Napoleon's army; his father had fought as an infantryman in the battle against the Prussian invader in 1870 before achieving fame as a historian with an interest in Czech nationalism.

As a student at the École normale at the turn of the century, Denis found his Protestant faith challenged, then reinforced, by exposure to the strenuously secular world-views of his mentors. He was excited by the new science of geography whose chief proponent, Vidal de La Blache, he had the good fortune to have as a teacher. His evident intellectual gifts brought him to the attention of the Jewish banker and philanthropist Albert Kahn, who took him on as an assistant in the preparation of an ambitiously conceived "Archive of the Planet," a proposed compendium of the contemporary world's scientific knowledge. This association brought three years of globe-trotting travel and reflection. Following his intellectual apprenticeship with Kahn, Denis accepted a teaching post at the lycée at Bar-le-Duc, in the Vosges, where his interest in geography and its influence on economic development within and beyond national boundaries was further developed. The outbreak of the war meant military service and, in 1917, an assignment to the counter-intelligence branch of the French General Staff in the Middle East. Peace brought with it a chance to visit the United States. The openness and the absence of rigid hierarchy and bureaucratic formality in American life left a permanent impression on Denis, who was henceforth a bitter critic of France's stratified politics and sclerotic economy. On his return from America, a chance encounter with France's commerce minister, Daniel Serruys, who was looking for an assistant to help draw up the economic clauses of the Versailles Treaty, led to a brief and rewarding diplomatic career for the intellectually versatile Denis.

After working directly under Serruys, Denis spent seven years in the League of Nations secretariat, shuttling back and forth between Geneva and London. Like other gifted men of his generation working for the League, including the Czech leader Edvard Beněs and his future Gaullist colleague René Cassin, Denis came to feel part of a truly international civil service, outside the immediate control of parochial national governments, working for world peace and order. Following World War II, he would regret the failure of Europe's sovereign nation-states to engage in their own "Night of 4 August," the moment in the summer of 1789 when the French aristocracy voted away its class privileges in the larger cause of French unity. Not surprisingly, given this perspective, Denis found Jean

Monnet, a devoted member of the League's economic and financial committees during the 1920s and a precocious proponent of European unity, a most congenial colleague.

In 1926, Denis left the League of Nations to start yet another career, this time as an employee of the Paris branch of the New York-based Blair Bank. In his new career, he experienced at first hand the impact on many nations of the monetary crisis which hit much of the Western world during the 1920s. When the Blair Bank let Denis go in the mid-1930s, he took on the task of restoring the financial stability of Venezuela, which had been bankrupted by the twenty-seven-year rule of the dictator Juan Gomez (1908–35).

Fifty-six years old when World War II began, Denis was called to the colours by the general mobilization of September 1939. For a few weeks, he commanded a unit of territorial reserves before being summoned to assist Jean Monnet in the coordination of French and British supply services. What Denis witnessed in the nine months between the war's opening and the French collapse of 1940 was in his view essentially a moral collapse, the disintegration of an outmoded political and economic system whose leaders were without intellectual or moral compass. The republican as well as the Protestant in him made Denis see his nation's defeat as the result of spiritual as much as structural decay. He attributed Europe's collapse after 1939 to "the basic flaw of those countries and those churches which are in need of reform, where individual sentiments have lost their spontaneity because they are constrained inside too rigid an administrative structure … Happy are those people whose national tradition is still fuelled with revolutionary enthusiasm."[2]

Denis' pessimism deepened as he shuttled between Paris and London on the eve of the French defeat. He was witness to the bitter rivalry within the cabinet between Prime Minister Reynaud and Finance Minister Daladier and shared the former's deep frustration at the failure of the United States to deliver desperately needed materiel for the Battle of France; but what really exasperated the patriot in Denis was the tendency of his superiors to fuss about administrative protocol as the military situation deteriorated in the spring of 1940.

On 9 June, Denis received an order to evacuate Paris and join the temporary headquarters of the Ministry of Finance in the Loire valley. Four days later, as news arrived of the French military collapse all along the front, he bought a bicycle to guarantee himself freedom of movement along the congested roadways. On 14 June, at the Château of Langeais, where the ministry was housed, he discovered (among other things) that his future colleague in La France libre, Maurice Couve de Murville, was worrying over the details of a new financial accord with Argentina!

Denis' disenchantment grew as he visited other ministries on the move. After listening to Pétain's speech suing for an armistice on 17 June, he realized that remaining inside a crumbling administration was pointless and set off on a bicycle trip which took him the next day to his property at Rauzan near Bordeaux. Along the zig-zag route which he followed heading south, he came to the conclusion that, among his fellow-citizens, "there was no longer any sense of community, no more civic sentiment."[3]

After surveying his estate, where he had rejoined his family, Denis left for Bordeaux. When he enquired of a cabinet official in the port city what he ought to do about a new order requesting him to head back to London, he was told, in a tone that suggested that a break with Great Britain was imminent, that he would be given further instructions in due course. At this point, Denis began to consider leaving for England on his own until he ran across René Pleven and Jean Monnet talking to Ronald Campbell, the British ambassador. When Monnet informed him that he was leaving that very night for England and that there was an empty seat on the plane, Denis made his decision. Having consulted his wife, who agreed to stay behind and look after their estate, he left France on 20 June.

At the time of his departure for what would be a four-year exile in London and Algiers, Denis had no idea that de Gaulle had already launched the Free French movement. Like most of his fellow-citizens, he had not heard the general's radio broadcast to France on 18 June.

The arrival of Denis in the British capital attracted the attention of General Edward Spears, Churchill's special emissary to Reynaud, who recommended him to de Gaulle. When the two men met, the general asked the new recruit to take on the financial administration of the fledgling organization he had just called into being. Denis accepted, and remained the chief financial officer of Free France (and its later incarnations) until the end of the war. To protect his wife and family back in France, he adopted the code name "Rauzan" throughout the war.

The task that Denis had agreed to take on after that first meeting with de Gaulle required tact, inventiveness, and stubborn resolve. The cash assets of La France libre on the eve of Denis' arrival in London amounted to fourteen shillings. This picayune sum having just been expended when the newcomer showed up at St. Stephen's House, Denis produced his own ten-pound note to cover the cost of two telegrams de Gaulle was eager to despatch.[4]

For the moment, the small contingent of volunteers the general had attracted could be paid from the commissariat of the French expeditionary corps which had been evacuated from Norway; and the British had come up with needed food supplies. The civilian staff at Gaullist headquarters depended meanwhile on personal loans and donations from sympathizers. To add to the malaise felt by the general's first recruits, there was no arrangement about the conversion of francs into sterling.

The parlous state of Free French finances contrasted sharply with the positive mood that had been generated by the agreement between Britain's Chancellor of the Exchequer John Simon and then French Finance Minister Reynaud in December 1939, by which the two governments pledged to share the cost of the war. The transfer of power to Pétain had rendered this pledge null and void. However, it is worth noting that one of the last acts of the same Reynaud, who became premier in March 1940, was to give de Gaulle 100,000 francs from a special government fund to finance the recently promoted general's trip to London. Writing about this discreet subsidy to the rebellious general sixty years later, François Delpha notes, "Some of (Reynaud's) partisans have since argued that this sum was just enough to turn the donor into one of the backers, if not *the* backer, of Free France. In fact, it was more like the gesture of a politician who is diversifying his investments. And the sum involved suggests the feeble return expected."[5]

As an immediate remedy to this financially desperate situation, Churchill ordered the British Treasury in July to open a special "General de Gaulle" account of one thousand pounds at the Bank of England. Later deposits provided the funding for Free France until June 1943, when de Gaulle and his colleagues moved to Algiers. A more formal financial arrangement was made on 7 August 1940, when Churchill and de Gaulle signed the accord Cassin had contrived committing La France libre on the one hand and the British government on the other to pay each other whatever wartime debts each might end up owing the other, thus preserving the principle (or the illusion) of their paritary partnership.

Following the signing of the accord, the War Office began granting a subsidy for the pay of soldiers serving under de Gaulle while the Admiralty offered similar monetary support for Free French naval personnel. Subsequent negotiations between British and Free French officials established equivalencies between British and French ranks and pay, uniform requisitions, mess supplies, and other related matters.

As of 19 March 1941, an agreement was reached between Denis and René Pleven and the British Treasury allowing for the direct transfer of British credit to the "General de Gaulle" account at the Bank of England on the understanding that La France libre would henceforth submit an annual budget to the Treasury by 31 March each year, a day before Britain's budget year began. Denis describes how the arrangement worked out on a monthly basis:

> Our expenditures were based on a budget which we drew up and submitted to the British Treasury at the beginning of each month. The funds needed to expend our budget were then deposited on a monthly basis in General de Gaulle's account. All expenditures made on our behalf by the various British ministries (for food, materiel and transport, etc.) were itemized in bills which we approved before they were sent to our services. These bills were then paid by the Treasury through a charge against the general's account without the British departments becoming directly involved in our financial administration. The Treasury limited itself to exercising a general supervision of our needs and expenditures … In this regard, tribute should be paid to the liberality and breadth of view with which the Treasury's control was exercised.[6]

Parallel to this 19 March arrangement, an agreement was reached to regulate the circulation of francs issued by Free France and to peg them to sterling at the pre-war rate of exchange, that is, 176 francs to the pound.

Reassured by a continuous line of British credit, the Free French Comité national in November 1941 created a Caisse centrale de La France libre (CCFL) of which Denis was made director. As a monetary institution, the Caisse (or Fund) issued a supply of bills to territories won over to the Gaullist cause and exchanged francs for pounds (or vice versa) in these areas as circumstances warranted. Possessed of all the financial assets of Free France, which were almost exclusively based on advances made by the British Treasury, the Caisse was obligated to account for all the expenses in its budget. Although the only regulatory agency that monitored the Fund was, incestuously, the Gaullist Commissariat aux Finances, no irregularities of any consequence occurred, a clear tribute to the integrity of Denis and his successors. Finally, the Fund was responsible for regulating exchange controls in areas of the French empire under Gaullist sway. The overall result of this arrangement was favourable to La France libre since, when operating on territory controlled by the Free French, the British paid their way in pounds while the Gaullists used francs. In addition, the United Kingdom made substantial purchases of raw materials in Gaullist liberated areas, helping create a favourable balance for the Fund.

Denis was delighted to discover that de Gaulle imposed no ideological test on those who volunteered to join him in the battle against fascism. Men of the Right as well as of the Left won quick acceptance, he observed, provided they were resolved to continue the fight.[7] Given these remarks and his own generally tolerant outlook, it is somewhat surprising that Denis was not above lapsing into condescending (if not racist) remarks about the substantial contingent of Jewish Gaullists. Some of these Jews, he observed, were "sufficiently evolved that they were able to share our general conviction concerning the pre-eminence of military virtues; in fact, they were not only able to understand their importance as the heart and core of our nationality but also to hear the call of military duty and respond to it!"[8]

As of July 1942, Denis was put under the nominal direction of the newly named *Commissaire aux Finances et Pensions*, André Diethelm, an *Inspecteur des finances* and fellow-Protestant who had made his way to London a year earlier. Born in 1896 at Bourg in the Ain department, André Diethelm was the grandson of an Alsatian who had left the province when it was annexed by Germany in 1870.[9] Protestant in background and belief, he attended lycées at Foix and Saint-Étienne then at Louis-le-Grand in Paris, where he prepared entrance exams for the *Ecole normale.* Enlisting at age eighteen when World War I opened, Diethelm fought at the battle of the Marne before being transferred to Salonika, where his bravery as a captain earned him the Croix de Guerre.

Following the war, Diethelm successfully competed for admission to the Inspection des Finances in 1920. After a mission to defend French financial interests in Yugoslavia in 1927–28, he served as director of finances in French Indo-China, where he helped stabilize the *piastre* and where his family developed important business interests. Leaving the public sector in the mid-1930s, Diethelm pursued a private career as a director of the insurance company Urbain-Vie and as an administrator of the Crédit colonial.

In 1938, Diethelm returned to public service as *directeur du cabinet* of Colonial Minister Georges Mandel, who was (among other things) determined to reform the internal organization of France's imperial possessions and reinforce their links to the mother country at a time when war in Europe seemed imminent. Shy and taciturn (perhaps in part because of severe myopia), the minister's aide was as strenuously opposed to the voices in cabinet favouring appeasement as Mandel himself in the months preceding the declaration of war.

When Mandel was shifted to the ministry of the interior on 18 May 1940, Diethelm remained as his *directeur du cabinet.* A month later, as France teetered on the brink of collapse, he was of course fully aware of Churchill's efforts to lure the feisty minister to London. Staying in France after the debacle (but, as an "Aryan," having of course much less to risk from the new regime at Vichy), Diethelm was part of what amounted to a patriotic *réseau Mandel* ("Mandel network") waiting for an opportunity to escape to rejoin the battle against fascism. Toward the end of August 1941, carrying government papers authorizing him to travel to Portugal, he made his way to London.

Arriving in the British capital just as the Comité national was being formed, Diethelm was named *commissaire à l'Intérieur, au Travail et à l'Information.* Quickly earning de Gaulle's confidence, the new commissioner drafted a plan of political action aimed at creating a Gaullist information network inside France.

In his later role as financial overseer of La France libre, Diethelm mandated his Protestant subordinate Denis to carry out an on-the spot review of the financial situation in those colonies which had gone over to (or been liberated by) Free France. The situation which Denis encountered often required diplomatic as well as financial finesse. In French Equatorial Africa, for example, he had to steer a course between the high commissioner and the governor as well as to overcome the initial hostility of Cunningham, Roosevelt's emissary in the area, who, taking him to be Jewish (his code name "Rauzan" being seen as a version of "Rosen"), snubbed him on first contact. In the end, after visiting Madagascar, Djibouti, Réunion, and Syria, Denis managed to regularize the finances in those parts of the French empire which had committed themselves to de Gaulle and to link them more effectively to the Caisse.

While Denis was away, he was replaced in London on an interim basis by André Postel-Vinay, a twenty-nine-year-old veteran of the internal resistance. Postel-Vinay, whose background was Catholic but who described himself in a letter to the author as a post-Vatican-II believer, "close to Protestantism,"[10] was born in 1911. Received into the prestigious Inspection des Finances in 1938, he had just begun his internship, auditing accounts for the government, when the war broke out.

Called up in September 1939, Postel-Vinay served as a lieutenant in France's 70th Artillery Regiment before being captured on 17 June as the Battle of France was ending. He escaped within a week and, for two years, beginning in October 1940, became engaged in a variety of highly dangerous activities in France's underground battle against Vichy and the Nazis.[11] He was part of a British organization devoted to the rescue and repatriation of downed RAF pilots; he established a link with the Paris-based resistance cell founded by researchers at the Musée de l'homme; and he managed at the same time to belong to a network providing military intelligence to the British.

On 13 December 1941, Postel-Vinay was arrested by the Gestapo and taken to La Santé prison near Paris. Dreading that he might under torture reveal the names of comrades, and determined not only to save them but to defend his honour, Postel-Vinay attempted suicide, seriously wounding himself, then feigned madness in order to resist interrogation, and finally tried to kill himself a second time before escaping the clutches of his captors in September 1942. With the help of friends in Paris, Postel-Vinay was able to make his way to Marseille, and then to Gibraltar, in the company of British airmen like those he had earlier helped on their way to freedom.

In England in October 1942, Postel-Vinay underwent the ritual process of interrogation at the Patriotic School. Once certified as a welcome alien, Postel-Vinay met Passy and Brossolette, the chief figures in Gaullist counter-intelligence, who wanted him to join the Bureau central de renseignements et d'action (BCRA). Turning down an offer which might well have brought him back into France, where he had suffered such excruciating physical and psychological anguish, Postel-Vinay was summoned to meet de Gaulle.

The general was courteous, if a bit distant, at this first encounter toward the end of October. After enquiring about the internal resistance, he informed Postel-Vinay rather abruptly that he was going to be appointed interim director of the Caisse centrale of Fighting France. Despite protests that he was ill-prepared, the general insisted "You are an *inspecteur des finances*! You will adapt easily to your new function." Postel-Vinay was still reticent, pointing out that he didn't speak English very well. Nor do I, the general remarked, before going on to say that "Rauzan," the current director of the Caisse, was about to leave for Africa for a number of months and that an immediate replacement was vital. Accordingly, the new appointee showed up the next day at 9 Princess Street, next to the Bank of England. "So here I am, a banker in the city! Well, after all, why not?" Postel-Vinay remarked to himself, noting that the new job offered a renewal of his earlier career in public service.[12]

In the weeks before Denis left for Madagascar on 19 December 1942, Postel-Vinay found the director a most congenial guide to the operation of the Caisse. Among other things, Denis introduced his deputy to Bartholomew, the elderly Englishman from the Treasury whom he described as "francophile, even Gaullist" and therefore an utterly reliable collaborator. Postel-Vinay found Bartholomew to be a kindly, grandfatherly type, like a character in a Dickens novel, always wearing a high collar and equipped with a pince-nez attached to his waistcoat. Relations with the other Englishmen with whom he regularly dealt – Penton at Treasury and

Lithiby at the Bank of England – were equally harmonious. A telephone call or brief note to either official would inevitably suffice to resolve whatever problems arose. In fact, Postel-Vinay notes, the many stormy personal crises between Churchill and de Gaulle during the war had no impact whatsoever on the constantly smooth relations between the administrator of the Caisse and his British counterparts.[13]

Left in charge of the Caisse, Postel-Vinay found the first three months extremely taxing, working so diligently that he violated a sacred convention of the City by showing up at the office on weekends. And, like other Gaullists in exile, he worried about family members still in France. So when a new issue of CCFL notes was being printed which required his signature, he fixed his code-name ("André Duval") to the paper to avoid retaliatory measures against his relations. Shortly after this well-intentioned deceit, when the deputy director ran across de Gaulle at Carlton Gardens, the general shouted to him in sarcastic tones, "Duval, why Duval? Did *I* change my name?" Happily, the reproach did not spoil subsequent relations between the two men.[14]

On 7 November 1942, a month before Denis' departure for Africa and his temporary replacement by Postel-Vinay, Operation "Torch," the American-led invasion of French North Africa, began. Before it was over, "Torch" would end up (Roosevelt's wishes to the contrary) ensuring the political triumph of de Gaulle over the American-backed General Henri Giraud and the transfer of Fighting France's headquarters to Algiers. For *Le Connétable*, this shift opened up the intoxicating prospect not only of basing his claim to represent French sovereignty on what was an integral part of the nation's territory but of reasserting a major role for France on the world stage.

By contrast, Denis was convinced that France had become so old and weary, so lacking in self-confidence and in the capacity to renew her civilizing mission that she would be unable to play a world role by herself. Like his Protestant colleagues André Philip and René Massigli, Denis came to place his hopes in the emergence of a United States of Europe through which old rivalries, continental as well as colonial, would disappear. "Nationalism is condemned," he confided to himself, challenging one of the central tenets of the Gaullist creed.[15]

Early in June 1943, Denis, who had just arrived in North Africa, discussed these and other issues with Massigli and Philip at Tipaza, a resort town on the Mediterranean coast near Algiers. All three, who saw themselves as "patriotic Jacobins," were concerned at the potential weakening of the Gaullist ethos which might come with the arrival among them of "opportunistic conservatives," including their co-religionist Maurice Couve de Murville, who had escaped to North Africa following the German occupation of what had been Vichy France in November 1942.[16]

Maurice Couve de Murville who, as *commissaire aux finances*, soon became Denis' superior, was born in Reims on 24 January 1907 into a severely Calvinist household where relationships tended to be formal, even between parents and children.[17] Quick-tempered as a child, he learned to repress the affective side of his nature, often hiding inner feeling with a sardonic smile which helped deflect indiscreet personal questions. The decision he made later in life not to write his memoirs was clearly designed, in part at least, to preclude revelations about the world of high politics and about Charles de Gaulle, who came to place total confidence in his discretion.

François Seydoux, a fellow-Protestant who shared Couve's experiences at the Lycée Carnot, observes about the youth who was to become his lifelong friend, "He stood apart from our group of lycéens through the subtle display of his thoughtful intellect which, together with an extreme reserve, made him attractive to those of us who took the trouble to get to know him."[18]

Couve de Murville graduated from the Lycée Carnot with a first prize in geography. A year of conscript service followed during which he showed little interest in military life. In time he obtained a doctorate in law at the University of Paris where he also earned a licentiate in arts and letters; but it was studies at "Sciences-Po" that prepared him for the career as an upper-level civil servant that lay ahead; in 1930, he became an *inspecteur des Finances.*

His 1932 marriage to Jacqueline Schweisguth, an Alsatian Protestant, brought the young Couve de Murville, at least symbolically, into the world of the Haute société Protestante (HSP), the small group of powerful banking families which had acquired a considerable degree of influence on French public life beginning in the nineteenth century and had, as a result, become the object of right as well as left-wing attack. Mme Couve de Murville, an amateur painter and sculptor, scoffed at the suggestion that she and her husband were members of the HSP, insisting that they were simply "de pauvres fonctionnaires" (humble civil servants); but the association, though tenuous, remained in the mind of those who analyzed the French establishment in religio-political terms. As the journalist and historian André Fontaine puts it, somewhat more charitably, Couve's strict upbringing, his natural reserve, his "Anglo-Saxon" manner in appearance and dress, helped condition him for membership in a self-conscious elite, persuaded of its intrinsic qualities and determined to put them at the disposal of the state.[19]

After a brilliant internship as *inspecteur des Finances*, Couve was moved to the Ministry of Finance by Wilfried Baumgartner who had been his examiner at "Sciences-Po." The new appointment was as deputy director of the Mouvement général des fonds, a post which he held between 1932 and 1935. His superior, Jacques Rueff, a passionate economic liberal, became his mentor and friend for life. Both men witnessed at first hand, and were equally distressed by, the fluctuating financial policies of French governments in the 1930s, from deflation at the beginning of the decade to the vacillating economic decisions of the Popular Front.

As of the end of July 1940, Couve was charged with examining France's overall financial position following the Nazi victory. A note of 7 August commenting on the German imposition of parity between the franc and the Reich mark resulted in his being named director of France's external finances by the Vichy Finance Minister Yves Bouthilier. This was followed on 12 September by Couve's appointment as vice-president of the French delegation to the German Armistice Commission meeting in Wiesbaden.

For the next thirty months, Couve de Murville put what were promising diplomatic skills to work defending France's interests from what was clearly a very vulnerable position.[20] German pressure on the French negotiators came on a wide variety of fronts: a demand for the surrender of gold reserves, some of them Belgian, that were then in French hands; payments exacted following the forcible annexation of Alsace and Lorraine; industrial collaboration; and the exploitation of French imperial interests in North Africa and Indochina. In protracted discussions on all these issues, Couve de Murville used patience, formal courtesy, dilatory tactics, and insistence that he must refer back to his superiors on all the major points of contention in order to stall the Germans and maintain France's long-term economic interests.

With the shift in power which brought Pierre Laval back to the premiership in April 1942 and the collaborationist Pierre Cathala to the finance ministry, Couve de Murville began to think that further participation in the Committee's work was going to be extremely difficult. He struggled on but, in January 1943, the French delegates to the Commission were recalled and Laval decided to deal directly with Berlin.

Couve de Murville left Vichy for Madrid in early March 1943 following an itinerary worked out in advance after the German occupation of the Vichy-controlled southern zone in November of the previous year. Once in the Spanish capital, he telegraphed London indicating his readiness to serve de Gaulle. On 24 March, the general wired this welcome news to his agent in Algiers, General Catroux.

Arriving in the Algerian capital while de Gaulle was still in London, Couve de Murville, always the pragmatist in terms of the state's interests, agreed to act as secretary-general in the American-backed administration of General Henri Giraud, then the dominant French figure in the Maghreb. This strategically placed post allowed the new arrival to help arrange the transfer of Fighting France to North Africa.

Not surprisingly, given his role as a senior mandarin in France's administrative apparatus (and therefore a very valuable political catch), Couve was a guest at de Gaulle's first luncheon party in Algiers on 30 May. A week later, obviously impressed, *Le Connétable* selected the veteran civil servant to be his *commissaire aux Finances* on the Comité français de libération nationale (CFLN), which had replaced La France combattante on 3 June, and over which de Gaulle and Giraud co-presided. Although he had committed himself (by wire at least) to the Gaullist camp, Couve was counted (together with Jean Monnet) as representing the Giraud interest on the Committee, balancing the unconditional Gaullism of René Massigli and André Philip, who had arrived from London on the same plane with de Gaulle. Although his sitting on the CFLN as a stand-in for de Gaulle's rival has led some historians to characterize Couve as a *giraudiste,* his earlier signal to *Le Connétable* from Madrid offers some evidence of his commitment to the Gaullist camp.

Among the priorities that Commissioner Couve de Murville was eager to tackle were the inclusion of France's African possessions (whether *gaulliste* or *pétainiste*) in the overall budget of the CFLN and the partial settling of the relatively modest debt which Free France had incurred as a result of the 7 August 1940 accord with the United Kingdom. British subsidy to the Gaullist cause having ended as of 30 June 1943, the CFLN relied henceforth upon the substantial resources of France's North African and other imperial dependencies. Couve kept the Caisse, however, so that it might continue to serve as an agency of currency emission and exchange control.

Despite his reservations about Couve de Murville, Denis agreed to continue to administer the Caisse under the newly appointed *commissaire aux Finances.* The two Protestants were, however, neither personally nor politically compatible. Denis, a *gaulliste de la première heure,* found the recently arrived mandarin indifferent to his successful reorganization of the finances of France's colonies and even unconcerned about the ultimate fate of these imperial holdings. And Couve's intractable nationalism, his preoccupation with the status and prestige of the French monetary system, augured badly, he felt, for the extension of Allied financial collaboration into the peace.[21]

His disagreements with Couve apart, the overall experience of Pierre Denis in Algiers was negative. The sense of moral commitment, the close collaboration of colleagues that he had found so rewarding in London, had given way to an atmosphere of divisiveness and scheming in the North African capital. "Gaullist camaraderie was slowly dissipated there," Denis wrote years later, adding, "We watched old administrative traditions resurface like weeds in a garden."[22] The Protestant who had been a devoted custodian of Free France's Caisse concluded that France, in 1943, ended up as much in need of moral regeneration as she had been three years earlier.

It was in these circumstances that Denis welcomed a proposal made to him by Pierre Mendès France (who replaced Couve de Murville as *commissaire aux Finances* in November 1943) that he go to London to serve as *attaché financier* of the CFLN in the British capital. Denis would as a result become involved in new tensions and disputes, brought about in part by American efforts to impose their own made-in-America banknotes on those parts of France they were planning to liberate. During this period of pre-Liberation anticipation, Denis was sharply rebuked by Jean Monnet for suggesting that, in recognition of the hospitality offered Gaullist forces during the war, France should consider helping finance the economic recovery of the United Kingdom when the conflict ended. And as he contemplated his own nation's challenges with victory in the offing, the Protestant Denis (like the Jew Mendès France) could only hope that his compatriots were up to the self-imposed austerity required of them in the period of moral and physical rehabilitation that lay ahead:

> We must reconstitute our elites, restore asceticism to its proper place, reaccustom every man and child to recognize that, in the French tradition, there is something more precious than money, comfort and material security. And, as for administrative reorganization, this too is a matter of moral reform. We must rid civil servants of a preoccupation with the state's duties towards them and get them interested in fulfilling their assigned roles.[23]

Meanwhile, Couve de Murville, who maintained a mandarin's detachment during the bitter power struggle between Giraud and de Gaulle, had no difficulty yielding up his role as finance commissioner to the Jewish Radical Mendès France in November 1943. As Couve observed to his biographer years later, de Gaulle's decision to replace him after only five months with an experienced politician was no doubt based on a politically strategic decision by the general "Having called upon me as a senior civil servant," Couve remarked, "he replaced me soon enough with Mendès France who was clearly of a different quality, politically speaking."[24]

Following his five months' service as *commissaire aux Finances*, Couve de Murville was sent to Italy in 1944 as CFLN delegate to the Consultative Committee, which had been created to oversee relations between the invading Allies and the Italian population. The experience proved frustrating since the Americans were clearly determined to set policy unilaterally and were using the committee as a foil; however, it gave the *inspecteur des Finances* a first exposure to the brilliant post-war political career which lay ahead.

When Pierre Mendès France took over the finance portfolio from Couve de Murville in November 1943, he inherited a situation largely free of the necessary but embarrassing debt toward the United Kingdom which Free France had assumed in the summer of 1940. Throughout the war, Vichy propaganda had pointed to this financial dependency as evidence of de Gaulle's treasonous submissiveness to "Anglo-Saxon" interests. In a 4 January 1944 speech before the Assemblée consultative provisoire, Mendès decisively refuted this charge.[25] To begin with, he pointed out, French holdings in the United Kingdom in 1940, the ultimate guarantor of loans extended to Free France, were far greater than those of the British in France. These holdings had of course been blocked as a precautionary measure by the Churchill government following the Armistice; they would be released as the liberation of the homeland got under say.[26]

A month after his speech to the Consultative Assembly, on 2 February 1944, drawing on a text prepared by Postel-Vinay, Mendès formally liquidated the CCFL and replaced it with a new entity, the Caisse centrale de la France d'outre-mer.

First piloted by Pierre Denis, then expertly managed by Postel-Vinay under the supervision of different finance commissioners, and solidly backed by agents of the British Treasury, the CCFL had allowed de Gaulle and his supporters to wage the war against fascism not as mercenaries of His Majesty but as proud and independent allies.

CHAPTER SEVEN

Jacques Soustelle: Huguenot Rebel Becomes Gaullist Propagandist

Born in Montpellier on 3 February 1912 to a working-class Catholic father and a Protestant mother, Jacques Soustelle was baptized in the Reformed communion. Although as an adult he drifted away from his childhood faith, Soustelle always saw himself as shaped by the Huguenot tradition. He never forgot early memories of itinerant lay preachers who travelled door-to-door throughout the Protestant heartland in the Cévennes distributing tracts with their message of eternal salvation. In writing about his wartime commitment to Free France, Soustelle recalls taking heart from these sometimes solitary pilgrims:

> I still remember one of them in particular, so vividly are his features still fixed on my childhood memory. He wore a dark blue overcoat made of cheap cloth and buttoned up to the chin, heavy boots and a well-worn hat fixed to his close-cropped skull. You guessed right away that his work in no way nurtured his body but after all "Man does not live by bread alone!" I have often thought back to those wandering pamphlet-vendors when, many years afterwards, I wandered the world myself, traveling light but full of a faith I was eager to spread to all those I encountered.[1]

Fleeing Paris in April 1961 after a falling out with de Gaulle over the Algerian crisis, Soustelle justified his non-conformist defiance of the government's policy by invoking the rebellious spirit of his Huguenot forebears:

> What I have always maintained is the right which we recognize in theory but not in practice of every citizen to speak out and support whatever he believes to be

just and not to let any authority, whatever its origin, try to impose on him an opinion contrary to his conscience. It is for this right that my Huguenot ancestors from the Cévennes fought and suffered as they confronted the all-powerful Sun King. It is for this right that the French Revolution overthrew the Old Regime.[2]

After undergraduate studies at the University of Lyon, Soustelle moved to Paris where he enrolled at the École normale supérieure. Three years later, aged twenty, he obtained both an *agrégation* in philosophy and a diploma in ethnology from that prestigious institution. Soustelle's field of research was Latin America, which he visited intermittently throughout the 1930s. His investigation resulted in the publication of *Mexique, terre indienne* in 1935[3] and the submission of a doctoral dissertation on pre-Columbian Mexican culture in 1937, when the brilliant young ethnologist was named deputy to Paul Rivet, the director of the Musée de l'homme. Several of his colleagues at the Musée (including Boris Vildé and Anatole Lewitsky) became members of the wartime resistance inside France. Soustelle's collaboration with Rivet was paralleled by a teaching appointment at the Collège de France, as well as at the École normale de la France d'outre-mer, in the years immediately preceding the outbreak of war.

His radical humanism made Soustelle a spontaneous supporter of the Popular Front. He was on the executive of the Comité de vigilance des intellectuels antifascistes and, shortly after the assumption of power by Léon Blum's left-wing coalition, he became a contributor to *Vendredi,* a newspaper launched by the Protestant novelist André Chamson to combat the influence of the influential right-wing weeklies. In the 26 June 1936 issue of the paper, Soustelle called for the democratization of France's museum policy. Given that only a highly educated minority frequented these temples of high culture, the progressive ethnologist argued, museums should be made more attractive to the public at large. Teachers' organizations and trade unions should be encouraged to sponsor visits to public museums and galleries which should in turn be kept open at night. Talks aimed at popular audiences would help make such visits more rewarding.[4] No action was taken in response to this suggestion by the Blum government; but the idea took hold a generation later when Soustelle's Gaullist contemporary, André Malraux, created a nation-wide network of Maisons de culture during the Fifth Republic.

In the spring of 1939, Soustelle was sent on a special mission by Premier Daladier to organize a French intelligence network in Mexico, where German agents were already well established but where the French community was also wealthy and influential. Familiar with the territory, but seen as a newcomer by those whose patriotism he was trying to arouse, the would-be agent had little success.

Following news of the armistice signed by Pétain, Soustelle thought of heading north to join the Canadian army, but when the Mexican press relayed the text of de Gaulle's 18 June appeal, he sent a telegram to the general, putting himself at the disposition of Free France. On 13 July, *Le Connétable* replied with thanks, pointing out that the chief representative of La France libre in the Americas was his old comrade from St-Cyr, Jacques de Sieyès, who was in New York, adding that Soustelle might best serve the cause by advertising its merits to the French in Mexico. Again, as he had done under Daladier's mandate, Soustelle tried to proselytize but without much success. Having decided he would be more useful in London, the student of Aztec culture nevertheless managed (thanks to his wife Georgette) to secure consular status for further potential visits not only to Mexico but to most Central American states.[5]

In London, after finding a room at the Hotel Piccadilly, Soustelle went at once to see de Gaulle. He offers a vivid description of this first encounter with the general in his post-war reflections on the Free French saga:

> He was perfectly natural with me, neither familiar, vulgar nor precious, in short, making clear he belonged to a type that doesn't tolerate fools … I was myself less excited than curious. And from the very beginning I had the impression that this man was not playing a role. He was quite simply himself, giving no thought to the idea of creating a special persona … He likes to ask questions and he's a good listener. He laughs rarely but heartily. His thoughts go instinctively toward broad trends in time and space, to basic shifts of opinion, to the long term movements of civilization, to the underlying currents that guide a historic period and a nation.[6]

Apart from military matters with which the general was obviously familiar, Soustelle concluded that de Gaulle was a masterful student of history, able to function like a physician who is at the same time an engineer. The cosmopolitan ethnologist also understood that the general was driven by an abiding belief in the overwhelming power of nationalism.

Having in turn impressed the general, Soustelle was assigned to act as second to Joseph Hackin who, as of September 1940, had been in charge of Free France's embryonic department of foreign affairs. Hackin had been director of a pre-war archaeological dig in Afghanistan, where he had uncovered a rich trove of Greco-Buddhist art. Tragically, this gifted scientist-turned-Gaullist agent was lost at sea in December 1941, when his ship was torpedoed in the Mediterranean. Like Soustelle, he saw in La

France libre the kernel of a regenerate French state in which moral revival would be matched by material reconstruction.[7] Soustelle served under Hackin from November 1940 until February 1941.[8]

Soustelle spent only part of these first days at Carlton Gardens working with Hackin. The rest of his time was given to collaborating with Jean Massip, former London correspondent of *Le Petit Parisien*, who had been put in charge of Free France's fledgling propaganda service. The overall responsibilities of Massip's new deputy included the organization of recruiting campaigns for La France libre in the United Kingdom and the devising of counter-propaganda to meet the slanderous campaigns against de Gaulle and his followers emanating from Vichy and Berlin.

After living through these rather chaotic conditions in his first weeks in London, Soustelle welcomed the creation at the end of January 1941 of Free France's first formal administrative structure, when René Cassin was made permanent secretary of the Conseil de Défense out of which in September would emerge the Comité national. He notes with a mixture of admiration and irony that this newly restructured organization rested on a very flimsy base: as of March 1941, the entire "civil service" of Free France, responsible for running departments of finance, colonies, propaganda, and foreign relations, consisted of a mere ninety-six people! His admiration was all the more roused for these early Gaullists, who were bound together not by any common ideology but by a collective repudiation of Pétain and collaboration, noting with interest that "traditional Catholics, Jews and Protestants rubbed shoulders in that microcosmic society."[9]

After his first three months in London, Soustelle was dispatched on a nine-month tour to set up Free French committees throughout the Americas. He began in Montreal, where he met the Catholic Elisabeth de Miribel, already engaged in a parallel mission of Gaullist evangelization. He soon confirmed the young woman's conclusions about attitudes toward de Gaulle in Canada:

> By a paradox which only the all-powered presence of the Catholic clergy can explain, French Canada was less favorable to our cause than British Canada. The province of Quebec held Pétain to be a great patriot and the slogan "Travail, Patrie, Famille" was regarded there as the last word in political wisdom for all time. As for Free France, it was seen as made up of a band of Jews, Freemasons and atheists.[10]

Fortunately, Soustelle's later reception in Mexico, Cuba, the Dominican Republic, and Haiti (where he ran into his fellow-ethnologist Claude Lévi-

Strauss) was far warmer, as were subsequent visits to Colombia, Venezuela, and the Central American republics.

During this roving mission across the Atlantic, Soustelle learned that, on the first anniversary of de Gaulle's 18 June appeal, Vichy had revoked his citizenship. The news made him worry about the fate of his parents living in a working-class suburb of Lyon.[11] At the same time, the decision to make him an alien in his own country reinforced his no doubt naive belief that since 18 June 1940 there had existed "a tacit contract between the French people and de Gaulle and that, as a result, the general had been given a mandate to conduct the war on their behalf and to work for the resurrection of their liberties."[12]

When he showed up again at Carlton Gardens in November, de Gaulle (who had originally planned to put him in charge of propaganda activities emanating from Radio-Brazzaville in French Congo) informed him instead that he would be named to sit on the newly created Conseil national français as *commissaire à l'Intérieur.* A few days later, the new commissioner took over the offices of the Protestant André Diethelm, who had been in overall charge of internal affairs and labour matters, as well as propaganda, since his arrival in London.

The journalist Jean Marin remembers the way in which the new arrival injected vitality and a decidedly leftist spirit into the small band of *gaullistes*: "Generous, light-heartedly witty, and intellectually self assured, he was full of plebeian energy which made his left-wing commitment immediately apparent."[13]

Soustelle's daily routine remained essentially the same until he departed for Algiers in the spring of 1943. Following a quick review of the press and Reuters news reports, he would join de Gaulle in a general discussion of the political and military situation. De Gaulle continued to impress Soustelle during these chats. "In a manner of speaking," the ethnologist wrote just after the war, "I was able to watch his thoughts flash forth in contact with the facts like sparks when a hammer strikes metal."[14]

At 9:30 a.m., after seeing de Gaulle, Soustelle presided over a daily "interministerial" conference which brought together Maurice Schumann, Georges Boris from the Commissariat à l'Intérieur, who brought along news provided by Gaullist counter-intelligence, and a staff of photographers, film experts, and publicity people.

The responsibilities of the "ministry" Soustelle had taken over were far-ranging. They included regular contact with British and American press services, daily directives to Free French media people in various parts of the world, the dispatch of war correspondents to Allied armies (especially where the Forces françaises libres were involved), the relaying back into France of information reaching London from the internal resistance, the overseeing of Free French publications, the organization of lecture tours to army camps and British war plants, and the mobilization of crowds for Gaullist rallies at Albert Hall and other public venues. The daily conferences chaired by Soustelle also aimed at ensuring that the BBC broadcasts to France not directly under Gaullist supervision were as fully informed and favourably disposed as possible. In this connection, Soustelle recalled spending one evening in the company of André Philip and Yehudi Menuhin when all three of them were shocked to hear the reactionary General Giraud extolled.[15]

Soustelle's personal rapport with the Catholic Maurice Schumann was particularly close during these months. The propaganda minister's close working relationship with Schumann was facilitated by the fact that they lived in the same South Kensington apartment building. The broadcaster regularly discussed his nightly "Honneur et patrie" talk with the information commissioner after returning from the studio. Soustelle was regularly given an advance copy of Schumann's text as soon as it was typed by the broadcaster's secretary, Annette Jackson. Before being aired, the script was also seen by British Intelligence which almost always approved it. It helped that Schumann was on good terms with Colonel Sutton, head of Britain's wartime propaganda service. Sometimes it was necessary for Soustelle or Boris to intervene with Sutton, and on a few occasions (most notably at the time of the Anglo-American landing in North Africa from which de Gaulle had been excluded), Schumann simply stopped broadcasting. In extremis, the Free French radio station at Brazzaville was put to use to relay the Gaullist message outside the reach of the British authorities.[16]

Soustelle ended most days at Carlton Gardens by paying a second visit to de Gaulle in the evening when the general briefed his commissioner on the high-level meetings with British and Allied officials, and sometimes handed over the draft of a text he was working on, eager to get Soustelle's critical opinion. Among the civilian associates whom de Gaulle saw on a regular basis during wartime, perhaps none was closer to him intellectually and psychologically than Soustelle.

One of the most exciting moments during Soustelle's experience with the Free French came in the summer of 1942, when de Gaulle told him that a key leader of the internal resistance, André Philip, then teaching law at the University of Lyon, would soon join the Conseil national as *commissaire à l'Intérieur.* Like so many others, Philip was spirited out of France with the aid of British intelligence. René Cassin phoned Soustelle on a Saturday in July to announce the arrival of this much-heralded Protestant and

Socialist newcomer, whose political assets included membership in the internal resistance. Soustelle, who had met Philip in Lyon before the war, showed up to greet the new arrival, quickly recognizing the feisty deputy, "a tall, swarthy man with darting eyes whose lips were always clamped tight around the stem of his pipe."

The next morning being a Sunday and Philip recalling that Soustelle was, like himself, Protestant in background, the newcomer phoned the information commissioner to find the address of the French Reformed temple in London and the time of worship. Soustelle gave directions, but was forced to confess that he had never attended services at the Huguenot church in Soho Square. He later attended a service to hear Philip who, he noted, "would have made a most eloquent pastor had he not been a deputy and later a government minister."[17]

Soustelle greeted Philip's presence on the Conseil with enormous enthusiasm. He recalled after the war, "We saw in him the professor, the fiery orator, the socialist true to his ideals, the man of the Resistance, whose role we tended to overestimate rather than misconstrue." Soustelle had been distressed, like other leftists, at the presence of many right-wing men among de Gaulle's early supporters. And he especially welcomed Philip's youthful energy and enthusiasm. This was surely the type of man needed, not only to help check the authoritarian tendencies in de Gaulle's entourage but also to reorient French civic life after the war. The general had promised a fundamental regeneration of the nation following liberation; Philip seemed just the right man to help deliver on this pledge.[18]

As we shall see, the hopes vested in Philip by Soustelle would soon be dashed, partly as a result of a radical difference in temperament between the two men, partly because of a clash over the shaping of post-war France. But in the months immediately following his arrival, the new *commissaire à l'Intérieur* reinforced what Soustelle judged to be a cohesive and effective team. He found René Pleven solid and "very Celtic," ideally suited by temperament to deal with the Anglo-Saxons; he admired René Cassin's dedication to republican principles and his determination to set La France libre on a democratic course. He sometimes felt startled but not put off by Diethelm's biting, even brutal, interventions. He respected the diplomatic skill and patriotic fervour of Maurice Dejean (an opinion de Gaulle did not share). He collaborated easily with the self-effacing and tireless Georges Boris, and he deeply appreciated the trade-unionist Henry Hauck, as solid physically as he was ideologically.[19]

Like Schumann with his nightly BBC broadcasts, Soustelle eagerly relayed news of Fighting France's exploits to the media. The victory at

El-Alamein in Egypt during May and June 1942, in which the Forces françaises libres played a key role, was generously publicized, as was the increasing militancy of the underground resistance across the Channel.

Some of Soustelle's most rewarding moments in London came when he had a chance to meet members of the resistance who managed to get to the British capital. He was much impressed by the contribution to the cause made by the journalist Pierre Brossolette, who arrived in the British capital in May 1942 to take charge of the BCRA. The propaganda minister shared the journalist's eagerness to transform *gaullistes* into a new political force superseding the old and factious party system of the Third Republic.[20] He felt an equal admiration for Brossolette's partner André Dewavrin ("Passy"), whose loss on a mission back in France he saw as a major blow to hopes for France's moral as well as political regeneration.

Before coming to London, Brossolette had met several members of the internal resistance, including the Protestant philosopher Jean Cavaillès, who had been Soustelle's *caïman* (director of studies) at the École normale. Soustelle was delighted when Cavaillès managed to reach London and they could share memories of their university days, which had included visits to the home of the scholarly pastor Maurice Leenhardt, an ethnologist with an interest in New Caledonian culture. He was all the more horrified after Cavaillès's return to France, when news reached London that the professor had been arrested and then shot at Arras.[21]

Another key member of the resistance whom Soustelle greeted in London in May 1942 was Philippe Roques, who had been secretary to Interior Minister Mandel in the Reynaud government and who was also a close friend of Diethelm. After two months in Britain, Roques was taken by submarine to the Mediterranean coast near Antibes carrying letters from de Gaulle to Mandel and Blum. This important mission was highly successful, producing a letter from Mandel unconditionally endorsing de Gaulle. Tragically, Roques was killed trying to cross back to freedom through Spain in 1943.[22]

Soustelle's keen interest in these contacts with the French underground was paralleled by an increasing focus on relations between Fighting France and the United States. Roosevelt's November 1941 decision to extend the Lend-Lease program to de Gaulle's organization seemed to augur well for the future; and on 9 July 1942, an American memorandum had contained a clear recognition of the contribution made by the Conseil national to the Allied war effort. Later that summer, however, rumours of an American decision to shift strategic focus from Europe to French North Africa, and to act there without consulting de Gaulle, re-excited old tensions.

Operation "Torch," the American-led Allied assault on French North Africa which began on the night of 7 November 1942, brought relations between Washington and Fighting France to the breaking point.[23] For a variety of reasons, chiefly in order to win over or neutralize the pro-Vichy French troops in the Maghreb, Roosevelt and his advisors were determined to exclude de Gaulle from the operation. Gaullists in Algeria were in fact few in number despite efforts by Soustelle and others to encourage anti-Vichy as well as anti-Axis sentiment there.

It was at a reception at the Russian embassy in London during the evening of 7 November that Soustelle learned from the Czech leader Jan Masaryk that "Torch" was already under way. He rushed at once to alert de Gaulle, who was understandably outraged at the news of the Allied attack on sovereign French territory without his foreknowledge. The general's first reaction was to wish that the invaders be thrust back into the sea. That evening, however, Soustelle and his colleagues gathered around the radio to hear a reinvigorated de Gaulle salute the Allied invasion of the Maghreb and urge the French in Algeria to support the invaders in a battle which, he assured his compatriots, would turn out to be the key to victory.

On Armistice Day 1942, just as news arrived that the Germans had occupied the so-called "Free Zone" of France governed by Vichy, members of the Conseil national gathered in the French Catholic church on Brompton Road for a memorial service dedicated to the French who had fallen in both world wars. That afternoon, Soustelle and Schumann organized a rally in Albert Hall where, standing under a huge banner displaying the Cross of Lorraine, de Gaulle offered a rousing speech urging French workers, soldiers, and intellectuals to rally to Fighting France:

> We will not allow anyone to divide our nation's war effort through so-called parallel, that is to say, separate, actions … Yesterday's established hierarchies, all the formerly venerated personalities, all the old-time rules of the game, no longer enjoy France's trust. The nation knows no other leaders but those guiding her towards liberation. As was the case during the Great Revolution, she only acknowledged the leadership of the Committee of Public Safety … Let popular sovereignty henceforth be fully exercised through the vote and through the overthrow of a socially and morally sclerotic regime which was first abandoned by the exploited masses and then betrayed by the ambition of the trusts and by those in power. Today's France is focused on one single hope and one single will![24]

Soustelle tells us that at the end of the speech, the crowd at the Albert Hall shouted with one voice, "Qu'importe le reste? De Gaulle est là!" (What else matters? De Gaulle is here!).

Soustelle's euphoria did not last. On 26 November, the BBC vetoed the text of the speech that de Gaulle had intended to give excoriating the

Allies for maintaining Vichyite elements in power in Algeria. The general retaliated by boycotting the British broadcaster until matters were smoothed out on 28 December. Meanwhile, incensed at the American-backed ascendancy of Darlan in Algiers, Soustelle issued a communiqué late in November denouncing the admiral whom Pétain had designated as his heir. Then, in mid-December, when de Gaulle named General Henri d'Astier de la Vigerie and Professors René Capitant and Louis Joxe as his representatives in the Algerian capital, Soustelle recovered his optimism, confident that the progressive forces in the territory, led by youth, small merchants, and the popular element would soon rally to Fighting France.[25] He soon enough discovered that the tortuous complexity of politics in Algiers were hard to fathom from a distance.

Soustelle welcomed the news that Darlan had been murdered by a young Catholic patriot, Fernand Bonnier de la Chapelle, on Christmas Eve. But he was quickly plunged back into despair when he learned that the reactionary Giraud, backed by the Americans, had replaced him. Giraud's ascendancy was particularly distressing, since he had ordered the arrest and detention of several of the Gaullists, many of them Jewish, who had been involved in the 7 November seizure of power in Algiers which had been designed to coincide with Operation "Torch."

Soustelle learned in detail about the 7 November putsch over lunch with Professor Capitant when the latter visited London. He was surprised to hear the professor urge support for some kind of power-sharing agreement between de Gaulle and Giraud. There is no chance of a one-hundred-percent Gaullist solution in Algeria, Capitant insisted, using what Soustelle describes as "all the diabolical cunning of a law professor as well as the fanaticism of a true apostle" in a vain effort to convince him. Given the propaganda minister's rigorously anti-fascist views, the lunch conversation was stormy, although, in time, the two Gaullists became close friends.[26]

The arrival in London in February 1943 of the experienced French diplomat René Massigli brought yet another Protestant recruit to the cause. De Gaulle named Massigli to replace Maurice Dejean as commissioner of external affairs in an effort to enhance what had been a relatively weak area of Gaullist influence and competence. Soustelle was not much impressed by the new commissioner, who dropped in on his office two or three times a day, always febrile and highly agitated. Massigli was anglophile in outlook and made clear his belief that Fighting France's policy ought to be more closely aligned with that of the United Kingdom. Eden and Churchill tried to take advantage of this bias, asking Massigli to urge de Gaulle toward more democratic ways. When, as a result, the new commissioner ventured to press the Conseil national to exercise more control over *Le Connétable,* Soustelle and his colleagues gave the suggestion short shrift.[27]

Massigli's attempt to conciliate the British was one thing. The Foreign Office's refusal to countenance a projected tour of the Middle East and North Africa by de Gaulle was quite another. The general reacted to this veto by leaving Carlton Gardens and not showing up for the next day's Council meeting when, with Pleven in the chair, Soustelle supported de Gaulle's act of defiance against Philip and Massigli.

Early in April, the diplomatically astute General Catroux arrived from Algiers with a proposal for the fusion of the territory's *gaullistes* and *giraudistes.* Clearly, the situation in Algeria was at a critical stage. De Gaulle, increasingly impatient to depart for North Africa, prepared an address on the subject to the French people to be broadcast on 20 April. Soustelle was brought into the general's office to help with the text. After the war, he recalled that "with my Protestant taste for scriptural quotations, I reminded [de Gaulle] of the biblical reference to *sépultures blanchies,* (whitened sepulchres), thinking that this would evoke a reflection of the news coming out of France and would expose members of the old-line parties which were so eager to reappear."[28] Following de Gaulle's reading of the text over the BBC, Soustelle recalls Massigli descending on him in a rage, his features contorted, his skin colour more bilious than usual, shouting out, "Well, I hope you're happy! Now everything is lost!"[29]

On 25 May, three days before de Gaulle's departure for Algiers, the Conseil national met in special session. General Catroux and Admiral d'Argenlieu joined commissioners Cassin, Diethelm, Massigli, Pleven, Philip, and Soustelle in giving de Gaulle a mandate to work for the unity of the nation in its struggle for liberation. All the commissioners handed in written resignations to the general, giving him a free hand to deal with the complex situation that would face him in Algiers.

Le Connétable left London three days later, taking with him the Protestants Philip and Massigli. A third Protestant, Diethelm, followed the next day. Staying on in London were Cassin and Schumann as well as Pleven, who replaced Massigli in handling Fighting France's external relations, and Soustelle, who took over the interior ministry from Philip on a temporary basis.

Newly empowered in de Gaulle's absence, Soustelle on 14 June dispatched a note to Eden, countersigned by those of his colleagues still in London, strongly urging that frequently promised funds be delivered to the resistance. Provocatively, he had arranged for broadcasts attacking Giraud to be relayed to North Africa through Radio-Brazzavile.[30]

News of intrigue and discord in Algiers prompted Soustelle to believe Fighting France should retain a base of operations in London even as it transferred its main offices to North Africa. At the end of June, the ad hoc interior commissioner was at last summoned to Algiers, where the struggle for France's future was already engaged on several fronts. Partisans of de Gaulle were battling devotees of Giraud; Fighting France was at odds with the Allies, who were reticent about recognizing de Gaulle as a full partner; and a shadow Gaullist government based in Algiers was vying for influence in France with the internal resistance. As we shall see, Soustelle would play a key role in ensuring that the intelligence services of what emerged as an embryonic French government in exile would reflect the progressive political vision of his colleagues as well as that of the men and women who were fighting for liberation inside France.

CHAPTER EIGHT

Blum's Disciples Become de Gaulle's Apostles

The synagogue sends me more recruits than the cathedral.
Charles de Gaulle

The presence of a contingent of Jewish Socialists in La France libre was a source of concern to de Gaulle, not because of any personal antipathy (he had great respect for Léon Blum) but because it caused deep resentment among many of the officers who had rallied to his cause and because it offered an easy target to Vichy propagandists, who tried to fix the blame for France's collapse on Blum's Popular Front administration (as well as on Jews in general). By contrast, Blum was the object of something close to veneration by the Socialists who showed up at Free French headquarters. The Jewish ex-premier had in 1920 assumed the mantle of Jean Jaurès, founder of the modern Socialist party, the Section française de l'Internationale ouvrière (SFIO), who had used an adroit mix of ideological synthesis, rhetorical skill, and parliamentary manœuvre to turn the party into the most powerful bloc in the Chamber of Deputies, and who might have come to power had he not been assassinated in 1914.

The ideology which these Socialists-turned-Gaullists brought with them to London included a commitment to achieve political power and transform French society through parliamentary means; a conviction that church and state must remain rigorously separated and that secular education was the only effective training ground for citizenship; a deep suspicion of France's military and clerical elites, intensified by memories of the role played by the Army brass and the Catholic clergy during the Dreyfus Affair; an ethnically inclusive civic nationalism coupled (until 1938 at least) with a search for international peace and collective security through the League of Nations or, in some cases, a commitment to pacifism; and a focus on individual rights, often reflected by membership in France's leading civil rights organization, the Ligue des Droits de l'Homme.

Most of the leaders of the SFIO were agnostics or Freethinkers like Jaurès and Blum. Others were assimilated Jews who, while respecting their cultural heritage, saw its religious component as secondary. Those who showed up at Gaullist headquarters in London were determined to stay true to the republican and democratic faith of Léon Blum as well as to his socialist convictions. They would have a profound impact on the political and socio-economic orientation of La France libre.

The Munich agreement of 1938, the high point of Franco-British appeasement of Hitler, created a deep rift within Socialist ranks.[1] Partisans of the agreement, led by Paul Faure, saw the war which broke out a year later as a conflict between capitalist states in which the proletariat had no interest; many of these *munichois* ended up voting plenipotentiary power to Pétain in July 1940, and some became *vichyssois*. On the other flank of the party stood Léon Blum, Vincent Auriol, Marx Dormoy, and Jules Moch, who remained in France, as well as those such as Georges Boris, André Weil-Curiel, and Jean Pierre-Bloch, who joined Free France.

The deep split in the SFIO left the party for all purposes dead at the time of the Armistice. Blum was taken into custody on 15 September 1940 and placed under house arrest in the village of Bourassol, where he remained until his trial for treasonous undermining of rational morale by the Vichy courts at Riom beginning in February 1942. Efforts to revive the party went unheeded until 9 March 1941, when a small band of militants with little popular support met at Nîmes to create the Comité d'action socialiste (CAS). Delegates from CAS in time made contact with their comrades who had joined de Gaulle.

The *munichois* among the socialists, in some cases, endorsed Pétain's so-called National Revolution and saw in Vichy's labour legislation a chance for proletarian emancipation. Those who joined Free France did their best (allied to the CAS) to propagate the gospel of social change within the Gaullist camp. In most cases they joined a resurrected SFIO at the war's end, intent on completing the socio-economic revolution they had begun during the Popular Front.

Georges Boris, who brought extraordinary skills as a tactician and propagandist to the Gaullist cause, traced his ancestry back to eighteenth-century Lorraine. Like many of the province's Jews, his father left for Paris following the German annexation in 1871 in order to escape the presumed anti-Semitism of the incoming Kaiser's regime. Ironically, the

Borises arrived (like the Dreyfus family) just a decade before the outbreak of virulent anti-Jewish sentiment in France!

At the time of Georges's birth, the Boris family were well-to-do and, like many other French Jews, fully assimilated, with only a nominal link to their religious tradition.[2] Georges attended Jeanson-de-Sailly lycée, but any hope of pursuing higher education ended when his father sent him on a six-month trip to Brazil to look after the family's business interests there. Following this experience, the young Boris traveled to Ceylon to supervise the tea and rubber plantations the family firm owned on the island.

His stay in Brazil had permanently undermined Boris's health, which precluded military service during the First World War. Instead, given his financial expertise, Georges was offered an assignment working with the French embassy in London, then transferred in 1916 to Berne to help serve with the Commission de ravitaillement and, finally, asked to work with the Inter-Allied Committee which had been established to oversee the economic blockade of the Central Powers. Following the war, Boris became secretary-general of the Tubize International Holding Company, owned by the Loewenstein interests, and engaged in the production of artificial silk.

In political terms, Boris saw himself, despite his capitalist connections, as "born on the left," embracing the socialist ideals of Jaurès and Blum, impressed by the British Labour Party's pragmatism and the economic theories of John Maynard Keynes, dreaming of "a union of the various elements of the left in the pursuit of an economic 1789."[3]

Given this leftist outlook, it is not surprising that Boris abandoned the business world for journalism, where his shyness would not impair the effective propagation of his socialist views. He began his newspaper career as a reporter for *Le Progrès économique*, published by the political philosopher Maxime Leroy, then became business manager as well as writer for Henri Damay's *Le Quotidien*. Finally, in 1927 and until June 1940, Boris founded and funded his own paper, *La Lumière*, to which he managed to attract a number of distinguished contributors. Among these were men who would be his colleagues in La France libre, namely, Pierre Mendès France, Pierre Viénot, Olivier Wormser, and Jacques Soustelle. Lieutenant-colonel Émile Mayer, the mentor of de Gaulle, was the paper's military critic.

Not surprisingly, *La Lumière* lent its support to the Rassemblement populaire, the broad-based left-and-liberal coalition which came together to elect Blum's Popular Front government in 1936. In articles for *La Lumière*, Boris supported the forty-hour work week while acknowledging that it might result in lower industrial production and expressing the hope that the working class would exercise due vigilance as a result.

In March 1938, Boris joined the second Blum government as *directeur du cabinet* of the prime minister and worked in close collaboration with Pierre Mendès France, under-secretary of state at the Treasury. Early in April, he fashioned a finance bill largely inspired by Keynesian economics. Had it not been blocked by the Senate, the bill would have aimed at increased arms production while controlling inflation and limiting the export of capital as well as enhancing family allowances and retirement plans for the elderly.

Following the collapse of the second Blum government, the new premier, Édouard Daladier, and his foreign minister, Georges Bonnet, presided over the climactic moment of the appeasement policy at Munich. Boris felt an overwhelming sense of shame and disgust at this betrayal of France's ally Czechoslovakia and committed himself and his newspaper to all-out resistance to further fascist aggression. When war was declared in September 1939, he followed words with action, bidding adieu to his readers, shutting down *La Lumière*, and enrolling in the army at age fifty-two. His decision to don a uniform as a lowly sergeant was reinforced by a malicious article in the right-wing anti-Semitic weekly *Gringoire,* which alleged in 1938 that Boris had shirked military service in 1914 out of sheer cowardice.

His linguistic gifts made Boris a logical choice to be a liaison officer with the British Expeditionary Force in Flanders. It was with these Allied troops that Boris embarked during the heroic evacuation at Dunkirk at the end of May. Arriving in the United Kingdom on 28 May, he accepted a proposal that he take a job in an Edinburgh munitions plant. Learning of the Armistice while in the Scottish capital, Boris headed at once for London, where, on the morning of 19 June, he read the speech de Gaulle had given the night before on the BBC. Perusing the general's text brought him a wondrous sense of hope reborn, honour saved and, even more precious, the ability to look people in the eye again, and a determination to respond to the general's appeal for volunteers.[4]

Boris's instant commitment to the Gaullist cause was reinforced by the equally passionate feelings of his friend and fellow exile André Weil-Curiel, who had made an earlier escape to Britain. Weil-Curiel's mostly Jewish ancestry included a number of mixed marriages, which allowed him later on in occupied France to pass for "Aryan."[5] He had become a lawyer before joining the SFIO in 1930, persuaded that the party's triumph would rid France of capitalist exploitation, moral decay, and war. Disillusioned by what he saw to be increased sectarianism within the Socialist camp as well as a lack of coherent doctrine and leadership, Weil-Curiel quit the SFIO in 1938, determined from then on to adopt an attitude of unconditional but non-partisan patriotism. By contrast with the shy and self-effacing Boris, he was vigorously assertive both about his Jewish background and his republican convictions. He enrolled in the army at the beginning of the war, joining an engineers unit of the British Expeditionary Force (BEF).

On 9 May, at the height of the German blitzkrieg, Corporal Weil-Curiel ran into Henry Hauck, a veteran French trade-union leader similarly linked to the BEF, who was about to leave for London to serve as labour attaché at the French embassy there. Having been persuaded by Hauck to join the exodus, Weil-Curiel crossed the Channel on 1 June. Shortly afterward, he ran across both his old friend Boris and Hauck, who suggested that the two newcomers show up at the Institut français in London where they might broadcast in support of Franco-British solidarity as the crisis deepened. Instead, the two established an ephemeral Services français d'information to prop up morale.

Weil-Curiel was delighted to learn that de Gaulle (whose *L'armée de métier* he had read with great interest) had been named on 6 June to the Reynaud ministry; and his spirits were further raised by Churchill's eleventh-hour proposal of a merger between the two Allied nations and their vast empires. He felt especially moved by what he felt was the willingness of the British people to assume and then expunge the sense of shame and humiliation experienced by the French they encountered in the street.

Weil-Curiel's optimism was soon dampened by the news of Reynaud's resignation. He tells us that while he and Hauck were deeply disturbed, they were still resolved to keep the spirit of resistance alive. Boris, however, was psychologically paralyzed, Weil-Curiel tells us, partly because of his lowly military rank, partly because of his Jewish background. To encourage Boris, who was alarmed by his "turbulent spirit," Weil-Curiel argued reassuringly, "We could be the little pebbles that start the landslide!"[6]

On the morning of 19 June, Weil-Curiel, having learned through Hauck of de Gaulle's arrival in London and of the speech the general had made over the BBC the night before, rushed to St. Stephen's House where the immediate reception was chilly. Colonel Rozoy, chef de mission of the fledging Free French air force, remarked to him in casual conversation that those who had thus far shown up to continue the battle in the air were a disappointing lot. "There is a majority of names ending in *thal* or *ski,* if you get my drift!" Rozoy observed with a complicitous wink. The would-be volunteer replied that this would surely mean more French planes in the air, to which the ineffable colonel replied that the volunteers in questions had come to park their planes, not fly them![7] Undeterred by this racist reception, Weil-Curiel pressed his case to de Gaulle in person. The general was a bit pensive, suggesting that the newcomer might for the moment help staff the improvised headquarters at St. Stephen's House. His first act was to call Boris.

On his arrival at St. Stephen's House, Boris introduced himself to de Gaulle's aide-de-camp, Geoffroy de Courcel and then, in an extraordinary signal of willingness to avoid provoking any anti-Semitic feelings that his presence might arouse, declared, "I wouldn't want my presence here to jeopardize the sense of unanimity among those volunteers who are showing up," adding that he would be quite willing to work "in the shadows."[8]

According to the leftist and anti-Gaullist André Wurmser, de Gaulle mumbled to his entourage shortly after this encounter, "Ce juif marxiste? Je n'en veux pas!" And we know from Weil-Curiel that a certain Major 'X' was so horrified at the notion of Boris being given any responsibilities in La France libre, that he protested to the general. "Don't you realize, mon général?" Weil-Curiel reports the major as saying, "This Georges Boris is a Jew, an apostle of the Popular Front! He was *chef de cabinet* of Léon Blum!" "Well now," we are told de Gaulle replied,

> Monsieur Boris is quite possibly a Jew and a supporter of Léon Blum. But, from my perspective, he is a Frenchman who is committing himself to do battle at fifty-two years of age, who fought in the Flanders campaign and who now wishes to join us to continue the fight for France. That's quite enough for me! I perceive no difference of race or of political opinion among us. I only recognize two categories of Frenchmen: those who do their duty and those who don't. Monsieur Georges Boris does his duty. He has his place here. And this is the last I wish to hear of that kind of comment![9]

Boris gives his own account of his first encounter with de Gaulle in a letter to Blum written two years later. He begins by dismissing the charge often levelled at the leader of Free France that he was either politically or racially prejudiced:

> I can assure you that on that day (19 June) when everyone was so easily given to passion, not only did de Gaulle not consider casting me aside, I was the one who felt an obligation to speak to him the following day on the matter, saying that, if my presence in his entourage became the object of such special attention that it might be exploited by the government in Bordeaux, it might be better for me to disappear for a while.[10]

De Gaulle assured Boris that he would be welcome in the ranks but conceded that for the moment it might be wiser if, together with his friend Weil-Curiel, he tried his hand at recruiting fighting troops for the cause in the camps around the country, where French army units from the Dunkirk evacuation were stationed.

Having been encouraged by de Gaulle to leave London at least temporarily, Weil-Curiel and Boris set off on a recruiting mission. Weil-Curiel notes in his memoirs about the attitude of most of the general's entourage toward them at this stage, "Boris and I represented to these fine gentlemen the abomination of desolation. Some of them had taken advantage of our presence (at St. Stephen's House) to undermine the movement by representing it as a leftover from the Popular Front and the so-called Judeo-Masonic conspiracy."[11]

At the Arrow Park base, the two recruiters found clear evidence of anti-Jewish sentiment. When Boris struck up a conversation with a Lieutenant de Sèze, who observed about those already enrolled in La France libre, "Hum. There are lots of Jewish names on the list," Boris replied, "I'm sorry if that displeases you but I'm Jewish myself." Undeterred, de Sèze pursued, "What I really don't like are Jews like Léon Blum, revolutionaries without a homeland." Boris ended this distasteful exchange by noting, "I'm even more saddened to have to tell you that I am a collaborator of Blum who happens to be my closest friend!"[12]

On his return to London on 1 July after a less than brilliant recruitment drive, Boris found a changed atmosphere at Gaullist headquarters. New enlistees, including Pierre Tissier, a *maître des requêtes* who was acting as temporary chief of staff, made access to the general more difficult. De Gaulle was not at first aware that a barrier had been put in Boris's way, but made a scene in front of the offending officer when he was made aware of the problem and resumed his dialogue with Boris, who became as a result a regular staff member at St. Stephen's House, albeit in what was at the beginning a modest function, as analyst of British press clippings.

From that moment on, Boris wrote to Blum two years later, he adapted his line of conduct to his new circumstances, confident that there was no alternative but to join La France libre even if the organization was dominated by politically reactionary elements.

After all, the organization represented France, and he had never repudiated his nation, whether the government in place pleased him or not. And his personal analysis led him to conclude that a non-conformist such as de Gaulle, full of contempt for the governing classes, the high command, and the upper bourgeoisie, a man who had not hesitated to commit an act of rebellion in 1940, would not hesitate to continue in this direction even if his background, his education, and his earlier prejudices might dispose him to take a contrary course of action.[13]

Meanwhile, also back in London, Weil-Curiel joined Hauck at one of de Gaulle's first press conferences. When the trade-union leader asked the general what role he saw for the working class in the current struggle, de Gaulle replied, "The working class? I cannot conceive of France, I cannot conceive of the present battle, without the working class having its place in the first rank. It should be associated in its own right in the governing of the nation as well as in the war effort."[14]

Unlike the self-effacing Boris, who agreed to work in the shadows, aware of but willing to ignore the racial prejudice he had experienced, Weil-Curiel decided that "the influence of Drumont" both at St. Stephen's House and among French troops stationed in Britain was too much to bear. And when his fellow-Jew René Cassin advised him simply to disappear and let himself be forgotten, the eager advocate of the cause felt deep outrage: "Now there's a singular reward for an absolutely disinterested devotion which had led to nothing more promising than a chance to serve as a corporal in some backwater barracks in the English countryside!"[15]

Despite his discouraging few weeks in London in the summer of 1940, Weil-Curiel professed an unconditional devotion to de Gaulle until the end of the war.[16] However, having concluded that Jews had no *droit de cité* in La France libre, he requested permission to return to France where, he argued, his Masonic connections and his "Aryan" appearance would allow him to work effectively for the cause among old friends and colleagues.

Weil-Curiel returned to France via Portugal, where he encountered a number of French Jewish refugees alarmed at losing their citizenship under the fledgling Vichy regime as well as Jean-Marc Boegner, son of the leader of the French Reformed church who had decided on repatriation after serving in the Norwegian campaign. In Vichy, the returning exile was distressed at the eagerness of the upper clergy to endorse the new regime but willing to believe that Pastor Boegner might exert a benevolent influence on his friend Pétain. He made bold to travel to Paris, aided by the right-wing lawyer Armand Grégoire who (no doubt fortunately) did not know he was Jewish. His spirits were kept high listening to the BBC broadcasts of Schumann and de Gaulle and establishing contact with potential supporters of resistance, including Paul Rivet of the Musée de l'homme and Colette Audry, niece of Gaston Doumergue, the Protestant president of the Republic in the mid 1930s.

Weil-Curiel left Paris in mid-October armed with false papers identifying him as "Neil-Curiel," hoping to recruit underground partisans of Free France. He returned to witness the 11 November protests on the Champs-Élysées. After efforts to organize small resistance cells linked to London, Weil-Curiel was arrested by the Gestapo. The would-be resistance agent soon gained his release, however, thanks to the intervention of Otto Abetz, Hitler's special emissary in Paris, whom he knew casually. Then, in January 1941, he fled south to unoccupied France and thence back to London.

Because of Abetz's role in his release, those in charge of Free France counterespionage insisted on his arrest when Weil-Curiel showed up in the British capital. De Gaulle demurred, remarking, "Surely you don't want to burden me with another Dreyfus Affair!"[17] and inviting the alleged miscreant to dinner at the Hotel Connaught. To satisfy those who remained suspicious, the general established a *jury d'honneur* which concluded, not surprisingly, that the zealous Weil-Curiel had been guilty of nothing more that imprudence. In the end, this "turbulent" friend of Boris was given an assignment promoting the cause of Free France in the Orient.

By contrast with his impulsive friend Weil-Curiel, Boris had been steadily at work promoting the cause. His experience in the world of Parisian journalism and the friendships he had developed in France's political milieu led Boris to try winning over some of the French intellectuals in London who had kept their distance from Free France.

Boris knew the staunch republicans who launched the newspaper *France* in the British capital on 26 August 1940. Two of them were, like himself, Jewish and republican. Georges Gombault had in fact been Boris's editor-in-chief at *La Lumière*. Louis Lévy had been military critic for *Le Populaire*, chief organ of Léon Blum. Pierre Comert, who had been press secretary at the Quai d'Orsay until the Munich crisis, was not Jewish but shared the antipathy his colleagues felt toward de Gaulle, partly because the general came from the notoriously reactionary officer caste, partly because he gave no clear sign of devotion to the republican and democratic tradition. That these three men were also members of the Groupe Jean-Jaurès, a cluster of SFIO veterans with close ties to the Labour Party, made them a particularly disturbing centre of anti-Gaullist dissidence in the formative months of La France libre. Had Boris been able to win them to the fold, de Gaulle would no doubt have had a better press in Great Britain, something which did not happen until deep into the conflict.

Boris fared no better in his efforts to win over the key figures behind *La France libre*, a monthly launched in November 1940. Despite its name, this periodical was not officially Gaullist, although it remained basically sympathetic to the cause. Raymond Aron, the nominally Jewish sociologist and political philosopher who arrived in Britain on the same ship as Cassin, had been invited to oversee the publication of a journal of opinion during a visit to Gaullist headquarters. Liberal in outlook, Aron cherished his intellectual independence too much to allow *La France libre* to become a partisan periodical. In addition, he dreaded the prospect of the feud between de Gaulle and Pétain becoming all-out civil war and urged reconciliation with moderate elements in Vichy and, later, an accommodation between *Le Connétable* and Giraud during the Algerian imbroglio of 1942–43. Aron justifies this sympathetic neutrality vis-à-vis the leader of La France libre by arguing that he was thus better able to preserve what he calls "ecumenical Gaullism."[18]

Among other French journalists in London in the summer of 1940 were two Protestant newspapermen – Paul-Louis Bret and Pierre Maillaud. Like Aron, both these staunch republicans were devoted to their absolute editorial autonomy and skeptical about de Gaulle's political aims.[19]

Boris made no headway in his effort to convert these independent-minded journalists, but political evangelization among the French exile community in London was not, of course, his main assignment. Most of the journalist's day was spent at St. Stephen's House and later at Carlton Gardens analyzing British press clippings. To further aid the cause, in September 1940, Boris helped produce *La France et de Gaulle*, a propaganda tract aimed at the French colonies in Africa and elsewhere, which the general was hoping to liberate from Vichy. An English version of the brochure (*De Gaulle's France and the Key to the Coming Invasion of Germany*), produced with the aid of Richard Crawford, a Conservative Party organizer, followed, aimed at the English-speaking world in Britain and the Empire.

Boris's regular perusal of British and French newspapers equipped him to help orchestrate the political message which La France libre beamed back across the Channel between the summer of 1940 and D-Day. From the beginning, Boris shared the information he had gleaned with Maurice Schumann, whose office he visited on a daily basis prior to the Catholic broadcaster's five-minute "Honneur et Patrie" talk over the BBC. Boris contributed a couple of talks himself on economic matters, setting them (as he had in the pages of *La Lumière*) in their global context. And, feeling emotionally involved, he offered a tribute to his political chief Léon Blum following the Socialist leader's brilliant defence at the 1942 Riom trial.

The close collaboration between Boris and Schumann was accomplished through much of the war by a friendly link the two men established with colleagues at the BBC. There were, however, times when relations became strained over fundamental differences in strategy between the "Anglo-Saxon" powers and Free France.[20]

The organization of Free France's propaganda, largely the product of Boris and Schumann during the first few months, took on a more structured form in April 1942, when de Gaulle named the Protestant André Diethelm *commissaire à l'Intérieur.* Diethelm set in place a Comité exécutif de propagande to coordinate radio messages aimed at France and named to it (among others) Boris, Schumann, Hauck, and another newly arrived Jewish recruit to the Gaullist cause, Jean-Louis Crémieux-Brilhac.

The newcomer, a Radical who had supported the Popular Front, had been an internationalist in the interwar years, tending, like many of his comrades, toward pacifism. Munich had mobilized the anti-fascist in him, and he had volunteered at the beginning of the war. Captured by the Germans, he had been interned in Pomerania before being taken captive by the Russians. Following a subsequent escape from the Soviet Union, he had made his way to London. His original misgivings about de Gaulle's commitment to democracy were overcome at their first meeting and, then, through listening to the general speak at the Albert Hall on 18 June 1942, the second anniversary of his original appeal over the BBC, when Crémieux-Brilhac had felt something close to rapture. He described his devotion to the general in an interview granted to Jean Lacouture in 1983:

> Those of us who worked in close collaboration with de Gaulle came every day more under his spell. We were literally in love with General de Gaulle. It is hard to imagine now what he represented at the time – such intellectual force, such breadth and depth of vision. I have occasionally wondered at our infatuation during those years in London. But, surprising as it may seem, that fascination was real![21]

Crémieux-Brilhac played a key role in the Propaganda Committee by serving as archivist, classifying and editing the increasing flow of material reaching Free French headquarters from inside France as well as from the Allies.

The newly created Propaganda Committee soon claimed an important psychological and political success. In concert with Schumann's radio talks, it urged French citizens to stage demonstrations throughout France on 1 May, the traditional day of working-class celebration. The results were substantial enough to warrant repeating the call for public manifestation of patriotism on Bastille Day, 1942.

Meanwhile, the journalist in Boris no doubt rejoiced in the launching on 14 June 1942 of *La Marseillaise,* the first official Free French newspaper, edited by François Quilici, a right-wing convert to the cause. Under the rubric "Ordre nouveau ou monde meilleur," and using the nom de plume "Alain Chambéry," Boris contributed some thirty-two articles on economic issues between 9 August 1942 and 31 January 1943, ranging from denunciation of the Nazi exploitation of French workers to the promotion of a social-democratic perspective for postwar France. What this latter series of articles projects is a liberated France given to overall economic planning aimed at guaranteeing full employment and comprehensive social security, all to be achieved within the democratic and parliamentary system.[22]

Further reinforcement to the contingent of Jewish Socialists serving the Gaullist cause arrived on 6 November 1942 in the person of Jean Pierre-Bloch, penniless and in worn-out clothes after spending seventeen months in Vichy and Gestapo jails.[23] The newcomer had joined the Jeunesses socialistes in 1927 following military service. A close friend of Pierre Brossolette and Blum's Socialist colleague Daniel Mayer, he was elected to the Chamber of Deputies in 1932. Pierre-Bloch describes himself as unashamed of his Jewish background but a Freethinker by conviction. Like many other fully assimilated left-wing Jews, he believed that the triumph of socialism would resolve all or most of society's problems, including racial and religious prejudice. Left-wing militancy led him to espouse the cause of the Spanish Republicans in 1936 and, at the time of the Munich crisis, to help found the socialist monthly *Agir.*

At the outbreak of war, Pierre-Bloch enlisted as a bombardier with the Artillery School at Poitiers. He was captured during the Nazi blitzkrieg while serving on the north-eastern front. Two days later, he was visited by a Catholic chaplain who brought a comforting letter from France's chief rabbi, Paul Haguenauer (who would die in a German concentration camp). More significant from Pierre-Bloch's perspective was the news of de Gaulle's 18 June radio address to the people of France. For the first time since the war's beginning, he tells us in his memoirs, he was hearing his fellow citizens described not as a miserable band of cowards but as members of a fighting nation.

Later, in the prison courtyard, Pierre-Bloch got confirmation of what he had been trying to warn his fellow Jews about when a Prussian officer, facing the assembled French captives, asked the Jews among them to step forward, then the North Africans, finally the Bretons, each group then being assigned to separate camps. After insisting that, as a member of the Chamber of Deputies, he had immunity, Pierre-Bloch was allowed to travel to Paris, where he visited a number of veteran Socialists, including Vincent Auriol, Daniel Mayer, and Félix Gouin. Later, he attended the 22 June 1941 clandestine meeting of the founding members of the Comité d'action socialiste, the first stirrings of a revived SFIO. In Vichy, he had several rendezvous with members of the nascent Catholic democratic resistance, including Georges Bidault, Paul Simon, Auguste Champetier de Ribes, and Francisque Gay. He was pleased to learn of Pastor Boegner's letter to the grand rabbi of France deploring Vichy's anti-Semitic legislation. Like other members of the SFIO, he made a pilgrimage to the village of Bourrasol, where his leader and idol Léon Blum was detained.

Deciding in the summer of 1941 to work in the internal resistance, Pierre-Bloch joined his friend and fellow-Jew Max Hymans, Socialist deputy for the Indre department, in locating suitable sites for parachute-drops by Allied planes bringing supplies, arms, bank notes, and occasionally letters from Gaullists in London. Arrested for this dangerous subversion in October 1941, he spent five months in prison at Périgueux. Escaping in July 1942, he learned with horror of the round-up of some 12,000 Jews at the Vel d'Hiver in Paris.

In Lyon, the escapee got in touch with key members of the underground movement Liberté, including the Catholic Emmanuel d'Astier de La Vigerie, future head of the Gaullist Commissariat à l'Intérieur, whose deputy he would become in 1943. Deciding at last to try flight, Pierre-Bloch crossed the Pyrenees only to be arrested by Franco's Guardia Civil and held captive until October 1942, when Britain's ambassador in Madrid secured his release. Travelling with a passport identifying him as "Captain Peter Martin," a member of the Canadian armed forces, and making easy use of his fluent English, Pierre-Bloch reached London on 6 November 1942.

Running across Pierre Mendès France wearing the uniform of the Free French Air Force one day, Pierre-Bloch was told, "In London, one has no choice but to be a Gaullist!"[24] A few days later, he attended an Armistice Day rally for Free France at the Albert Hall, where de Gaulle made a rare public speech. Thrilled by the general's delivery and now fully converted, Pierre-Bloch showed up the following morning at Carlton Gardens. His first encounter with de Gaulle left him stunned: "Sitting at his desk, the general was very intimidating, wearing a simple uniform without any decorations … He was tall, even taller that I had been led to believe. I was struck by all of this, feeling suddenly very small but very moved. He greeted me without a smile."[25]

The general offered the new recruit the usual bird's-eye view of the world conflict, then listened to Pierre-Bloch without any change in expression.

As the would-be volunteer surmised: "It was evident that the arrival of a Jewish Socialist parliamentarian was not in that environment to be classified as a happy surprise." Pierre-Bloch adds, "I felt curiously timid, handicapped by a very real inferiority complex, something I had only felt once before, in the presence of Léon Blum."[26]

When he mentioned his idol by name, de Gaulle exclaimed, "Ah, monsieur Blum! Now there's a great man!" But when the general went on to observe that political parties seemed to belong to the past, his visitor insisted that they were still very relevant, referring to his own role in the emergence of the CAS and the recent rebirth of the Communist Party in the underground.

In the end, when their conversation was over, Pierre-Bloch asked himself if there had been any real dialogue with this man of glacial reserve, who made no offer of a post in the Fighting France organization. Fortunately, the would-be recruit ran across Schumann a few days later and was assured that he had made an excellent impression. Later meetings with the inner core of de Gaulle's advisors – Boris, Diethelm, Cassin, Pleven, and Soustelle – were equally encouraging. The result was an invitation to Pierre-Bloch to join the staff of the Bureau central de renseignements et d'action (BCRA) with the rank of captain. At the Hill Street headquarters of the BCRA, he found his old Socialist comrade Pierre Brossolette, who had written for Blum's organ *Le Populaire*, and Brossolette's superior, André Dewavrin, whose code-name "Passy," like that of many of those working at Hill Street, was taken from the Paris metro system.

Dewavrin, a graduate of the École polytechnique and former professor of artillery at St-Cyr, had volunteered for the Allied campaign in Norway in April 1940. Evacuated from Narvik following the collapse of the Franco-British effort, he arrived in Britain in time to show up at St. Stephen's House on 1 July. Perceiving his qualifications (which included perfect fluency in English), de Gaulle had immediately put him in charge of Free France's intelligence service.[27]

Pierre-Bloch was eager to become the third member of the BCRA team, which met daily to decipher telegrams and cryptic radio messages emanating from the internal resistance and arranged for the abduction of key figures from the underground, whose presence in London was deemed useful. Also put in charge of screening new recruits for the BCRA, Pierre-Bloch was outraged to discover that the application form for the organization included the questions, "Êtes-vous juif? Êtes-vous franc-maçon? Êtes-vous communiste?" Effective lobbying brought an end to this egregiously "vichyssois" part of the questionnaire.

The general atmosphere at Gaullist headquarters showed some signs of improvement as the months passed, although Pierre-Bloch always remained on his guard. When he ran across the devout (and future Carmelite) Admiral Adrien Thierry d'Argenlieu one day, he was asked point-blank if he was a believer, to which he replied, straightforward fashion, that he was a deist, but that he remained faithful to the values of Judaism. The admiral, apparently reassured, declared, "Well, then, we'll get along splendidly!"[28]

A chance to progress from amicable relations to full-fledged ecumenical celebration was lost in the spring of 1943. Supporters of La France libre were invited to participate in a shared Easter/Passover service at the Huguenot Church in Soho Square, where André Philip would preach. The nominally Protestant Soustelle attended; Pierre-Bloch tells us he would have joined too, had he been asked. After all, he observes in his memoirs, his fellow Jew Maurice Schumann regularly attended mass while in London. And, had he been invited to share a Seder celebration with a family of English Jews, he would gladly have accepted![29]

Three months after working as Brossolette's colleague in counter-intelligence, Pierre-Bloch, who found the job frustrating, requested a transfer and was assigned to the coordination of political activity inside France. He and other BCRA staff members met daily to orchestrate the efforts of the many resistance cells that had begun to spring up all over France by the fall of 1942. Pierre-Bloch was particularly proud to have helped alert France's prefects about an alarming summons to Vichy, which he had learned about in advance.[30]

Until the summer of 1942, Pierre-Bloch, like the rest of the BCRA personnel, had worked under the overall direction of the Protestant Interior Minister, André Diethelm. As of 28 July, 1942, the staff were given a new commissioner, André Philip, even more devotedly Protestant than Diethelm and clearly more leftish in orientation. Philip had arrived in London the day before. De Gaulle, who had signalled his desire to have the brilliant young lawyer, resistance activist, and parliamentarian come to London, met the newcomer that same day and immediately confirmed him in his new post. Brossolette was delighted to meet the new appointee as was Pierre-Bloch, who shared Philip's Socialist perspective. Two others Jews who were soon to join the BCRA staff – Jacques Bingen and Jean-Pierre Lévy – reinforced the progressive outlook of the intelligence organisation.

Bingen was born in 1908 to an Italian Jewish couple who had settled in Paris.[31] His father's financial success allowed the family to enjoy a solid middle-class lifestyle in the fashionable 16th arrondissement. Both parents were detached from Jewish faith and practice as would be the case with Jacques.

Like his future Gaullist colleague Maurice Schumann, Bingen attended the Janson-de-Sailly lycée, where a solid intellectual performance prepared him for later success at both the École des Mines and "Sciences-Po." He arrived at maturity with charm, good looks, and an engaging sense of humour, as well as proficiency in English, qualities which would serve him well in wartime. Jacques's older sister having married the automobile manufacturer André Citroën, Bingen came to know one of the captains of French industry in the interwar years. In 1935, following Citroën's death, he became director-general of the firm, which he steered toward the production of ocean-going vessels. As tensions mounted in Europe, he was appointed secretary of France's national committee of ship-owners. At the outbreak of war, Bingen was director of the Société française de gérance et d'armement. Despite his social background and his career choices, Bingen had developed a socialist perspective through the 1930s. It would be farfetched to call him a disciple of Blum; but he would become a devotee of de Gaulle and a partisan of an ideological shift to the left as the prospect of Liberation approached.

Following the declaration of war, Bingen, who was a reserve lieutenant in the artillery, joined the Fifty-First Scottish Division as liaison officer. Wounded during the German blitzkrieg, he managed to escape capture and find his way to Morocco and then, after considerable difficulty, to reach Liverpool on 16 July 1940. René Pleven, one of de Gaulle's earliest collaborators, saw in Bingen a man ideally suited to take charge of Free France's merchant navy, whose formal creation took place on 12 August 1940. The new recruit spent the next two years organizing the French ships and crew which rallied to the Gaullist cause. By the year's end, roughly one-third of France's merchant ships were serving the Allied war effort. This not inconsiderable contribution helped offset the financial liability which de Gaulle's government-in-exile had assumed in asking for credit from the United Kingdom in 1940 and helped facilitate the repayment of Free France's wartime obligation at the Liberation.

After two years as administrator of Free France's merchant navy, Bingen was named deputy head of the non-military branch of the BCRA. In the autumn of 1942, he oversaw the creation of a four-man committee to be presided over by de Gaulle's delegate-general Jean Moulin, which aimed at co-ordinating the strategy of the three main resistance movements inside France – Combat, Franc-tireur, and Libération.

At the beginning of 1943, Bingen assumed full control of the non-military section of the BCRA, where he faced two grave problems: a number of resistance agents inside France had been arrested or frustrated from communication with London; and, in North Africa, Giraud and his American backers had for the moment marginalized de Gaulle's partisans, putting in jeopardy the future of Fighting France. Meeting Moulin in London on 18 February 1943, Bingen agreed that Fighting France's control of all elements in the Resistance was of paramount importance. The result was an understanding which Moulin would take to Paris and which would lead, on 27 May 1943, to the creation of the Conseil national de la Résistance (CNR), bringing together anti-Vichy trade-unions, political parties, and resistance movements under the aegis of General de Gaulle.

Like his close friend and colleague Claude Bouchinet, Bingen was at this stage eager to engage in the combat inside France, as he told Moulin. De Gaulle's delegate-general persuaded him that for the time being he would better serve the cause by helping to keep the internal resistance under the tutelage of Fighting France. When the news of Moulin's arrest and death at Caliure on 21 June 1943 reached London, Bouchinet (who had been parachuted into France in mid-June) replaced him on a temporary basis. Shortly afterward, Bingen was named Bouchinet's deputy for the southern zone. Parachuted into France on 16 August 1943, he ended up taking over much of the delegate-general's responsibility for the whole of the nation.

Based in Lyon, then in Paris, Bingen was involved in a wide variety of tasks: he participated in meetings of the Comité général d'études, a think-tank of intellectuals, many of them Catholic, who were drawing up position-papers on a variety of issues for post-Liberation France; he joined Michel Debré, head of the Commission des désignations administratives, to discuss the selection of future prefects to replace Vichy appointees; he talked with the Protestant resistance leader Gaston Defferre and with José Aboulker, the twenty-four-year-old Jewish hero of the 7 November 1942 rising in Algiers; and he sent urgent messages to London complaining about the lack of financial and materiel support for the *maquis*.

On 12 May 1944, on the point of being apprehended at Clermont-Ferrand, Bingen swallowed the cyanide pill which was part of the kit of underground agents, committing suicide rather than risk arrest and torture, which might have forced him to reveal vital information to the enemy.[32]

Jean-Louis Crémieux-Brilhac, who had the occasion to observe Bingen at close quarters during his heroic and ultimately tragic participation in the struggle for French liberation, salutes his comrade with special fervour:

> What a charming man he was, this Jew who didn't believe in heaven but put his faith – with his eyes wide open – in de Gaulle, this brother-in-law of Citroën who

wanted to contribute through and beyond liberation to the birth of a broad-based labour party, uniting Blum's and Mayer's Socialists with the new forces born out of the Resistance, a seeming dilettante who hid his anxieties under a nonchalant joyousness and found his fulfilment in action; a touching figure because no one seemed better suited for happiness and so little fashioned for suffering that he preferred death to it.[33]

Unlike his colleague Bingen, Jean-Pierre Lévy came to Fighting France from the internal resistance. In 1939, he had been a textile executive and an army reserve officer. In 1941, he became a founding member of Franc-tireur, an underground organization with its own newssheet whose supporters tended to be (like Lévy) anticlerical, passionate defenders of *laïcité*, and often veterans of the Ligue des Droits de l'Homme. This ideological perspective originally set partisans of Franc-tireur apart from supporters of the other two major resistance groups – Combat, which included a number of Christians, and Libération, which brought together militant trade-unionists, Christian and secular alike.

Jean Moulin, sent into France at the beginning of January 1942 to bring these three groups together and to get them to agree to the general's overall leadership, met Lévy at the end of the month. The leader of Franc-tireur consented to put his organization under the overall control of de Gaulle. When Moulin presided over the first meeting of the Conseil national de la Résistance in May, Lévy was in the British capital, where he had arrived on April 15. Two months later, Lévy and Emmanuel d'Astier were sent into France on a mission.

Although Lévy's presence in London was limited, he was an integral part of the substantial contingent of Jewish Socialists who rallied to de Gaulle and helped create an intimate link between *Le Connétable* and Léon Blum. This support would prove vital in forging the unity of purpose and strategy which would carry Fighting France and the CFLN to victory.

The Jewish presence within the Gaullist camp and, with it, the influence of the Left, increased markedly following the transfer of Fighting France to Algiers in the spring of 1943. When de Gaulle departed for North Africa taking with him the Protestant Socialist André Philip, Boris remained in London, aided by Pierre-Bloch and, for a while, by Bingen, to oversee the day-to-day operation of the Commissariat à l'Intérieur. In November 1943, when Philip was replaced by Emmanuel d'Astier who was frequently absent from London, Boris's effective control of policy vis-à-vis the internal resistance was – if anything – consolidated.

Boris's mandate and his use of it involved organizing parachute missions into France, directing radio propaganda beamed across the Channel in collaboration with Schumann, and welcoming new arrivals, whose escape to London became every month easier thanks to Allied domination of the skies.[34] As Crémieux-Brilhac puts it, Boris, who had been in the shadows since his arrival, was, as of mid-May 1943, the dominant figure, together with the Catholic Schumann, in the formulation of Gaullist strategy from London and the key orchestrator in its transmission to the people of France: "From 1942 through 1944, (Boris was) the most intuitive as well as the shrewdest mind upon which de Gaulle was able to rely as far as political action inside France was concerned. He was, together with Closon, the counsellor of André Philip in 1942–1943, then of Emmanuel d'Astier in 1943–1944. He held the Commissariat à l'Intérieur together by himself for a whole year, in part because there was a very serious shortage of manpower."[35]

The Jewish Socialists who rallied to the Free French cause (with the exception of Crémieux-Brilhac and Jacques Bingen who had had no formal connection with the SFIO) did their best to reconcile their allegiance to Charles de Gaulle with their unconditional devotion to Léon Blum. Their special perspective as both Gaullists and Socialists equipped them admirably to provide Blum with an ongoing analysis of *Le Connétable*'s reliability, not only as leader of the united Resistance but as promoter of republican and democratic values.

For his part, Blum, under house arrest in the village of Bourassol following his trial at Riom (February through April 1942), managed not only to receive a number of Socialist colleagues from the Popular Front days (including his fellow-Jews Daniel Mayer and Jules Moch) but to exchange a number of messages with de Gaulle. On 5 May 1942, less than a month after his successful defence at Riom, Blum gave a letter endorsing de Gaulle ("A transitional government can only be brought together around one man, one name – that of General de Gaulle") to the Socialist deputy Edouard Froment, who was about to leave for London.[36]

Boris encouraged this endorsement (albeit not without reservations) in a letter to the Socialist leader on 22 June.[37] Boris began by congratulating Blum on the superb defence of his Popular Front government during his recently completed trial. He went on to assess the evolution in de Gaulle's leadership over the last two years, arguing that, even if the general was not the ideal leader from a socialist perspective, he must be accepted as the indispensable symbol of the resistance on both sides of the Channel. It is our duty to proclaim our faith in this symbol and then to work hard so that it becomes a reality, he wrote, until others more worthy can take charge of France's destiny. France's internal divisions and the continuing hostility of the Americans require that, on the day of our liberation, we show persistence in the right path by rallying around this iconic personality. His presence in a position of power will expunge any accusations of abandonment or treason which may be made against us and will avenge us of all our humiliation.

Boris went on to assure Blum that the radicalization which the war had produced, including within the Gaullist camp, meant that workers' demands dismissed as outrageous in 1936 now seemed eminently reasonable. He even ventured to say, "Presumably socialism will impose itself, perhaps in some new formulae."

Although basically positive, the portrait of de Gaulle offered by Boris was far from totally flattering. Like others close to the general, Blum's former colleague criticized de Gaulle for a lack of tact and understanding in dealing with those who had volunteered to serve under him, conceding that there was some justification for this insensitivity given the mediocrity of most of his supporters, none of whom had the moral strength to challenge him. It was no doubt true, Boris conceded, that de Gaulle was not instinctively drawn to democratic ideas and methods; he had, however, been persuaded by a combination of personal reflection and experience to adopt less authoritarian ways. The utter contempt the general felt for the old elites had also oriented him in the right direction, as had his conviction that the healthiest element in the French nation remained the people at large. Boris added here that, during the fall of 1941, de Gaulle had confessed to him in a private conversation that he had felt constrained from making any overtly democratic declarations because of the serious protests such professions would stir up in the military and colonial world, but that he was beginning to feel freer in this regard. All the more reason, Boris summed up, for the veteran Socialist Blum to give de Gaulle his blessing.

Three months after Boris's note, one of Blum's colleagues, Felix Gouin, arrived in London at the beginning of September 1942 with a letter from Blum to de Gaulle and a mandate to examine at first hand the conduct and outlook of Fighting France. Gouin had excellent credentials: he had voted against giving Pétain plenipotentiary powers in 1940; he had been one of Blum's counsellors at Riom; and he had been chosen president of CAS, the underground Socialist party. Unfortunately from the Gaullist point of view, Blum's emissary was taken in hand on his arrival in London by the Jean-Jaurès group as well as by Raymond Aron, who did their best to influence him against La France combattante. The result was a highly critical report carried back to Blum at the end of the year, in which Gouin alleged that most supporters of de Gaulle were from the Right or the Far Right, men "who have brought into the movement their prejudices, their convictions and their hatreds … creating here a kind of scaled-down version of the Pétain government."[38] Men of the Right such as Passy and Diethelm, Gouin went on, were the dominant clique around de Gaulle; true democrats such as Boris, Cassin, Hauck, and André Philip were playing only secondary roles. Blum's emissary added that an oath to de Gaulle had been exacted from all those who joined Fighting France and that the organization had been highly exclusionary from the beginning, rejecting good men such as Pierre Cot.

Gouin went on to say that de Gaulle, who had "put on Napoleon's boots," would do anything to confirm his personal power, and the republicans who supported him risked becoming one day victims of their good faith or their naiveté. What was needed, the president of CAS concluded, was to put blocks in the path of this would-be Bonaparte. De Gaulle should be granted military command of the external Resistance; but overall control of the struggle to restore French democracy should be in civilian hands, a process which might best be achieved through slow but steady infiltration of positions of influence around the general. Finally, Gouin noted, while it was necessary to check de Gaulle's overwhelming power, nothing should be done which would threaten to divide the Resistance as a whole.

In a 21 October 1942 note, Blum warned Gouin against giving too much credence to the Jean-Jaurès group, who clearly suffered from "émigré pathology," and expressed his own conviction that the general was determined to commit France to radical political and social change. It was of course important, Blum added, that de Gaulle not violate democratic sovereignty in the process.[39]

In November, in response to an appeal by the general, Blum penned a letter of support for de Gaulle addressed to Roosevelt. In a separate note to the general, he deplored the apparent persistence of an anti-Socialist attitude among Gaullists and argued the case for the vigorous presence of political parties in the regenerate France both of them were fighting for.[40]

The November 1942 letter to Roosevelt which Blum had agreed to write on de Gaulle's behalf, contains an almost unconditional endorsement:

> It is fortunate, a joy, in the midst of so many disasters, that this man exists. His authority is fully recognized by us at the present time … If General de Gaulle incarnates this unity, it is because he is in large measure its creator … I have been, like millions of French people, a daily witness to his work. In a France struck down and benumbed as a result of an incomprehensible disaster and stifled under a double oppression, it is he who, bit by bit, revived our national honour, our love

of liberty, our patriotic and civic conscience ... I make this profession of faith not only in my own name; I know that I am in this respect the interpreter of all the socialist groups in France in the occupied as well as in the so-called free zone. I am convinced that I express the view of the mass of republicans – bourgeois, workers and peasants. Those who are now helping de Gaulle to assume the role of leader are serving democracy.

Blum added,

When I speak in this fashion, I am not throwing France into the arms of a new dictator. I am a republican and a socialist. I am considering the vital interests of my country during what may be an imminent moment ahead of us and I cannot hesitate before making a decision. This decision is subject to one condition alone – that is, that the intermediary nature of de Gaulle's government be expressly clarified or, what amounts to the same thing, that the ultimate claim to sovereignty remains entirely and fully reserved. In this regard, the general has adopted a categorical position in repeated declarations and I trust his word.

The Socialist leader concluded,

It is possible that, in the mind of the public, de Gaulle may increase the authority he already enjoys and the confidence he inspires by presenting himself with this guarantee from a man who is particularly representative of the republican ethos and of "the spirit of resistance." As far as I am concerned, I am ready to furnish this guarantee unreservedly, as I am doing today.[41]

Needless to say, given the American president's disdain for de Gaulle, no response was given to Blum's appeal and, as Jean Lacouture points out, no effort was made in Washington to come to the aid of the Socialist leader who was soon carried off to Buchenwald.[42]

By passing the torch of Republican faith and legitimacy to the devout Catholic general, the agnostic Jewish socialist, symbolically at least, brought the Two Frances, driven apart by the Revolution, together again.[43]

Determined to allay continuing doubts about his intentions to create a Conseil de la Résistance subsuming all political parties, de Gaulle wrote in February to Blum, insisting that the new structure was simply an essential co-ordinating tool in the battle against fascism both inside and outside France. Parties would not be eliminated or swamped in this new organism, wrote de Gaulle, adding, "It is not only normal but desirable that the

Resistance, while keeping its unity and coherence, should reflect the nuances and distinctions of our traditionally diverse political tendencies."[44]

Verbal assurances were one thing; on-the-spot validation of de Gaulle's commitment to republican and democratic value was another. Encouraged by Blum to try to create a counterweight to de Gaulle's arbitrary power within Fighting France, Gouin returned to London and on 22 March 1943 summoned to a special meeting the twelve men elected to the French parliament in 1936 who were in the British capital to support the general. With Gouin in the chair, the twelve constituted themselves the Groupe des parlementaires adhérant à La France combattante. Acting as a crypto-parliamentary body, they informed de Gaulle of their existence and requested to see the budgets for Fighting France drawn up by commissioners Diethelm and Philip.

Alerted, the general rejected any claim that the group was the repository of republican sovereignty or legitimacy, which only a fully constituted national assembly could represent; but he agreed to heed its advice and to consider drawing from its ranks in appointments to his executive. *Le Connétable* added pointedly that conceding any further weight to the group's existence would give Fighting France an unwarranted leftish colouration.[45]

From the beginning in fact, the Socialists (Félix Gouin, Max Hymans, Pierre-Olivier Lapie, André Philip, and Jean Pierre-Bloch) were the most numerous and most vocal members of the group, and their relative strength was increased with the arrival of Pierre Viénot and Jules Moch later in the year. The Radical Pierre Mendès France would be, with his fellow Jew Pierre-Bloch and the Communist Fernand Grenier, the most ardent Gaullist among those who met under Gouin's presidency. All three fought hard against any resolutions which threatened de Gaulle's leadership.

In addition to the mandate to convene the French deputies in exile, Gouin had brought with him a 15 March 1943 letter from Blum to de Gaulle, which made clear that the Socialist leader's anxieties had not yet been fully put to rest. Blum conceded that the whole concept of political parties had to be revisited, but he insisted that no democracy could survive without their participation. The general could learn at first hand from André Philip and Gouin just how much young blood had been infused into Socialist ranks; he no doubt knew that the party's paper, *Le Populaire,* was circulating again, if clandestinely. As for the Resistance movements, however vital, they were no substitute for well-structured parties and, in the case of the Communists, who had created a parallel military organization of their own, they posed a real threat outside the purview of Fighting

France and subject to the Soviet Union. Following the liberation, Blum continued, France must formulate a new constitution, a process which must come from below, from the people, rather than be imposed from above or from outside. This process must wait upon the establishment of peace and order.[46]

Meanwhile, under Gouin's presidency, the group of deputies continued to meet twice-weekly in London from March until 22 August 1943. As a kind of crypto-parliamentary assembly, they passed a series of resolutions designed to guide Fighting France and its successor, the Comité français de libération nationale (CFLN), toward the restoration of a fully democratic system. Pierre-Bloch, who helped formulate many of these resolutions, sees them as laying the foundations of the Fourth Republic.[47] The failure on the part of the group to recognize the need for a strong executive branch reflected the group's preference for a return to *gouvernement d'assemblée*, the domination of the state by an all-powerful legislature, something which was clearly bound to create a rift between de Gaulle and even his most zealous partisans among Blum's disciples.

At the beginning of June 1943, just as the parliamentarians were becoming more assertive, an article in the Gaullist newspaper *La Marseillaise* (quite possibly inspired by Jacques Soustelle) denounced them as partisans of a "renewed old regime ... nothing but legislative flotsam and jetsam."[48] Incensed, the deputies wrote to de Gaulle on 7 June, reminding him that most of their number had voted against Pétain on 10 July 1940, adding that anti-parliamentary rhetoric was standard practice in fascist circles. The general replied haughtily on 19 June, "Tout ce qui est exagéré ne compte pas (You're making a mountain out of a molehill)."[49] The group responded to this condescending dismissal by sending off a telegram insisting on the indispensable role to be played by parliamentarians as well as members of the resistance in the Consultative Assembly which was to meet in Algiers in the fall of 1943.

Meeting for the last time in August 1943, the group of French parliamentarians insisted on their early transfer to Algiers, where many of them would soon sit as delegates to the Assemblée consultative provisoire. Pierre-Bloch would play a key role in selecting those who ended up as delegates to the Assembly. In this crypto-parliament, he and his colleagues would do their best not only to offer a critique of the CFLN, but to prepare the way for what would become the Fourth Republic.

In the three-year period between the creation of La France libre in June 1940 and the transfer of Fighting France to Algiers at the end of May 1943, the Jewish Socialists who joined de Gaulle, together with their Radical colleagues, served as guarantors of the general's ultimate republican and democratic commitment. Their close personal link with the captive Socialist leader Léon Blum, as well as with *Le Connétable,* helped establish trust between the former Jewish premier of the Third Republic and the future president of the Fifth, and between the internal and external elements of anti-fascist resistance.

CHAPTER NINE

Pierre Mendès France: A Jewish Radical Joins the Battle

The strong Jewish presence in the ranks of the Free French was hardly surprising. Jews had been consistent defenders of the republican ideal since 1848. They had participated in the ephemeral government of the Second Republic in 1848, and the quintessentially assimilated Léon Blum had become the first Jewish premier of France in 1936 (albeit, not without infuriating disciples of Maurras). Pierre Mendès France, who played a secondary role in Blum's Popular Front government, would join La France libre following his escape from Vichy. His presence in General de Gaulle's wartime organization would be the prelude to a long, mutually respectful (if sometimes stormy) relationship based on the recognition by each man of the other's high integrity, political courage, and capacity to make bold decisions.

The descendant through his father of Jews who fled Portugal in the seventeenth century and on his mother's side of a Jewish family that left Alsace following its cession to Germany in 1871, Pierre Mendès France was born in Paris on 11 January 1907. His parents, thoroughly assimilated and detached from their ancestral faith, provided Pierre with a happy as well as a materially comfortable upbringing and left him to choose his own career.[1] Intellectually gifted, the young Mendès prepared himself for the baccalaureate on his own, then studied law at the University of Paris. In 1926 he obtained both his law degree and a diploma from the prestigious École des Sciences politiques. Political militancy during these years led him to become president of the Ligue d'Action universitaire républicaine et socialiste (LAURS).

In 1924, at age seventeen, Mendès joined the Radical party, matching this commitment with a deep and ongoing concern about the economic policy of successive French governments. Like other left-wing Radicals, he was ready to recognize that the Third Republic had brought political democracy to France but lamented its apparent indifference to the ongoing struggle for economic and social justice.

In 1930, the young Radical criticized the American-backed Young Plan, which had been instituted to govern the flow of German reparations to France and Belgium, for not going beyond this limited goal by creating a Europe-wide financial entity to balance the American domination of post-war Europe's economy. Mendès was equally concerned about the hegemonic power of trusts worldwide and urged a degree of state intervention to curb their power.

Running for election to the Chamber of Deputies in 1932, Mendès had his first encounter with the publicly expressed anti-Semitism which he was to face throughout his political career. His adversary having hinted that Mendès France was not his real name, the candidate responded in an open letter declaring that the name could be traced to his great-grandfather. In any event, he pursued, being Jewish surely brought with it no shame. His ancestors had left Alsace rather than live there following the German annexation. Their descendants, like other French Jews, had been eagerly welcomed into the army in 1914; their exploits in battle had been appropriately applauded.[2]

The overall platform on which Mendès ran, and which helped make him the youngest deputy in French history, was based on themes which would be a constant before and after World War II: budgetary discipline, fiscal justice, increased production, and a strenuous opposition to protectionism.

Almost from the beginning of his parliamentary life, Mendès became associated with a group of progressives in the Radical party known as the Young Turks, men who were ready to join others further to the left in promoting social reform. Several of them – Paul Bastid, Jacques Kayser, Pierre Cot, and Jean Zay – became or, in Cot's case, tried to become, Gaullist supporters during World War II.

Two years into his mandate, Mendès, like all devotees of the Republic, confronted the crisis of 6 February 1934, when mass demonstrations by right-wing organizations led to what many regarded as an intended coup against the regime. The crisis was resolved through the appointment of a government headed by the conservative Protestant Gaston Doumergue with the support of a majority of Radicals. Mendès (who was convinced that the 6 February constituted a genuine fascist threat) was part of a

Radical minority who refused to endorse the new government, calling instead for new, younger men to save the Republic through moral renewal as well as bold social reform.

Re-elected in 1936 as part of the Rassemblement populaire, which led to the creation of the Popular Front government headed by the Socialist Léon Blum, Mendès presided over that government's Customs Committee (Commission des douanes) for the next two years. He supported the Matignon accords of 7 June 1936 which produced substantial wage increases, shorter hours, and better bargaining power for France's industrial workers and then argued that a similar deal ought to be negotiated with the nation's farm labourers. Mendès insisted then (and later) that a reduced workweek historically ended up increasing rather than limiting productivity, a matter which was debated during the wartime trial of Blum by a Vichy court.

In the second Blum government, formed in March 1938, the premier chose Mendès to be his under-secretary of the Treasury. In the weeks that followed, Mendès began a lifelong collaboration with Georges Boris, then serving as Blum's *directeur du cabinet.* Together, the two men drew up a finance bill with a moderately socialist slant. Unfortunately for the government, the bill was defeated in the Senate on 7 April 1938. The epigonic version of the original Popular Front experience had been brief. The government of the Radical Edouard Daladier, which followed, had no Socialist representation. A year and a half before the outbreak of war, France had clearly moved to the Right.

In September 1939, Mendès, who was a reserve lieutenant in the air force, volunteered to join the expeditionary army of General Maxime Weygand stationed in Syria, where in April 1940 he became a licensed flight observer.[3] Granted leave shortly afterward, he returned to Paris on 4 May, seeking an opportunity to join the ongoing battle in Norway. Six days later, however, the German blitzkrieg began, frustrating any such move. While still in the capital, Mendès was shown the 9 January 1940 memo submitted to his superiors by then Colonel de Gaulle stressing the need to bring into play the concentrated use of tanks and aircraft in the ongoing Battle of France.

As German troops neared Paris, the would-be combatant left for Bordeaux, where the Reynaud government had relocated. On 17 June, he listened heavy-hearted to Pétain's speech requesting an armistice. "In the immediate moment," he wrote two years later, "the blow was too hard to sustain. One was simply stunned, incapable of any reaction." During the evening of the following day, out of curiosity at how the British government might be reacting to France's new capitulationist administration, Mendès asked his Bordeaux cousin to turn on the BBC. Then came an epiphany as the deputy-turned airman listened to de Gaulle's 18 June call to arms, which he was long after able to recite from memory "At the very moment when all was lost, there came over the airwaves this message of unvanquished will, of faith, of hope reborn," Mendès recalled.[4]

Thrilled by the general's appeal and frustrated at the lack of any clear guidance from his military superiors, Mendès, like other members of the French parliament, decided to board the *Massilia* on 26 June on the assumption that the Pétain government (which had sanctioned the ship's departure for North Africa) was thus unmistakably signalling its intention to pursue the battle against the Third Reich. It was, as it turned out, a cleverly contrived trap. Some forty hard-line anti-capitulationist parliamentarians (including the Jew Georges Mandel, whose arrival in London Churchill would have eagerly welcomed and whose departure Pétain had specifically encouraged, as well as Daladier and such future Gaullists as Pierre Viénot and Paul Bastid) were thus removed from the scene on the eve of the Marshal's agreement to sign the Armistice. News of this humiliating development was received with gloom by those aboard the *Massilia* while the French press, on the urging of the new ministry, was quick to denounce those headed to North Africa as deserters!

The *Massilia* arrived in Casablanca on 24 June. Like his fellow-passengers (many of whom were not allowed to disembark or were put under house arrest when they landed), Mendès felt hopeful that the European settler community in North Africa would press for continuing the war against Germany. On the 25th, he paid a visit to Casablanca's Cercle juif, a contact which was later used as evidence of his complicity in a plot against France's national interest (the same charge was levelled against Mandel). Mendès's hopes in the local community's resolve quickly faded. They were further dashed when Washington recognized the Pétain regime and when, on 10 July, in the absence of the forty parliamentarians in Casablanca and the seventy-three Communist deputies who had been dismissed from parliament by the Daladier government, a truncated version of the pre-war French parliament voted plenipotentiary power to Pétain. The real nature of the new regime established at Vichy and backed by the authorities in North Africa became evident on 25 July, when Mendès was arrested, interrogated, charged with deserting his post in the face of the enemy, and imprisoned at Rabat.

Following a decision to try him on these charges in France, Mendès and his fellow-accused were transferred to Clermont-Ferrand in October 1940.

Isolated from his colleagues, the Radical deputy received intermittent visits from the prison chaplain. On Christmas Eve, following one of these visits, he listened from his cell to midnight mass, noting, "Christianity added other, more noble, aspirations to what had been the preoccupations of the pagan world."[5]

In February 1941, Mendès learned of the new Vichy decree denying elective office to French Jews and obliging all those currently holding such positions to declare themselves as such to the regime. The prisoner penned a fierce letter of protest to Pétain, denouncing the collective outrage (*brimade*) to which all French Jews were thus exposed and reminding the Marshal that the Mendès family had been ready to sacrifice for France for generations.

The particulars of the case drawn up against Mendès included his remaining in Paris during the German spring offensive, his delay in heading for Bordeaux, and "his cowardly flight to Morocco when he ought to have fulfilled his soldierly duty." On 12 June 1941, the prisoner was sentenced to six years in prison.

Happily, on the eve of the court's ruling, Mendès managed to escape and, with the help of forged identification papers, to flee Clermont-Ferrand. He felt ashamed to have to inscribe "Non" on these papers which demanded an answer to the question "Êtes-vous juif?" but there was no alternative in order to avoid instant arrest. And, writing years later, he expressed regret that he had not followed up his escape with an active commitment to the Resistance, insisting rather defensively that his aim throughout had been to return to his fighting unit.

For the next several months, Mendès made his way around France incognito, noting the efforts of certain Christian personalities (among them Cardinal Saliège of Toulouse and Pastor Marc Boegner) to limit the repressive impact of Vichy's racial legislation and applauding the resistance offered the regime in the academic world as well as by clandestine Christian trade-unions who had rediscovered their dedication to the true interests of the French working class. During his undetected rambling throughout occupied and unoccupied France, Mendès also managed to read copies of the opposition press (*Esprit, Temps nouveau, Valmy*) before these "subversive" periodicals were suppressed (in August 1941), and he rejoiced in listening to the familiar voices of his friends René Cassin and Georges Boris over the BBC.

In the end, Mendès made his way to the Swiss border, where he contacted Francis Bertholet, code-named Pierre Robert in the underground. Bertholet, a *passeur* who helped Jews and others fleeing Vichy France to cross into

Switzerland, belonged to a Protestant sect descended from the Waldensians and given to a strict vegetarian and prohibitionist lifestyle; he had aided Spanish Republican refugees in the late 1930s and now prepared new false papers for Mendès, identifying him as a Polish Jew named Jan Lemberg who was heading for Havana. The artifice worked: Mendès crossed back into France in a sealed train bound for Spain and ended up in Barcelona, whence he travelled to London, arriving on 20 February 1942.

A week later, on 1 March, Mendès was received by de Gaulle, who offered his standard overview of the world conflict in progress before musing aloud about several of his own military initiatives. "Was I right in my decision about St. Pierre and Miquelon? Was I justified in Syria? Did I make the right choice on 18 June?" Reflecting years later on what might have motivated the general to pose such questions aloud, Mendès concluded that de Gaulle was unconsciously querying his own wisdom in committing himself and his cause to the British in the first place![6]

In the end, although his intention in coming to Britain had been to rejoin his air unit, Mendès set off with de Gaulle's blessing for the United States, where he stayed from April until September 1942. This journey had two purposes. Mendès wanted to see his wife Lily, who had managed to find refuge there thanks to the intervention of his colleague Pierre Cot; and he had been encouraged by de Gaulle to drum up support for the Free French cause in the American public, where a band of anti-Gaullist exiles, including the poet-diplomat Alexis Leger (who did his best to discourage Mendès from rejoining de Gaulle), had been encouraging Roosevelt's antipathy to *Le Connétable*. With this second mission in mind, Mendès published *The Pursuit of Freedom* in the United States. Later translated into French as *Liberté, liberté chérie, 1940–1942*, this work focused largely on Mendès's own wartime ordeals and adventures but included an indictment of the Vichy regime as based on a coalition of fascists, big banking interests, frightened bourgeois, and academicians "whom no one reads."[7] The Radical-turned-Gaullist also made a point of naming the intellectual celebrities under attack in Vichy such as Henri Bergson and the scientist Paul Langevin, both of whom were well known in the American academic community, and paid exaggerated tribute to the achievements of the Resistance.

Mendès returned to the United Kingdom in September 1942 and, after months of additional combat training, resumed active service with his air squadron. Between 3 July and 18 November 1943, he flew bombing missions over industrial and military targets in France. Horrified by the inevitable loss of civilian life that followed, and denounced for his part in these raids by Radio-Paris, Mendès soldiered on, convinced that they were strategically vital to the war effort.

Mendès the flight observer kept a *Carnet de notes* during these months.[8] They record, not surprisingly, the anti-Semitic whisperings behind his back which accompanied him on many of his missions. The notes also offer us a glimpse into Mendès's life in London between sorties. He saw himself as a loner, somewhat reserved, even forbidding, lacking in warmth at first contact, tending despite himself to seek the company of other Jews. He records with mixed emotions a dinner-party of seven at which four of the guests (Pierre-Bloch, Philippe de Rothschild, the writer Maurice Druon, and himself) were Jewish, then adds that, as during other such meetings, none of those present ever thought of raising the issue of anti-Semitism within the Gaullist camp. At one point in the journal, he even goes so far as to say that he would be ready to change his name if this would help to attenuate anti-Jewish prejudice![9]

It is not surprising, therefore, that Mendès welcomed the arrival in London of Jacques Kayser, a fellow-Jew as well as a fellow-Radical and, like himself, one of the Young Turks who had fought to sustain the Republic against internal as well as external threats in the 1930s. The newcomer was embittered at being snubbed at Fighting French headquarters despite his diplomatic training, which would normally have qualified him for a key appointment. Mendès was not only sympathetic but saw this rejection of an obviously competent and enthusiastic recruit as typical of de Gaulle's entourage, which had by contrast eagerly promoted such mediocrities as Dejean and Diethelm.[10] Happily, Kayser eventually served under Viénot in the complex negotiations leading up to Fighting France's involvement in the June 1944 landings.

Confident in the victory of the Allied cause, Mendès and Kayser spent much of their time together sharing thoughts about the postwar world. Kayser favoured a purge of pre-war Radical party leadership, ready to see both Herriot and Daladier cast aside. Mendès agreed that Daladier might have to go and conceded that Vincent Auriol was "old hat" (*vieux jeu*), but thought the veteran Herriot had a key role to play in the restoration of parliamentary democracy.

Mendès spent his first days back in London with Georges Boris and his wife, old friends from the days of the Popular Front. The new arrival came to feel enormous sympathy for the modest but tireless Boris who was clearly on the verge of collapse, so overwhelmed by work that he was unable to find any relief. Blum's former *directeur du cabinet* shared the newcomer's concern about de Gaulle's authoritarian streak, noting that the general might enjoy a glorious political career if only he could adjust to more democratic methods of decision-making.[11] In mid-August 1943, Mendès and Boris were joined by the Catholic resistance leader François de Menthon (who had managed to reach London) for a thoughtful review of the bitter internecine debates which had divided them and weakened French democracy in the 1930s.

Mendès also spent time with the Catholic Maurice Schumann, who pleaded with the politician-turned-airman to be taken on one of Mendès's bombing missions. Why didn't he enlist then, like me, Mendès asked himself before telling Schumann that his frail health – and in particular his poor eyesight – precluded any such ventures. Then, as though to underline the distinction he drew between active combat and propaganda, Mendès turned down Schumann's invitation to speak over the BBC.[12]

Whenever he was able to manage it, Mendès turned up at meetings of the French parliamentary group in London, which had been convened by one of Blum's trusted emissaries, Félix Gouin. While ready to support this rump assembly in its attempt to act as a kind of check on de Gaulle's authoritarian leadership, Mendès made clear that the group must not call into question *Le Connétable's* overall direction of the French fight against fascism.[13]

In notes written between flights over France, Mendès summed up his personal reasons for supporting de Gaulle. By his act of defiance in June 1940, the general had given his fellow-citizens pride in being French again, a contribution even more valuable in moral and human terms than in its purely political dimension; he had nullified the defeatist message of Vichy; and he had for three years maintained a steady and consistent course.[14]

Throughout his stay in London as well as later, in Algiers, the problem of de Gaulle's entourage remained a source of anxiety and anger for Mendès. He deplored "the cautious, measured tone that they adopt whenever they discuss the Jewish question," adding, "In the end, they are desperately afraid of appearing to resemble the men of the Popular Front, the so-called Judeo-Masonic gang, the society of the Third Republic."[15]

Mendès's overall perception of de Gaulle would undergo a series of shifts following the Liberation, most notably during the debate in 1958 about the constitution of the Fifth Republic and, a decade later, in the wake of the student-worker rising of 1968. Even so, the long tribute which the one-time Gaullist published in *Le Monde* following the general's death reflects the enthusiasm with which he originally committed himself to the leader of Free France.[16] The legitimacy to which the general laid claim in 1940, the former Free French airman wrote, had taken into account republican tradition and had clearly aimed to restore it. The enemy he denounced had clearly been fascism rather than the demonized Germany of Maurrassian mythology; the dictatorship he condemned and the popular sovereignty he proclaimed were heartfelt expressions of a deep conviction. In de Gaulle, the French Resistance had found its leader, a man whose pure heart and unflinching hope made him a reincarnation of the great soldiers of 1793.

Following the shift of Fighting French headquarters to Algiers in May 1943, the transformation of La France combattante into the Comité français de libération nationale and the subsequent decision to call together an Assemblée consultative provisoire in North Africa, Mendès and his friends entered into increasingly earnest discussions about how they might best advance the democratic cause within the Gaullist camp. The Consultative Assembly was to be made up of a mix of personalities representing the internal and external Resistance as well as those political parties which had managed to resurrect themselves since 1940. At least five seats were to be assigned to delegates from the Radical party. Kayser urged Mendès against becoming part of the Radical deputation, arguing that he would be better able to influence events from outside the Assembly. Still in uniform, Mendès was upset about what he heard concerning the quality of the delegates from the internal Resistance who, whatever their qualities of courage and resolve, were utterly lacking in parliamentary experience. For his part, Boris dismissed the overall selection as an unworkable mix of "Boy Scouts" and old-style political manipulators.[17]

Given de Gaulle's deeply suspicious views about parliamentary assemblies, both Boris and Mendès were convinced that an impasse between the general and this awkwardly contrived crypto-parliament was inevitable. On the other hand, Mendès confided to his notebook, since the absence of any such parliamentary forum at Vichy had produced absolute political stultification, its presence in Algiers could only help in the desired transition toward full-fledged democratic government as Liberation approached. It might even help de Gaulle accept the need for ongoing critical debate. In addition, Mendès noted, it would give some reassurance to the Allies about the general's overall commitment to democratic values.[18]

Early in November 1943, Mendès's musings about the future ended when de Gaulle summoned him to Algiers, not as a member of the Provisional Assembly, but as commissioner of finance in the CFLN. The deputy-turned-pilot was hesitant, especially after listening to the Protestant Gaston Defferre, a leading figure in the Resistance from the Marseille area, who had managed to get to London. The Socialist Defferre insisted that the atmosphere in Algiers was more *vichyssois* than Vichy itself and revealed that, while de Gaulle was indeed personally eager to appoint Mendès to the CFLN, he was nervous because, having already made René Mayer a commissioner, this would mean a second Jew in his administration![19] Defferre's co-religionist André Philip had already given Mendès a pretty glum picture of the situation in Algiers back in July, when he reported that the political confusion in the North African city had given the most reactionary elements on the scene a chance to advance their interests.[20]

Quite apart from these disheartening reports about the situation in Algiers, Mendès had by the late summer of 1943 concluded that the original idealism behind the Allied war effort had been substantially eroded. The American dealings with Darlan in North Africa and the Allied acceptance of General Pietro Badoglio in Italy were surely evidence of the triumph of cynicism and Machiavellian calculation over liberal and democratic conviction. Mendès even went so far as to commit to his notebook the conviction that the cult of mindless violence on the Allied side meant that, whatever the military outcome of the conflict, Hitler had won out on the moral and philosophical plane.[21] As he shed his airman's uniform and committed himself to dealing with the convoluted politics that faced him in Algiers, Mendès was fully forewarned. The skepticism which his friends had conveyed to him in London would soon enough be intensified.

CHAPTER TEN

Louis Closon, Jean Moulin, Georges Bidault: Binding the Resistance to de Gaulle

As the resistance to fascism within France gathered momentum beginning in 1942, the Free French in London faced the challenge of trying to bring it under the overall command of General de Gaulle or of letting it develop autonomously, which might lead to a very different representation of the Republic when liberation came, especially if the communist vision of post-war France were to prevail. To further the first option, de Gaulle and his advisors found three remarkable men – Louis Closon, Jean Moulin, and Georges Bidault – who would between them help secure the general's claim to lead all French forces committed to the liberation of their homeland.

The son of a prominent Marseille doctor, Louis Closon was born on 18 June 1910. After lycée studies in his native city, he took courses in law and letters at the universities of Aix-en-Provence and Paris. In 1932, he began a career in the Ministry of Finance where he helped draft future legislation.[1]

Closon expressed his opposition to Hitler from the outset, an opposition that was intensified when he witnessed Nazi fanaticism at the annual party rally in Nuremberg in 1936. His progressive Catholic outlook was reinforced through the mid 1930s by friendship and collaboration with the Dominicans, whose Paris headquarters on the boulevard de Latour-Maubourg he regularly visited. Like Schumann, the activist civil servant wrote a number of articles for the Dominican journal *Sept* and, after its condemnation by the papacy, its successor publication, *Temps présent*.

Impressed by Roosevelt's application of Keynesian economics to the Depression crisis, Closon published a favourable assessment of the New

Deal in 1937.[2] A year later, at the time of the Munich crisis, he headed to the United States on a Rockefeller Foundation scholarship, carrying with him a letter of recommendation from the Protestant André Philip. He learned of the war's beginning while doing research in Alabama. Soon after, Paul Reynaud, minister of finance in the Daladier government, got in touch with him to ask if he would take charge of France's wartime purchasing mission in New York. Over the next eight months, Closon bought everything he could that might sustain his government's war effort. The collapse of June 1940 brought a request from Paris that Closon oversee the transfer of all materiel still in French hands to British purchasing agents in the United States, an operation which he stayed on to supervise.

The appeal issued by de Gaulle on 18 June had almost no impact on the French community in New York, which was by and large sympathetic to Pétain. A tiny band of Gaullist sympathizers came together, nevertheless, among them Closon, who volunteered his services to Free France's agent in the city, Jacques de Siéyès. After a long wait, the eager recruit was told to pack his bags in April 1941, when he set off for Washington to inform the ambassador of his intentions. The two men had a bitter exchange, which no doubt helps explain the Vichy government's subsequent decision to strip Closon of his citizenship.

Leaving his family with Franco-American friends, Closon travelled to Britain via Canada. Early in May, he showed up at Carlton Gardens where, after signing up for military duty, he was told to report instead to Free France's chief financial officer, the Protestant Denis ("Rauzan"). Closon ended up serving as Denis's deputy then, in 1942, when the director left on a tour of Free French territories in Africa and Oceania, he assumed the directorship on an interim basis.

Soon after joining La France libre, Closon was summoned to his first meeting with de Gaulle who would become, together with André Philip and Jean Moulin, a key figure in his subsequent career. To the new arrival, *Le Connétable* seemed all cordiality, far from the *monstre sacré* of later legend, blunt and direct, but neither aloof nor affected, providing his thirty-year-old supporter with a reassuring sense of confidence in the future of La France libre.[3]

Closon was delighted to run into Maurice Schumann at Gaullist headquarters. The two men had come to know each other as contributors to progressive Catholic periodicals in the 1930s. Both were concerned at the damage done by Vichy propaganda, which condemned La France libre as an organization run by a small band of faithless men and women among whom Jews and Freemasons played the dominant role. Fortunately,

Schumann told Closon, as they discussed how to deal with this problem, there already existed in London a French-language periodical, *Le Glaive de l'Esprit*, which might be used to counter this Vichyite allegation.

Le Glaive de l'Esprit was in fact the French-language version of *Sword of the Spirit*, a paper sponsored by Cardinal Hinsley of Westminster Cathedral with a view to encouraging English Catholic participation in the war effort. The first issue, edited by a bilingual Englishwoman, Mira Benenson, had appeared in December 1940.[4]

Schumann and Closon got permission to take over the English paper, which they renamed *Volontaire pour la cité chrétienne*. As editor-in-chief, Closon signed himself almost transparently "F.-L. Courbon"; Schumann resorted to the pen name "André Sidobre," which he had used when writing for *Sept* and *Temps présent* in the 1930s. Under their joint direction, *Volontaire* appeared roughly once a month between October 1941 and July 1944. The overall aim of the paper was set forth clearly in the first issue:

> to bring together all those in La France libre, whatever their former belief, who believe in Christian civilization and to reassure them that they are not alone but that they reflect the mass [and] … to proclaim to Christians in other nations who are not always sure of it that Free France fully and truly expresses that part of France which escaped enemy domination and which is determined to continue the tradition of Liberty, Equality and Fraternity, to give a full account of our wartime activity on our return to France, and to aid in the reconstruction of a France where public morality as well as our political and social institutions will allow our children to live as Christians.[5]

Challenging Vichy propaganda on its own ground from the outset, *Volontaire* portrayed the war as a spiritual conflict, a crusade against the corrosive materialism and the philistine elements in church as well as state which had undermined French society in the interwar period, setting the stage for defeat and collaboration.

Two of the leading Catholic intellectuals of their generation – the philosopher Jacques Maritain and the novelist Georges Bernanos, both of whom supported La France libre from exile in the Americas – made this case in *Volontaire* with great eloquence. Maritain blamed France's defeat on the governing classes and placed his hope in the still-to-be-released energy of the people. The debacle had its positive side, he wrote: it meant an end to the selfish individualism of the bourgeoisie and the narrow class interest of the proletariat. Meanwhile, the parties of the Right were self-destructing through collaboration. In these circumstances, the moral authority of La France libre would surely redeem France, helping to bring into being a truly Christian civilization.[6]

In its 15 November 1941 issue, *Volontaire* reprinted a letter from Bernanos to an American friend. In apocalyptic mood, the novelist declares France to be in a state of mortal sin, controlled by the same band of Pharisees whose ancestors had martyred Joan of Arc. "Mediocre Christians, mediocre priests, have sold us out, smug Christians who, more often than not, are well-to-do," Bernanos wrote. "They have gone bankrupt and Hitler has come as bailiff to oversee the liquidation."[7]

While Bernanos and Maritain lent impressive intellectual support to the crusade against fascism being waged in the pages of *Volontaire,* Christian intellectuals inside France were fighting a far more dangerous battle against Vichy and the Nazis. Understandably, Closon and Schumann seized every opportunity to celebrate the courage of these thinkers as well as their ecumenical solidarity. In its 20 May 1942 issue, *Volontaire* reprinted several pages from *Témoignage chrétien,* the most significant underground paper produced by the Christian resistance. Schumann had been informed about this clandestine publication by his old friend Stanislas Fumet, with whom he managed to keep in contact. The paper had been founded by a Jesuit, Pierre Chaillet, who taught theology at Lyon. The paper's original name, "Témoignage catholique," had been changed out of respect for the Protestants, most notably Pastor Roland de Pury, who joined in launching it.[8]

The aim of those involved in what had to be a perilous publishing enterprise was to create "a front of spiritual resistance" inside France. The first (November 1941) issue, of which 5,000 copies were printed, carried a daring text ("France, prends garde de ton âme!") written by the Jesuit Gaston Fessard and justifying resistance to fascism, even arguing that collaboration might well imperil the soul. Like later issues, it was distributed by courageous sympathizers. As we shall see, Simone Weil would help deliver copies in the Marseille area while waiting to take ship for America and, in 1943, some issues were printed in the basement of Marc Sangnier's Paris apartment.

Schumann was of course thrilled to learn that his old friends were carrying on the battle inside France. Shortly after the Liberation, he expressed his gratitude to Father Chaillet: "You offered us a 'spiritual 18 June' on that day when a 'missionary' from the internal resistance gave me a copy of your *Témoignage.* I felt the same liberating shock that I had experienced on the evening on what seemed like an endless retreat when I listened to General de Gaulle."[9]

The reprinting of the 20 May 1942 issue of *Témoignage chrétien* not only established an intellectual link between the internal and external Christian resistance to Vichy and the Nazis; it allowed readers to appreciate the truly ecumenical approach which characterized Christian opposition to fascism on both sides of the Channel. Alongside Father Chaillet's admonition to action, *Volontaire* reproduced two key letters of sympathy addressed by Christians to the Grand Rabbi of France, which had appeared in *Témoignage chrétien.* Writing on 26 March 1941, Pastor Marc Boegner condemned Vichy's anti Semitic legislation and indicated to the Jewish leader that the Protestant minority was well placed to be compassionate, given its own history of persecution at the hands of the French state. The distinguished diplomat and playwright Paul Claudel, in a letter of 24 December 1941, informed the rabbi that, like all true Catholics, he was aware "that Israel remains the oldest son of the promise just as much as the herald of human suffering." Finally, Closon and Schumann chose to include in this issue of their paper the full text of *Mit brennender Sorge* (With Deepest Emotion) Pius XI's 1937 encyclical denouncing Nazi racist ideology.[10]

Two months after giving their readers evidence of the heroic anti-fascist propaganda being circulated inside France by the Christian resistance, the editors of *Volontaire* were able to report a new level of collaboration among their colleagues across the Channel. The directors of the Protestant underground newsletter *Présence de l'Église* (sometimes called *La Feuille*), which had been founded by Professor René Courtin at the suggestion of W.A. Visser't Hooft of the World Council of Churches, had decided to suspend publication and join forces with the more widely distributed *Témoignage chrétien.* Closon and Schumann reprinted the final editorial of *La Feuille,* which began with the assertion that all Christians were now not only in agreement about the essentials of doctrine but also in their struggle against fascism, as had been made clear after the publication of *Mit brennender Sorge.* There were no doubt some deplorable cases of collaboration within the Christian community, but in the present struggle Catholic leadership had proven itself: "We have no hesitation in declaring that Catholic militants have assumed a preponderant role in the resistance movement. They have often taken the initiative and they still provide the essential inspiration. As of today, we can only bow before so much courageous and radiant spirituality."[11]

Not without a hint of triumphalism, Closon and Schumann, who titled their lead editorial "La Fille aînée," a term reflecting French Catholic assumption of a leading role inside the Roman communion, hailed the decision of "our separated brethren" (again, a reference to the charge of schism conventionally levelled at Protestants) to recognize that France's Catholics are "in the vanguard of our common struggle."

While Schumann's remarks about the French Protestant minority seem rather patronizing, they in no way detract from the journalist's genuinely ecumenical outlook. The co-editor makes this fraternal feeling clear by citing a reply made by his mentor Péguy to a friend who had criticized the poet for having too many Protestant acquaintances: "I'm a man of the fifteenth century. So how can you expect me to take into account what might befall my friends a century after my death!" Péguy, Schumann added, represented in his life and thought the perfect convergence of Catholic and republican beliefs.[12]

If, for the editor of *Volontaire*, Péguy reflected a new Catholic approach toward Protestants, René Cassin represented the willingness of some contemporary Jews to see and welcome the waning of anti-Semitism among leading representatives of the Catholic hierarchy. The eulogy written by Cassin in the pages of *Volontaire* following the news of Cardinal Verdier's death was ample testimony to this new-found sense of spiritual convergence in the face of the fascist menace.[13]

As partisans of social Catholicism, Closon and Schumann were delighted to extend an ecumenical welcome to André Philip and Albert Guigui, both of whom were devotees of the Reformed version of *Christianisme social*. Early in September 1942, Schumann hailed the arrival in London of Philip, emphasizing the very special role played by this man of profound faith inside the aggressively agnostic SFIO. Philip contributed his own message to readers of *Volontaire* the following month, stressing the "profound moral unity" transcending the ideological differences which lay at the heart of the internal resistance. Whether nurtured by rational conviction or by Christian faith, those doing battle against fascism shared a belief in the sacred rights of the individual.[14]

Closon, during these same months, expressed the hope that the centripetal forces inside La France combattante would in the end prevail despite new-found divisions and tensions. He insisted that no one serving in Fighting France had disobeyed an order simply because his superior was a monarchist or a republican, a Jew, Catholic, or Freemason. The yearning for unity was in fact increasingly apparent in the combat "to further French glory and bring joy to the world."[15]

Although the calamitous fate of European Jews did not figure prominently in the wartime discourse of de Gaulle or, for that matter, of the Allies, it was given substantial space in the pages of *Volontaire*. Denunciations of anti-Semitism by Cardinal Saliège of Toulouse, whose prayers to the Sacred Heart of Jesus on behalf of those suffering persecution or martyrdom during the war were cited in the first issue of *Volontaire*, were regularly reported. In the Christmas 1941 issue, Schumann and Closon offered the view that racism, like class hatred, resulted from a debasing of the idea of liberty, whose benefits cannot be properly experienced unless accompanied by a sense of social responsibility. In this same issue, the editors included extracts from a sermon denouncing racism given by Britain's Cardinal Hinsley on 7 December at a pontifical mass attended by de Gaulle. To further emphasize the importance they gave to the race theme, Schumann and Closon offered their readers the text of a radio address given by Maritain to French youth, praising students and workers who had openly protested German persecution of the Jews.[16]

In the June 1942 issue, Paulin Bertrand, who had edited an ephemeral Paris underground paper (*Valmy*) before escaping to London where he adopted the name Paul Simon, joined in denouncing anti-Semitism. He began by pointing out that he was Christian despite having a family name common among French Jews. It was wrong to assume that French intellectuals were prejudiced, he insisted, pointing out that the clandestine newspaper *Valmy*, which had put the case for racial understanding in the boldest terms, was edited by practicing Christians. Simon went on to make clear his own abhorrence of the discriminatory laws which now barred French Jews from most professions. And, in an effort to reassure his readers, he did his best to portray the Nazi propaganda film *Juif Suss*, which offered grotesque Jewish racial stereotypes, as a box-office failure in France.[17]

In September 1942, Closon denounced the Vichy government's decision to deport some 10,000 foreign-born Jews to Germany in violation of France's traditional respect for the sacred right of asylum. If those in power in Vichy were truly Christian, Closon added, they would see how wrong this decision had been; even as men, they should have understood their grievous moral error.[18]

At the end of the same month, *Volontaire* published part of a sermon condemning racial persecution ("Contre l'odieuse persécution des Juifs") preached at Lourdes by Cardinal Saliège, and cited remarks by the bishop of Montauban who had spoken to his flock about the fraternal bonds which linked Aryans and non-Aryans. Both clerics had joined in signing a letter to Pétain about the grave crisis of conscience which Vichy's racist legislation had created for all France's clergy.[19]

Gabriel Francis, in "Le massacre des Innocents," informed readers about a train which had left Lyon on 6 September 1942 carrying 4,000 Jewish children on what had to be a grim journey, denouncing Vichy for its complicity in the Third Reich's campaign of persecution.[20] "F.B.," a chaplain serving with the Free French forces, addressed himself to "Mes frères français," citing St. Paul to the effect that, ever since Christ's sacrifice on Calvary, there was neither Jew nor Greek, slave nor free, and stressing the need for all those fighting for freedom to establish solidarity with their Jewish brothers and sisters.[21] The same theme was picked up in an article ("Les Juifs nos frères") reprinted from the underground paper *Combat*. As the author of the article pointed out, Jews were ethnically very diverse, making the racial basis of persecution utterly irrational. In any event, French Jews had amply displayed their faith in the nation by sacrificing their fair share of blood during the wars of 1870, 1914, and 1940.[22]

Following the liberation of North Africa in the winter of 1942–43, Schumann and Closon pointed to the perverse impact of Vichy propaganda, which had undermined the will of Muslims to join in the fight for freedom by suggesting that Jews, Freemasons, Communists, and Anglo-Saxons rather than fascists were the true enemies of France.[23]

Although the Cross of Lorraine was prominently displayed on its front page and although *Le Connétable* appears to have been one of its regular readers, *Volontaire* was not primarily an organ of Gaullist propaganda. De Gaulle is rarely mentioned, and the military exploits and political advances of Free France are given little space.

Contributors to *Volontaire*, like the paper's editors, are primarily concerned with the spiritual resurrection of their homeland. At the same time, they are "good Europeans," eager to see Germany purged of her demons and readmitted to the Christian commonwealth of nations. They denounce the philistinism and collaborationist tendencies of the French ecclesiastical hierarchy, and at the same time celebrate (when they do not exaggerate) the exploits of the heroic minority of Christians in the internal resistance. The editorial perspective adopted by Closon and Schumann reflects more than anything else their shared *sillonniste* past and the views both men had expressed about fascism and about social justice in the pre-war progressive Catholic press. The tone was at once intensely Catholic and profoundly ecumenical.

While editing *Volontaire*, Closon continued to serve in the Commissariat of Finances until July 1942. When Commissaire Denis was replaced by André Diethelm and when the new director relieved him of responsibility for the funding of the organization's secret service, Closon resigned and requested a special audience with de Gaulle. *Le Connétable* expressed his sympathy, agreeing that Diethelm was hard to work with.

The hiatus in Closon's career did not last. It coincided happily with the arrival in London in July 1942 of his Protestant and Socialist friend André Philip whom de Gaulle immediately named as his commissioner of the interior. As the editor of *Volontaire* puts it, "What I knew about him was the intensity of his Protestant faith which at that point in time made him a creature apart in the Socialist Party." When they greeted each other again in the summer of 1942, Philip confided that, having been advised against showing up at Protestant places of worship after 1940 because his easily identifiable features would have led to instant arrest, he had taken to attending Catholic mass out of a profound spiritual hunger. Closon adds that, in their shared conviction of the role of faith in politics, they were "precocious ecumenists."[24]

Working under Philip, whom he served in many ways as mentor, Closon spent much of his time analyzing information reaching London about the state of opinion inside France and drawing up tentative plans for the nation's post-war renewal. Then, at Christmas time 1942, eager to move from reflection to action, he requested an assignment to the home front, where the battle against fascism was being more and more actively engaged. Philip agreed, and the journalist-turned-activist was attached to the ongoing mission of de Gaulle's delegate-general to the internal resistance, Jean Moulin, whom Closon would come to revere as much as he did *Le Connétable.*

Moulin, who had arrived in London in October 1941, was born at Béziers in southern France in 1899.[25] His father, a schoolteacher, Freemason, and founding member of the Radical party, transmitted his secular republican faith to his son; his mother was a devout Catholic who saw to it that he was baptized and catechized prior to his first communion.[26] After beginning to study law at the University of Montpellier, Moulin served briefly in the army at the end of World War I. With the coming of peace, he began a career as sub-prefect, then prefect, in various jurisdictions throughout France.

In 1925, Moulin met the Young Turk Pierre Cot. Seven years later, he became Cot's *chef de cabinet*, a role that took on considerable significance when Cot became air minister. Moulin had witnessed the 6 February 1934 demonstrations against the regime from the Pont de la Concorde and saw Premier Édouard Daladier's subsequent resignation as an abandonment of republican responsibility when confronted by the mob. An earlier tendency toward pacifism on the young prefect's part was soon replaced by militant anti-fascism and by concrete efforts to come to the aid of the embattled Republicans during the Spanish Civil War.

In February 1938, Moulin was named prefect of the Eure-et-Loir department, headquartered at Chartres. During the mass exodus from the city which followed the French military collapse of June 1940, he was one of the few prefects who remained at his post in order to confront the Germans as a representative of the duly constituted republican authority.

Moulin's republican devotion was quickly tested when German officers arrested him and demanded that he sign a statement affirming that Senegalese soldiers in French uniforms had raped and slaughtered a number of local women and children. The prefect's refusal led to charges that he had insulted the Third Reich and to subsequent beatings and torture. When Moulin denounced the German soldiers for shaming their uniform by such acts, they locked him up with the bodies of the dead French victims, then with the corpses of the Senegalese who, Moulin assumed, had been murdered to cover up what he was convinced had been a German, not a Senegalese, atrocity. Unbearably distressed by the situation in which his loyalty to the Republic and its soldiers had plunged him, Moulin attempted suicide by slitting his throat, only to be saved by nuns at the local hospital.

In September 1940, when the collaborationist Marcel Peyrouton became interior minister and thus his immediate superior, Moulin began planning to join de Gaulle in London, a decision made easier by his dismissal from office two months later. After making contact with key republican figures throughout France and evaluating their commitment to resist Vichy and the Nazis, the ex-prefect managed to reach the British capital in the fall of 1941.

Moulin's first meeting with de Gaulle, on 24 October 1941, has been described as "symbolic and historic ... the reconciliation of right and left, of the French military and political tradition of state service and the tradition of rebellion, and, more immediately, of the external and internal resistance."[27]

Unlike most encounters between de Gaulle and would-be volunteers to the Free French cause, the meeting with Moulin was a dialogue between equals.[28] In any event, as a consequence of their 3 November 1941 exchange, de Gaulle designated Moulin to be his personal emissary in France at the level of prefect. On 2 January 1942, having been assigned the nom de guerre "Max," Moulin was parachuted into France to fulfill a complex mission: to unify both the political and military elements of the resistance under de Gaulle's command and to help set in place the structures of the regenerate Republic which would be built following Liberation.

Despite the cordial relationship he had established with de Gaulle, Moulin still asked himself whether the general had *la tripe républicaine* ("a gut-feeling for the Republic") and wrote to Cot (whom *Le Connétable* had snubbed in London), "Don't worry! I haven't forgotten Pilsudski!", a reference to the Polish general who had taken effective control over Poland during most of the interwar years.[29] It did not take long, however, for Moulin to regard the Free French leader as worthy of comparison with Gambetta and Clemenceau.

During his eighteen months inside France, "Max," given a new code name ("Rex") on 16 February, achieved all that was asked of him, and more. To begin with, he undertook to provide funding and weaponry for the Armée secrète, an underground force of partisans who, by the time of the Normandy landings, numbered some 100,000 fighters. In October 1942, these partisans were put under the command of General Georges Delestraint, a tank specialist known to de Gaulle.

On the political front, in January 1943, Moulin persuaded the leaders of the three key resistance movements in the *Zone sud*[30] (the area formerly under Vichy control which German forces occupied in November 1942) not only to unite as the Mouvements unis de la Résistance (MUR), but to accept de Gaulle's overall command.

Finally, at a clandestine meeting in Paris on 27 May 1943, Moulin convinced seventeen representatives of political parties (including those of the centre and right), as well as delegates from trade unions and resistance movements, to join in one umbrella organization – the Conseil national de la Résistance (CNR), again under de Gaulle's overall leadership. Together, these three initiatives taken by Moulin bound the internal political and military resistance to the Free French leadership and legitimized de Gaulle as the standard-bearer of the republican cause.

Within a month of this last extraordinary success, General Delestraint was arrested in Paris on 9 June and Moulin himself was apprehended twelve days later in a safe house at Caluire near Lyon where a special meeting had been called to find a replacement for the leader of the Armée secrète.

The complex circumstances surrounding the arrest and subsequent execution of these two key figures in the united Resistance have led historians to search for the culprits who betrayed their whereabouts to the Gestapo. This search became more passionate and personal when the wartime leader of Combat, Henri Frenay, alleged on French television in October 1977 that Moulin had acted on his mission inside France as a crypto-communist, betraying both de Gaulle and the Resistance.

Daniel Cordier, the young ex-Maurrassian who had been parachuted into France in July 1942 to serve as Moulin's secretary, was driven by this charge to write an exhaustive analysis of Moulin's career as well as to come to a judgment, based on circumstantial evidence, that "Rex" was in all probability betrayed by René Hardy, another member of Combat who gave up information about the movements of key Resistance personalities to the Gestapo following his own arrest and torture. Cordier's account of Moulin's service to the Resistance, thoroughly detached and impersonal, ends nevertheless on an irrepressibly panegyric note: "In the grand chronicle which is the History of France, the role of Jean Moulin bears comparison with that played by Joan of Arc four centuries earlier as she prepared the way for the coronation of her king at Reims."[31]

Moulin not only fulfilled his original mandate in linking the internal resistance to London; he created two political bodies which were designed to aid in the process of liberation and post-war reconstruction. The first of these initiatives, taken in April 1942, was the selection of Georges Bidault to head a Gaullist Bureau d'information et de propagande (BIP).

Bidault had been a committed Catholic from his earliest childhood.[32] To provide him with a proper religious upbringing following the 1905 Separation law, his parents sent him to a Jesuit school in Italy – just as de Gaulle's family had sent young Charles to receive guidance from the Jesuits in Belgium. Bidault pursued his higher education at the Sorbonne, was called up at the end of World War I without seeing combat, then, with the coming of peace, began a teaching career at the Lycée Louis-le-Grand in Paris.

During the interwar decades, Bidault, as a militantly engaged Catholic, was involved in a wide variety of activities. He joined the Action catholique de la jeunesse française (ACJC), founded by the comte de Mun in 1886; he wrote for the review *Politique* until 1934 when he became a key editorialist for *L'Aube;* he became a member of the PDP in 1931 and ran as a candidate for this middle-of-the-road Catholic party in the 1936 election.

Several key themes pervade Bidault's writing and speeches in the interwar years. He denounces Charles Maurras, consistently deploring the right-wing polemicist's xenophobic nationalism, his cult of the "Goddess France" as well as his promotion of "politique d'abord," unthinkable in a believing Christian; he preaches the cause of Franco-German reconciliation; he denounces Catholic non-participation in the parliamentary system and urges his co-religionists to accept and even promote the Republic, including its advocacy of *laïcité,* so long as this is aimed at ensuring tolerance and not irreligion; he presses Radicals to abandon their outmoded anticlericalism and ends up praising Premier Blum (1936–38) for not exploiting this old-fashioned shibboleth to gain popular support.

Running for the PDP in 1936, Bidault found himself, ironically, competing not only against a Communist but also against two other Catholics, one on the Right, backed by the Church hierarchy, the other on the Left,

Philippe Serre, carrying the JR banner. Interestingly, Serre was elected and soon became a devotee of then Colonel de Gaulle.

The Munich settlement in 1938 induced Bidault, an increasingly vigorous anti-fascist, to aim at achieving a broad political coalition which might ward off further threats to peace. Together with his future Free French colleague René Cassin, he helped found a Comité d'action franco-tchecoslovaque and suggested the creation of a vast rassemblement of citizens loyal to the principles of Christian democracy. Finally, in this same period of pre-war anxiety, he urged the formation of Nouvelles équipes françaises (NEF), a group which was committed to democratic as well as family values.

Called up early in World War II, Bidault was soon captured. He learned of de Gaulle's 18 June 1940 appeal while a prisoner of war and, knowing almost nothing about the general, felt drawn to him instinctively.[33] Liberated in July 1941, he ended up teaching history at the Lycée du Parc in Lyon, the de facto capital of the French Catholic resistance. Progressive Catholic journalists and politicians from the 1930s, including François de Menthon, Stanislas Fumet, and Louis Terrenoire (who had written for *L'Aube*), were natural companions for Bidault; unfortunately, Charles Maurras was also there and made sure in a malicious article in the *Action française* of 30 June 1940 to stigmatize the new arrival as a poisonous influence on the nation's youth.

His impulse to become actively engaged in the battle against Vichy and the Nazis led Bidault to join Combat, led by Henri Frenay. His first direct contact with Free France came in October 1941 when he met Léon Morandat, the Catholic trade-union leader whom de Gaulle had sent into France on a recruiting mission. Three months later, the professor met Moulin whom he saw regularly over the next sixteen months and came to revere. Such dedicated souls might profess agnosticism, Bidault observed, but they were surely destined to be met by angels at Heaven's gate![34] Moulin offered a less rapturous, more nuanced view of his latest recruit, describing Bidault as "likeable, skilful and supple," qualities which would help lead the professor toward, and then away from, *Le Connétable*.[35]

Following the Allied landings in French North Africa in November 1942, Bidault sent two messages to London. The first of these, despatched on 25 November, urged that a firm declaration be issued affirming that the fight against fascism was being waged in the name of universal rights and that solidarity with the Anglo-Saxons would be a prevailing element in Free French policy through and after the war. Bidault's second message, sent on 13 January 1943, suggested that the Republic be proclaimed in all those territories so far liberated from Vichy.

As was noted earlier, Bidault's meeting with Moulin led to his being chosen to head a Bureau d'information et de propagande (BIP). Jacques Dalloz describes this new entity as "the first common institution of the internal resistance" and notes that its staff was predominantly Christian Democrat in outlook. The *Bulletin de La France combattante*, which Bidault soon began to produce on an underground press in Lyon, relayed news from London and sent back in its pages analysis of events inside France to Free French headquarters in the British capital. In October 1943, the *Bulletin* shifted its operations to Paris.

Bidault represented the PDP at the first meeting of the CNR in Paris on 27 May 1943 with Moulin presiding. He opened the proceedings with a motion which urged that all parties, movements, and unions represented in the Council endorse General de Gaulle as overall leader of the internal as well as the external resistance.

Bidault did not know in advance of the 21 June meeting at Caluire that Moulin was apprehended. Daniel Cordier, Moulin's secretary, brought the news of "Rex"'s arrest and murder ("Our God is dead!") to him immediately. Shortly afterward, Claude Bouchinet, de Gaulle's temporary replacement for Moulin as his delegate-general inside France, recommended that Bidault be made president of the CNR, noting that "as a Catholic, he will reassure the right, while the friendly relations he has with the Communists will cover him on the left."[36] The unanimous support for this suggestion meant that, as Jacques Dalloz has remarked, "For the first time in French history, a Christian Democrat acceded to a political function of the highest order."[37] Bidault certainly saw himself henceforth as the paramount voice of the internal resistance and as a result felt bitter about the way in which Free French headquarters treated him as "no more significant than a worker ant"; his frequent messages to London were either ignored or responded to with an enigmatic "Slow traffic!"[38]

On his own, Bidault took a number of significant initiatives as president of the CNR: he arranged for contacts with disaffected *pétainistes* who were ready to join the resistance; he produced a Charter of the Resistance, setting forth what may be seen as the agenda of the Fourth Republic; and he maintained a good relationship with the Communists while helping to ensure that they would not control key areas of power as the war ended. As we shall see, however, his first meeting with de Gaulle in Paris in August 1944 would reveal differences of outlook and personality which would increase over time and lead to a split over the Algerian question in 1962.

Apart from the establishment of the CNR, over which Bidault presided until Liberation, Moulin had set in place during his mission a Comité général d'études (CGE) whose purpose was to prepare position papers on the political and socio-economic perspective of what would become the Fourth Republic. The CGE turned out to be a remarkably ecumenical group of academics, including three Catholics known to Closon – the jurists Pierre-Henri Teitgen, François de Menthon, and Michel Debré (a *juïf d'origine* who had converted) – and two Protestants – the Radical deputy Paul Bastid and the economics professor René Courtin.

Louis Closon, meanwhile, who had been undergoing basic training for his role as a key member of Moulin's original Délégation générale, did not receive his own *ordre de mission* from Philip until 5 April 1943. Parachuted into the Loire valley, he made his way first to Lyon, then to a number of other cities. In Paris he had long talks with key members of the CGE (Teitgen, de Menthon, Courtin, and Bastid). Bastid, he noted, still maintained, despite the circumstances of their clandestine rendezvous, the outward calm and austere manner of the proper Protestant bourgeois, sporting white or black spats according to the weather![39]

Closon's first experience inside France was brief. Toward the end of May, he was flown to Algiers just as de Gaulle and a few close associates were transferring their headquarters from London to North Africa. He was present as La France combattante was transformed into the Comité français de la libération nationale (CFLN).

Back in London in July 1943, Closon wrote in great distress to Philip in Algiers that the situation in France following the death of "Rex" was increasingly serious. Were the Allies to land on the Continent now, he reported, the CFLN had no one on the ground capable of exercising effective command either of local partisan groups or of the Resistance as a whole.

It was in these trying circumstances that Closon (whose code name was "Fouché") was sent back into France in September on what would be an eight-month mission.[40] His special responsibility during this assignment was to oversee the establishment of comités de libération (CDL) in each of France's eighty-six departments. These committees, based on local resistance groups which were often resentful of the efforts by the CFLN to prevent them from playing what they felt was their rightful role in the Liberation, saw themselves as agents of popular sovereignty whose powers should be above those of the traditionally dominant prefect.

Closon was relatively pleased by the situation in the *Zone sud,* where both the Christian and Socialist resistance had been well organized. He was particularly happy to make contact with the Protestant Francis Leenhardt, who represented the "new outlook" of the resurrected SFIO and whom he would choose as his deputy for that region.[41] Paris and the surrounding area were a very different case, given the hegemonic position of the Communists and their allies in the local comités de libération and the inferiority complex they had managed to create among their bourgeois colleagues.[42] Closon felt confident, nevertheless, that the threat of a revolutionary push by the Communists was minimal.

By February 1944, Closon had managed to find a formula which reconciled the aims and interests of both the CFLN and the CDLs. The departmental committees would coordinate the *action immediate* in their zone; they would direct the local insurrection at the Liberation; and they would represent the local population before the *commissaires de la République* who were chosen by the CFLN to govern larger regions as they were freed from the enemy. They would not, however, be authorized to set up fully autonomous "soviets," nor were the risings they orchestrated to degenerate into anarchy. Ultimately, then, as Closon defined things, it would be the *commissaires* who were to be responsible for the administration of law and order until representatives of the new republican regime were duly elected.

By early May 1944, his main assignment completed, Closon had overseen the creation of comités de libération in seventy-one of the nation's eighty-six departments. If setting up these committees took up much of Closon's time, he was also concerned at the way in which the CFLN had selected the eighteen *commissaires de la République* who were to assume power as French territory was freed from the enemy. Too many of the appointees were unknown to the internal resistance, whose feelings and interests needed to be taken into account.

What preoccupied Closon above all during his critical eight-month assignment was the overarching need to find a replacement for "Rex" as delegate-general, an overall strategist who enjoyed the confidence of the internal resistance as well as the CFLN. In the end, it would be Closon who created a consensus in favour of Alexandre Parodi, a member of the CGE who was both the son and grandson of democratically minded academics and the brother of a magistrate who, after joining the Resistance, had been arrested and shot by the Germans.[43]

While on mission, Closon also talked with fellow-Catholics about the role of the Catholic church during the Occupation and worried about how compromised the venerable institution would be as a result of its wartime conduct. In a memorandum written on 5 December 1943, while he was hiding out in Paris, Closon notes that, from the moment when the Vichy regime was founded, the Assembly of French Cardinals and Archbishops, citing the 10 July 1940 vote in the National Assembly granting plenipotentiary powers to Pétain, had enjoined the faithful to obey the established authority (*le pouvoir établi*). The prelates had even added that this attitude should not be modified without their prior consultation. This ecclesiastical resolution had been exploited by Pétain (a man not known for his Catholic piety) who had made an ostentatious pilgrimage to Lourdes following the Armistice. Later, even more provocatively, the Marshal had recalled religious orders previously proscribed from France and given subsidies to Catholic private schools (*écoles libres*), highly provocative acts which flew in the face of republican opinion.

A further nefarious collusion between the upper clergy and the Vichy government had occurred in February 1943, Closon adds, when the Assembly of Cardinals and Archbishops offered no protest against the arbitrary transfer to Germany of French workers through the Service du travail obligatoire (STO). The French episcopate had, on the other hand, condemned the Allied bombing of French cities. As a result of these and other provocative acts, Closon warned, the highest officers of the Church in France risked stirring up a new wave of anticlericalism or, worse still, the marginalization of their role in the nation's civic life.

It was vital, of course, Closon concluded, that while criticizing those clerics who were guilty of betraying the faith, the government of post-war France must respect the independence of the Church and "its sacred character in the eyes of the faithful from which some members of the episcopate have clearly strayed." Closon also made a point of stressing the heroic role often played by the lower clergy and by the Jeunesses catholiques in the struggle against fascism.[44]

When Closon talked about ecclesiastical delinquency, he did not always limit himself to generalizations. At one point in his sojourn in France, he drew up a list of upper clergy known for their *pétainiste* leanings ("Liste des évêques non-résistants"), putting Archbishop Feltin of Bordeaux among the top delinquents.[45] Philip's roving delegate was also fully aware of the courage shown by a few bold members of the upper clergy and made a point of citing the pastoral letter denouncing both racism and forced labour sent by Archbishop Jules-Geraud Saliège of Toulouse to his diocesan flock during Lent in 1944.[46]

In a series of separate reflections ("Les catholiques français et notre temps"), Closon makes the general observation that those Catholics currently seduced by Vichy propaganda "have a predisposition which one might be tempted to call innate except that it clearly derives from a deformation of the original Christian teaching (which itself is often given a bourgeois gloss) and not from the essence of Christianity." Those currently in office in the État français, for instance, including Darlan and Laval, were only nominal Catholics. It was within the ranks of the Resistance, among *catholiques sociaux* and *démocrates chrétiens* such as François de Menthon, that the true gospel was being followed. What we must now do, Closon pursues, is "work in an entirely new spirit, freed of all the filthy deposit left on our Christian faith by the passage of time, by encrusted habit and by a lot of middle-class conformity (*bourgeoisisme*) to the point that it is barely recognizable."

Those of us involved in our future liberation, Closon concludes, must attend to a number of problems left unresolved in pre-war France – the rights of property and of the worker, the school question, and the role of the family – deriving our answers from scripture and Christian tradition. Beyond this, more ambitiously, Closon yearned for a "rechristianization of the masses" to counter the very real threat of civil war based on anticlerical reaction to the Church's wartime actions. For this, Philip's emissary warned, we can count only on a small band (*petit troupeau*) to help us. Fortunately, there were elements in the Christian resistance, especially in the South of France, to allow for hope.[47]

Discussions with old and new friends in the CCE and perusal of the many texts submitted to the committee brought Closon to jot down on paper what he saw to be an emerging consensus concerning a new French constitution. While he acknowledged that there were clear differences of opinion between those who favoured a rather authoritarian regime and those who clung to the Jacobin myth of popular sovereignty and the vesting of ultimate power in a single legislative assembly, most of those who had submitted draft proposals agreed that France needed a stronger executive and a better definition of the three branches of government. There was a general consensus that votes for women and the right to work ought to be inscribed in the new constitution. Closon noted that, in his view, there should be an explicit commitment to religious freedom, code-language for family rights and the strengthening of the *écoles libres*. Moulin's aide also emphasized the need to avoid any dependency on a professional as opposed to a conscript army. The editor of *Volontaire* concluded by suggesting that most of his fellow-citizens seemed ready, following their liberation, to live in a system which was halfway between the rigorously statist Soviet Union and the radically individualist United States.[48] In many ways, these reflections of Closon anticipate the program of the post-war MRP, the party led by Schumann, over which Marc Sangnier presided as honorary chairman.

Georges Bidault, Louis Closon, and Jean Moulin – two devout Catholics and a militantly secular republican – together produced not only a formal agreement by the various elements of the internal resistance to recognize de Gaulle's leadership; they set in place inside France a communications network and an administrative structure which, when liberation came, could ward off any revolutionary threat by the Communists while ensuring that the Anglo-Americans would find it difficult to treat France as occupied territory subject to their will.

CHAPTER ELEVEN

Simone Weil: Would-Be Martyr to the Free French Cause

Of all those drawn to the Gaullist cause, Simone Weil must surely be counted the most spiritually exalted.[1] Born in Paris in 1909 to a determinedly agnostic Alsatian-Jewish father and a mother whose family was only nominally linked to Judaism, Simone developed an early antipathy to the faith of her ancestors and an equally powerful fascination for the Catholic version of Christianity. This spiritual outlook was based partly on an aversion to the Old Testament which she saw to be ethnocentric in focus[2] and partly on a fascination for Catholic ritual. Visits to the Benedictine abbey at Solesmes at Easter 1938, when she spent ten days listening to Gregorian chant, helped convince the already sympathetic demi-convert of the "supernatural power of the sacraments."[3] However, unlike Maurice Schumann (whom she had befriended as a fellow-student at the Lycee Henri IV), Weil never crossed the baptismal threshold into full participation in the Roman communion. She remained a *catholique virtuelle*, unwilling to surrender the intellectual autonomy which she was convinced she would lose with formal conversion, and equally resolved not to detach herself from the unbelieving masses she revered. Weil did, however, find great spiritual satisfaction through vicarious participation in the Church's key sacrament, the Eucharist.

The attraction which Weil felt for the Christian mysteries was accompanied by an obsessive yearning to share the afflictions of the dispossessed. In a posthumous testimony to Weil's extraordinary compassion, Schumann notes that, after reading Plato's description of crucified slaves, she was for the rest of her life moved by all those suffering oppression.[4] The near-convert consistently denounced French imperialism and urged greater autonomy for the colonized; in 1929, she toiled as a field hand in southern France in order to experience the way farm workers were being exploited; in 1934 and 1935, she spent months as an assembly line worker and came to feel at first hand the alienation[5] of the industrial proletariat. This plunge into the soulless life of those who toiled with their hands oriented Weil toward communism but, after long conversations in the early 1920s with French leftists who had returned, bitterly disillusioned, from the Soviet Union, she ended up instead a grass-roots syndicalist, mistrustful of the PCF and the Communist-dominated Confédération générale du travail (CGT). Early in the Spanish Civil War, Weil joined the Trotskyist Partido obrero de unificación marxista (POUM) in Barcelona where, like George Orwell, she hailed what would be the ephemeral coming to power of the working class. Her stay was interrupted when Weil stepped into a pot of boiling oil. After returning to France, she wrote admiringly to Georges Bernanos whose *Les grands cimetières sous la lune* (1938) expressed the wrath of a conservative Catholic at the atrocities committed in Christ's name by Franco's men.

Weil's compassion was extended from the very beginning to the German people who, she felt, had been far too harshly dealt with by the Treaty of Versailles. This concern helped persuade Weil to adopt an unconditional pacifism until the eve of World War II. As late as 1938, she suggested that the Third Reich be granted all the territorial claims put forward by Hitler. Even after Munich, she backed Neville Chamberlain's pursuit of peace through negotiation. The violation of the Munich pact in March 1939 persuaded Weil that her pacifist stance was no longer tenable. The outbreak of war later that year bolstered her new-found militancy.

Following the collapse of the French army in the field, Simone and her family fled Paris in mid-June 1940, enraged and ashamed at Premier Reynaud for handing power to Pétain and denouncing the Marshal for signing the Armistice. The ex-pacifist, now intent on getting to Britain to help in the ongoing battle against fascism, applied for a teaching post in North Africa as an oblique means of reaching the United Kingdom. When Jacques Chevalier, the Vichy minister of education, made no response to her request, Weil inferred that this decision might be based on the new regime's *Statut des Juifs* (issued on 3 October 1940) which denied public office to anyone with predominantly Jewish ancestry. To make clear her own position vis-à-vis Judaism as well as to mock the absurdity of Vichy's effort to give the term "Jew" a legally meaningful definition, Weil wrote Chevalier, asking,

> Does that term designate someone who belongs to a religious group? In that regard, I have never entered a synagogue and have never been present at a Jewish religious ceremony. Indeed, if there is a religious tradition which I consider to be part of my inheritance, it is the Catholic tradition, the Christian, French and Hellenic tradition. The Hebrew tradition is foreign to me and no legal text can alter that.[6]

Weil goes on to say that, if Jews are to be defined in racial terms, she does not fit the description, having learned from Josephus that the Emperor Titus had exterminated all those living in Palestine 2000 years ago! She concludes by observing that, if the term "Jew" must nevertheless be applied to her, she would accept it but only if she were to be informed officially to this effect. Perhaps not surprisingly, this challenge was left unanswered.[7]

In Marseille during the fall of 1941, while waiting for an opportunity to leave France, Simone Weil attended mass regularly without, however, participating in the sacrament. She turned up at local meetings of the *jocistes* (members of the Jeunesse ouvrière chrétienne), detecting among these young Catholic workers a *pur esprit ouvrier* which gave her new confidence in the possibility of real spiritual renewal when the war ended. She also began her role as an active *résistante* by distributing copies of the clandestine newspaper *Témoignage chrétien* in the region. On 18 October, she wrote to Xavier Vallat, Vichy's *commissaire aux questions juives*, noting with delicious irony that her failure to meet a teacher's qualifications under the new regime's racial legislation had forced her to find employment as a vineyard worker, taking on the kind of productive manual labour which Vichy clearly encouraged!

Early in July 1942, Weil was finally able to board ship for the United States, the only way to begin the complex wartime voyage to Britain. By month's end, settled in New York, she began an intensive lobbying campaign with Gaullist friends in London (Maurice Schumann, Jacques Soustelle whom she had known at the École normale, and Pierre Mendès France) to enlist their aid in securing transport to the United Kingdom. To nurture her spiritual hunger during this stay in Manhattan, Weil not only turned up for mass at Corpus Christi Church on 121st Street but attended services of worship at a Baptist church in Harlem and even, on occasion, visited a synagogue frequented by Ethiopian Jews.

The would-be recruit to La France libre had already thought up two ways in which she might serve the cause: as an organizer of front-line nurses or as a member of a team of saboteurs who might be parachuted into occupied France.[8] Weil made clear to her friends that, by volunteering for such hazardous missions, she was seeking to atone for her earlier passive complicity in the rise of fascism. She also insisted that she was intent one way or another on enduring the living conditions of those condemned to live under Nazi rule. To Schumann she wrote, "I beg you to try to find the proper degree of suffering and danger which will save me from being needlessly consumed by remorse."[9]

Happily for Weil, Schumann spoke on her behalf to André Philip, Free France's *commissaire à l'Intérieur* who, while skeptical about the new recruit's prospective projects, saw a possible role for her in his own jurisdiction. Then, by a lucky accident, Weil was able to meet Philip in October when he stopped over in New York en route to a fateful encounter with President Roosevelt. The *commissaire* assured the eager supplicant that she would be given a critical assignment under his deputy, the Catholic Louis Closon, a journalist and civil servant before the war who had joined Free France in May 1941 and who happened also to be a close friend of Simone's brother André. On 10 November, encouraged by this assurance, Weil boarded a Swedish freighter bound for Liverpool.

On her arrival in Britain, Weil was taken into custody and kept in detention at the Patriotic School near London, where all alien arrivals were kept pending careful screening. After eighteen days, she was rescued by her friend Schumann who was well placed to testify to her anti-fascist zeal. In London on 14 December, she was introduced to Schumann's editorial collaborator Closon and his wife, who remained close friends for the remaining months of Weil's life.

Within a few days of her arrival, Weil settled in at 17–19 Hill Street, headquarters of the Commissariat à l'Intérieur. The property, which belonged to the Duke of Portland, had been rented to the Free French for a nominal fee. Weil's office was in an annex built to accommodate the family's servants and coachmen. During her stay at Hill Street, Weil attended daily mass at a nearby church on Farm Street. On Sundays, sometimes joined by Schumann, she walked to Brompton Oratory but always asked her friend to leave her at the entrance so that she might meditate privately during mass.

As the protégée of Philip, but under the immediate supervision of Closon, Weil was required to analyze and comment upon the position papers being forwarded to London from the Comité général d'études (CGE), the "think-tank" set up by Jean Moulin (de Gaulle's delegate-general inside France since January 1942) to allow members of the internal resistance to develop plans for post-war France. Stimulated by what she read and eager to let her own lively mind play over the issues raised by her unseen collaborators in the underground, Weil produced a remarkable series of her own reflections between December 1942 and April 1943. When circumstances permitted, these reflections were sent back to France. In addition, during these last months of her life, passed in wilfully induced semi-starvation, Weil penned a discursive essay (*L'enracinement*) which effectively summed up her view of the civilizational crisis through which contemporary France was passing as well as her radical thoughts about its resolution.[10]

In *L'enracinement*, Philip's associate argued that France's defeat was the ultimate consequence of the social and psychological uprooting (*déracinement*) of all sectors of society. What might have ended or at least attenuated this serious social dislocation, Weil argues, was the presence among the French of an overarching faith, the kind of mystical bond which she felt had helped keep British society together in the modern age. Instead, since the Revolution, the French had waged a bitter battle over their school system, the training ground for civic life. Here Weil blames the partisans of *laïcité*, who had transformed France's public schools into breeding-grounds of agnosticism, discouraging the development of a shared sense of transcendent values. Rather extravagantly, she writes, "If one habituates children not to think of God, they will turn into fascists or communists out of a need to surrender to something outside and beyond themselves."[11]

Fully aware that most defenders of the republican tradition were anti-clerical and deeply suspicious of the teaching methods followed in the Catholic schools (*écoles libres*), Weil conceded that a Catholic education, by its very nature, excluded the consideration of rival faiths. On the other hand, she noted, a purely secular education excluded all religious teaching! The author of *L'enracinement* went on to confess that

> Christians are defenceless against the secular spirit because they must either give themselves over entirely to political action with a view to handing over temporal power to the clergy; or else they must resign themselves to become irreligious in the secular part of their lives. In either case, the proper function of religion is to infuse with light profane life, both public and private, without ever trying to dominate it.[12]

While blaming militant secularists for sowing disbelief among the nation's youth and thus undermining any feeling of overall spiritual solidarity, Weil was convinced that the process of *déracinement* had begun far earlier, during the administration of Cardinal Richelieu. By launching an idolatrous worship of the state, the cardinal had helped engender among the French a contempt for all other institutions, including the church. As a result, religion, which had played a cohesive role in earlier generations, had become a purely private affair for most citizens. "The idea of a nation called into being as such belongs only to the Old Law,"[13] Weil concluded, returning to her old charge that the teachings of the Old Testament were essentially ethnocentric.

Having analyzed the long-term causes of national uprooting, Weil went on to recommend ways by which the various uprooted elements in French society might be reintegrated. For the proletariat, this *enracinement* could be promoted by involving blue-collar workers in the process of technical innovation and automation and by bringing them into close communion with intellectuals who might join unions as volunteers and establish *universités ouvrières* near industrial centres. Weil dreamed of a "new type" of French worker, realizing the vision propagated (and then subverted) by the Soviet Revolution. She foresaw working-class participation in management, an idea advanced after the war by *gaullistes de gauche* such as René Capitant. She imagined workers fulfilling themselves intellectually and culturally, enjoying the kind of camaraderie that artisans knew in pre-Revolutionary times, owning their own houses and small plots in a society that was neither capitalist nor socialist but transcended both ideological systems. Moreover, Weil insisted there was a concrete base for this radical transformation in the Jeunesse ouvrière chrétienne which ought to be encouraged since it was "perhaps the only clear sign that Christianity is not yet dead among us."[14]

Weil was equally concerned with the French peasantry which, she noted, the leaders of the Resistance had all but ignored and which both Vichy and the Nazis had cultivated. She suggested a series of remedies for peasant alienation including the proper training of priests to serve as *curés de village*, prepared to become an integral part of the local scene rather than simply to officiate at Sunday mass. The introduction of New Testament readings into the curriculum would do wonders in terms of the moral edification of the nation's youth and would end the destructive conflict which perennially pitted curé against schoolteacher. Our age, Weil argued, has as its primary task the creation of "a civilization founded on the spirituality of labour."[15]

To complement the socio-economic and cultural reforms she was advocating, Weil proposed a radical, even revolutionary, change in France's political system – the abolition of political parties. Weil developed this indictment in a separate essay, in which she cited Rousseau's argument that democracy, to be effective, depends on the free and independent views of the largest possible number of citizens expressing reasoned opinions before arriving at consensus. This expression of the general will (*la volonté générale*) could not be articulated through political parties, she argued, even when they were mass-based, because such formations were by their very nature partisan and divisive. In the summer of 1943, *L'enracinement* was as yet unread while Weil lay dying in a hospital near London. Published by Gallimard in 1949, it helped establish Weil's reputation as a brilliant if erratic intellectual. Some critics on the left, such as Philippe Dujardin, see in *L'enracinement* not only a betrayal of Weil's early commitment to communism but an unconscious tribute to the values of the "New Order" established at Vichy in 1940.[16]

While Weil's colleagues were unable to read her negative comments about political parties in *L'enracinement*, they could uncover the same hostile assessment in a paper she managed to submit before her death. Whatever their original mode of operation, she wrote, France's parties had become machines designed to generate collective passion, to pressure individuals to conform, and to expand their own membership and power, all characteristics tending toward totalitarianism. Were parties to be abolished, Weil concludes, and the free flow of ideas encouraged, candidates for election would present their own individual views to the electorate unconstrained by party discipline. Natural affinities between candidates and citizens would lead toward a freely accepted consensus, thus realizing Rousseau's goal of a general will openly expressed.[17]

Weil's attack on political parties came in the wake of a lively debate on the subject within the Gaullist camp. The matter had been raised by Pierre Brossolette, a socialist and free-thinker who had joined La France libre after escaping to London in September 1942 when he was made deputy to André Dewavrin, the head of the Free French intelligence service.[18]

The disenchantment Brossolette had felt about the role of parties in pre-war France was based partly on the view that most of them were venal, susceptible to bribery by the monied interests. This lingering contempt was reflected in a sensational article published in late September 1942 in the Gaullist newspaper *La Marseillaise.* Condemned by some Gaullists for recommending the liquidation of France's traditional party system and by others for urging the creation of a single hegemonic Gaullist party with fascist overtones,[19] Brossolette insisted that his aim was to bring together under the Gaullist aegis all the vital elements in the Resistance – communists, socialists, Free-Thinkers, Catholics and patriotic nationalists. After all, the intelligence chief argued, "Léon Blum is a Gaullist; André Philip is a Gaullist; Paul Reynaud is a Gaullist;" and, even more important, the consensus around which France's national revival would be achieved had already been arrived at. There already existed "a fusion of all the resistance elements among political parties in a more or less broad-based Gaullism," and it was "in the context of the resistance and within the framework of Gaullism that France planned to effect a political transformation following the Liberation."[20]

If Brossolette's disparaging views about the role of France's political parties were close to those of Simone Weil, it might be noted that de Gaulle himself had retained from his early reading of Charles Maurras, as well as from personal observation and experience, an abiding contempt for the pre-war parliamentary system. This contempt is clearly articulated in an Armistice Day speech in 1942, delivered at the Albert Hall before a rapt audience, in which *Le Connétable* declared, "It is within Fighting France[21] that the whole nation must be brought together."[22]

In *L'enracinement*, Weil had analyzed France's long-term ills and suggested means by which they might be remedied. In a variety of separate texts submitted to Philip, she proposed ways in which Fighting France might improve its wartime strategy while at the same time working toward France's spiritual rehabilitation.

In "Réflexions sur la révolte," Weil offered concrete advice about the strategy which she felt Fighting France ought to adopt if it wished to establish France in a morally as well as politically strong position after Liberation.[23] The real revolution which all of us are working for, she argued, must come from the mass of the population which had been spiritually dead even before 1940 and which Vichy's spurious "National Revolution" had left eager for redemption. What offered promise in these grim circumstances was the underlying fury which the Third Republic, then Vichy and the Nazis, had generated among the French and which, if properly orchestrated, could trigger a mass uprising. Weil cited Clausewitz to the effect that it was the popular rage of the whole French people at the end of the Old Regime which produced the levée en masse and a people's army, more than a match for the soldiery mustered by Europe's reactionary powers.

In the present circumstances, Weil suggested that La France combattante propose the creation of a Conseil suprême de la Résistance made up of representatives of all the oppressed peoples of Europe, who might together plan a generalized insurrection against the Nazi regime. Two elements were necessary for such an insurrection to succeed: an effective propaganda war, which would be better managed by radio from London (a clear tribute to her friend Schumann's BBC broadcasts) than by the courageous but limited work of the underground press inside France; and disruption of the enemy's communications and production networks through sabotage. Ultimately, Weil argued, the aim would be to impose on the current masters of the Continent the exhaustion and demoralization which had overwhelmed the French population in 1940. It was vital that Europe be liberated through the exercise of its own will and energy, through some *grande action* of its own, which could come spontaneously once bands of partisans began collaborative efforts at undermining Nazi power all over the Continent. The alternative – domination by an alliance between American money and the brute power of the Soviet Union – would end any hope that France would regain the "liberty, honour and freedom" that she had lost in 1940.

Rather surprisingly, Weil insisted that, to carry out the grand strategy she proposed, La France combattante needed a whole new set of leaders. De Gaulle was a remarkable symbol, she conceded, but he lacked the leadership qualities needed to establish the bond between the Resistance and the French masses which was indispensable if her projected mass rising were to be carried out. New cadres would arise spontaneously, she insisted, as the generalized revolt began; their presence would preclude the kind of compromising arrangements which the Americans had made with Pétain's deputy, Admiral Darlan, in North Africa. Finally, these new men would heal the wounds left over from the action of the French *ligues* and the Popular Front, an oblique reference to the presence in Gaullist ranks of conservatives as well as partisans of Léon Blum.

After receiving Weil's provocative essay, André Philip took it to de Gaulle and read him the entire text. There is no evidence of any clear reaction on the general's part (after all, he had treated the author of "Réflexions" as a madwoman and had refused to meet her).[24] It is probable, however, that Weil's text was considered at the first clandestine meeting of the Conseil national de la Résistance in Paris on 27 May 1943. The perspective of the CNR was, however, exclusively French, not pan-European.

The reservations which Weil expressed about de Gaulle's leadership through the period of Liberation and beyond were matched by her doubts concerning the legitimacy which *Le Connétable* and the CFLN would have as victory approached. These doubts were set forth in a paper ("Légitimité du gouvernement provisoire") which she submitted to Philip.[25]

Weil allows that few would contest de Gaulle's yearning for legitimacy (*désir de légitimité*). Should the general continue to act over the next two years with probity as well as efficacy, this conditional legitimacy would be strengthened. He might, in the meanwhile, enhance his role by issuing a *Déclaration fondamentale*, updating the 1789 Declaration of the Rights of Man, thus providing a guideline for France's post-war civic life and ensuring that all those henceforth holding office would be held accountable to the principles it set forth. The *Déclaration*, to which de Gaulle should pledge himself personally, ought in time to be ratified in a general plebiscite.

Weil added the suggestion that de Gaulle announce his intention henceforth to govern France in trust, making his future actions subject to review by a specially designated tribunal pending the convocation of a constituent assembly. He should also make clear that he had no intention of creating a political party of his own partisans and, more important, he should declare that he had no interest in pursuing a post-war political career. The leadership of France beyond the Liberation, Weil insisted, must come from among those who had lived in France throughout the war. De Gaulle's acceptance of the conditions she had set forth, Weil suggested, would give him the highest possible degree of legitimacy and would free him of any challenge by the constituent assembly. His consent to her proposals, Weil believed, would provide the people of France with a salutary shock, "une injection de bien pur."[26] Meanwhile, the very strength of Gaullism derived from its expression as a purely spontaneous movement embodied in ad hoc structures.

Although most of her time was spent analyzing documents reaching London from inside France, Weil was also mandated to review texts produced by the Commission de réforme de l'État, one of several bodies created by La France combattante to draw up plans for post-Liberation France. On the recommendation of René Cassin, this committee was chaired by the socialist Félix Gouin, elected to the Chamber of Deputies in 1936. Gouin had helped recreate a clandestine version of the SFIO in the south of France in 1941 before escaping to London in September 1942.

Like the Jean-Jaurès group of Socialists living in London, Gouin favoured a return to the pre-war parliamentary system which set serious limits on the executive branch of government.[27] In response, the author of *L'enracinement* felt that, by conceding too much power to the Assembly, Gouin had left ill-defined and therefore relatively impotent both the executive and judicial branches of government, thereby opening the way to chaos. *Gouvernement d'assemblée* had produced corruption enough at the end of the Third Republic, when Premier Daladier resorted to *décrets-lois* to suppress the Communist Party in 1938.[28]

Weil's reading of the Socialist Gouin's text reinforced a conservative element in her political outlook. Like Edmund Burke, she deplored the failure of France's revolutionary leaders of 1789 to include a clear definition of responsibilities alongside their ambitious and ill-defined declaration of individual rights. If the political order were to function effectively, those who assumed the role of governing must take on the burden of ensuring the basic human needs of the governed; and citizens who asserted their rights must similarly agree to fulfil their civic obligations.[29]

If her constitutional meditations tended to move from radical to conservative toward the end of her life, Weil's thoughts on the spiritual drama through which her compatriots were passing were increasingly exalted. In "Cette guerre est une guerre de religions," Weil warned, "Enslaved and oppressed Europe will not enter a new and happier day at the moment of liberation unless between now and then the virtue of spiritual poverty takes root there."[30] Such an inspiration could only come, in Weil's view, from inspirational elites living among the masses, willing to accept spiritual as well as physical privation. Again, by implication, Weil was suggesting that de Gaulle and his comrades, who had lived through the war apart from the people of France, were unlikely guides through the kind of regenerative experience she longed to see happen.

In one of her final texts, this one a study specially commissioned by de Gaulle on the Statut des minorités françaises non-chrétiennes et d'origine étrangère, Weil again displayed deep reservations about the historic role played by her own ethnic group. Of the Jews, she wrote, "The existence of such a minority does not constitute a boon. Our objective then ought to be to hasten their disappearance; every temporary accommodation with them should be seen as a transition toward this end." Mixed marriages, Weil suggested, together with a Christian education, should be encouraged as means toward such assimilation in the coming generations. If only true Christian inspiration without dogma were made manifest in the world, she added exaltedly, "not only Jewish religious belief but atheism as well would disappear."[31]

Last but not least, Weil submitted to Philip a succinct text "À propos de la question coloniale dans ses rapports avec le peuple français,"[32] in which she suggested that a review of the nation's future relations with its colonies required a set of objective assessors. French settlers were obviously incapable of detachment in the matter, as were missionaries who had brought the gospel to people already subdued by military force. As for the partisans of *laïcité* who had urged the colonized to thrust aside their gods, they had done only harm by sowing skepticism, a plague worse than alcoholism or syphilis. Weil challenged Gaullists to develop a policy detached from such nefarious influences.

The cultural impact of colonialism was of particular interest to Weil. The general uprooting of French society, which she had analyzed in *L'enracinement*, applied equally well in her view to peoples living under imperial domination. She cited the classic cliché, the phrase "Our ancestors the Gauls," which schoolchildren in Hanoi or Dakar were urged to recite, noting that even those who tried hard to assimilate were snubbed by the dominant culture which pretended to want to absorb them. Inversely, apart from a few Arabic specialists (*arabisants*) in Morocco, there were few French people interested in or able to understand indigenous culture. In these circumstances, why should France not follow the lead of Père Foucauld, the Catholic soldier-monk who had learned so much from Islam?

Addressing the specific issue of her paper, Weil recommends that France, together with the other European colonial powers, consider a protective outlook toward those peoples under her control, leaving them neither totally dependent nor fully autonomous, rather along the lines of the Communauté française which would have an ephemeral existence following the war.

There is no evidence that Weil's thoughts on the colonial question reached de Gaulle, whose views in the matter would remain ambiguous. But, as we shall see, by making the liberal General Georges Catroux governor-general of Algeria in 1943–44, *Le Connétable* opened the way (however briefly) to a radical reform in the political, socio-economic, and cultural life of the Muslim masses in Algeria.

Still putting her ideas to paper even as her condition continued to worsen, Weil received a welcome visit from Jean Cavaillès, a fellow-graduate of the École normale, who arrived in London for a two-month stay beginning in February 1943. The Protestant Cavaillès, born in 1903, had had a distinguished career as one of France's leading philosophers of science during the interwar years. He had come to know about and admire de Gaulle through Emmanuel d'Astier de La Vigerie, an ex-naval officer turned journalist and resistance leader. The two men, joined by the Protestant philosophy graduate Lucie Aubrac and the banker Marcel Zerapha, had put together the resistance network Libération-Nord, while Cavaillès took charge of an underground information group in occupied France.

After welcoming Cavaillès, Weil did her best to win him over to her plan for a parachute-drop into France, pointing to the aviation manual and special crash-helmet which she had procured for such a mission. Her obviously failing health made any support for such a project absurd but, like her other friends, Cavaillès hesitated to point out that her "Semitic" features made her especially vulnerable in the racist atmosphere created by Vichy and the Nazis and that, if captured, she had no strength to resist torture and might well confess, exposing all others in her unit.[33]

During the spring of 1943, as her tuberculosis, now complicated by what some have seen as anorexia,[34] became even more critical, Weil was still considering baptism. She was extremely anxious to know whether this vital sacrament of the Church could be administered to someone with her theological reservations. In an effort to help her deal with this dilemma, a friend asked one of Fighting France's chaplains, the abbé René de Naurois, to discuss the matter with her. The priest was glad to oblige, seeing Weil on at least three occasions during May and June 1943. In the end, however, Naurois was just as troubled by Weil's idiosyncratic theological outlook as she was by his reiterating the Church's position that unbaptized infants were condemned to eternal limbo. Nothing conclusive emerged from these conversations and there is no evidence that, even as life slipped away from her, Weil asked to be baptized. Perhaps she requested that the sacrament be administered if she dropped into a coma; but even Mme Closon, who had come to be on very intimate terms with the dying woman, could not be sure. What was clear at the end, as well as during most of her adult life, was that Simone Weil felt as close to the Roman communion as one could be while still remaining outside.[35]

The most explicit profession of faith made by Weil may well be in the text titled "Théorie des sacrements," which she bequeathed posthumously to Schumann: "I believe in God, in the Trinity, in the Incarnation, in the Redemption, in the Eucharist and in the teachings of the Gospel." But, she added, she could not yield to the Church the right to limit the operation of her intelligence or "the illumination which love brought to the world of thought."[36]

At the end of May 1943, Schumann left for Algiers just ahead of de Gaulle, Philip, and Closon, who were anxious to join in establishing a base for Fighting France on sovereign French soil. Rumours soon reached Weil about the bitter rivalry in North Africa between *Le Connétable* and the conservative General Henri Giraud and about the return of the factious divisions which had traditionally plagued French parliamentary politics. To Closon, who returned to London at the end of June, she confided her increasing distress at the internecine battles which were undermining the mystique of the cause she had committed herself to defend. A month later, in a letter to the editor of *Volontaire*, she expressed her continuing frustration at being denied a chance to be sent into France on a mission, adding that she no longer wanted anything to do with La France combattante or with the government apparatus being set up in Algiers. Instead, Weil declared, she would like to rejoin the teaching corps from which she had been expelled by the Vichy regime. Surely Philip could at the very least find a research post for her?[37]

At the end of July or early in August, Schumann, back in England, came to see Weil, whose physical condition had steadily worsened. The two old friends ended up quarrelling violently over de Gaulle's leadership, Schumann defending the general's claim to represent the whole French people, Weil utterly disenchanted with what she saw to be the radical abuse of a once nobly held mandate.

On 17 August, severely weakened, Weil was taken to Ashford Sanatorium on the outskirts of London. A week later, she was dead. Weil was buried in the New Cemetery at Ashford in an area reserved for Catholics. Just seven people attended the service, including Schumann, his secretary Mme Rosin, Mme Closon, Mme Raymond Aron, and an Englishwoman, Mrs. Francis, who arrived with a bouquet of red, white, and blue flowers. The Catholic priest who had been asked to officiate failed to show up, having missed his train. In his place, Maurice Schumann and Mme Closon read from the Catholic burial service.

At the time of Weil's death, the cause for which she had so desperately sought to sacrifice herself was, as she observed, undergoing a radical transformation. The high idealism which had attracted Catholic, Jewish, and Protestant patriots to join La France libre had begun to fade; mundane politics were beginning to determine Gaullist strategy. Political parties, which Weil saw to be an integral part of the nation's decline, were starting to reassert their divisive influence. At the first meeting of the CNR in mid-May 1943, parties had been invited to play a role in designing France's future. Two weeks later, Fighting France played midwife to the creation of the Comité français de la libération nationale (CFLN), bestowing on the racist and reactionary Giraud co-presidency with de Gaulle. Men who had served or endured the Vichy regime (among them the Protestants Couve de Murville, René Massigli, and the Jew René Mayer) turned up in Algiers to serve the state apparatus being recreated there.

Simone Weil had from the beginning eagerly identified with the small band of Gaullists whose readiness to combat fascism was largely based on the sheer Nietzschean resolve of their leader and their collective refusal to be contaminated by compromise. With equal passion, she had empathized with the suffering mass of the French people, purified by deprivation and ready (like herself) for redemption.

The madcap schemes she conjured up as head of a front-line nursing organization, or as part of a guerrilla group dropped into France by parachute, helped make Weil the object of derision at Gaullist headquarters. On the other hand, some of her constitutional reflections are not too far removed from de Gaulle's own vision of a political order in which party and faction would give way to a transcendent vision of an entire nation freely bound to a common goal. Crémieux-Brilhac calls Weil a *chercheuse d'absolu,* a seeker after the absolute.[38] In however flawed a fashion, she incarnates Peguy's mythic Joan of Arc, at once Christian, patriot, and republican, a symbol of the ideological and spiritual union de Gaulle would spend his remaining years attempting to achieve.

CHAPTER TWELVE

André Philip and the Christian Left Commit to Free France

Given the longstanding devotion of the vast majority of French Protestants to the Republic and to democratic principles, it is not surprising that a substantial proportion of those who showed up to enrol in La France libre were linked to the Reformed communion.[1] None of these Protestants had a more significant role in shaping wartime Gaullist policy than André Philip, the only practicing Christian among the pre-war leaders of the SFIO.[2] Before arriving in London, Philip had been active in the internal Resistance. Through his initiative, two more Protestant *résistants* familiar with the French trade-union movement – Albert Guigui and Louis Vallon – would show up at Carlton Gardens. Intellectually brilliant and rhetorically impressive, with a bluntness of expression that sometimes caused more resentment than affection among his colleagues, Philip radically reinforced the passion for social justice within the Gaullist camp, helped animate the struggle against fascism, and clarified the vision of a morally regenerate France which had already brought so many to rally to Free France.

André Philip was born in 1902, at Pont-Saint-Esprit in the Gard department, Cévenol country, the site of the Calvinist revolt against Louis XIV in defence of freedom of conscience. His father, a Catholic army captain, died when the boy was just nine, leaving his Protestant mother, Gilberte, to raise him in the Reformed faith.

After studying at the lycée in Marseille, Philip moved with his mother to Paris in 1919. In a letter written to a friend a year later, reflecting on the paroxysmic patriotism which had led so many young men to death in

World War I, the future Gaullist made a profession of what was to be his lifetime creed:

> As far as patriotism is concerned, I believe that one must choose between two totally contradictory world-views. To begin with, I consider a patriot the man who pursues above all else the interests of his country. Similarly, I call a Christian or revolutionary (these terms being synonymous for me) the man who obeys only his conscience. The choice being set before me in this fashion, I do not hesitate to say that I am clearly an anti-patriot … I must confess to you that I feel solidarity with all those internationalists, all those revolutionaries who, from the beginning of time have, each in their own country, struggled for a fuller unity. Yes, my fatherland is to be found in the union of all those souls who, freed from every limitation and prejudice, are solely in search of the truth. But, even then, I cannot call such a union my fatherland because I am unable to place any limit on my love which must reach out to all humankind.[3]

This grandiloquent profession of faith reflects the powerful mix of evangelical Protestantism and international socialism which would characterize Philip's thoughts and actions from the interwar years through the Free French experience to the crusade for a United States of Europe in the 1950s and the campaign on behalf of the Third World which he waged in the final decade of his life.

Philip's university studies in the 1920s in Paris and Lyon included the pursuit of graduate degrees in political economy, philosophy, and law. Research for what would lead to a doctorate in political economy took the young Protestant to Great Britain in the summers of 1921 and 1922 to prepare a dissertation on Guild Socialism and the British trade union movement.

Philip was disturbed at the naive assumptions about human nature which he encountered in British left-wing circles. He had already come under the influence of the Protestant theologian Karl Barth, who warned his contemporaries about the peril of founding political systems on an illusory belief in human perfectibility.

If the refusal of British leftists to take human fallibility into account disturbed Philip, he was even less sympathetic to the orthodox Marxists' conviction that the proletariat was the vessel of human redemption. In any event, for Philip, socialism had to be more than the expression of working-class grievances and aspirations: it was and must always remain "the manifestation of a permanent yearning after justice and freedom, finding different forms of expression in different periods of history, but always pursuing a fixed moral ideal." True socialists must commit themselves to work for the proletariat broadly defined, that is "for the most miserable and most exploited human beings."[4]

Although he made a successful defence of his thesis on Guild Socialism in 1926, Philip was considered at twenty-four to be too young to receive the *agrégation*. The result was a Rockefeller-funded two-year stay in the United States, where he mixed some theological study with a critical on-the-job study of the American labour movement.

On his return from America, Philip became an *agrégé* and began his career as a professor of law at the University of Lyon, a post he held for more than fifteen years. Teaching was interrupted for six months in 1930 when Philip visited India, where he met Gandhi and was much impressed by the Mahatma's advocacy of passive resistance to oppression. Although the Protestant professor never became an integral pacifist himself, the encounter with Gandhi undoubtedly helped inspire him to take up the cause of two French conscientious objectors – Jacques Martin in 1932 and Philippe Vernier in 1934–5.

Apart from the law, Philip had been drawn to political life ever since the beginning of his student days when he joined the SFIO. During these same years, Philip joined and then became president of the Fédération des étudiants Protestants, often a training-ground for a political career at the national level. It was at a Federation meeting that he met Mireille Cooreman, daughter of a Protestant pastor, whom he married in 1923. In meetings which the young couple attended together, Philip honed his oratorical skills, addressing working-class as well as student rallies, unembarrassed to proclaim Christ the precursor of the socialist ideal and Karl Marx a Christian who didn't recognize the source of his own ideological inspiration (the German thinker was at least nominally Christian since he was the child of Jewish converts).

Philip's first opportunity to translate his Christian socialism into concrete action came with his successful campaign for election to the Chamber of Deputies from the 4th electoral district in Lyon in the May 1936 election which brought to power the Popular Front government headed by Léon Blum. The presence later that year of a practicing Christian at an SFIO convention dominated by free-thinkers and anticlerical militants was in itself an anomaly. But when Philip stood up before his fellow-delegates and professed himself to be a Christian socialist, he was quickly informed by one comrade that he would never again be invited to a party convention. In fact, that startling speech of Philip's still resonated years later. Welcoming Philip to London in 1942, the Catholic Maurice Schumann recalled a conversation he had had just after that speech with Marcel Déat, at that time a passionate socialist as well as a zealous atheist. Déat had laughed out loud as he repeated Philip's declaration "that he was a socialist because Jesus Christ dwelt within him," adding with a guffaw that the SFIO might take inspiration from these words and sally forth to recruit new converts in the nation's insane asylums! Schumann followed up this anecdote by remarking that, while religious conviction had helped inspire Philip's commitment to de Gaulle, Déat, the socialist turned fascist, still proudly atheist, was now living under the protective custody of the Gestapo![5]

Philip made his parliamentary debut on 12 June 1936 as *rapporteur* for the committee which recommended the introduction of the forty-hour week, legislation which Premier Blum regarded as the keystone of his government's program. The Protestant deputy championed the bill on psychological as well as economic grounds, arguing that its passage would give workers an opportunity to fulfill themselves spiritually as well as to improve themselves materially.[6] Blum applauded Philip's oratory with an enthusiastic "Très bien!"; the implementation of the forty-hour week, together with the granting of paid summer holidays (*conges payés*) produced something of a social revolution, bringing much of the French proletariat the beginnings of an *embourgeoisment* which would be radically accelerated after the war.[7]

André Philip volunteered to serve in uniform when the war began in 1939 and was given an assignment as a liaison officer with the British army before being sent on a brief mission to the United States. Back in France at the time of the Armistice, he thought of joining those who left Bordeaux on the *Massilia* to continue the combat against fascism from North Africa. In the end, however, Philip stayed in France and was one of the eighty members of the Chamber of Deputies who voted on 19 July against the award of special powers to Pétain. The following day, he joined seven other parliamentarians from the department of the Rhône in drawing up a manifesto, the text of which was later taken by Philip to London and broadcast over the French-language service of the BBC. The signatories denied that it had been the National Assembly which brought on the debacle now facing France; it had been the ineptitude of the military elites; the proposed ceding of plenipotentiary power to an aging army hero was, in these circumstances, hardly calculated to remedy the situation! The deputies and senators ended up with a categorical declaration of defiance: "Undeterred by threats and resisting any efforts to corrupt or seduce us, we prefer to endure the heightened sufferings which a dictatorship imposed by force will bring to the dishonour of a tyranny to which we would have given our consent."[8] On the Sunday following this act of defiance, which happened to fall on Bastille Day, Philip was much heartened by a sermon by Pastor Roland de Pury, then in Lyon, who encouraged those willing to take risks in the struggle against tyranny.

In the fall, Philip resumed his academic life as a professor of law at the Université de Lyon. Shortly afterwards, on 29 November, by showing up at a meeting of Paris-based intellectuals, many of them Catholic (the philosophers Emmanuel Mounier and Gabriel Marcel and the Jesuit Gaston Fessard, who had deserted the capital for the still relatively free atmosphere of the south-eastern city), he took a first tentative step into the necessarily secret world of the internal resistance.

In March 1941, Philip attended a clandestine meeting of socialists opposed to Vichy at which all present declared "that they would be unconditional Gaullists." Three months later, Philip and his wife Mireille sent their children off to the United States. From that moment on, the couple became more and more involved in various forms of resistance, including the sheltering of refugees (most of them Jewish) which had been organized by the Protestant relief organization Comité inter-mouvements auprès des évacués (CIMADE). Chambon-sur-Lignon became the most celebrated of these refugee centres; Philip and his wife had a country house there and knew Pastor André Trocmé, the key figure in providing asylum for those fleeing persecution.

It was also during the summer of 1941 that Philip met the nominally Catholic Emmanuel d'Astier de la Vigerie, founder of the underground resistance movement Libération. D'Astier was keen to learn of the contacts Philip and his friends were making with representatives of the Confédération générale du travail (CGT) and Confédération française des travailleurs chrétiens (CFTC). In fact, secret meetings were being held in a number of cities at which representatives of political parties, unions, and churches were present. In Lyon, Philip's colleague Olivier de Pierrebourg had met François de Menthon and Marcel Poimbeuf of the CFTC. A discussion group dealing with philosophical issues as well as post-war politics brought together in Lyon Pastor Roland de Pury and the Radical-Socialist deputy Paul Bastid, of Protestant background. A similar gathering at Marseille included the Protestants Pierre Grosclaude and Francis Leenhardt. At Montpellier, the Catholic Pierre-Henri Teitgen joined the Protestant professor René Courtin and Marc Bloch, a historian of Jewish background, in a truly ecumenical dialogue on France's future; and in Clermont-Ferrand, the Protestant Jean Cavaillès met with the Catholic René Capitant.

Until the fall of 1941, when Philip began to consider joining de Gaulle in London, the internal and external elements of the French resistance knew little of each other. More significantly, what they did know or imagine did not lead to mutual admiration or respect. By the fall of the year, however, two factors changed this for the better. RAF domination of the skies over the Continent allowed for the parachuting of Allied agents into France, where they could evaluate the internal resistance at first hand and spirit out those in the underground who were ready to examine the political perspective of Free France and its leader. Meanwhile, the German assault on the Soviet Union, beginning in mid-June, brought the French Communist Party to abandon its formal neutrality and commit itself wholeheartedly to the battle against fascism, sufficiently swelling the ranks of the resistance that those in London could no longer pretend to dismiss it.

At the end of October, the Catholic trade-unionist Léon Morandat (who assumed the code-name "Yvon") was parachuted into France near Toulouse, bearing a mandate from de Gaulle to recruit prospective new supporters and to encourage the coming together of all internal resistance groups under the general's overall command. During his mission, "Yvon" met the Catholic Georges Bidault and the agnostic socialist Robert Lacoste as well as Philip. The Protestant leftist was an eminently desirable object of de Gaulle's solicitation: he was a key member of the Socialist resistance; he was a leading figure in the Reformed community; and he had a well-established reputation for moral and spiritual integrity. For his part, Philip was impressed by the Catholic syndicalist and by Morandat's favourable disposition toward Free France and its leader.

This positive reaction to de Gaulle was reinforced when Philip made a secret trip to Paris at the beginning of 1942 and met another special emissary of the general, Gilbert Renault, a film maker by profession known as "Rémy" in the underground. Renault was the leader of the Confrérie Notre-Dame, a Free French network of information gatherers. For the first time during this meeting, Philip indicated a willingness to go to London. For his part, "Rémy" was much impressed with the new recruit, although the portrait he drew of Philip was not altogether flattering: "Philip has a shock of black hair, thick black eyebrows and a heavy black moustache. He is verbose and somewhat muddled in speech as well as very warm-hearted. He is troubled by a nervous tic around the mouth which makes those near him very uncomfortable."[9]

The decisive factor in Philip's decision to travel to London was a meeting with an old friend, Christian Pineau, son-in-law of the brilliant novelist and playwright Jean Giraudoux, France's minister of propaganda at the beginning of the war. Pineau was a militant syndicalist with close links to the British trade-union movement. A Catholic by upbringing, he had ceased to practice his faith since adolescence, finding the rich liturgy a distraction from the intellectual reflection which he thought the church should inspire in its followers. In his mature years however, especially during the war, he describes himself as still obsessed by the idea of God.[10] Pineau's social and political radicalism in the 1930s was paralleled by his wife's integral pacifism.

In the aftermath of France's military collapse and the advent of Pétain, the Pineaus knew without articulating it that they were committed to resist the new order. Undeterred by the *pétainiste* outlook of most of their comrades, they joined with a few close friends, including the Socialist Robert Lacoste, in drawing up a *Manifeste du syndicalisme français* in defence of basic liberties and in denunciation of national socialism. They became active in the underground organization Libération and contacted Professor Jean Cavaillès, a Protestant who was deeply engaged in the resistance; and in Paris they met Pierre Brossolette, who was on the point of travelling to London to explain the work of the internal resistance to de Gaulle.

Encouraged by his friend Philip as well as by Emmanuel d'Astier and Henri Frenay, Pineau travelled to London in February 1942 to transmit the plea that de Gaulle draw up a manifesto in favour of democracy aimed at the internal resistance. Speculating about the general's reaction, Philip noted, "If his response is in the main consonant with our ideas, we will be able to make it our own formulation and thus unify the spirit of the resistance." If, on the other hand, all de Gaulle had to offer was another form of fascism, it would make any collaboration with him pointless.[11] Sitting at a café in Lyon, Pineau and his friends drafted the outline of what they hoped de Gaulle might accept as the core of a future post-Liberation program for France.

Flown off to London on a Lysander, Pineau met first with the chief of Gaullist counter-intelligence, "Passy." The conversation convinced the visitor that links between the external and internal resistance were still in the embryonic stage. In the end, all that those fighting fascism inside France knew about de Gaulle came from the BBC; the general served as a "flag," an emblem of the common combat against Vichy and Berlin, nothing more.

Pineau's first meeting with de Gaulle was not reassuring. The general presented himself to the trade-unionist rather like an authoritarian prince of the church, at once unctuous and stern. Instead of the message of unity and ideological harmony which he had hoped to hear, Pineau found himself listening to a diatribe against the "Anglo-Saxons" from a man whose perspective was military rather than political. The general clearly saw the current war in terms of History, while his would-be supporters inside France conceived it as a struggle for Liberty.

When Pineau brought up the question of the manifesto he and his colleagues were looking for, de Gaulle frowned, making clear he would do nothing to resurrect a regime based on the primacy of political parties. However, when his Socialist visitor urged the need for democratic representation in the battle against fascism and cited the role his friend André Philip might play, a role in guaranteeing this, the general exclaimed, "So, then, he's with us! That gives me great pleasure! Perhaps I'll invite him to join me!"[12]

Following this first conversation with *Le Connétable*, Pineau made the rounds of Free French notables. He was much impressed by Pleven but even more by Henry Hauck, who had been counselling de Gaulle on working-class questions and in whom he knew he would find a helpful collaborator in the campaign for the desired Gaullist manifesto. Hauck remained cautious about the general's long-term commitment to democracy ("The general is a maurrassian," he insisted), but agreed to join Pineau and his Socialist comrade Adrien Tixier in a second (although not much more successful) effort to win over de Gaulle.

At his third meeting, the general produced his own three-page text, which began with a severe indictment of the Third Republic. Pineau, borrowing Philip's idea, suggested that the manifesto include a reference to the need for post-war economic planning. The final version of de Gaulle's text, issued following this meeting, retained a still troubling statement that "the French people condemn with equal vigour the regime which led to the collapse of 1940 and the system at Vichy which replaced it," but the general clearly tried to offset this denunciation with a pledge to Pineau that he would not betray the working class, and in the end he modified the text to make this guarantee more concrete.[13]

When Pineau returned to France and relayed the details of his meetings with de Gaulle, including the general's hesitations about including any reference to post-Liberation economic policy, Philip professed indifference. What was important was the creation of a new political and social order, with or without the general, and based in any event on the strength of the internal resistance. But when Pineau made mention of de Gaulle's suggestion that Philip travel to London, the Protestant Socialist was so excited that he decided on the spot to draw up a fully articulated new constitution to take with him to the British capital.

Now irrevocably committed to join de Gaulle in London, Philip was involved in several botched attempts to leave France by plane in the spring of 1942. Having become suspect to the authorities because of his involvement in the Resistance, he did his best to avoid public appearances; on at least one occasion, full of ecumenical warmth, he attended Catholic mass rather than risk being seen at a Protestant temple.[14]

In the end, the Socialist deputy left from the Mediterranean coast near Cassis late in July, boarding a British corvette disguised as a Portuguese trawler. The same small craft would also transport to freedom Gilberte Brossolette, wife of de Gaulle's deputy chief of counter-intelligence, and Louis Vallon, a trade-unionist of Protestant background who would play a key role not only in Free France but who, unlike Philip, would remain a passionate *gaulliste* after the war.

Born in 1901, Louis Vallon was the child of a mixed marriage: his mother was Catholic, his father Protestant. Vallon *père,* a school principal and later mayor of Crest in the Drôme department, was a member of the SFIO and took Louis to hear Jean Jaurès when he was just thirteen.[15] The Socialist leader's oratorical power had a lasting influence: whatever his ideological shifts later in life, Louis Vallon always regarded himself as a socialist. His lifelong friend Francis Raoul describes Vallon as possessed of "a passion rising up from the Huguenot atavism that had dwelt within him since childhood," adding that by family tradition, Vallon was "a republican, a patriot and a socialist."

Vallon's education included studies at the École normale as well as the École polytechnique. The latter prepared him for a career as an engineer with a keen interest in research. In the mid-1930s, he proudly displayed one of France's first television sets in his Boulevard St. Michel apartment. His skills led him to be made director of the Compagnie des Lampes, part of the huge Thompson chain of enterprises. Although Vallon's career linked him to the capitalist world, his heart and mind were oriented toward efforts to transcend class conflict and work for a social order based on harmony between workers and employers.

Unlike most of his generation with left-wing views, Vallon actually read Marx, concluding that, while the communist theorist's analytical method might still be valid, his historical projections no longer held up. *Prolonger le marxisme* ("Extending and updating Marxism") became a catchword in the engineer's approach. The advanced stage of capitalism, he concluded, had created the conditions for the democratization of wealth by forcing increasing numbers of former bourgeois into the proletariat. Perhaps influenced by his Protestant background, Vallon saw the monetary system as essentially Catholic in structure, based on decisions handed down by a few from the apex of an economic pyramid, as opposed to credit arrangements which were basically Protestant, rooted at the base in trust.[16]

Vallon joined the SFIO in 1923, actively involving himself in the reformist wing of the party, bitterly opposing the orthodox who insisted on fighting class war and opposing the collaboration of Socialists in bourgeois governments. During the Popular Front, Vallon played no active political role but made a few radio broadcasts and contributed articles to *L'homme réel*, an anarcho-syndicalist review. Following the collapse of the second Blum government in 1938, dismayed at the increasing sense of drift and division in French public life, he indicated support for Gaston Palewski's effort to promote a government of national unity led by Paul Reynaud.

At the beginning of the war, Vallon was called up as captain of a company of army engineers and fought on even after the Armistice before being captured and taken off to prison camp in Germany. The intervention of his wife, Suzanne, and a professional friend, who insisted that his skills were needed in Paris, brought his release in the summer of 1941. Following contact with Pierre Brossolette in January 1942, he met André Philip and began collaborating with Christian Pineau in Libération-Nord. At a secret meeting in his Paris apartment, Vallon met with Pineau, Cavaillès, and de Gaulle's special agent "Rémy," who persuaded him to work as a spy for the Confrérie Notre-Dame by relaying information about French rail movements for transmission to London. When this network was threatened with exposure, "Remy" urged "Passy," the head of the BCRA, to arrange for the transfer of Vallon to London. Hastening south, Louis and Suzanne Vallon boarded the British corvette at Cassis which was taking Philip and Gilberte Brossolette to Britain.

Reflecting years later on his mental state as he left for the United Kingdom, Vallon remarked,

> The debacle of 1940 had created a wall in front of us behind which we were cut off from the present by a distress which seemed without remedy. Our past was suddenly lost to view. Then de Gaulle rose up, rousing us to action through his words and acts, giving back to the people the energy required in order that France remain a nation able to play a role on the world stage … So I became a Gaullist.

I was still a socialist and I would remain one. Together with André Philip and in concert with Pierre Brossolette, I joined de Gaulle in July 1942, faithful at one and the same time to my country and my upbringing.[17]

Embarking together late in July, Philip, Vallon, and Mme Brossolette arrived in England on 25 July. De Gaulle received Philip on the 27th. A three-hour conversation ensued, beginning with one of the general's classic reviews of the world-historical struggle in progress and France's role in resolving it. The new arrival was suitably impressed, seeing in *Le Connétable* more of an intellectual than a military figure. Fully conscious of his own symbolic as well as political value as a link to the internal resistance, Philip talked frankly of the need for more democratic representation and practice in the Comité français. His intellectual brilliance and his energy delighted de Gaulle; Bouchinet talks of a "reciprocal seduction" between the two men.[18] In 1947, however, Philip (who had by then broken with the general) told Lacouture that at the conclusion of this long talk he had declared, "*Mon général*, as soon as the war is over, I will part company with you. You are fighting to restore our nation's greatness, I am fighting to build a socialist and democratic Europe."[19]

To help him overcome any lingering doubts about serving under de Gaulle and to define more clearly his mandate as Free France's interior commissioner, Philip found a letter from Pierre Brossolette, dated 30 May 1942, waiting for him in London.[20] The deputy head of counter-intelligence began by making clear that, in his view, Philip's presence in the British capital as a representative of the internal resistance was far more valuable than that of any of his predecessors, including Pineau, Cassin, Pleven and Dejean. The Protestant leftist was clearly better equipped to put the case for Free France in Washington as well as London, where the image of de Gaulle as "tomorrow's monstrous dictator" was doing grave harm. Hostile elements in the British Labour Party who had been misled by the Jean Jaurès group, as well as Roosevelt and his entourage, needed to be informed that the resistance inside France as well as in London saw the general as their *chef total*, their moral as well as political leader.

Brossolette ended his letter by declaring, "De Gaulle sees in you the deus ex-machina of our drama," urging Philip to use this unconditional endorsement to assert full administrative control of all Free French operations inside France. Although "Passy" would prove a less than perfect collaborator, Philip would rely heavily on both Boris and Hauck as well as on the Catholic Louis Closon, whom he had come to know as a fellow-recipient of a Rockefeller fellowship. There thus emerged at the core of Free France's interior ministry a remarkably ecumenical team.

Encouraged by Brossolette's letter and putting aside all doubts about de Gaulle's political outlook, the new commissioner addressed his compatriots over the BBC, declaring, "My presence here … as a member of one of those organizations which are leading the struggle against the occupying power and the Vichy traitors in both zones of France, signifies that we recognize General de Gaulle as our military and political chief."[21]

Philip's commitment to de Gaulle was further established soon after his arrival in London when a second major figure in the SFIO, Félix Gouin, showed up in the British capital to examine the republican credentials of *Le Connétable.* Carrying a mandate from Léon Blum, Gouin ended up joining Philip in an effort to persuade the Groupe Jean-Jaurès to end their dissidence and rally to the Gaullist banner. The effort failed, and Philip showed his anger and contempt for the small band of Socialists in exile by branding their attitude as treasonous.[22]

Philip's failure to modify the hostility of the Jean-Jaurès group toward de Gaulle was, as we shall see, far less serious than his disastrous attempt to win the American president to the cause during a fall 1942 visit to the United States.[23] Fortunately, the peculiar skills of the Protestant Socialist were far better employed in handling the domestic aspect of the responsibilities Brossolette had urged him to take on.

From London, Philip did his best to further the work of the Comité général d'études, the underground group of intellectuals inside France who were drawing up plans for the socio-economic and political structures of post-war France. And in July 1943, he sent his fellow-Protestant Émile Laffon ("Guizot"), a mining engineer and lawyer by profession, back across the Channel to start discussions with the internal resistance about who might best act as *commissaires de la République* and prefects during and immediately after Liberation. In this regard, Philip himself played a key role by confiding the creation of Comités de libération in the northern part of France to Closon and charging his friend and co-religionist Francis Leenhardt ("Lionel") with the same responsibility in the southern zone. He also arranged for the abduction from inside France of key figures in the resistance, such as the Protestant Albert Guigui and the Catholic labour leader Marcel Poimbeuf, whose presence in London, he felt, would better serve the cause.

Inevitably, in his efforts to orchestrate a closer relationship between the external and internal resistance, Philip came (like his colleagues) to consider the role of political parties in the further pursuit of the war effort. In the aftermath of the debacle of 1940, the old-line parties which had failed to deal with the fascist threat were almost as much discredited in London as they were in Vichy. By the summer of 1942, however, this negative attitude had begun to change as a result of three key developments: the re-emergence of the Communist Party, which abandoned its wartime neutrality following the German invasion of the Soviet Union in June 1942; the arrival in London of emissaries from newly resurrected parties inside France and their demand for recognition and acceptance; and the direct observation by de Gaulle's delegates inside France of the real contribution made to the common cause by party cadres and supporters.

Despite their shared concern about the long-term revolutionary intent of the Communists, Philip and de Gaulle were by the fall of 1942 both convinced of the wisdom of integrating representatives of the PCF into the Fighting France organization. As a result, the BCRA, in collaboration with the Protestant François Faure ("Paco"), who had been a lieutenant-colonel in a tank regiment before joining "Rémy"'s confrérie Notre-Dame, arranged for the Communist Fernard Grenier to be brought out of France in January 1943 to serve as an advisor to Philip in the Interior Commissariat.

This closer link to the Communists brought with it a vigorous debate about the use of sabotage and about how to reply to the Nazi demand for French conscript labour (the Service du travail obligatoire was imposed by Vichy on 15 February 1943). The Communists incited workers to refuse to respond to this arbitrary call-up, while Philip's friend Guigui urged compliance on the ground that this might in time lead to the creation within Nazi Germany of a pro-Allied fifth column.

The Communists were not alone in putting pressure on de Gaulle and his colleagues to sanction an armed rising inside France. In May 1943, to preclude being outflanked on the Left by this pressure, the general sent secret instructions across the Channel permitting guerrilla actions where they were deemed feasible. This policy went against Philip's strong belief in "resistance through patience," but the control of military actions of La France combattante was essentially outside his jurisdiction. As a result, he focused more and more on the problems associated with national reconstruction, a focus which intensified following the transfer of Fighting France to Algiers at the end of May.

Not surprisingly, given his background, Philip's religious faith remained as fervid as his new-found Gaullism. This became startlingly clear to his one-time co-religionist Jacques Soustelle, a casual acquaintance from pre-war Lyon, whom (as we have seen) he met again in René Cassin's office on the day of his arrival. Assuming that the ethnologist was still a believer, Philip asked for direction to a Protestant place of worship; fortunately, the commissioner for propaganda was able to give him directions to the Reformed church in Soho Square.

This temple, as it turned out, was the only French-speaking Reformed church in London – or for that matter in Britain – during the war. Its pastor, Frank-Henri Christol, had assumed charge of the congregation in 1928 after spending a number of years as a missionary in Africa. In 1938, on the urging of Marc Boegner, he had agreed to stay on in the British capital, where he spent the war years separated from his family.[24] As soon as he was made aware of de Gaulle's presence in London in the summer of 1940, Christol decided, with the backing of his presbytery, to join the Free French movement. However, when he went to see de Gaulle's aide-de-camp with this news, he was told by a Catholic chaplain who happened to be present that such volunteering was pointless since there were no Protestants in the ranks of La France libre! The tone changed radically when the pastor met de Gaulle himself on 27 December to offer his services as Protestant chaplain to the Free French forces. The general accepted, although it was not until May 1941 that Christol was appointed chaplain with the rank of captain.

On one occasion, probably during the late summer or early fall of 1942, Pastor Christol invited André Philip to preach the sermon in his place. Philip persuaded his colleague Soustelle to come and hear him, quite possibly because of the theme, based on James 1:2–3. In testing times such as those being faced by the people of France, Philip told the congregation, the Gospel according to James counselled neither passive resignation to evil nor violent revolt but resistance through patience based on confidence that God's will must prevail. (As Jacques Poujol sees it, Philip was aiming his message directly at Soustelle, urging the Propaganda Commissioner to avoid inciting gratuitous revolt inside France and to steer away from measures which too closely resembled those being used by the enemy).[25]

Spiritually anchored at the temple in Soho Square, Philip agreed to Maurice Schumann's request that he record a number of talks to be broadcast to France via the BBC; he greeted Protestant volunteers to the Gaullist cause from all over the French Empire; he helped to produce and distribute a French-language Protestant periodical (*Le Lien. Organe Protestant de La France combattante*); and through his fellow exile and parishioner, the trade-unionist Albert Guigui, he facilitated links between Gaullism and the CGT.

Philip had arranged for the air rescue and transfer to London of Guigui, a fellow-Protestant as well as a vigorous champion of trade-union power.

Born in Algiers on 26 March 1903, the son of a painter-decorator, Guigui moved with his parents to Paris in his infancy and completed his primary education there in 1915. After training as a mechanic, the young Protestant worked for three years in the aeronautical field until 1918. There followed a series of jobs in the metallurgical trades paralleled by a rising interest in working-class literature, especially in anarchist theory. In 1921, Guigui's involvement in strike action and his distribution of anarchist pamphlets led to his arrest. That same year, he was chosen by the metal workers' union to represent them at the CGT congress at Lille; later, he headed to Moscow to represent the Confederation there but, after running into comrades returning from the Russian capital who were discouraged by the labour policies of the new Soviet government, he turned back.

During the Popular Front period, Guigui joined Georges and Émile Lefranc in launching the Centre confédéral d'Éducation ouvrière and, in December 1936, gave a lecture on the right to strike to its members, arguing that workers must always retain their autonomy, no matter what concessions they might win in capitalist states. In June 1940, just before he resigned as premier, Paul Reynaud requested that Guigui travel to the United States to help inform the American labour movement about what was at stake in the Battle of France. The trip never materialized and, after a brief arrest as a subversive, Guigui travelled to Toulouse where, meeting with his trade-union colleagues, he sought permission to leave for the United States with his family. While waiting for his passport, he worked as a proofreader for the newspaper *Paris-Soir.* Many months later, Guigui was circulating in the south of France when Jean Moulin ("Max") arrived in the area on a mission from de Gaulle to make contact with the internal resistance. As a result of this meeting, the Protestant militant and the Socialist Robert Lacoste were assured that money would be forwarded from London to help the underground trade-union movement, and Guigui was chosen to go to the British capital to represent the CGT there.

During the night of 12–13 February 1943, in an open field in the Jura department in south-central France, two Lysander aircraft picked up Guigui and three companions – Moulin; General Delestraint, head of the underground army loyal to de Gaulle; and the Protestant agent Jacques Kalb – and airlifted them to Britain. Kalb, code-named "Jacques d'Alsace," born in Colmar, became the spokesperson for Alsace-Lorraine in London and a frequent speaker on BBC programs beamed in France.

A few days after his arrival in London, Guigui went to see de Gaulle in the company of André Philip. The general expressed his delight at the message transmitted to him by Guigui that the underground CGT was committed to Fighting France. For his part, Guigui pressed on *Le Connétable* the continuing need for financial support to the underground union movement. An agreement was reached that Britain, the United States, and Fighting France would together subsidize a *Fonds de soutien* to be administered by the CFN. As a result, beginning on 1 March 1943 and continuing until 1 July 1944, an "envelope" containing money for a designated representative of the underground CGT was dropped over France at the beginning of every month.

Following his meeting with de Gaulle, Guigui was introduced to the British and Allied Press by Philip on 26 March 1943. Playing the Gaullist propagandist to the hilt, he declared rather improbably, "Beginning with the first appeal of General de Gaulle in June 1940, the working class has let its heart speak and, without reservation, has rallied to his cause." Although Vichy had destroyed France's regular unions, the workers had kept the CGT in their blood. Guigui insisted they still expressed "a kind of faith, a religion whose catacombs are in our workshops."[26]

On 29 March, three days after his press conference, Guigui informed his compatriots over the BBC that he had been mandated by all of France's workers, whatever their union affiliation or ideology, to transmit their unconditional support to de Gaulle and that the general had been proud to receive their endorsement. Although the underground CGT and its supporters were being hunted down all over France, he pursued, they were everywhere present, in privately owned factories as well as throughout the public sector.[27]

A week later, on 8 April, in a second radio broadcast, Guigui urged his listeners to join together in resisting the Nazi demand for conscript labour under the STO, to distinguish in their dealings between patriotic and collaborationist employers, and to forget all internal factional disputes in the common combat against fascism.[28]

Guigui's presence in London was hailed by the Catholic editors of *Volontaire pour la cité chrétienne* in their 29 April 1943 issue. And, soon after his arrival, the Protestant trade unionist joined the committee chaired by André Philip at the Huguenot church in Soho Square, which welcomed French Protestants who had come to London to join in the battle against Vichy and the Third Reich.

Guigui, like Louis Vallon, had come to London thanks to André Philip, who was anxious both to reinforce the progressive element in Fighting France and to forge a closer link between the internal and external resistance. Philip, whose arrival in the British capital de Gaulle had eagerly solicited, had come to put his faith in the general largely through reassurances given him by the Catholic trade unionists Yvon Morandat and Christian Pineau. Named commissioner of the interior and backed by an ecumenical team headed by the Jew Boris and the Catholic Closon, he had encouraged the work of the Comité general d'études, a group of mostly Christian intellectuals engaged in drawing up blueprints for a politically and socially progressive post-war France. He had given a plenipotentiary mandate to the Catholic Closon in the northern zone of France and to the Protestant Leenhardt in the south to coordinate resistance efforts and prepare the way for the transition government which would accompany the liberation. What resulted was a well-orchestrated structure, which would also block any revolutionary attempt by the highly disciplined Communists. In short, when liberation came, Philip and his associates would help ensure that Christians, including the overwhelming majority of Catholics among them, would enjoy the *droit de cité* which they had so long been denied.

CHAPTER THIRTEEN

De Gaulle's Protestant Emissaries: René Massigli and André Philip

In the aftermath of his 18 June 1940 appeal over the BBC, Charles de Gaulle expected to rally to his cause key members of France's military and political elites. Nowhere was the reaction to the general's challenge more disappointing than among France's senior diplomats, whose responses ranged in tone from indifferent to openly hostile. As a result, at least during its first year, Free France's external relations were entrusted to a variety of well-intentioned intellectuals and two men with a background in business.

The absence of experienced diplomats at the outset of the Free French saga and the peculiar vulnerability of the Gaullist enterprise (especially before its transfer to Algiers) meant that relations between La France libre and its wartime allies very much depended on the idiosyncratic outlook and world view of de Gaulle. However much he might have repudiated the ethnocentric nationalism of Charles Maurras, the general clung to the view that, in the final analysis, relations between states were based on the primacy of national rather than ideological interests. "La France seule," a Maurassian formula, would be the hallmark of Gaullist diplomacy throughout the war. Quite apart from this governing principle (supplemented by the conviction that Russia, whatever its ideological outlook, was France's natural geopolitical ally on the Continent), de Gaulle harboured an abiding anglophobia, a deep antipathy transmitted by his father and intensified by childhood memories of Fashoda, the Sudanese watering-hole which Colonel Marchand had yielded to the British in the summer of 1898, following a brilliantly successful rupture of the imperial life-line that

Britain had established between Capetown and Cairo. Throughout his four years of exile in London and Algiers, de Gaulle's underlying prejudice against "perfidious Albion" would be reinforced by "Anglo-Saxon" threats (both real and imagined) to French interests around the world and by Churchill's willingness to yield to Roosevelt's insistence that Free France be excluded from the formulation and execution of Allied policy.

Fortunately for the Free French cause, Churchill was as inveterate a francophile as the general was anglophobic.[1] The young Winston had witnessed and admired both the power and the elegance of French troops marching down the Champs-Élysées before 1914. He had been very much impressed by both Marshal Foch and Premier Georges Clemenceau during World War I and, in the interwar years, had maintained close and friendly relations with Generals Georges and Maurice Gamelin. The prime minister's links to France's political establishment were just as strong: he made clear to intimates during the war that he would have preferred to see Reynaud, Herriot, or Mandel at the head of the anti-Vichy cause in Great Britain. In the end, however, despite an increasingly bitter relationship with de Gaulle (who had cultivated no close friendships with British figures, political or military, before 1940), Churchill retained his fondness for France and did his best to ensure that she recovered major power status after the Liberation.

If relations between de Gaulle and Churchill were at times brought close to the breaking point by differences of personality and outlook, the wartime rapport between the general and President Roosevelt was even more seriously undermined by mutual prejudice and misunderstanding.[2] The American head of state had concluded in 1940 that, as a result of her rapid collapse, France had been permanently relegated to second-power status, unworthy of equal partnership in the battle against the Axis. His perception of de Gaulle as authoritarian, if not fascistic, and therefore to be kept at arm's length, had been largely shaped by French exiles in the United States, most notably the émigré diplomat Alexis Léger who used the pen-name "Saint-John Perse" as a poet. Overall strategic considerations led Roosevelt to maintain a link to the Vichy regime where the president's personal envoy, Ambassador William Leahy, a practicing Catholic, became a champion of Pétain. Finally, scruples about the need to consult the whole French population about their future meant postponing any recognition of Free France until the Liberation, and Machiavellian calculation dictated that Washington deal with the realities on the ground, whether in French North Africa in 1942 or Normandy in 1944.

Following his 18 June call to arms, de Gaulle had naturally enough hoped for the collaboration of the French ambassador in London, Charles Corbin, who had devoted most of his career to the promotion of the Entente Cordiale. Belonging to one of France's most conventional establishments and being in any event close to retirement, Corbin, while conceding that the Gaullist cause was just, decided not just to resign but to remove himself permanently from all political activity.[3] Meanwhile, the writer Paul Morand, who directed the cultural section at the embassy, arranged for the transport back to France of most of his colleagues under the protection of the Red Cross. This mass departure deprived Free France of experienced diplomats who had established the kind of close and confidential relationships with their British counterparts that few Gaullists would be able to develop.

In the absence of trained professionals, de Gaulle had perforce to turn to men who, in some cases, brought more than mere enthusiasm to this improvisational phase of Free French diplomacy. The Jew René Cassin (as we have seen) arrived in London early enough to lend his expert legal mind to the formulation of the 7 August 1940 accords with the British government, which gave de Gaulle recognition as "leader of the Free French" and allowed for the transfer of funds from the Treasury and permission to recruit for the Forces françaises libres. Cassin was supported in these early days by Pierre-Olivier Lapie, who had been elected to the Chamber of Deputies in 1936 to represent Nancy, in Lorraine, on behalf of the Union socialiste et républicaine, a small left-wing party.

Lapie was replaced in this embryonic foreign affairs branch of Free France by Jules Hackin, a captain in the army reserves, who had shown up at the British legation in Kabul on 19 June to put himself at the disposal of de Gaulle. A World War I veteran, Hackin had made a reputation as an archaeologist and conservator at the Guimet Museum of Orientalia in Paris during the 1920s. An interest in the origins of Buddhism brought him to take part in the celebrated *Croisière jaune* in 1927. Although Hackin and his wife were both involved in an archaeological dig in Afghanistan when they learned of de Gaulle's appeal, they did not hesitate to respond.

Hackin assumed the direction of the skeletal diplomatic mission at Carlton Gardens in September. Two months later, he was joined by the ethnographer Jacques Soustelle, who had responded to de Gaulle's appeal from Latin America and who served under Hackin from November 1940 until February 1941.[4]

The disappearance of Hackin in the Mediterranean when his ship was torpedoed was in some ways compensated for by the arrival in London that same month of the first professional diplomat to join the Free French cause. Maurice Dejean, a son of a merchant whose agnostic outlook he came to share, was born on 30 September 1899 in the Paris suburb of Clichy. After earning a licentiate in letters and a diploma in philosophy at the University of Paris, he entered the diplomatic service in 1930. Dejean spent the entire pre-war decade in Germany as press and information officer of the French embassy in Berlin and was thus able to observe the takeover of power by the Nazis and the subsequent dismantling of France's diplomatic and strategic position in Europe. Like every one else in the embassy, he was overwhelmed by the imposing presence and style of his superior, Ambassador André François-Poncet. Hardworking and modest but showing no particular flair, Dejean proved an excellent second. Recalled to Paris at the outbreak of hostilities in September 1939, he joined the personal staff of Daladier, then Reynaud. Together with Gaston Palewski, he formed part of the determined and courageous minority in the ministry who urged Premier Reynaud to ignore the pleas of his mistress Hélène de Portes and other defeatists and maintain France in the war.

Staying in France following the defeat, Dejean grew increasingly restless as Vichy turned toward collaboration. After managing to travel to Morocco with his wife, he arrived in London on 27 February 1941. His first meeting with de Gaulle lasted over two hours, quite remarkable in itself. The two men got along famously. The general was much impressed both by the newcomer's evident zeal for the Free French cause and by a vitriolic diatribe which Dejean delivered against Pétain. The chief result of this mutually gratifying encounter was that de Gaulle named Dejean *directeur des affaires politiques*, a portfolio so broad that, Bouchinet insists, *Le Connétable* had not properly defined it in his own mind! A lack of administrative acumen was a perennial problem for the Free French leader, who was usually too preoccupied with grand strategy to pay any heed to its day-by-day application; in any event, in June, he added to Dejean's responsibilities by putting him in charge of Free France's external relations.

Between March 1941 and January 1943, when he was replaced by René Massigli, Dejean was little more than a frustrated bystander during a series of diplomatic crises with the "Anglo-Saxons," which de Gaulle took it upon himself to resolve. To begin with, reports reaching London concerning the vacillating and, in the end, disastrous diplomatic style of de Gaulle during and after the Syrian campaign (June–July 1941) alarmed Dejean and Bouchinet with whom he shared his distress. Bouchinet agreed that the general's efforts at negotiating had been consistently "on the edge of the abyss, full of rhetorical extravagance and lacking in balance."[5]

While the Syrian crisis was creating new tensions between Free France and the British, Operation Barbarossa, the German attack on the Soviet Union which began on 22 June 1941, allowed Dejean to give a first demonstration of his skills, although it was, as usual, de Gaulle who orchestrated Free France's overall diplomatic strategy. On 24 June, two days after the Nazi invasion, *Le Connétable*, then in Jerusalem, telegraphed Dejean with instructions to issue a bold statement of support for the Russians. The commitment of the Soviet Union to the war effort, he noted, offered new hope for a France that had been seriously weakened; just as important, it introduced an element of balance in the world in the face of the overweening "Anglo-Saxon" powers.[6] To transform these long-term meditations into reality, de Gaulle mandated Dejean and his colleague Cassin to enter into a dialogue with the Soviet ambassador to Great Britain, Ivan Maisky.

The result, after a series of meetings, was a joint declaration of 26 September 1941 in which Maisky, on behalf of his government, recognized de Gaulle as *chef de tous les Français libres* (the *tous* designed to cover the internal as well as external resistance) and pledged Moscow's aid in the struggle to guarantee the full restoration of France's independence and grandeur. The declaration, still offering less than full diplomatic recognition, was followed by the accreditation to Fighting France of Alexander Bogomolov, former chargé d'affaires of the Soviet Union in Vichy and by de Gaulle's naming of General Émile Petit, a former classmate of the general at St-Cyr, to Moscow, where he would establish military liaison with his Russian counterparts. In a 20 January 1942 radio broadcast, de Gaulle celebrated the renewal of the historical bond between France and Russia which "had too often been prevented or undermined by intrigue and incomprehension" and described the "new Russia" as the predestined ally of France.[7]

At the end of a year which had allowed Maurice Dejean to play a limited role in the shaping of Gaullist relations with the Allies, a new diplomatic challenge emerged, this time over the French islands of St. Pierre and Miquelon in the New World. It was a crisis that would sorely strain the already troubled relations between Carlton Gardens and Washington.

In the first formative weeks of its existence, de Gaulle had entrusted the propagation of the Free French message in the United States to another old comrade from St-Cyr, Jacques de Siéyès. A year after naming de Siéyès, however, de Gaulle realized that the veteran *saint-cyrien* had been a thoroughly inept promoter of the cause. Pro-Vichy propaganda by French exiles in New York and Washington, reinforced by sympathetic views of the État français relayed to Roosevelt by Ambassador Leahy, made the prospect of reaching an understanding with Washington increasingly difficult. To remedy this problem, de Gaulle in May 1941 selected the experienced businessman and devout Catholic René Pleven. Although he lacked formal diplomatic training, Pleven had a keen sense of the limits of what he might accomplish. He would try to win recognition of the Comité national français without, however, suggesting that the Americans cut their links to Vichy: he would encourage Siéyès; the Protestant Raoul Aglion, a trained diplomat who had volunteered to serve as secretary in support of the cause; and others to recruit for the Free French, and he would actively promote the evacuation from France to America of key scientists and others who could help the Allied war effort.

Pleven's sojourn in Washington brought mixed results. On the one hand de Gaulle's emissary was able to secure permission for Free French agents to establish offices in New York and Washington and to have the use of a diplomat's pouch and franking. On the other hand, while Pleven managed to arrange economic cooperation between the United States and the French colonies liberated from Vichy, the extension of the Lend-Lease program to Free France itself was refused[8] and neither Secretary of State Cordell Hull nor his deputy Sumner Welles deigned to meet him. What was even more frustrating was the refusal of major figures in the French exile community to chair a committee representing Free France in America. In the end, on the advice of the British ambassador in Washington, Pleven selected Étienne Boegner, the industrialist son of the French Protestant leader Marc Boegner, to play this role. The other committee members were Raoul de Roussy de Sales, a gifted artist in failing health; Jacques de Siéyès; Raoul Aglion; and Adrien Tixier, a Socialist with strong links to the French trade union movement.

From the beginning, meetings of the five-man delegation were stormy and divisive. Boegner soon made it clear that discussions within the group were futile given that, apart from Siéyès, none of them knew anything about de Gaulle, whose authoritarian and anti-democratic musings (as he saw it) had been clearly set forth in *Au fil de l'épée*, and whose anti-American prejudices were likely to undermine their mission.

Boegner flew to London in June 1942 to discuss American Free-French relations with *Le Connétable* directly. The meeting between the two men was a disaster, both resorting to personal invective before it was over. Beyond the clash of personalities, the difference of perspective was unbridgeable. As Boegner saw it, de Gaulle was incurably hostile to the "Anglo-Saxons" at a time when American aid was indispensable to the restoration of France's position in world affairs;[9] Boegner was in fact so disheartened by the failure of his effort to bridge the gap between Free France and the Americans that he withdrew permanently from any involvement in political life.

Boegner having deserted the cause, Siéyès having proved his inadequacy, and Pleven being summoned back to London in September 1941, de Gaulle ended up selecting Tixier as his chief American lobbyist. De Gaulle chose Tixier because "he had a reputation as a loyal and solid man" and because as a Socialist he understood and could reflect the views of French unions, Communist as well as Catholic, a vital asset given that the social question would clearly be a key issue with the coming of peace.[10]

As Aglion saw it, however, Tixier was from the outset a most unsatisfactory defender of Free France's interests.[11] The new appointee had little support in the United States, even among Gaullists. He made public his doubts about de Gaulle and the CNF (as well as his own anti-American feelings) to compatriots he met there. His openly disparaging attitude toward the CNF which had mandated him were ironically similar to those made by Alexis Léger, who had helped to shape Roosevelt's prejudice against Free France! Not surprisingly given this outlook, Tixier frequently adopted positions at odds with the instructions he received from Carlton Place, as during the grave crisis between the CNF and Washington which opened in late December 1941 in the Gulf of Saint-Lawrence.

De Gaulle had considered the possibility of liberating St. Pierre and Miquelon almost from the beginning of the Free French experience. His interest in the islands was, predictably, matched by that of the State Department which, invoking the Monroe Doctrine, was determined to prevent any European intrusion in the New World. On 14 December 1941, just a week after Pearl Harbor, desperately anxious to keep the French navy in the Old as well as the New World from falling into enemy hands, Roosevelt reassured Pétain that the status quo would be maintained as far as France's possessions in the western hemisphere were concerned.

At the end of November 1941, a few days before Pearl Harbor, mandated by de Gaulle, Admiral Muselier set out across the Atlantic carrying secret instructions to rally St. Pierre and Miquelon, a mission he accomplished on Christmas Eve, to the great delight of the islanders and the enormous distress of Washington.

In the end, *Le Connétable*'s unilateralism only served to confirm negative impressions of his acceptability as a political partner by the White House. It also embarrassed Churchill and exposed the dependency of the British government on strategic decisions reached in Washington.[12] Finally, it angered and frustrated Dejean and made clear that those who attempted to exercise conventional diplomacy on behalf of La France libre were engaged in a largely gratuitous exercise.[13]

Four months after the tense situation generated by Muselier's action in the Gulf of St. Lawrence, another crisis, this time triggered by the British and involving the island of Madagascar, challenged those in charge of Gaullist diplomacy. In the end, determined to secure their sea-lanes to the East at a time when the Japanese were on the borders of India, the British acted alone, invading Madagascar early in the morning of 5 May 1942, declaring subsequently that the island would revert to France at an appropriate time. De Gaulle's suspicions about British motives had now reached a new intensity. As Pierre Brossolette put it following one of the general's bouts of anglophobia, "We had to remind the general on a regular basis that our principal enemy was the Germans because, if he followed his first instinct, it would have been the English!"[14]

By June 1942, de Gaulle had at last been convinced that Adrien Tixier was an ineffective advocate of the Free French cause in the United States, no doubt, the general surmised, because he had too long been out of touch with developments in France. In an attempt to convey an up-to-date image of the combative mood of his supporters inside France, *Le Connétable* selected the nominally Catholic veteran resistance leader Emmanuel d'Astier de la Vigerie to present the cause for La France libre to the American people. The results were highly disappointing. D'Astier had no luck, either in Washington or in the French émigré community, and ended up resorting to a dubious publicity device. Interviewed by *Life* magazine, which featured him on the cover, posing with his back to the camera, and identified only by his code name, "Bernard," d'Astier declared himself ready to draw up a list of French collaborators who should be shot when France was liberated.[15] The impact, six months after Pearl Harbor and American involvement in the war, was disastrous and made the diplomatic challenge for Free France even more complex.

So, with a view to strengthening the tenuous links between the Comité national français and Washington, as well as to dispel his own unfavourable image on the other side of the Atlantic, de Gaulle decided in the fall of 1942 to send yet another emissary to Washington, this time a man with a high political profile, the Protestant Socialist André Philip.

On the face of it, Philip seemed an eminently suitable intermediary between de Gaulle and Roosevelt. To begin with, like most key personalities in the SFIO, he had admired the New Deal. He had come to know something of American life and culture during his two-year stay in the

United States on a Rockefeller Fellowship. He had sent his children to live and study in America. His English was fluent. Perhaps more important than any of these factors, he had been strongly recommended by two key Roosevelt appointees who had observed him in London – Admiral Harold Stark (the president's personal emissary to de Gaulle), and Ambassador John Winant.

No doubt a subtle psychologist might have detected some of the problems which, despite these assets, would make the French Socialist a less than ideal interlocutor with the American president. Philip came from a modest background, lacking the tact and polish which would have better prepared him for a conversation with a Hudson Valley patrician. He tended to adopt a lecturing – not to say sermonizing – style, hardly appropriate when addressing the supremely self-confident leader of the Allied cause. He was a lay preacher in the Reformed tradition, seeing a direct connection between the Gospel and radical political action, about to face an Episcopalian with a Machiavellian streak for whom such a link was less than evident. Finally, despite his political cosmopolitanism, Philip was intimately acquainted with the heroic struggle of the partisans, and not ready to listen in silence to disdainful or cynical references to contemporary French politics, especially when they included a rationale for American collaboration with Vichyites.

Seeing himself as a goodwill ambassador, Philip arrived in Washington toward the end of October bearing a personal letter from de Gaulle to the American president, which he transmitted to Under-Secretary of State Sumner Welles. The general began his 26 October letter by reminding the president that it was the terrible suffering and sheer demographic loss she had suffered during World War I, not internal division and parliamentary corruption, which had caused France to collapse two years earlier.[16] The humiliation which the French had suffered as a result would have been easier to bear had they not felt abandoned by their allies. Should his compatriots continue to feel disparaged, the general warned, they might risk being turned from their traditional democratic path, a clear hint at the possibility of a shift in French opinion toward sympathy with the Communist party and the Soviet Union.

He had assumed temporary trusteeship of the national interest in 1940, *Le Connétable* went on, because France's traditional elites had clearly manifested their incapacity to lead. I am a soldier, he wrote, not a politician, but I have nevertheless rallied the vast majority of my compatriots to the Free French cause. In fact, "we have witnessed the emergence of a kind of mystique of which I am the nucleus and which is bit by bit uniting all the elements of the resistance." There is no question here of my seeking personal power, de Gaulle insisted. We are exercising a purely provisional authority; we are applying the laws of the Third Republic; and we will yield to the will of the sovereign people when they are again free to decide France's political future. Our present preoccupation, the general concluded, is to defend France's interests in Europe and the world. It is with this in mind that we seek a meeting with you to discuss overall strategy.

Ray Atherton, head of the French desk at the State Department, to whom Welles had transmitted de Gaulle's letter, was unfortunately not sympathetic to the Free French cause.[17] The text clearly reflected the general's intention to establish his personal power with the aid of Allied arms, Atherton noted; de Gaulle showed no understanding of Washington's decision to keep the lines open to Vichy, nor could he see that this policy would better ensure that France's empire survived the war intact; finally, the leader of the Free French was obviously unaware that American intelligence concerning developments inside France was just as good as that provided by his own services. The tone of de Gaulle's letter, as rendered by Atherton, could only reinforce Roosevelt's antipathy.

Events following Philip's presentation of de Gaulle's letter in late October added further tension to the atmosphere by the time Philip and his colleague Tixier met Roosevelt almost a month later. The 7 November launching of Operation "Torch" in North Africa, without de Gaulle's prior knowledge, made abundantly clear not only Washington's paramount role in Allied strategy but the deliberate exclusion of Free France from its formulation and execution. On 9 November, Philip, who had taken for granted that de Gaulle had been involved in the operation, made an impromptu radio address to the American people, making clear that de Gaulle and his supporters in North Africa were urging full support to "Torch." Subsequent revelations that the Americans were ready to deal with Darlan and Giraud caused him to feel deep resentment and a sense of betrayal.

Philip and Tixier were given no satisfaction when they made these feelings known during successive meetings with Welles on 12 November and, two days later, with Cordell Hull. As a result, the two Gaullists pressed for an immediate meeting with the American president. A date was quickly found but, when the two emissaries turned up four hours late (an unforgivable lapse of protocol at the best of times), the meeting had to be rescheduled.

When it finally took place, the 20 November exchange between Roosevelt and Welles representing the United States and Philip and Tixier representing de Gaulle soon turned into what might well be seen as the nadir in the always troubled Free French -Washington relationship. After some preliminary exchanges, during which Roosevelt expressed his understanding of de Gaulle's reticence about sending an emissary to confer with Giraud and indicated his willingness to receive *Le Connétable* in Washington at some later date, the mood soon deteriorated.[18] Philip had heard about the base in Virginia where Americans were being trained to act as prefects and mayors in liberated France and made clear that this arrangement was utterly unacceptable to the Comité national français. Then, when the Protestant emissary went on to protest the current American collaboration with Darlan, Roosevelt broke in abruptly. "What matters to me," the president declared, "is to reach Berlin. The rest doesn't matter. If Darlan gives me Algiers, long live Darlan! If Laval gives me Paris, long live Laval! I'm not like Wilson! I'm a realist!"

Years afterward, Philip recalls saying at this point that, as a Frenchman, he had heard the word "realist" all too often coming from the mouth of Pétain and his kind, who used it to rationalize their acceptance of the Armistice and collaboration with Nazi Germany. Philip was in fact so agitated at this point that his jaws broke right through the pipe he was clenching, from which he had been blowing dense clouds of smoke in the direction of his seriously ill host.

Roosevelt responded to Philip's complaints by making doubly clear that, as long as the United States was the occupying power in North Africa, it would make all final policy decisions there and that, until all of France was liberated, the American government alone would decide which officials would administer areas under Allied military control. Tixier struggled to interrupt Philip at this point to explain that Fighting France understood the need for Allied commanders to be fully in charge of military operations but felt that the civil administration might be given over to the French. Philip then burst in to declare that France was not a colony and the CNF "would not allow a single parcel of our national territory to be administered by a foreigner!" For that matter, he added, French North Africa should be transferred to the Committee within three weeks!

Then, pushing undiplomatic behaviour even further beyond the limit, de Gaulle's delegate suggested that, if France were betrayed by those she had considered her allies, she would be obliged to turn for support to the Soviet Union. This was too much for the president who had expected, among other things, that Philip or Tixier would in the course of the conversation express some gratitude for the American commitment to the battle to free the Continent.

When at this point, almost an hour into the conversation, Philip and Tixier began shouting at the top of their lungs and at cross-purposes, without paying any attention to what the president was saying, Welles decided that it was pointless to continue the meeting but, to prevent a total fiasco, he suggested that de Gaulle himself might come to Washington to resolve the vexatious issues that had just been raised.

Relaying his impressions of his bitter encounter with Roosevelt to Aglion, Philip described the president as having been "olympian, biting and disdainful, acting like the Sun King on his throne," before going on to insist (no doubt to Aglion's distress) that, as de Gaulle's emissary, he had given as much he got during the lively dialogue. Roosevelt, the Protestant envoy insisted, seemed unable to understand that the war was a moral conflict between two different types of civilization in which military power was not the ultimate weapon.[19]

For his part, Roosevelt concluded that Philip's behaviour as well as his remarks might best be explained as deliberately designed to alienate him from the leader of the Free French. In a letter to Admiral Stark, who had recommended Philip as a sympathetic envoy, the president commented bitterly, "Why did you insist that I receive that man Philip? He uttered not a single word of appreciation [for the commitment of American troops to liberate North Africa]."[20] Half a year later, on 5 May 1943, Roosevelt wrote to Churchill suggesting that the CNR be purged of "unacceptable elements" such as Philip, whom he had found to be full of ill-concealed personal ambition.

When news of the diplomatic fiasco suffered by Philip and Tixier reached London, Soustelle correctly surmised that both men had come away from it thoroughly devastated; in any event, the telegram in which they relayed their reaction to de Gaulle, Soustelle, and Pleven created the same feeling of anguish in London. And, when Philip showed up in the English capital on 9 December, Soustelle found him "morally traumatized" by his transatlantic experience as well as bitterly disenchanted at the way the State Department, in its ignorance of French politics and its cynicism about moral values in diplomacy, was turning to men such as Alexis Léger and Darlan for guidance in handling arrangements for the post-war disposition of French affairs.[21]

In Soustelle's view, Philip was totally lacking in diplomatic skills and had therefore been from the beginning ill-suited to bring about the Franco-American rapprochement de Gaulle had been hoping for. The man in charge of the largest army in history, Soustelle wrote in his memoirs, had found himself talking to "a wordy intellectual, a Protestant professor of law who spoke to him of nothing but abstract principles." The result, not surprisingly, had been an increase in the American president's contempt for the Free French, seen as "that little band of irritating theoreticians which manifested itself in the person of Philip."[22]

The frustration Philip and his colleagues felt following his failed mission to Washington was balanced at year's end by the high hopes placed in René Massigli, whose arrival in London had been impatiently awaited for months. The most impressive and certainly the most experienced diplomat to join La France libre, Massigli reached the British capital in January 1943, replacing the ineffectual Dejean, who was made CFLN representative to the other governments-in-exile based in London.[23] Born in Montpellier in 1888 to an academic father and a mother who conditioned him to accept the rigorous self-discipline of the Reformed faith,[24] Massigli attended local primary public schools before spending the years 1910–13 at the École française de Rome. Studying under the School's director, Mgr Louis Duchesne, a mentor he came to cherish and admire, Massigli specialized in the history of early Christianity. This academic preparation led to a brief career in 1913–14 as *chargé de cours* at the University of Lille, where Massigli taught a course in the history of religion. Following the outbreak of World War I, the young lecturer joined the French Propaganda Office, where he analyzed the Swiss and German press and developed an interest in diplomacy.

In 1920, Massigli was named general secretary of the Conference of Ambassadors at the Quai d'Orsay; then, from 1924 until 1928, served as *maître des requêtes* at the Conseil d'État. Beginning in 1928, Massigli headed the Service français de la Société des Nations which, among other things, acted as liaison between the League of Nations and the French government. While in Geneva, he helped shape France's policy during the Disarmament Conferences of 1932 and 1933 as well as during the League debates on the Italian invasion of Ethiopia and on German violations of the Versailles Treaty. In the 1930s, Massigli joined "les protestants du Quai," a group of co-religionists in the diplomatic corps.

In March 1933, Massigli was appointed Assistant Director of Political Affairs at the Quai d'Orsay; from 1937 through October 1938 he served as Director. On 19 September 1938, at the beginning of the Munich Conference, Massigli took a stand against the appeasement of Nazi Germany, insisting that Czechoslovakia not be partitioned or forced to yield any territory. His subsequent categorical condemnation of the Munich settlement brought Massigli into direct conflict with the secretary-general of France's Department of External Affairs, Alexis Léger, who became his lifelong nemesis. As punishment for his outspoken attack on the appeasement policy, Massigli was relieved of his post and on 24 October 1938 made ambassador to Turkey in what was in effect a serious demotion.

Aware of the ambassador's commitment to the Republic and its values, the Vichy government recalled him from Ankara at the beginning of 1941, following which Massigli ceased all contact with the new regime.

In mid-1942, frustrated at the absence of effective diplomatic counsellors in London, de Gaulle expressed the wish that Massigli (whose *antimunichois* sentiments he had learned about) join the CNF. The candidate was willing enough, but his airlifting out of France was not effected until January 1943, when Massigli (who had gone underground, protected by the Resistance, following the German invasion of Vichy France in the previous November) was spirited out of Lyon by partisans and escorted across France to a clandestine rendezvous whence he took flight for England.

Massigli was introduced to de Gaulle in London on 23 January 1943. He had not met *Le Connétable,* but knew of his writings; and he had sat in on a pre-war meeting of the parliamentary defence committee at which the then Colonel de Gaulle had made a vain appeal for a radical shift in French military strategy. The general's welcome was somewhat formal, if not chilly. After all, Massigli had taken a full six months to respond to the great man's summons! Moving directly to the business at hand, de Gaulle set forth at some length the critical state of relations between Fighting France and her allies, deploring the way in which the United States had marginalized him, especially during the North Africa landings.

Developments in Algeria reflected an overall American plan, the general insisted. Roosevelt and Cordell Hull were determined that the United States would dominate the wartime strategy of the Allies and the post-war shape of Continental politics; and they had meanwhile made imprudent promises to Vichy. The Protestant diplomat noted to himself that the Free French had not been faultless in their dealings with Washington: among other things, they had needlessly provoked the Americans by liberating St. Pierre and Miquelon without giving the United States prior notice.

His subsequent mixed verdict concerning de Gaulle's diplomatic strategy indicates the difference in perspective of the two men and the difficult task Massigli would assume as Fighting France's commissioner of foreign affairs:

> I would come in time to understand that events often came to pass in conformity with the general's long-range vision which, curving over the horizon, let him know tomorrow's reality before anyone else. Present reality, however painful, even threatening, was of little importance to him; at worst, it might retard the inevitable. The strategist in him was clearly little concerned with tactics ... The genuine disdain for compromise, even for the most legitimate and normal psychological precautions, together with the legends about him and about the fascistic tendencies in

the Gaullist camp which were being relayed across the Atlantic, had created a dangerous element of mutual incomprehension.[25]

Before agreeing to apply his diplomatic skills in the service of Fighting France, Massigli asked for a fortnight's reflection. This being granted, he made the rounds of the French exile community in London (much of which was hostile to de Gaulle) and renewed his acquaintance with Anthony Eden, whom he had met before the war.

The British leaders – Churchill as well as the foreign secretary – were more welcoming to Massigli than de Gaulle, treating the new arrival as "one of their own," an anglophile to boot who, unlike *Le Connétable*, understood the advantages of old-style diplomacy.[26] On 5 February, having completed his round of talks, Massigli met de Gaulle and agreed to become commissioner of Fighting France's external affairs. As he put it in his memoirs, the veteran diplomat was determined from the outset that the responsibility he was taking on should be above party and in no way based on an unconditional attachment to de Gaulle: "Fully persuaded that I would be working within the Committee (of National Liberation) on behalf of France and not in the service of one man's ambition (as some of our refugee intellectuals suggested), I brought the general my acceptance."[27]

Four days later, on 9 February, the new appointee was received by Churchill. The prime minister was still seething with rage over de Gaulle's truculent conduct in the presence of Roosevelt at a conference held in Anfa, an elegant suburb of Casablanca, the previous month to plan Allied strategy following the successful American landings in North Africa in November 1942. Churchill was even considering a total break with *Le Connétable* and had penned a press release with this in mind.[28] After greeting his visitor, he declared that he would no longer deal with the Fighting French leader alone, but treat him only as the spokesperson of the CNF, thus implying a need for radical change in administrative style and responsibility at Carlton Gardens, a change which he urged Massigli to promote. In the meantime, the prime minister made clear, the British government would not accede to de Gaulle's request to leave Britain on a tour of French colonial territories, where he was clearly intent on stirring up trouble. When, three days after this troubling conversation, Massigli ventured to propose to his colleagues that the CFN change its modus operandi in line with Churchill's demand for more transparency and less authoritarianism, his remarks were greeted with a glacial silence.[29]

Massigli, who had arrived in London full of optimism, was deeply troubled by the analysis of Free French relations with the British, which he had heard from de Gaulle as well as Churchill. His colleague Soustelle, no doubt a bit cruelly, describes the resultant distraught state of mind of the foreign affairs commissioner in those early days in London when Massigli would often drop by for a chat:

> Two or three times a day, the door of my office at Carlton Gardens would open to let through a very tall man of almost skeletal thinness, making abrupt and nervous gestures. It was Massigli who had arrived in London after "Melpomene perfumed herself with roses" (the BBC radio signal to prepare the diplomat to be lifted out of France by plane). He sat, or rather threw himself, into an armchair. Everything about his person and his expression revealed the chagrin of a tormented soul. His precipitate and syncopatic conversation was regularly punctuated by outbursts of "But it's sheer madness!" accompanied by desperate shrugs and hands raised to the heavens ... A demonic pessimism would plunge him into the abyss from which he would emerge only to announce yet another catastrophe.[30]

Soustelle's sarcastic comments reflect the feeling of many in the Gaullist camp that Massigli was an outsider, a non-ideological servant of France's interests as he perceived them, rather than an unconditional believer in the Free French cause.

Also, like his co-religionist André Philip, Massigli was a "good European," convinced that, when the war ended, the Continent's political leaders must abandon their nationalist outlook and concentrate on the mobilization of Europe's moral and political resources against the hegemonic pretensions of the United States and the Soviet Union. In this regard, he deplored the absence of any vision of a united post-war Europe either in the Free French press or in the position papers of the Comité général d'études.[31]

One of the first major tasks assigned the foreign affairs commissioner was to draw up a text outlining the respective responsibilities of de Gaulle and Giraud (who had been forcibly brought together at Anfa) in their prospective joint administration of anti-Vichy forces outside Europe. While negotiations between Algiers and London concerning such a power-sharing agreement were in full swing, Massigli had been working patiently to persuade the irascible Churchill to let de Gaulle travel to Algiers. On 23 March, visiting Charles Peake, the prime minister's liaison with exiled governments in London, the French diplomat conceded that de Gaulle was a difficult personality who kept grudges and that, by contrast, Britain's leader was magnanimity itself; but he cautioned that, given the general's overwhelming popularity inside France, it would be ill-advised of His Majesty's government to frustrate the move to North Africa.[32]

When permission was finally granted at the end of May 1943 to move Fighting French headquarters to Algiers, de Gaulle included Massigli (as well as a second Protestant, André Philip) in a small advance party. A few hard-line Gaullists commented sarcastically that the decision to quit the British capital amounted to "a new *Massilia*" (a reference to the ill-fated attempt by a group of parliamentarians in June 1940 to board ship at Bordeaux for French North Africa in order to continue the struggle against fascism there). The sturdily republican foreign affairs commissioner took the intended insult as compliment.[33]

Soon after arriving in Algiers, Massigli established a miniature version of the Quai d'Orsay at the Lycée Fromentin, rebaptized "Le Nid" ("The Nest") by the building's new occupants. Raphaële Ulrich-Pier has described the many challenges which faced the veteran diplomat in this new environment and the compromises through which he tried to resolve them.[34] To begin with, there was the contingent of right-wing diplomats already on the scene, which Massigli inherited from the Giraud administration. To meet this challenge, the commissioner proposed the creation of parallel cadres made up of men without diplomatic training who had solid academic backgrounds and who had played an active part in the struggle against fascism. After consulting with his colleagues Cassin and Mendès France about its legal and financial implications, this innovation was sanctioned by a decree of 26 April 1944, which underwrote diplomatic roles for such gifted Gaullists as the trade unionist Christian Fouchet; Jacques Kayser, a leftist radical; and Olivier Wormser, who became ambassador to the Soviet Union after the war. The latter two were thus able to act as deputies to Pierre Viénot, the CFLN's "ambassador" in London, Kayser helping in relations with the media and the House of Commons, Wormser acting as liaison with other foreign missions and providing Viénot with counsel in matters judicial and military.

Backed by an enlarged corps of professional diplomats, Massigli used calculated prudence in dealing with the Anglo-Americans. This approach was sorely tested in Algiers, where it was as often as not in conflict with de Gaulle's highly personal diplomatic style and purpose. Fortunately in these circumstances, the British resident minister in the city, Harold Macmillan, was ready to play the role Eden had played in London, acting as sympathetic intermediary between representatives of Fighting France and its English-speaking allies, including the heretofore anti-Gaullist Robert Murphy, Roosevelt's special emissary in North Africa. Murphy's successor, Edwin Wilson, more favourably inclined, was unfortunately unable to win over Cordell Hull.

Relations with the Anglo-Americans seemed to take a turn for the better on 26 August 1943 when Britain, the United States, and the Soviet Union recognized the CFLN as the de facto administrator of those overseas French territories which acknowledged its authority. De Gaulle was unimpressed by this concession, but Massigli put a positive reading on it, suggesting in a 30 August memo to the Allies that they henceforth include Fighting France in their plans for Europe's liberation.[35]

The continuing marginalization of Fighting France in the overall orchestration of Allied military strategy was brought home to Massigli on 8 September 1943, when he was informed by Murphy and Macmillan about the terms of the armistice with Italy signed by Eisenhower and General Badoglio on 22 August 1943, to which Giraud had been made privy. The foreign commissioner made his objections to this dismissive attitude known at once, which no doubt explains why, a few days later, the CFLN was invited to name a representative to the Comité de la Méditerranée. Although this Committee, formed to supervise Allied policy in Italy, was to have only a nominal role, Massigli helped launch the diplomatic career of his fellow-Protestant, Couve de Murville, by naming him to it.

The neglect of the CFLN in the evolution of Allied policy in the Italian campaign was a natural derivative of the dependency vis-à-vis the Americans, which Admiral Darlan, Pétain's heir-apparent, had agreed to in a 10 November 1942 deal with General Mark Clark by which, in return for his renunciation of allegiance to Vichy, he was made High Commissioner for North Africa. This dependency was particularly frustrating for an anglophile such as Massigli. It became all but intolerable as Anglo-American plans for the invasion of the Continent began to take shape through the winter of 1943–44. From August 1943 until the eve of D-Day, the foreign affairs commissioner did his patient but unavailing best to persuade his British and American counterparts in Algiers to revise the Clark-Darlan accords, only to encounter delay and unfulfilled promises.[36] In the end, thanks in large measure to the sheer intractability of de Gaulle rather than to the subtler diplomatic approach of Massigli, the accords became a dead letter, as *Le Connétable* noted publicly on 15 May 1944, just three weeks before D-Day.

Under constant critical surveillance by de Gaulle and the more radical members of the CFLN during his time in Algiers, Massigli took some comfort from the confidential letters he exchanged with the Catholic Pierre Viénot, who was acting as the Committee's informal ambassador in London. Over a sixteen-month period (from February 1943 to June 1944), the two men (who address each other with the familiar "Cher ami") provide a remarkable insight into the frustrations they face as devoted servants of the Republic, defenders of French national interests, and champions of a new Entente Cordiale.

During these diplomatically hectic months, Viénot was gravely ill, suffering from a blood clot around the heart and taking morphine injections to sustain a fragile nervous system, but determined nevertheless to carry on. Most taxing of all, the "ambassador" had to deal with Churchill's increasing hostility toward de Gaulle. Rather aptly, Viénot describes the prime minister in the fall of 1943 as acting like an aging "John Bull in love with the France he knew when he was twenty."[37]

In January 1944, in the middle of this period of intense personal frustration, Massigli was much heartened when Harold Macmillan was replaced in Algiers by the equally francophile Alfred Duff Cooper, named British representative to the CFLN with the rank of ambassador. As minister of information in the summer of 1940, Duff Cooper had put the BBC at the disposal of de Gaulle. Although the new ambassador never developed a close relationship with *Le Connétable,* he liked and admired the man and refused to share his friend Churchill's increasing antipathy toward the Fighting French leader.

An opportunity to promote a renewal of the Entente Cordiale came in the fall of 1943, when de Gaulle invited his colleagues in the CFLN to offer their views on the political and economic design of post-war Europe. Submitting his own reflections on the matter on 12 October, Massigli advised against too close a collaboration with the Soviet Union and suggested that the United States would in all likelihood revert to isolationism after the war while Germany would remain a source of anxiety to France, even in defeat. In these circumstances, Massigli urged, a solid understanding with Great Britain was well worth exploring, especially given that, apart from the Levant, there were no outstanding sources of fiction between London and Paris.[38]

The other commissioners having spoken, de Gaulle commented that France must always seek her own interest in the years ahead, with no illusions about the motives of her present or future partners. A Franco-Soviet treaty made some sense, *Le Connétable* concluded, adding that it might be complemented by an understanding with the British. The memorandum drawn up by Massigli on 30 October reflected the consensus in the CFLN in favour of a British alliance, with the rider that a tripartite French-British-Soviet understanding might be even more advantageous.

In the meantime, acting on his own, de Gaulle, who had become thoroughly disenchanted with Churchill and had no illusions about the official American attitude toward Fighting France, had begun to explore the possibility of reaching a separate understanding with the Soviet Union.[39] In taking this step, the general not only ignored Massigli's repeated warnings but, even more ill-advisedly, dismissed as unimportant the lack of any reciprocal interest on the part of Foreign Commissar Molotov or his chief agent in dealing with representatives of the Allied government in London, Alexander Bogomolov.

De Gaulle's bold exploration of a pact with Moscow was not taken up by Bogomolov, who not only did not like the general but listened sympathetically to the left-wing French exiles in London who denounced him as both clerical and monarchist. Unaware of or indifferent to such hostility, de Gaulle kept to his resolve, convinced that, whatever means were required, France must regain her place among the world's great states. (It might be noted here that the general's one-time mentor, the germanophobe and fascistic Maurras, had eagerly embraced the Franco-Russian alliance of 1894).[40]

While defending the need for post-war Western European unity in the Assembly and working bilaterally to ensure that the key to this unity must be a solid Anglo-French alliance, Massigli and his equally anglophile colleague Viénot were deeply distressed by a new crisis between the CFLN and Great Britain which erupted in the Middle East in the fall of 1943. By then, both London and Algiers had become preoccupied with the growth of effervescent nationalism throughout the Arab world. The creation of the Arab League in Cairo, the proclamation of the United Nations charter with its promise of universal liberation, and Roosevelt's indictment of Europe's colonial regimes brought pressure on de Gaulle and his colleagues to decide on short- and long-term responses to the Arab question. Should they try to nip any nationalist movements in the bud, or should they attempt to accommodate the demand for political enfranchisement? There was a clear precedent for concessions: nationalist leaders in Beirut and Damacus had signed an accord with Paris during the Popular Front (when Viénot was under-secretary of colonial affairs) only to see it blocked by the French Senate. To inform himself more fully concerning recent developments in the Middle East, Massigli could turn to an extensive file opened by the foreign affairs department of the CNF in London.[41]

While Massigli was pondering the long-term implications of different approaches to the Arab question, General Catroux, sent on a mission to Beirut by de Gaulle, had persuaded his colleagues in the CFLN to issue a March 1943 decree restoring the pre-war constitutions of Syria and Lebanon. The elections which followed produced nationalist majorities in both mandates. Things came to a head at the end of October, when the newly formed governments demanded full legislative and administrative authority. Concession to this demand would have effectively terminated French rule. On 11 November, Ambassador Jean Helleu, the CFLN administrator in the mandate, suspended the Lebanese constitution and ordered the arrest of the territory's key political leaders.

Following Helleu's repressive action, the British government, supported by both Washington and Moscow, notified the CFLN that they would not tolerate prolonged turbulence in a region of such critical strategic interest. De Gaulle reacted in a note to Massigli that the disorder, which he insisted was being over-dramatically reported, was clearly designed to test French strength. When, to make this point, the CFLN threatened to pull its troops out of the area, Viénot in London signalled that such a move would simply allow the Anglo-Americans to fill the ensuing vacuum and, in a 16 November telegram to Massigli, denounced such a proposed unilateral measure as both retrograde and counter-productive:

> Such an attitude would amount to declaring to the French people, even before their liberation, our acceptance of the basic principle of the Action française; "France and France alone! (La France, la France seule!)." The explosion of gallophobia which I have witnessed here over the last five days is all too revealing. I accepted, even asked for, the posting I now have in order to achieve quite a different result. If we are about to launch a war on England, someone else will have to be found.[42]

To deal with the ongoing crisis, de Gaulle again despatched Catroux to Beirut. The Catholic and pro-Arab general agreed to free the captive Lebanese and, in a 22 November telegram to his colleagues in Algiers, made clear that he would not implement their hard line policy. In a separate personal memo to de Gaulle, Catroux noted, "People no longer see in us the spiritual heirs to the French Revolution ... All the more reason, then, that our political recovery should be brought about on the moral plane, in those areas where we have sinned against the spirit by using force."[43]

Going over the head of Massigli, de Gaulle sent a telegram that same day to Catroux, making clear that the CFLN should not sanction the release of the Lebanese, especially under pressure from London. The next day, Catroux made some concessions to his colleagues in Algiers but nevertheless allowed the Lebanese president to resume office, making clear to the CFLN that he would simply ignore orders from Algiers in the matter. That same day, Massigli read a telegram from the defiant Catroux outlining his continued recourse to personal on-the-spot diplomacy; but, when the foreign affairs commissioner indicated his own support for it, de Gaulle flew into such a rage that Massigli offered to resign on the spot. Subsequent discussion in the Committee was, however, followed by a twelve-to-three vote endorsing Catroux's policies and, by implication, condemning *Le Connétable* for going over Massigli's head in dealing with the Lebanese crisis.

The liberal Catroux was now in a position to proclaim the full restoration of the Lebanese constitution. A month later, on 22 December, the insubordinate general concluded an agreement with both Beirut and Damascus, transferring so-called "shared interests" to the two mandates, thus preserving (formally at least) the ultimate trusteeship over them assigned to France by the League of Nations.

Despite Catroux's progressive intervention, however, the effective end of French control over both Syria and Lebanon would come at the end of May 1945 when General Oliva-Roget, in command of French troops in the Levant, ordered a massive bombardment of Damascus. Earlier that same month, French troops had ruthlessly repressed demonstrators at Sétif and elsewhere in Algeria in what some consider was the beginning of that territory's war of independence. With these parallel measures, any hope that the ecumenical vision of Gaullists such as Catroux would bring about the political and social enfranchisement of France's "fourth religious family" had been effectively extinguished.

Despite the best efforts of Massigli and Viénot, the struggle for political ascendancy in the Levant divided the Fighting French from their British allies until the war's end. Equally troubling for the relationship was the well-founded suspicion in the Gaullist camp that the British and Americans were wilfully excluding them from secret plans for the liberation of France. A 4 April 1944 meeting at 10 Downing Street which brought together Viénot and his advisor J.-C. Paris on the one hand, Churchill and his personal secretary Major Morton on the other, reinforced this feeling. The prime minister opened with the by now familiar assertion that he had been a lifelong friend of France but that he no longer recognized de Gaulle as embodying that nation's values, adding that, while he admired the general, he did not consider him to be a friend of the United Kingdom. Viénot replied by insisting that all France was now behind *Le Connétable* and that, beyond the question of personalities, what would be at issue in France as she was liberated was a choice between the CFLN and its leader on the one-hand and anarchy on the other.

Churchill then reminded his visitors that, since June 1940, he had consistently defended France's interests but that, in the long term, these depended on the Americans and, given Roosevelt's seriously deteriorating health, the CFLN must simply learn to be more accommodating. After receiving a résumé of this meeting from Viénot, Massigli decided that, given its tenor, it should not be passed on to de Gaulle.[44]

On 21 April, the CFLN was informed that coded communication between Algiers and London was suspended as well as the sending of confidential messages through diplomatic pouches. Massigli made clear that these acts by the Anglo-Americans were "an absurd slight" and on 12 May pressed in vain for the need to conclude an agreement dealing with the inevitable problems and challenges that would accompany the imminent invasion of France.

In these extremely strained circumstances, as the British imposed an effective veto on exchanges between the CFLN in Algiers and London, Duff Cooper gave Massigli his word of honour, backed by assurances from Eden, that once in London, de Gaulle would have unrestricted freedom of communication, offering to tender his resignation if this were not granted. Then, during the tense deliberations within the CFLN, which decreed itself to be the Gouvernement provisoire de la République française (GPRF) on 3 June, over the wisdom of de Gaulle's acceptance of Churchill's request that he travel to London on the eve of D-Day, Massigli in turn told Duff Cooper that he would resign from the Committee if *Le Connétable* spurned the prime minister's invitation.

Following the 6 June Normandy landings and the subsequent irrefutable evidence of de Gaulle's popularity in the French population at large, Washington began to press the general to visit Washington. When the GPRF debated the wisdom of accepting such an invitation, Massigli, backed by Pleven and Mayer, urged a positive response. In the end, after insisting that there could be no negotiation of his government's recognition during his sojourn, de Gaulle left for Washington on 5 July. The trip was a great success. In a private meeting with *Le Connétable,* Roosevelt, who had from 1940 on judged his visitor to be authoritarian if not fascistic, was cordiality itself, at least on the surface. Yet, although the path to full and formal American recognition of the GPRF seemed open at last, Washington's decision in the matter did not come for another three months.

On 9 September 1944, shortly after the transfer of the Provisional Government to Paris, de Gaulle made a number of cabinet changes, including the acceptance of Massigli's resignation and his appointment as ambassador to the Court of St. James. The following month, the anglophile diplomat received a telegram from Churchill's counsellor Sir Alex Cadogan informing him that recognition of the GPRF by the United States was imminent. Roosevelt had been holding off on this decision because of his preoccupation with the campaign for his re-election in November but in the end had decided that he might lose more votes than he would gain by further spurning pro-Free French feeling in the United States. Churchill, who had been threatening to recognize the Provisional Government unilaterally, was stunned but hastened to follow suit. In the end, on 23 October, the Soviet Union joined Britain and the United States in granting the GPRF the full recognition de Gaulle and Massigli had so long and passionately sought.

The chance to turn British recognition into a full-blown renewal of the Entente Cordiale came soon after when Duff Cooper, similarly minded, persuaded Massigli that an invitation from de Gaulle to the British prime minister to join in Armistice Day celebrations in Paris would be welcome. Massigli convinced his successor, the Catholic Georges Bidault, who in turn won over a somewhat hesitant de Gaulle, not overly eager to have French attention during the visit distracted from himself. The visit was a great success. Everyone in the Provisional Government, apart from the incurably anglophobe de Gaulle, was in jubilant mood.

In the end, however, despite the persistent efforts of the francophiles Eden and Duff Cooper, Churchill, while sympathetic to post-war European unity, opted to commit Britain first and foremost to the cousinly American camp, while de Gaulle, in parallel fashion, ignored Massigli's strenuous efforts to promote a special bond with Great Britain, favouring instead a pact with the USSR or a loosely federated Europe in which France would play a dominant role. On 9 September, in an interview with *The Times* of London, de Gaulle made clear that, given the differences between London and Paris over the German question and the future of the Levant, there was no possibility of forming an alliance between the two nations.

Concerning this failed attempt to revive the Entente Cordiale as the war ended, the British historian Martin Thomas writes, "The absence of a general agreement between London and Paris facilitated the predominance of the Americans and Russians at the decisive peace conferences of 1945. Another lost opportunity!"[45] The parallel failure by the leader of Free France to establish a friendly relationship with Washington (which was predisposed in any event to regard him with a mixture of suspicion and contempt) was due in some measure at least to the ineptitude of de Gaulle's emissaries to the United States, including André Philip. It would contribute to a durable mutual antipathy.

CHAPTER FOURTEEN

Operation "Torch": Jews, Muslims, and the Limits of Political Ecumenism

In sharp contrast to the aims of those who planned it, Operation "Torch," the American-led assault on the North African coast which began on 8 November 1942, would end up radically enhancing the status and influence of La France combattante.[1] Yet while the liberation of the Maghreb, accomplished with the aid of Jewish Gaullists inside Algiers, was followed by the ascendancy of de Gaulle over his American-backed rivals and the restoration of Jewish rights which Vichy had revoked, it did not deliver to Algeria's Muslims the political and social emancipation which they hoped for and which progressive Gaullists such as Georges Catroux laboured in vain to promote. Gaullism had gathered to its bosom members of France's three traditional religious families; it was not yet ready to welcome a fourth.

The strategic aims of "Torch" were clear: to apply military pressure on General Rommel's Afrika Corps, which had crossed into Egypt in the summer of 1942 and was threatening not only Suez but the entire Middle East; to open a second front against the Axis by using the Maghreb as a base for an assault on the "soft underbelly" of Hitler's Europe, thereby satisfying Stalin's demand for military relief; to dissuade Franco from any thought of seizing Gibraltar and cutting the Allies' strategic lifeline; finally, but critically, to rally the substantial French army stationed in North Africa to the Allied cause or, at the very least, to ensure its benevolent neutrality in the ongoing conflict.

It was assumed by those planning the operation that the French military leadership in North Africa, as well as the notoriously reactionary settler community, would be alienated if de Gaulle were involved in "Torch." After all, *Le Connétable* had been condemned as a traitor in a Vichy court and he had committed troops under his command to do battle with men loyal to Pétain at Dakar in September 1940 and again in Syria, in the spring of 1941. In addition to these military considerations, there was the deep antipathy toward de Gaulle felt by the American president. Encouraged by a coterie of anti-Gaullist French exiles living in the United States,[2] Roosevelt wanted to assure the people of France a free political choice at war's end, uncompromised by what he saw to be the general's authoritarian designs. Finally, the president had deeply resented the Gaullist coup in St. Pierre and Miquelon in December 1941, particularly irritating because it was carried out in the name of a nation which, he felt, was in radical decline.

Resolved to sideline de Gaulle and to conciliate the Vichyite authorities in the Maghreb and the equally reactionary settler community, those planning "Torch" hoped at first to secure the collaboration of the area's military commander, General Maxime Weygand. When Weygand was dismissed in November 1941, they turned in the spring of 1942 to General Henri Giraud, who had just escaped from a German prison. That neither of these men shared the democratic values which had been widely advertised as central to the Allied war effort was a matter of supreme indifference to the planners of "Torch." Either one of them, it was felt, could serve as a "temporary expedient," a pro tem ally until the battle for North Africa was won and the question of what, if any, democratic rights might be granted to French North Africa could be debated.[3]

To prepare the way for a favourable reception from French forces on the ground, the Americans worked through the consular offices all along the Mediterranean coast which they had set up at the end of 1940 to help funnel food to the civilian population. These thirty-three points of contact were under the supervision of Robert Murphy, a devout Catholic who had served under Roosevelt's ambassador to Vichy, the equally pious Catholic Admiral Leahy.

As of January 1942, Consul Murphy and his colleagues had come to rely on the "Group of Five," a cluster of patriotic right-wing French businessmen and army officers who were anything but Gaullist in outlook. Jacques Lemaigre-Dubreuil was an industrialist who had backed the 6 February 1934 Paris street demonstrations against the Republic; his close friend and advisor Jean Rigault wrote a financial column for the *Jour-Echo de Paris,* published in the unoccupied zone; Colonel Van Hecke was a retired army man who supervised the Chantiers de la Jeunesse, a Vichy-sponsored youth organization; the diplomat Tarbé de Saint-Hardouin had served in the French embassy in Berlin; Lieutenant Henri d'Astier de la Vigerie worked in the French intelligence service or *Deuxième Bureau.* To these five would be added in the months ahead two invaluable associates – Lieutenant-Colonel Germain Jousse,[4] who commanded the Algiers garrison, and *commissaire* André Achiary, in charge of counter-espionage in the Maghreb, both of whom were sympathetic to de Gaulle.

A veteran of the security forces, André Achiary had been made chief of Algerian counter-intelligence (*Commissaire du Bureau de Sécurité du Territoire*) in September 1939. In this post he came to know the top civilian as well as military officials in Algeria and acquired a keen understanding of both Muslim and European communities. Like his politically activist father, he was on the left; at the time of the Armistice, he was president of the Jeunesses socialistes d'Alger.

Following the debacle, Achiary, who was sure that the Vichy regime would be ephemeral, waited for an opportunity to act against both Pétain and the Nazis. A regular listener to the 8:15 p.m. Free French broadcast over the BBC, he learned quickly about de Gaulle's 18 June appeal and signalled his interest at once. In October 1940, a British plane left Gibraltar for Algiers bringing Gaullist agents as well as a radio transmitter which Achiary installed in his apartment, submitting the bill to his Vichyite superiors! Shortly afterward, the *commissaire* came to know Lieutenant-Colonel Jousse who, like himself, was impatient to defy the Vichy system.

The conservative military and civilian elites with whom Roosevelt and Murphy were so eager to collaborate were certainly more representative of the European settler community than the tiny band of Algerian Gaullists who were to play a key role during the execution of "Torch." Given the pro-Vichy outlook of the *colons,* Charles de Gaulle's 18 June 1940 broadcast evoked little response in Algeria. Evidence of the reactionary attitude of the French authorities in the Maghreb and of their European constituents had been clear from the moment of France's defeat. The mission of the *Massilia* on which some twenty-four members of the National Assembly sailed from Bordeaux to Casablanca on the eve of the Armistice in an effort to continue the war effort, only to be placed under house arrest, was a foretaste of official Algeria's pro-Pétain sentiment. The British assault on the French fleet at Mers-el-Kébir had turned hearts against any fellow-citizens willing to ally themselves with the United Kingdom.

There were, however, positive reactions to de Gaulle's appeal from two sources. Algeria's Jews, devoted to the Republic which had emancipated them, had felt the newly aroused anti-Semitism of their settler neighbours following Vichy's legitimizing of discrimination; and a small band of *métropolitains,* including two Catholic academics, René Capitant and Louis Joxe, had become anti-fascist in large measure because of their religious upbringing.

As of the 1940s, the Jewish minority in Algeria (roughly 125,000 in all) made up roughly one-tenth of the settler population.[5] The French conquest of Algeria beginning in 1830 had brought with it a promise of religious freedom. This was given an institutional framework in 1845 when the government of Louis-Philippe created Jewish consistories in Algiers, Oran, and Constantinople, placing all members of the community under rabbinical authority. Within a generation, Jews had become commercially active and their sons had begun to enter the liberal professions.

As they joined the economic and social mainstream, Algeria's Jews were increasingly anxious to become full-fledged citizens and thus to be released from rabbinical supervision. This aspiration became part of the agenda of Adolphe Crémieux, the first Jew to be elected to France's Chamber of Deputies. During the Provisional Government of what would become the Third Republic, the Crémieux Decree of 24 October 1870 granted Algerian Jews a comprehensive bill of civil rights. Not surprisingly, the newly enfranchised Jews voted solidly in favour of candidates pledged to defend the often beleaguered Republic in the decades that followed. The settler majority, meanwhile, which had opposed Jewish emancipation, elected Edouard Drumont, author of the virulently anti-Semitic *La France juive,* to represent Algiers in the Chamber of Deputies in 1898 at the height of the Dreyfus Affair.

Algerian Jews, as much a part of the Union sacrée as other settlers, served with honour during World War I. However, the rise of fascism re-excited old enmities. The triumph of the Popular Front and the subsequent Blum-Viollette proposals to offer full assimilation to Algeria's Muslim elites created major unrest in the territory. The defeat of this reform initiative exacerbated feelings on all sides. The settler community damned the Jewish premier Blum for challenging the status quo, while the educated Muslim minority, represented by the pharmacist Ferhat Abbas, was embittered, convinced that republican France would never accept them as equals. In these circumstances, the charge that Jews were behind the assassination of the mufti of Algiers poisoned relations between the two communities.[6] In a vain effort to prevent a further deterioration in inter-confessional feelings, an enlightened minority of ecumenically minded Algerian Christians, Jews, and Muslims came together in the Union des Croyants monothéistes to combat both racism and fascism. In February 1937, a number of Jewish intellectuals led by Dr. Henri Aboulker, a prominent neurosurgeon, revived the Comité juif algérois d'études sociales, an ad hoc organization founded in 1917 to defend the rights and interests of Algeria's Jews in the face of heightened racial tension. Effective lobbying by the Comité, supported by Algeria's liberal governor-general Georges Le Beau, produced the Marchandeau Law in 1939, which effectively prohibited racial and religious incitement until it was repealed in 1940 by Le Beau's successor, Admiral Abrial, a Vichy appointee.

The transfer of power to Pétain was followed by a series of anti-Semitic laws, beginning in October 1940 with the abrogation of the Crémieux decree. Algeria's Jews, thereby deprived of French citizenship, became "French national subjects," inferior in status to their Muslim neighbours who could still apply individually for citizenship. The chief rabbi of Algeria was made responsible for the territory's Jews, who were again subjected to rabbinical regulation. A census of the Jewish minority was taken in September 1941, and laws were subsequently passed excluding Jews from most professions and limiting them to the ownership of purely private property. In March 1942, all Algeria's Jews were told that they must adhere to the General Union of the Jews of Algeria, a ruling that had still not been effectively enforced at the time of the Allied landings. Finally, on a variety of pretexts, hundreds of Jews were arrested and placed in detention camps in the months prior to "Torch." Yet, even in the face of this discrimination, as Amipaz-Silber has noted, the Jews of Algeria were an extraordinarily resilient community:

> Anti-Semitism did not psychologically ravage the Algerian Jews as it did Western Jews. Algerian Jewry, like their brethren in Eastern Europe, were accustomed to anti-Jewish manifestations and did not suffer from an inferiority complex. On the contrary, they did not hide their Jewishness but were openly proud of it and closed ranks when faced with anti-Semitism.[7]

In similar vein, Lucien Steinberg writes, "Jews of Algiers, contrary to many of their brethren in France, were not at all split between their Jewishness and their Frenchness. Since 1940, they reacted not only as French republicans, shocked by Vichy's imposture, but also as Jews attacked directly by it."[8]

This resiliency was quick to surface in the fall of 1940, when a number of Algerian Jews who had been demobilized following the Armistice bought a ship with a view to sailing to London to join the Free French.[9] When the authorities confiscated this and other vessels, Dr. Raphaël Aboulker, a prominent physician who had been involved in the escape plan, persuaded his compatriots that they could in any event better serve their nation's cause by staying in Algeria. If properly organized and trained, they could challenge the para-military power of the Légion des combattants, a *pétainiste* veterans' organization; even more important, they could prepare to participate in any putative Allied assault on the Maghreb. Dr. Aboulker opened a nightclub (*Le Cabaret de Paris*) in the elegant Hotel Aletti as a front for his fellow-conspirators until its subversive purpose was exposed and the authorities closed it down in April 1941.

In the meantime, the would-be conspirators had found convenient cover for their plans thanks to a non-Jew, Géo Gras, an Olympic wrestling champion, who offered them the use of his gymnasium in Algiers. The presence of men of varied ethnic and social backgrounds at the gym gave the plotters the camouflage they needed. As their numbers grew, recruits to the operation were divided into units of five men or less, each group being kept in total ignorance of all others in the best conspiratorial mode. When the challenge came, the units would be brought together to form a full combat-ready company. By the summer of 1942, some of the 250 Jews who were involved in these training exercises were distributing clandestine tracts and inscribing "V" or "Vive de Gaulle" graffiti on the streets of Algiers; others were sabotaging shiploads of supplies headed for France; still others were relaying BBC messages to anti-fascist groups inside Algeria.

During that same summer a Captain Alfred Pilafort, who knew Dr. Raphaël Aboulker, arrived in Algiers on leave from the French army. The newcomer's intention to sound out the possibility of mobilizing anti-fascist resistance in Algeria fit ideally into the bold but amateurish Géo Gras project. The leaders of the combat units based in the gymnasium agreed to serve under Pilafort, giving the conspiracy a clearer military structure and mode of operation. Pending an Allied landing, the priority of the clandestine force would be the neutralization of the work of the Italian and German commissions operating in Algeria to police the terms of the Armistice. Meanwhile, a separate resistance organization was being put together by José Aboulker, a medical student at the University of Algiers, and his cousin Roger Carcassonne in Oran. Aboulker recruited a number of his fellow-students to join the resistance with the benevolent support of André Achiary.

Jean Daniel, future editor of *L'Observateur*, was one of the young Aboulker's first recruits. The child of an army officer who was also a practicing Jew, Daniel grew up revering the agnostic André Gide, supporting the Popular Front, and tending toward pacifism. The shock of France's defeat and the discriminatory legislation which followed it changed all that. One day in 1941, following the abolition of the Crémieux decree,

Daniel joined other students, including José Aboulker, at a protest meeting. Proud of his Jewish background as well as of his status as a Frenchman, Daniel declared, "Since I've always considered myself to be French, I won't allow this country to abrogate my citizenship twice." Aboulker rose to reply, arguing that this was no time to dissipate one's energies by stressing ethnic differences. Taking Daniel aside afterward, Aboulker added that, at a time when Freemasons, Communists, and other potential resistance groups were also being deprived of citizenship, it was both arrogant and self-defeating to take a "Judeo-centric" approach, adding, "I don't like to give my adversary the power to decide the nature either of my struggle or of my death. They wish us to die simply because we are Jews but I will die because I am an anti-Nazi and it will be in a manner of my own choosing!"[10]

Daniel both admired and somewhat resented José Aboulker, whom he saw to be a cold, aloof figure belonging to a community of upper-middle class Jews so self-assured that they could treat anti-Semites with contempt. José Aboulker's ascendancy over the band of conspirators would nevertheless, he conceded, provide unity of command and direction.

Apart from Jean Daniel, Aboulker was able to recruit a number of eager Jewish volunteers including his cousin Bernard Karsenty; Pierre Alexandre, the son of wealthy Alsatian-Jewish industrialists who had fled to Algeria following the French military collapse of 1870; and the brothers Guy and Elie Calvet, who had created a fashion house in Algiers before the war. This small nucleus gathered almost daily in the home of Henri d'Astier de La Vigerie, whom the young Aboulker had met through Achiary. The link with the Group of Five was strengthened when Lieutenant-Colonel Jousse was introduced to the young Jewish volunteers. Finally, when Captain Pilafort, whose Géo Gras organization was being separately readied for combat, was brought into the secret deliberations at Henri d'Astier's home, the chance for effective and concerted action was vastly increased.

As the conspirators grew in number, the small apartment of Henri d'Astier de La Vigerie where they had been meeting became too small to hold them all. José Aboulker asked his father Henri if it would be possible to use their more substantial home as headquarters for planning the rising.[11] The house at 26 rue Michelet thus became the command post for the early November operation. José Aboulker, Bernard Karsenty, and Pierre Alexandre spent a good deal of time during these weeks with Consul Murphy, hoping for news of the arrival of American submarines bringing arms and ammunition for the conspirators. At night, they regularly headed for the beaches, hoping to catch sight of these ships as they surfaced.

While José Aboulker was recruiting friends and fellow-students in Algiers, his cousin Roger Carcassonne was creating the nucleus of a resistance cell in Oran. A number of anti-Vichy officers, most notably Henri d'Astier de La Vigerie, joined this *groupe de choc* as did the abbé Louis Cordier, a Jesuit who happened also to be attached to army intelligence and was thus admirably suited to play double agent.

A direct link between this Oran cell and José Aboulker's group was created when Roger Carcassonne sent his brother Pierre on a mission to Algiers. Jean Rigault of the Group of Five subsequently met Aboulker to work out a common strategy as they waited for a signal that the Americans were about to attack. It was agreed by the Jewish Gaullists and their conservative military partners that a French officer acceptable to both parties (presumably Giraud) would, at an appropriate time, be designated to represent the overall patriotic interest of the conspirators, who would put aside their ideological differences until the Maghreb was liberated.

This link between the Jewish underground and the Group of Five allowed for collaborative action in Algiers to coincide with the expected American invasion. Less important militarily, but of considerable significance psychologically, was the presence in Algiers of two Catholic and Gaullist professors eager to propagate the gospel of progressive republicanism.

René Capitant, professor of law at the University of Algiers, was one of the few well-placed non-Jewish champions of the Gaullist cause in Algeria.[12] Born in Grenoble in 1901 to a Catholic mother who made sure that he received an education in the Roman faith, Capitant remained a nominal if not a practicing Catholic throughout his life. Following his family's move to Paris during his childhood, the young Capitant prepared a career in law, then began teaching at the University of Strasbourg in 1930. During the Popular Front government, he was named prime ministerial consultant for public works. Capitant grew increasingly disillusioned with Léon Blum's non-interventionist policy toward fascist aggression in Spain and openly denounced the Munich pact in 1938. With the coming of war, his friend Jean de Lattre de Tassigny, a St-Cyr graduate and tank expert, intervened personally to see that Capitant was assigned to Fifth Army headquarters in Alsace, where he served as lieutenant in a tank division and where he first met Colonel de Gaulle.

Following the Armistice, Capitant resumed his teaching career, this time at Clermont-Ferrand, where the University of Strasbourg had re-established itself following the German annexation of Alsace-Lorraine. He helped found the resistance group Liberté which by 1941 had transformed itself into Combat. Then, with a percipient feeling that there would be an Allied landing in North Africa, he requested a transfer to the University of Algiers. With the help of his friend and colleague, law professor Alfred Coste-Floret, the move was effected in February 1941.

Capitant resumed his resistance activities in Algiers. Together with a fellow-Catholic, Louis Joxe, he founded Combat-Algérie, the only branch of that key resistance organization outside metropolitan France. Joxe notes that his colleague's contribution was above all based on an exalted moral sense: "His unwavering enthusiasm, his constant demands on himself as well as on others, kept our small band of rebels (*contestataires*) in a state of constant alert,"[13] and his propagation of the republican ideal in a colonial culture which had been all too ready to welcome Vichy authoritarianism was invaluable. Whenever Joxe brought up the subject of Pétain's government, Capitant would burst out, "There is no longer any legitimate authority in France. Everything that emanates from there these days is null and void."[14]

It appears that the authorities in Algiers were fully aware of Capitant's outspoken Gaullism. In any event, his sympathies for La France combattante were made manifest to the students who attended his lectures. While most of those preparing law careers were sons of *colons*, a few were Muslim, including two future ministers in the 1960 Provisional Government of the Algerian Republic, as well as Ali Boumedjel, who would become a distinguished lawyer in his own right.[15]

Whenever, during his lectures, Capitant made clear his conviction that the only legitimate government in France was in London, not Vichy, thereby outraging the settlers' sons in his class, Boumedjel would come to his defence. And when the flag was raised at the beginning of each academic day and faculty and students were expected to intone the Vichy anthem "Maréchal, nous voilà!" Capitant (who insisted that the Marseillaise was the nation's proper *hymne national*) would stand stony-faced, while his Muslim students, wearing the traditional fez, refused to bare their heads. These overt expressions of opposition to the regime resulted in a number of temporary suspensions of Capitant's lectures. But no more serious sanctions were applied. Operation "Torch" would afford Capitant an opportunity to give his Gaullist convictions even more open expression.

Louis Joxe, co-founder with Capitant of Combat-Algérie, was born to parents with strong Catholic as well as patriotic convictions. He describes his mother as a *quarante-huitarde* in outlook, convinced, like many of the participants in the 1848 revolution, that Catholic and republican values were complementary. After a brief teaching career in the Paris area, Joxe accepted a post as *chef adjoint du cabinet* to Pierre Cot, the minister of air in the first Popular Front government. Journalism was, however, just as appealing to the young civil servant as politics and Joxe ended up joining other leftish Catholic intellectuals (including Georges Bidault and Francisque Gay) who had launched the periodical *L'Aube.* Recalling the atmosphere in the editorial room almost a generation later, Joxe wrote, "We were clearly participating not only in a new phase of French Catholic social thought but also in the definitive *ralliement* of Catholics to the Republic as well as in the intense internal debate of contemporary liberal intellectuals."[16] As *Inspecteur des services étrangers de l'Agence Havas* between 1934 and 1939, Joxe was able to expand his personal and political connections. He knew both Julien Cain of the Bibliothèque Nationale and the historian Jules Isaac, and used his influence with the Agency to intervene in favour of these as well as other Jews seeking appointments.

Following the defeat, and sensing that his philosemitism and his other activities at Havas might jeopardize his career, Joxe asked for a transfer to Algiers, where he taught history at the local lycée. Like other liberal-minded exiles, he found the settler community arrogant and irremediably colonialist in outlook. In any event, he saw that the real power in the territory lay with the military, who were also overwhelmingly *vichyssois* in attitude.

What Joxe saw as a rather hopeless situation began to change with the first tentative signs of a pro-Gaullist feeling, partly among those who had come as patriotic settlers following the German annexation of Alsace-Lorraine in 1871. When invited to speak over *Radio-Alger,* he made his patriotic sentiments known, talking in glowing terms of the great revolutionary victory of Valmy in 1792 and of other clearly republican as well as national triumphs. In these bold sallies, Joxe was encouraged by the voice of Maurice Schumann over the BBC, which he was occasionally able to hear. Not surprisingly, Joxe responded eagerly to the invitation to join René Capitant's Gaullist circle. The third member of what became known as a Gaullist triumvirate in Algiers was the Catholic and monarchist Henri d'Astier de la Vigerie.[17]

While José Aboulker and his companions, as well as the three Catholic Gaullists, waited for a clear signal that their conspiracy would be supported by American arms, Murphy's colleagues requested that the Group of Five arrange a rendezvous with top representatives of General Eisenhower to finalize the details of "Torch." As a result, a seaside villa near Cherchell on the Algerian coast was chosen for an extraordinary encounter on the night of 21–22 October between three of the Group of Five backed by the Americans – the Gaullist Colonel Jousse, his superior General Charles Mast, and a Captain Barjot on the one hand, and members of Eisenhower's staff led by General Mark Clark on the other. Two impressions, both of them false, were taken away from this meeting by those representing the plotters – that the American invading force would number roughly half a million men (in the end, some 110,000 were involved, of whom only 35,000 were disembarked at the time of the rising inside Algiers); and that, by dawn on the morrow of the landings, the invaders would relieve the conspirators who were to neutralize the 12,000-man French army in Algiers as "Torch" got under way.

Meanwhile, on 19 October, Murphy had written Giraud, committing the United States to treat France as an ally, to restore her territorial integrity in Europe and the Empire, and to award the recently escaped general overall "command coordination" during "Torch." Giraud replied on 28 October, adding his own condition to what became known as the Murphy-Giraud accord – that the "dissident French" (i.e. the Gaullists) should be excluded from the impending operation.

A week later, on 5 November, in a totally unexpected development, Admiral François Darlan arrived in Algiers out of concern for his son Alain, who was being treated for poliomyelitis there. The arrival of Pétain's second-in-command, and potential successor, added to the rumours of an impending coup.

On 7 November, the afternoon preceding the coup, Professor Capitant and Joxe arrived at the Aboulker apartment, followed by André Achiary, who had been exiled to Sétif for arresting too many German Armistice agents.[18] As the deadline for action approached, only 377 (most of them Jewish) of the anticipated 800 conspirators showed up. Even more alarmingly, none of the arms promised by the Americans had been delivered, which meant that the plotters had to rely almost entirely on bluff. Then, at the very last minute, the anti-Vichy officer, Colonel Esquerré, who was to have led the insurgency, deserted the cause. Fortunately, José Aboulker, armed with the only seriously effective weapon available to the rebels, a Sten gun which had arrived via Consul Murphy's diplomatic pouch, was ready to assume command. As they crowded into the Aboulker apartment, the volunteers were given armbands bearing the letters V.P. which identified them as Volontaires de la Place, ex-servicemen devoted to Vichy, on call whenever public order was threatened with subversion.

As the American fleet approached in the early evening of 7 November, José Aboulker kept in touch with the lead ship by a telephone in his bedroom. Toward 7 p.m., all the section chiefs involved in the conspiracy were brought together, some of them meeting for the first time. Colonel Jousse laid out a map of Algiers in the bedroom of José's sister Colette and assigned specific tasks, insisting that if at all possible no blood be shed during the hours ahead. The group leaders then dispersed, picking up outmoded Lebel rifles waiting for them in a garage just down the street.

At 11 p.m., the plan was put into operation and small "shock groups" began fanning out all over Algiers. An hour later, José Aboulker, in control at the central police station, reported that the city's political, military, and communications centres had all been taken and that Admiral Darlan and General Juin had both been arrested at the latter's home.

Tragically for the conspirators, this swift and brilliant success was followed by a military and political fiasco. To begin with, American troops (a few thousand of whom had disembarked at the nearby shoreline town of Sidi-Ferruch) were circling the city perimeter at a considerable distance from the men they were supposed to relieve. Far more critically from the viewpoint of the conspirators, Robert Murphy, still intent on winning over the substantial French army in the Maghreb to the Allied cause, had begun negotiating with Juin and Darlan! In an effort to induce Darlan to come to terms with the invaders, the consul had declared that there were some 500,000 US troops moving on the city. Unimpressed, the admiral not only rejected Murphy's proposal but even managed to send a message to his superior, Pétain, urging resistance to "Anglo-Saxon aggression." In the meantime, administrators loyal to Vichy in Algiers recovered their nerve. By 3 p.m., a number of conspirators had been arrested and some (including Pilafort) had been killed in street skirmishes.[19]

The limited number of American troops committed to the operation, together with their lack of battle experience, might well have turned "Torch" into a total fiasco. Instead, intervention by the predominantly Jewish shock groups played a key role in neutralizing the 12,000 regular French army units loyal to Pétain inside Algiers and gave the invading forces time to recover from their initial ineptitude. Finally, the transfer of the port of Algiers with its facilities intact would not have been possible without the brilliantly executed coup of the night of 7–8 November. Jacques Soustelle, *commissaire de l'Information* at the time, describes the heroic exploits of the young men led by the "adolescent" José Aboulker in glowing terms: "Never before were more vast and dangerous undertakings discussed with more composure by more amateur conspirators who nevertheless, as proved by their success, surpassed the most experienced specialists in this field."[20]

In the meantime, following his release by the Americans, Darlan agreed to a cease-fire; and, three days later, he was made high commissioner for French North Africa, while Giraud was given command of the area's military forces. The Germans meanwhile, alarmed at the strategic implications of "Torch," occupied Vichy France on 11 November, thereby eliminating what remained of its pretended sovereignty. The struggle to represent France's national interest would henceforth pit Darlan and then Giraud, both one-time servants of the Vichy state, against de Gaulle. Inadvertently, "Torch" had created a situation in which *Le Connétable* emerged as an even stronger champion of a France uncontaminated by collaboration.

This complex political imbroglio soon became simpler. On 20 November, meeting in the countryside near Algiers, four members of Van Heck's Chantiers de la jeunesse who had been involved in the 7 November rising met to discuss plans to eliminate Darlan, whom they saw to be a traitor to the national cause. Twenty-year old Fernand Bonnier de la Chapelle, as zealous a Catholic as he was a monarchist, insisted on carrying out this assignment. In the days that followed, Bonnier contacted the monarchist Henri d'Astier and the abbé Cordier, as well as a number of Gaullists, all of whom urged him on. On 24 December, armed with a revolver provided by Cordier, Bonnier presented himself at Darlan's headquarters under a false name, then surprised and killed the Admiral. Arrested on the spot, the patriotic assassin was shot on 26 December. Cordier, Henri d'Astier, and Achiary were taken into custody at once on the grounds of complicity in Darlan's murder. Whether Bonnier was acting on behalf of the monarchist cause (Henri, comte de Paris, pretender to the throne,[21] had arrived in Algiers on 10 December) or on behalf of Fighting France remains a mystery (Levisse-Touzé calls Bonnier a "Gaullist at heart"[22]). What is pre-eminently clear is that Darlan's removal from the scene set the stage for a duel between his successor Giraud and the far more politically skilful de Gaulle. Renée Pierre-Gosset adds that the Americans' cynical support of both Giraud and Darlan helped increase support for the Gaullist cause in Algeria.[23]

Pleven and Soustelle had learned about "Torch" from the Czech Jan Masaryk at a Soviet embassy party in London on the evening of 7 November. The news was conveyed to de Gaulle early the following morning. The general's first reaction was to wish that the "Anglo-Saxons" be thrown back into the sea for this outrageous violation of French sovereignty. An early afternoon meeting with the British prime minister brought a radical shift of mood, Churchill insisting that the Americans had forced him to keep de Gaulle from any advance knowledge about the North African operation and assuring his visitor that the Anglo-French accord of 1940 still held.[24]

Reassured by this conversation, de Gaulle prepared the text of a speech to be delivered over the BBC that evening. The tone was serene, full of generosity toward the Americans who had demonstrated their contempt for him throughout the planning of "Torch." France's allies were to be commended for helping to ensure: "… that our Algeria, our Morocco, our Tunisia, serve as the springboard for the liberation of France. French leaders, soldiers, sailors, airmen, civil servants, settlers! … Rise up! Help our allies! Pay no heed to names or formulae! Scorn the appeal of traitors who try to persuade you that our allies wish to take our empire for themselves."[25]

De Gaulle's endorsement of "Torch" was a calculated act of political realism. The Americans and their "expedient" – if reactionary – French allies were fully in control of the situation in Algeria. The general had not yet learned of the heroic role played by José Aboulker and his band of young Gaullist partisans in helping to ensure the success of the American landings. Nor could he know at this stage that many of these conspirators were to be arrested following the recovery of Vichyite forces in Algiers.

The repression of the Gaullist elements in Algeria, begun on 8 November, was followed by a larger crackdown at the end of December. The pretext for this new repression was the alleged involvement of the tiny band of Gaullists in the murder of Darlan. This so-called assassination plot was said to have originated on Christmas eve, when José Aboulker invited a number of Allied officers to dinner in celebration of their heroic involvement in "Torch."[26] When the suckling pig which was to be the piece de resistance of the feast had not arrived by late afternoon, Dr. Henri Aboulker phoned to inquire, sarcastically, whether the pig had yet been slaughtered. The dinner, much delayed, proceeded without a hitch. But five days later, on 29 December, just after he had been visited by the American journalist A.J. Liebling, the police showed up to arrest the doctor on the ground that his sarcastic telephone query of 24 December ("Eh bien, ce cochon de lait n'est donc pas encore tué?") was a clear reference to his involvement in the murder of Admiral Darlan which took place at roughly the same time as the dinner party!

Eleven other participants in the 7 November plot were apprehended at the same time, among them José Aboulker, Dr. Raphaël Aboulker, Father Cordier, Pierre Alexandre, André Achiary, and Esquerré. René Capitant narrowly escaped arrest that same day, while Louis Joxe was transported to the Tunisian border and left to fend for himself. During the night that followed, Giraud announced over the radio that those arrested had been about to take concerted action to assassinate Robert Murphy and that as a result they would be shot. Fortunately, Collette Aboulker was able to reach Liebling, who alerted the Anglo-American press corps, which in turn went in a body to inform Giraud of their concern. Although their lives were spared, the detainees were taken on a long trek toward the edge of the Sahara and imprisoned at an army base at Laghouat. Three weeks later, all but the seven Jews in the party were released.

The detention of José Aboulker and a number of his fellow-conspirators was part of a general program of reaction and repression by Giraud and his associates, who were determined to keep in place Vichy's anti-Jewish laws. Outraged at this cynical betrayal of the cause for which they had risked everything, Algeria's Jews refused to return to the discriminatory situation they had too long endured. On 12 November, Chief Rabbi Maurice Eisenbath, who had been asked to calm his co-religionists, declared that any return to the old repressive situation was cause for indignation, not submission. Two days later, he challenged Governor-General Châtel to rescind the territory's racist laws. Châtel replied that neither the Americans nor the Muslims would accept such a move. Algeria's Arabs, he argued, resorting to what had become familiar casuistry, did not wish Jews to be given back their citizenship.

In direct contradiction of this duplicitous argument, a group of Muslim leaders, including Maître Boumendjel and the spiritual leader of Algeria's Muslims, Sheik el-Okbi, wrote to Dr. Loufrani, a leader of the territory's Jewish community, declaring their solidarity with the newly threatened Jewish minority:

> By putting down the Jew, one only brings him closer to the Muslim. It was no doubt assumed that the Muslim would rejoice at the abrogation of the Crémieux decree but the Muslim can easily perceive the dubious worth of a citizenship that the granting authority can take away after seventy years of enjoyment. If there had been antagonism between Muslims and Jews, it would not have failed to show itself during the events of the past few years. Yet nothing has been spared to set the Muslim and Jewish communities against each other.[27]

When Roosevelt's treasury secretary, Henry Morgenthau Jr., who was Jewish, visited Algiers during these tense times for his co-religionists, he asked Murphy to arrange a meeting with representatives of the local Jewish community. Murphy selected a group of conservative delegates who only partly reassured the visitor. Shortly afterward, the anti-Semitic propensities of the authorities became overt when Giraud ordered that Jews were to be kept apart from regular army units and placed in special Pioneer Battalions where they would not carry weapons. As a result, Jews were regularly assigned to manual labour, often under the supervision of the notoriously anti-Semitic Foreign Legion. Those who volunteered were offered a chance to serve in Senegal, replacing men from that colony heading for the Tunisian front.

The vengeful actions of the *Vichyssois* following the failed coup persuaded key members of the Jewish community in Algiers to revive the Comité juif algérois d'études sociales, which had been disbanded in November 1940. Professor Henri Aboulker, re-elected president, informed Dr. Stephen Wise of the World Jewish Committee in New York that the situation for Jews in Algeria was even worse than before. It was vital that the Pioneer Battalions be disbanded. Jews who had managed to escape these ghettoized battalions had already joined Fighting France units in Tunisia. Meanwhile, Jews were being discouraged from enrolling in the regular French army stationed in North Africa, no doubt to prevent them from lobbying for their rights as veterans.

Ironically, on the very day (24 December) when Dr. Henri Aboulker submitted a letter of protest to Giraud, Darlan was murdered by Bonnier de La Chapelle. Two days later, Giraud (who was more openly anti-Semitic than Darlan) was made High Commissioner of North Africa in charge of both military and civilian affairs. The new appointee's race policy is summed up in the cryptic phrase "Le juif à l'échoppe, le musulman à la charrue (The Jew in his little shop, the Muslim behind the plough)"[28] with which he responded to all questions on the subject.

In January 1943 meanwhile, Murphy replaced Governor-General Châtel with Marcel Peyrouton, the former Vichy minister of the interior. This was hardly calculated to conciliate Algeria's Jews since it had been Peyrouton who had abrogated the Crémieux decree in the first place! The new appointee had the effrontery to repeat his predecessor's justification for the status quo by telling a delegation of Jewish leaders on 28 January that the Muslim community would be incensed at the full restoration of their rights at a time when Muslims were still categorized as subjects, not citizens.

Peyrouton, who blamed Léon Blum for the anti-Semitism which swept through France during and after the Popular Front, suggested that the re-establishment of the Crémieux decree would be best dealt with at war's end and promised that the *numerus clausus* affecting Jews in the professions would in time be abolished. This attempt at conciliation was rejected out of hand, and Jewish professional corporations declared themselves unwilling to accept anything less than the integral restoration of their rights.

While ex-Vichyites stalled, British and American reporters revealed the persistence of racist legislation in Algeria, and the World Jewish Congress (including its French representative in New York, Baron Edmond de

Rothschild) also voiced its outrage in a 10 February 1943 statement asking for "the complete restoration of human rights to those who have been robbed of them in North Africa."[29]

These expressions of indignation, together with the defeat of the German army in Tunisia and the turn of the tide against the Axis on the Russian front, caused the French administration in the Maghreb to change course. On 14 March, the High Commissioner declared that all laws governing Algeria passed since the summer of 1940 were null and void but added that, in order to eliminate all racial legislation, the Crémieux decree which in 1870 established a difference in status between Muslims and Jews was abrogated.

Algeria's Jews were anything but happy with this apparent liberalization which gave them only "subject" status – that is, property rights, access to education, and the possibility of serving in minor military positions, but not the right to hold public office. Just as important, Jews would again, as before 1870, be made subject to rabbinical courts in matters of marriage and divorce. Made aware of Giraud's duplicitous move, Dr. Stephen Wise lobbied for American intervention with American Undersecretary of State Sumner Welles, while Edmond de Rothschild publicly condemned the annulment of the Crémieux decree.

One of those keeping a watching brief on the anti-Semitic bias of Giraud and his associates following "Torch" was René Cassin, Fighting France's justice commissioner. As much as any of de Gaulle's team, Cassin was devoted to the principles of 1789 and the republican ideal of a society open to all the world's races and faiths. On 15 March, the day after Giraud's decree, Cassin issued a communiqué declaring that the reactionary general's ruling violated the acquired rights of Algeria's Jews, who had in any event made abundantly clear that, unlike their Muslim brothers and sisters, they wished to live under French civil law. The commissioner expressed himself forthrightly: "Equality between the indigenous peoples of Algeria, whether Muslim or Jewish, cannot be interpreted to produce a levelling down to the lowest common denominator."[30] A week later, in a separate note to de Gaulle, Cassin reminded *Le Connétable* that Fighting France was committed to avoiding all compromises with *vichyssois* elements. And drawing a historic parallel with Louis XIV's infamous abrogation of Protestant civil rights in 1685, he noted that Giraud's rescinding of the Crémieux decree amounted to "a revocation of the Edict of Nantes."[31]

If de Gaulle did not act at this juncture to counter Giraud's decision, it was no doubt in large part because he was preparing to move Fighting France to Algiers and needed for the moment at least to conciliate his rival. Following the transfer of Fighting France to the North African city and its subsequent transformation into the CFLN, pressure to restore Jewish rights intensified. Cassin, who had stayed behind in London until August, was delighted to discover on his arrival in Algiers that his own views about the restoration of Crémieux had been expressed in a report submitted to the CFLN by his Protestant colleague André Philip, the interior commissioner. Philip had concluded, "Jews presently resident in Algeria are not French by virtue of the Crémieux decree but by virtue of the normal rules of civil law, of descent and of possession of status. They are French because they are children of French parents according to the law of 10 August 1927 concerning French nationality."[32]

Despite these strongly expressed liberal opinions, changes in the status of Algerian Jews came very slowly. By July 1943, the segregated Pioneer Battalions were at last disbanded and Algerian Jews were accepted into regular French combat units as the campaign to liberate Italy began. Rabbi Eisenbeth obtained an audience with de Gaulle on 15 September 1943 and was assured that Jewish rights would be restored but warned that it would take a long time to change the anti-Semitic outlook of settlers in the Maghreb. A signal that such prejudices were absent or muted in the Gaullist camp came when Roger Carcassonne was made *chef de cabinet* of the war minister and put in charge of security, including de Gaulle's personal safety.

Under rising pressure from Cassin and the World Jewish Congress as well as from Professor Aboulker, de Gaulle wrote to Dr. Wise in New York on 27 September promising that "in the war for human rights ... we shall continue ... to make it possible for all men to participate in the benefits of victory."[33] Finally, on 21 October, on the eve of the opening of the British section of the World Jewish Congress, the CFLN put the Crémieux decree back into force, restoring to Algeria's Jews the citizenship which had been taken from them since July 1940.

Frustratingly however, although their citizenship had been fully restored, Algeria's Jews were still not free of discrimination. In February 1944, Cassin received a disturbing letter from a Jewish sergeant who had enlisted in an infantry battalion in June 1943 to pursue the war against fascism. After serving under a Free French officer for whom his ethnic background posed no problem, he was now under the command of a captain who wanted Jewish soldiers to be placed in segregated units and who had been overheard damning his predecessor and his "gang of *youpins*."[34]

Meanwhile, across the Mediterranean, as the liberation of France proceeded apace and as anti-Jewish persecution was reaching paroxysmic intensity, Cassin learned with great anguish about the summary execution by Joseph Darnard, head of the Vichy *Milice,* of his old friend and fellow-Jew Victor Basch, president of the Ligue des Droits de l'Homme. To commemorate Basch and to signal Free France's commitment to universal human rights, the justice commissioner reopened the Algiers office of the Ligue. At the same time, Cassin submitted an apposite article ("Les droits de l'homme et La France libre") to the *Cahiers anti-racistes,* an Algiers-based review, including, with his own reflections on the subject, citations from de Gaulle's 1940 and 1941 texts denouncing racism.[35]

If, after half a year of procrastination by Giraud and his American protectors (as well as by a still cautious de Gaulle), Algeria's Jews had recovered their full civil rights, the Muslim majority, which had remained essentially neutral between the collapse of France and Operation "Torch," was showing signs of restlessness following the American landings in the Maghreb.

The leaders of the Third Republic, who had launched France on a path of extraordinary colonial expansion, began in the early years of the twentieth century to consider mobilizing native troops to help face the challenge of an increasingly aggressive Germany.[36] Key members of Algeria's Muslim elite saw army service for their countrymen as opening the way to assimilation into French society. The most celebrated partisan of this cause, the pharmacist Ferhat Abbas, was much encouraged by the Blum-Viollette proposals of 1936 and remained hopeful even in 1939 that this process might still be furthered.

The opening of World War II posed new challenges to the French military in its relationship with Muslim soldiery. Pacifist and Communist propagandists in the 1930s had done their best, albeit without much success, to undermine loyalty and discipline among indigenous soldiers, preaching *insoumission,* acts of disobedience which ranged from insubordination to desertion. Nazi Germany tried to detach Muslims from the French by inciting or encouraging anti-Semitism, again without much success.

A change in attitude toward the colonial administration came about as the war progressed. Reflective of this shift was Ferhat Abbas, who had exhorted his fellow-Muslims to join in the battle against fascism in 1939 but who had become embittered when the French army brass refused to promote him to officer status. A group of more radical Muslims, the Étoile nord-africaine (ENA), led by Messali Hadj, was vigorously nationalist and close to the Communist Party. Dissolved as subversive in 1937, the ENA re-emerged as the Parti du peuple algérien (PPA) and campaigned against Muslim recruitment until its dissolution in September 1939. Radical dissidents with the PPA went even further, creating the Comité d'action révolutionnaire nord-africaine (CATNA) in January 1939 with the aim of proposing an alliance with Nazi Germany to secure independence from France.

In the aftermath of Operation "Torch," German propagandists did their best to undermine the Allied effort to enrol Muslims for the campaign to liberate Tunisia and urged that instead they declare their continuing fealty to Pétain. And, noting the restoration of the Crémieux decree, the Germans suggested to the Muslim majority in Algeria that, while Jews had benefited from the "Anglo-Saxon" invasion of North Africa, the condition of Muslims had in no way been ameliorated. Yet, in the end, despite their persistent efforts, the Germans were unable to cause any significant desertions or mutinies among France's Muslim troops during the war.[37]

If the military repercussions of Muslim restiveness during the war were minimal, the social and political consequences for the future relationship between the European minority and the Arab/Berber majority were enormous. The Armistice of July 1940 radically reduced the number of men in the French army, with the result that thousands of Muslims were demobilized, bringing social dislocation and unemployment and exacerbating tensions with the settler community. Soon after the French surrender, the civil authorities in Algeria reported signs of a *mauvais esprit* in the Muslim population, an ill-tempered attitude towards settlers, sometimes accompanied by a threat to pay taxes to Germany because *La France est perdue* ("France is finished").

Faced with rising tensions, the government of Marshal Pétain was unable or unwilling to develop a coherent policy vis-à-vis the Arabs and Berbers of the Maghreb. The existing political structure in Algeria (local conseils généraux and an overall administration known as the Délégations financières) was abolished, and, in December 1940, replaced with a Financial Commission which included six Muslim delegates, local notables with little or no education, utterly disconnected from the territory's sophisticated elites. Undiscouraged, still believing in the merits of assimilation, Ferhat Abbas in April 1941 submitted a brief to Pétain asking for a series of reforms. This text, in which the pharmacist simultaneously invoked the pacifist Gandhi and the ethnic nationalist Maurras, was essentially a revised, more liberal version of the Blum-Viollette proposals. In a passionately worded conclusion, Ferhat Abbas makes clear his continuing faith in the possibility of bringing about "in the heart of the European community as well as in the conscience of our potentially regenerate (Muslim) masses, a yearning to live together, the kind of shared yearning which, according to Renan, constitutes the founding element in a nation."[38]

Sixteen months later, on 27 August 1942, Dr. Mohamed Bendjelloul, a graduate of the Paris faculty of medicine and president of the indigenous Fédération des Élus, submitted a series of demands to Pétain and Laval as well as to Algeria's Governor-General Châtel. France had blocked all efforts at internal reform in Algeria, the doctor protested, adding that he personally favoured "total assimilation with France," a process which would involve the removal of all existing political structures in which European and Muslims had separate representation.

Following the Allied liberation of Algeria, General Juin was able to mobilize some 30,000 indigenous troops for the ongoing battle in Tunisia. By the fall of 1944, when the struggle to free France itself was fully engaged, more than 134,000 Algerian Muslims were fighting alongside European French comrades.

The conclusion of the leading specialist in the field, Belkacem Recham, is that the participation of Muslim troops in World War II stands out as "one of the rare moments in the history of colonization when the colonized and the colonizer made common cause against European totalitarianism, in the process turning upside down old myths and legends."[39]

While Muslim soldiers serving in the French army made a substantial contribution to the victory over fascism, and although the Arab and Berber population in Algeria remained basically neutral during the war, the political elites which Vichy had done little to appease emerged from the conflict determined to assert their people's right to self-determination. Operation "Torch" encouraged this new assertiveness in two ways: the demonstration of American power added to the evidence that France's imperial role, already diminished by the Nazis, was in radical decline; and the Rooseveltian pledge to oversee the liquidation of Europe's colonial empires encouraged Algeria's Muslim leaders to abandon their traditional assimilationist views in favour of a call for full-fledged independence.

Ferhat Abbas and his colleagues, having made contact with the American authorities soon after the success of "Torch," came up with a new federalist concept of Franco-Algerian relations. Darlan, and, later Giraud, responded by urging the Muslim leaders to earn consideration for any change in the old colonial relationship by committing themselves more fully to the war effort. Ferhat Abbas responded in turn on 20 December 1942 by publishing a *Message aux autorités responsables*, followed two days later with a similar submission, this time specifically aimed at the French administration in Algeria.[40] In both documents, Ferhat Abbas insisted that, before any new commitment to the war effort, the French administration must summon a purely Muslim assembly, which would be mandated to define a new social, economic, and political statute for Algeria which France would undertake in advance to sanction. Neither Giraud nor Governor-General Peyrouton deigned to reply to this bold departure from the militant pharmacist's views.

The silence of the French authorities resulted in what would become a key document in the evolution of Algeria's struggle for independence – the *Manifeste du peuple algérien,* published in February 1943 and addressed to Peyrouton along with copies to the fledgling United Nations, with the obvious aim of attracting the attention of the Allied powers.[41] The authors of the Manifesto made a point of rejecting assimilation, declaring that they were proudly Muslim and wished to remain so and that they were intent upon promoting Algeria's right to self-determination with its own constitution and official language (Arabic).

Seeing the mobilization of Muslim troops as his highest priority, Peyrouton not only accepted the Manifesto as the basis for future reform on 31 March 1943, but allowed fifty-six Muslim dignitaries and elected representatives to sign the Manifesto and established a Commission d'études musulmanes to look into means of reshaping Algeria's social and political future.

On 26 May, however, these same Muslim delegates made public a more radical program in the form of a *Projet de réformes faisant suite au Manifeste.* This supplemental text proclaimed that, at war's end, following the calling of a constituent assembly elected by all the territory's inhabitants, Algeria would become an autonomous state. Meanwhile, the *Suite au Manifeste* noted, the existing administration in the territory (the *gouvernement général*) should be transformed into a truly Algerian government, made up of an equal number of French and Muslim officeholders chaired by the French ambassador, who would assume the title of high commissioner. The *Suite* also proposed a North African federation with no reference to any link to France. This radical initiative was immediately rejected by de Gaulle and the newly appointed governor-general, General Georges Catroux.

Catroux, one of de Gaulle's most prestigious recruits, had met *Le Connétable* in a German prisoner-of-war camp in 1916. During a distinguished interwar career, he had come to know the Arab world intimately both in the Middle East and in Morocco, where he became a disciple of Lyautey, whose fervid Catholic faith he shared. Aristocratic in bearing and diplomatic in style, he possessed the very gifts of tact and flexibility of mind which de Gaulle so obviously lacked.

At the time of the Armistice, Catroux, by then a four-star general, was governor-general of Indo-China. Through his son René, then in London, he offered his congratulations and encouragement to the leader of the

Free French, substantially his inferior in grade. Then, dismissed by Vichy, no doubt in part because of this indication of his disaffection from Pétain, Catroux made his way to London on 31 August 1940. Soon after, he met de Gaulle in Chad and was named to the Conseil de l'Empire. Later, having been selected as *Le Connétable's* delegate-general for the Middle East, he helped orchestrate the Free French attack on Syria in the spring of 1941, promising that territory as well as Lebanon (mandates of France under the League of Nations) their independence as the campaign got under way. Later, Catroux was chief negotiator for de Gaulle in discussions with Giraud at Anfa in January 1943. Then, appointed Delegate of the CNF for North Africa, he arrived in Algiers on 25 March 1943. A little more than two months later, following the resignation of Marcel Peyrouton, de Gaulle named Catroux governor-general of Algeria.

On 11 December 1943, on Catroux's initiative, the CFLN resolved that France's policy vis-à-vis Algeria's Muslims would henceforth be based on a pledge to elevate their social and political conditions to those of the European minority. Three days later, the governor-general announced the creation of a commission which would report to the CFLN within six weeks on the means required to realize this radical change in European-Muslim relations. Four principles were to guide the deliberations of the commission: Muslim elites should be granted French citizenship while being permitted to retain their legal status under the Koranic code; Muslim representation at all levels of political assembly and deliberation should be increased and their suffrage extended; more Muslims should be named to administrative posts; finally, the socio-economic advancement of the Muslim majority should be actively promoted.

In submitting his final report to the CFLN on 4 April 1944, Catroux made clear the visionary aim – the full assimilation of Algeria's Muslim majority into French society – which had inspired the members of his commission:

> As of now, the Committee [CFLN] has before it a real program of social uplift and economic progress aimed at improving the lot of the indigenous Muslim population. The various elements in this programme proceed from a single inspiration … The aim of France here is effectively to assimilate the indigenous peoples within France, to make them French in mentality through an appropriate form of public education and to provide for their leveling upward to us in social and economic terms. This presupposes a large diffusion of teaching offered strictly in the French language. It also presupposes putting Muslims and non-Muslims on a paritary basis in terms of health and public assistance, working conditions, social benefits,

> housing, credit and a guaranteed minimum wage in both the industrial and agricultural sectors. In other words, the policy of assimilation is based on the promotion of social equality which is in any event demanded by the humanistic outlook of the French nation. It is on the basis of these fundamental precepts (to which should be added the pressures produced by Algeria's well-known demographic expansion), that the commission on Muslim reforms has based its conclusions.[42]

Tragically for future Franco-Algerian relations and for any long-term understanding between the European minority and the Muslim majority in the territory, this bold set of reform proposals, building on the failed Blum-Viollette reforms of 1936, was given only partial endorsement and inadequate funding.[43] Meanwhile, on 14 March 1944, a new organization, the Amis du Manifeste de la liberté, was founded with the express aim of promoting the emergence of an Algerian nation federated with a post-colonial France.

Events outside Algeria and beyond French control contributed to the new headiness of Algerian nationalists. On 22 March 1945, the Arab League was founded, offering Algeria's Muslims the dream of freedom in communion with the whole Arab nation, while those inspired by religious fervour envisioned an International Islamic Brotherhood. This sense of rising expectations was further encouraged by the high-flown rhetoric at the founding meeting of the United Nations in San Francisco (April through June 1945), when promises were made to end colonial oppression and give freedom to all those aspiring to national liberation.

Catroux's fear that the failure to meet these rising expectations would provoke a violent response was borne out in May 1945. On the first of the month, the ritual day for working-class and revolutionary celebration, impatient nationalists called for Algerian independence. Demonstrations followed throughout the territory, bringing retaliation from the French military and police. Eager to take advantage of this popular mobilization, radical nationalists called for a general insurrection on 8 May. The rising which followed that day at Sétif in the Kabylia region east of Algiers degenerated into a bloody riot. Some 8,000 to 10,000 Muslims, many of them armed, some brandishing replicas of the green-and-white banner first hoisted 110 years earlier by Abd-el-Kader, leader of what was to be a jihad against France's colonial invaders, provoked terrible repression. The army brought in tanks and planes and, before the confrontation was over, more than 100 Europeans and thousands of Muslims had been killed or wounded and several nationalist leaders, including Ferhat Abbas and Messali Hadj, had been arrested. Charles-Robert Ageron, the leading

French authority on modern Algeria, describes the clash at Sétif as "a failed attempt at national insurrection" while Algerian historians identify Sétif as the opening shot in their war of independence.

However traumatic, the violent clash at Sétif did not end efforts to find a solution to the complex relationship between France and Algeria and between the territory's Muslim majority and European minority. During sessions of the Provisional Consultative Assembly, which moved from Algiers to Paris in September 1944, Dr. Bendjelloul tried in vain to persuade his fellow-delegates to vote for a single integrated electoral college along the lines proposed by Catroux's commission. On 17 August 1945, on a proposal by José Aboulker, the Assembly, maintaining the former dual college structure, agreed to award the Muslim electoral college the right to choose as many deputies to the National Assembly in Paris as its European counterpart. However generous in intention, this grant of equal but separate representation subverted Catroux's basic principle. And, giving parity to the European minority which was intimately linked to the settlers' lobby in Paris, Aboulker and his colleagues were offering the *colons* an effective veto over any change in the status quo.

During the second Constituent Assembly meeting in Paris between June and November 1946, a proposal that France and Algeria form a federal union was soundly defeated, even though Ferhat Abbas was willing, in return for this transformation of the old colonial relationship, to accept the double college system. In the final vote, a majority of the deputies representing Algeria rejected this formula, thus repudiating the principles set forward in the 7 March ordonnance. They did so, it should be noted, with de Gaulle's blessing.

Orchestrated by Americans, with the support of a small but dedicated band of mostly Jewish Gaullists inside Algiers, Operation "Torch" had been less than brilliantly executed. Unable to seize the city swiftly, the invaders had reached a deal with Vichy's local representatives, whom Roosevelt in any event favoured. The new lords of the city had remained passive as their Vichyite colleagues rounded up, detained, and humiliated their would-be allies. Vigorous lobbying by the WJC, together with the removal of Darlan and the ineptitude of Giraud, had resulted in the restoration of Jewish rights in Algeria. The lot of the Muslim majority was, however, left unsettled in spite of urgent pleas by moderate Algerian nationalists and the liberalizing efforts of Catroux. The insurrection of May 1945 followed. A decade later, the Gaullist Jacques Soustelle would make a vain attempt to impose the radical integration of Algeria with France which Catroux had done his best to promote.

CHAPTER FIFTEEN

From Mystique to Politique: The Emergence of a Gaullist Administration

In London, where he was kept long after the success of Operation "Torch," *Le Connétable* declared on 2 January 1943 that the interests of France required the creation of "an enlarged provisional central authority based on the principle of national unity, inspired by a fighting spirit and a desire for liberation and guided by the laws of the Republic until the nation is able to make known its will."[1] This bold demand was seriously challenged at a conference two weeks later at Anfa, an elegant residential suburb of Casablanca, where Churchill and Roosevelt met to discuss wartime strategy. The role of French forces in the ongoing conflict and the future disposition of France itself were secondary issues for the "Anglo-Saxon" heads of government.

Giraud showed up at Anfa on 17 January accompanied by ferociously anti-Gaullist advisors. He made clear to his American sponsors that, while he had no objection to reaching an accord with de Gaulle, "the rebellious spirits from 1936" with whom his rival had surrounded himself in London ought clearly to be kept at arm's length.[2] *Le Connétable* arrived at Anfa on 22 January, accompanied by four Catholic counsellors – Catroux and Palewski would guide him in matters diplomatic, while Admiral d'Argenlieu and Boislambert (who had recently escaped from the prison camp where he had been held since the failed coup at Dakar) would provide military advice. From the beginning of his stay in Morocco, de Gaulle was made to understand that, although he was on sovereign French soil, he was effectively in the custody of the Americans.

De Gaulle and Giraud met on 23 January but failed to reach an understanding about how they might concert their efforts in the common cause. Nevertheless, an "Anfa Memorandum" signed by Roosevelt, Murphy, and Giraud the next day proclaimed that de Gaulle and his rival had reached an agreement which implicitly recognized Giraud's superior authority. Outraged when he learned of this text, de Gaulle penned his own "Testament d'Anfa," which he transmitted through the loyal Boislambert to Commandant Loys Tochon, a former student who was on garrison duty at Casablanca.[3]

Backed by his four advisors, de Gaulle refused to sign the final communiqué announcing the results of the Anfa meeting, including the statement that he and Giraud had agreed to form a committee to administer France's imperial interests for the duration of the war. Nevertheless, albeit reluctantly, he agreed to pose for a photograph with Giraud in the presence of Churchill and Roosevelt, so that the appearance of harmony in the French camp might be presented for propaganda reasons. Afterward, he drew up his own communiqué expressing his solidarity with Giraud in pursuing the battle for French sovereignty and democracy. Giraud agreed to sign the text provided the words *libertés humaines* replaced the phrase *principes démocratiques.*

Relations between de Gaulle and the "Anglo-Saxons" reached a new low following the Anfa conference. Churchill talked of the need to marginalize de Gaulle politically and to restructure the CNF so that more malleable figures could play a key role, while Roosevelt discussed with his wartime confidants the creation of a new state ("Wallonia") based on the areas straddling France, the Low Countries, and Germany. Unaware of these distressing developments, de Gaulle agreed with the CNF that Catroux be dispatched to Algiers to resume discussions with Giraud about power sharing. There were, however, de Gaulle made clear, areas in which no compromise with his rival was possible: "I represent for France a certain number of ideas: the Resistance, the battle against Vichy and the punishment of collaborators. If I were to go to Algiers without a guarantee that these problems are to be dealt with, I would betray the confidence placed in me. And I cannot betray France."[4]

Early in February, Soustelle expressed his concern at the reactionary policies which Giraud was continuing to pursue unilaterally, without any prior consultation with Catroux. The American-backed general was clearly intent on consolidating "a *pétainiste* regime without Pétain" supported by Vichy appointees.[5] In a confidential note of 17 February, Soustelle reminded de Gaulle that he, not Giraud, represented French legitimacy and that this legitimacy was based, not only in the revolutionary proclamation of 18 June, but on the mandate he had been given by the Resistance. Meanwhile, raw power politics dominated the Mahgreb, where Machiavelli and Talleyrand were in fashion, while "for us, the moral basis of Fighting France is our reason for being, our armor and our treasure."[6]

On 30 May, accompanied by Massigli, Philip, and Palewski, de Gaulle landed at Boufarik airport near Algiers, where he was greeted with an insulting "Bonjour, Gaulle!" by Giraud. As *Le Connétable* recalled years later, in the battle for dominance which was about to begin, his adversary possessed all the apparent military, political, financial, administrative, and propaganda advantages.

The day after his arrival, de Gaulle made clear that the CNF would cede no power except to a body pledged to establish political control over the military, to defend French sovereignty, and to insist on the dismissal of North Africa's Vichy-appointed governors. This obduracy produced one immediate result: *Le Connétable* received a letter of resignation from Marcel Peyrouton, the Vichy-appointed governor-general of Algeria, who had earlier served as Pétain's interior minister. De Gaulle unwisely accepted the resignation without consulting his colleagues. A brief crisis followed on 2 June when rumours of a putsch against de Gaulle circulated throughout Algiers.

The next day, emerging from an atmosphere of near civil war, de Gaulle seized the initiative, proclaiming unilaterally the creation of a Comité français de la libération nationale (CFLN). The new body, whose presidency de Gaulle agreed to share with Giraud, would guide France's wartime efforts while exercising sovereign control over all French territories already freed from Vichy control. The CFLN, de Gaulle made clear, would yield power to any future provisional government constituted in conformity with the laws of the Republic. Meanwhile, it was pledged to work toward the restoration of the nation's traditional liberties.

As finally constituted on 7 June, the CFLN was made up of partisans of the two rival generals. From the beginning, however, supporters of de Gaulle formed a clear majority in the new body and occupied its key administrative posts. Gaston Palewski was *directeur du cabinet* (private secretary) to the co-presidents and Louis Joxe, veteran of the small band of de Gaulle's supporters in Algeria and a participant in the November 1942 putsch, was the Committee's secretary-general. René Massigli was assigned the foreign policy portfolio and General Catroux was given Muslim Affairs. Pleven was put in charge of colonial policy while Philip took over domestic affairs.

Two recent converts to the Gaullist cause, both of them republicans with typically anti-clerical and anti-militarist prejudices, were chosen to sit on the CFLN, giving that body an added leftward tilt. Henri Bonnet, named to the information or propaganda portfolio, had been president of the Institute of Intellectual Cooperation, an organ of the League of Nations, before the war. He arrived in London just days after de Gaulle's 18 June appeal but, like most of the French intellectual community then in Britain, was deeply suspicious of a general with political ambitions.

Rather than join Free France, Bonnet spent his first weeks in London trying to organize a Centre français d'études politiques et économiques which would put the case for the preservation of French democracy to those trapped inside the Vichy regime. This effort proving fruitless, Bonnet left for the United States where, after some reflection, he joined France Forever, a New York-based pro-Free France organization. Summoned to Algiers, Bonnet, now fully converted to the Gaullist cause, successfully oversaw the propaganda battle against the *giraudistes*.

The second neophyte Gaullist in the CFLN, Adrien Tixier, an outspoken Socialist, was given responsibility for labour and social welfare in the newly formed crypto-ministry. Wounded in World War I, he was serving as deputy director of the International Labour Organization in Washington in 1939. Although he shared Bonnet's doubts about de Gaulle's democratic credentials, Tixier accepted the general's request that he replace René Pleven in Washington in the fall of 1941. Only in April 1942, during a lengthy sojourn in London, when he had a chance to talk with René Cassin and Christian Pineau, did Tixier become a true convert to the cause. Summoned to Algiers to deal with social and economic issues, he served on the CFLN as an able advocate for the French working class and for a post-war program of social democracy.

By contrast with de Gaulle's partisans on the CFLN, Giraud's supporters were clearly in the minority. General Joseph Georges, who had shared supreme command with General Maurice Gamelin during the debacle of 1940 and had been spirited out of France in May 1943 at the request of Churchill, who hoped that he might play a key role in a new anti-Vichy government-in-exile, was a *commissaire d'État* on the Committee. Georges did his best, if not very effectively, to back Giraud in the Committee's deliberations. Like his sponsor, he was dropped from the CFLN in November.

Dr. Jules Abadie, a surgeon from Algiers with a colonel's rank in the French army, was put in charge of justice (replacing Cassin, still in London) as well as education and public health. His nominal presence in the Giraud camp did little to alter the political balance on the CFLN. By contrast, three figures of proven administrative competence, two of whom might best be described as *giraudistes gaullisants*, were given substantial administrative responsibilities. Maurice Couve de Murville's skills in handling the finance portfolio have already been noted. René Mayer, a practising Jew, was given responsibility for the reorganization of the nation's merchant marine. Jean Monnet, who had served as Roosevelt's chargé de mission in the Giraud camp in Algiers after working for the American government's wartime supply administration since 1940, was given responsibility for the reorganization of armaments, supplies, and post-war reconstruction.

Monnet found working with de Gaulle extremely difficult. He admired the general's overall strategic perceptions but deplored his fits of pique. The view of *Le Connétable* which he had already developed in London in 1940 was reinforced in Algiers. "His impatience and intolerance would seem to predispose him to seek certain forms of personal power,"[7] Monnet concluded before accepting an offer to go to the United States in mid-November to take up a post as administrator for France of the United Nations' Relief and Reconstruction program (UNRRA). Once in Washington, however, Monnet also did his best to get the Americans to recognize the CFLN and to modify Washington's plans to impose its own currency in France after D-Day.

Born in Paris in 1895 to a devoutly Jewish businessman, René Mayer was, on his father's side, the grandson of the Grand Rabbi of Paris. His mother's family was linked to the Rothschilds. The young René attended the Lycée Carnot before studying for a *licence* in both law and letters at the University of Paris. He served with distinction in the First World War, winning the Croix de guerre and being made a Grand Officer of the Legion of Honour. After acting as its auditor during the early 1920s, Mayer was made a *maître des requêtes* on the Conseil d'État. Mayer's public career included a role as a consultant for the Port of Strasbourg, as secretary-general on the superior council of France's rail network, as vice-president of the Chemin de Fer du Nord, and as professor at the École libre des Sciences politiques.

Mobilized in 1939 as a commissioner, then as chef de mission, of the Arms Ministry's London office, Mayer found himself in Canada at the time of France's collapse.[8] He made his way back to France through the United States and Spain, anxious to comply with Vichy legislation requiring all French nationals to return to the homeland. While in Madrid, he told friends and associates that he had decided not to join de Gaulle out of a sense of obligation to his co-religionists, whose uncertain fate depended on Vichy and the Nazis.

Back in Paris, Mayer rejoined his family and, having been demobilized, found himself subject to the *Statut des juifs*, promulgated on 19 October 1940. Since the new legislation precluded him from continuing to engage in any of his pre-war professional activities, Mayer depended on the generosity of colleagues, who arranged for him to serve on the board of the Compagnie générale de Navigation rhénane, the Wagons-Lits, and other enterprises, and to move about the country with appropriate documentation. His itinerant business activity allowed Mayer to maintain contact with the increasingly anxious Jewish communities in Marseille and Lyon.

The situation of French Jews grew even more tense on 29 November 1941 when the Vichy government created the Union générale des Israélites de France (UGIF), in which all members of the Jewish minority were obliged to register. In mid-December, after reports reached Mayer of the deportation and execution of Jews in the German-occupied zone, he headed to Marseille to discuss the situation with the city's Comité israélite.

Early in 1942, Mayer received a summons from Xavier Vallat, Vichy's *commissaire general aux affaires juives*, which he ended up ignoring without reprisal. There followed a three-month period of relative calm; then, after Pétain named Pierre Laval head of government, Mayer decided to leave France whenever the opportunity presented itself. The German occupation of Vichy-held territory following the Allied invasion of North Africa made departure an urgent necessity. Before leaving, Mayer did his best to ensure the survival of his wife and daughter by arranging that they be given residency permits in Monaco, then left for Perpignan and, after a hazardous passage across the snow-covered Pyrenees, found his way to Barcelona.

Arriving in Madrid early in February 1943, the reluctant exile sent a telegram to Fighting French headquarters in London putting himself at the disposal of de Gaulle. Receiving no response, he made the same offer to Giraud, who invited him to come at once to Algiers. On 7 March 1943, Mayer reached the North African capital, where he found his old friend Jean Monnet.

Named secretary of communications in the Giraud administration on 26 March, Mayer set about reorganizing the civil as well as military transportation grid of Algeria and Morocco, including the rail network, civil aviation, the merchant marine and, later, the post office. When de Gaulle arrived in Algiers on 30 May, Mayer had clearly identified himself as a *giraudiste*, an effective member of the team the United States counted on to maintain social peace in the area and to collaborate in the forceful prosecution of the Allied war effort.

Given that Giraud's supporters on the CFLN – General Georges, Dr. Abadie, Monnet, and (less categorically) Couve de Murville and Mayer, were in the minority, de Gaulle ventured on 8 June to repeat his demand that civilian control be established over the army. When Giraud refused, *Le Connétable* wrote a letter of resignation to each of his colleagues on the CFLN. A week later, backed by threats of action against de Gaulle by Churchill and Roosevelt, Giraud and Georges urged the Committee to accept this offer to resign. Two days later, assured that his views would soon be reinforced by the arrival of some of the CFLN *commissaires* who had remained in London, de Gaulle resumed the co-presidency of the Committee. A tentative compromise worked out on 22 June awarded Giraud overall command of the soon to be merged North African and Fighting French forces, while granting de Gaulle direct supervision of the latter. This compromise, backed by several *giraudistes* as well as all the *gaullistes* on the CFLN, put an end to all efforts by the British and Americans to eliminate de Gaulle.

Still uncertain about the wisdom of accepting this compromise, which was endorsed by a bare majority in the CFLN, de Gaulle had a stormy conversation with André Philip on 26 June in which he again expressed an inclination to resign. The following morning, Philip penned a brutally frank letter to the general, pointing out that, if he stuck to this resolve, Giraud or someone else would take over the presidency of the CFLN, which would inevitably become an instrument of American policy. You have been the incarnation of our nation's unity above class and party divisions, Philip wrote. Your departure would signal a renewal of old social conflicts and political partisanship. On the other hand, if your persistent threat to resign is merely a ploy to force us to recognize your omnipotent authority, the result will be even more catastrophic for our democratic cause.

Philip then proceeded to give the general a severe lecture on democratic governance. If your decision to resign was based on a refusal to allow for free debate about policy matters, an open vote on the CFLN, and the assumption of collective responsibility for the result, then you are ignoring one of the most fundamental principles of democratic rule. Your decision in the Peyrouton case, when you acted arbitrarily and on your own, is a case in point. What was needed before each meeting of the Committee, Philip pursued, was a caucus of the Gaullist group to think through their position and agree to hold to it.

The Protestant commissioner pointed out that, quite apart from tactical faults, there was a purely human flaw in the general's personality that needed correcting: de Gaulle simply refused to see his colleagues on the

Committee as equals. In the more informal circumstances that obtained in London, this might have been tolerated, but in the radically different situation in Algeria such an attitude was unacceptable.

Toward the end of this extraordinary letter, Philip charged the general with failing to act in line with the Christian values both men shared:

> To begin with, you have total disdain for human nature. I can understand this in light of the disillusionment and suffering which you have experienced but, as a Christian, you should scarcely be troubled by cowardice, ingratitude and other manifestations of human sin. Throughout history, both the Christian and democratic traditions have always observed a deep respect for, even a degree of confidence in, humankind. Since you do not appear to share this fundamental respect, this keeps you from having a democratic outlook.[9]

Whatever influence Philip's letter may have had upon him, de Gaulle returned to the Committee. Circumstances soon enough justified this decision. Giraud in fact helped assure his own political eclipse by visiting the United States and the United Kingdom in July, allowing de Gaulle to act as de facto president in his absence.

On Bastille Day 1943, with Giraud out of the picture, de Gaulle was greeted with rapturous acclaim in front of a huge crowd at the Forum, the principal public meeting place in Algiers. As though to signal the coming together of the Two Frances in the mixed throng of European settlers and Muslims who had come to hear him, the general invoked the protection of "Notre Dame la France" following the singing of the Marseillaise. The scene thrilled Soustelle, who saw in it the communion of a regenerate multi-ethnic Algeria devoted to France and the ideals of 1789;[10] the memory of that moment would inspire him when he took on the task of governor-general of the territory in 1955. De Gaulle himself was sufficiently encouraged by the spontaneous response to his 14 July speech that he henceforth acted as de facto leader of the CFLN. Lacouture speaks of this shift as the founding moment of "l'État gaulliste," the emergence of a hegemonic Gaullist government.[11] To transform psychological victory into reality, *Le Connétable* proclaimed himself sole president of the CFLN on 31 July, while confirming Giraud as commander-in-chief of French forces in the field. Diplomatic success soon followed. On 26 August, the Soviet Union recognized the Committee, while Britain and the United States offered a conditional but symbolically significant form of recognition.

Returning to Algiers at the end of July, and finding himself very much on the defensive, Giraud agreed to replace the rotating co-presidency of the CFLN with a clear division of powers which would allow him to retain nominal control of matters military under the supervision of a Comité de défense nationale while conceding high policy in political affairs to de Gaulle. Then, early in September, following the signing of an armistice with Italy and a subsequent rising of resistance groups on Corsica which he had orchestrated, Giraud made one last effort to outflank his rival politically by promoting the island's liberation unilaterally. The CFLN countered by appointing its own civil personnel, including the faithful Gaullist François Coulet, to take over the territory's administration.

Incensed by Giraud's duplicity, de Gaulle on 18 September attempted in vain to end the increasingly untenable dyarchy. A week later, two of Giraud's original backers, Couve de Murville and René Mayer, proposed the creation of a *commissariat de la défense* and a reduced role for Giraud in overall policy-making, in effect preparing the ground for a unified executive under de Gaulle. It was two months, however, before the *ex-pétainiste* general and his most loyal supporter, General Georges, were finally removed from the CFLN following a 6 November request that all members of the Committee submit their resignations to de Gaulle to allow for a comprehensive administrative shuffle.

While Giraud was being slowly marginalized within the CFLN, de Gaulle proceeded, beginning in September 1943, to add a number of representatives from the Resistance recently arrived from France to positions on the Committee. François de Menthon, a Christian democrat, co-founder of the movement Combat and key member of the Comité général d'études, became *commissaire de la justice* in a 9 November "cabinet shuffle." André le Troquer, Socialist deputy and defence lawyer for Léon Blum during the Riom trials, was given the war and air portfolios. René Capitant, organizer of Algeria's Gaullists and a key figure in the 7–8 November 1942 putsch, was entrusted with education. Henri Frenay, who hoped for a more significant appointment, was put in charge of prisoners of war, deportees, and refugees. The veteran André Diethelm became commissioner for supply and production.

Meanwhile, even without Giraud, the conservative influence, represented within the CFLN by men such as Massigli, Mayer, and Monnet, was reinforced in November 1943 with the arrival of the veteran Radical politician Dr. Henri Queuille, an agnostic. A member of the Reynaud government in 1940, Queuille had escaped to London in April 1943 in a plane which also carried Emmanuel d'Astier. From the beginning, he insisted that he was joining Fighting France in his own name, not as a representative of the Radical party.

Having assumed that there was an ideologically diverse coalition around de Gaulle, Queuille was distressed to learn that the general was surrounded by what he describes as an intransigent band of partisans, including Diethelm, Philip, Pleven, and Schumann. Despite his reservations about the presence of these militants in Fighting France, Queuille, while still in London, accepted a post as president of the Commission d'embarquement, created by the CFLN in May 1943 to help plan supplies for what would become the D-Day operation a year later.

In August 1943, Queuille travelled to Algiers, where he would do his best to temper what he saw as a Socialist plot to achieve hegemonic control of the external resistance. Not surprisingly, given this outlook, he was gratified that, after moving to Algiers, de Gaulle had come under the moderating influence of men such as Massigli, Mayer, and Monnet. Named to sit as a delegate from the Radical party to the Constituent Assembly, he did battle there against Philip, Tixier, and Pierre Bloch, speaking in favour of the broadest possible coalition in the battle against fascism and condemning what he saw to be the partisan "Popular Front atmosphere" in Algiers, urging that those who had deserted in 1940 be pardoned and that even those who had been misled into supporting Vichy be considered for inclusion in the struggle to redeem France.[12]

Queuille's prestige as a "notable" who had served in a number of pre-war governments, as well his natural sense of political balance, led to his being made interim president of the CFLN during the absence of de Gaulle. In April 1944, in what he regarded as an ideologically motivated plot by Diethelm, Philip and Pleven, Queuille was removed from his position as president of the Commission d'embarquement.

The presence of pragmatic moderates such as Mayer, Massigli, Monnet, and Queuille in the Gaullist administration posed problems for those of the general's associates who were anxious to keep to a militant anti-fascist policy throughout the conflict and beyond. On the other hand, the replacement of André Philip as interior minister by the nominally Catholic aristocrat Emmanuel d'Astier de la Vigerie on 3 November 1943 offered substantial comfort to leftists in the Gaullist camp.

Born on 6 January 1900 to the baron Raoul d'Astier de La Vigerie and Jeanne Masson de Montelivet, Emmanuel d'Astier attended the Lycée Condorcet in Paris, then the École Sainte-Geneviève before graduating from the Naval Academy at Versailles. After a career in the navy, he resigned his commission in 1931 to begin a new career as a journalist. Called up in 1939, d'Astier found himself in Brittany with a few comrades as the French collapse began. Boarding a frigate at St-Nazaire, the group headed down the Atlantic coast toward the Spanish border to avoid capture by the advancing Germans. In the end, the young naval officer decided to stay in France, where he spent months travelling about the country looking for signs of resistance, dreaming that the defeat would be followed by a mass rising. Instead, he found a number of heroic individuals with whom he would establish a long-term bond. These included de Gaulle's emissary, the Catholic Yvon Morandat, and Daniel Mayer, the Jewish secretary of the underground Socialist party, as well as the Jewish leftist Raymond Aubrac and his Protestant wife Lucie. Among other "subversive" activities, d'Astier helped launch the resistance movement Libération Sud.

In May 1942, d'Astier escaped to Gibraltar and then by submarine to Britain. He describes his first meeting with de Gaulle with a mixture of amusement, disdain, and reluctant admiration. Even taller than expected, he noted, *Le Connétable*

> has gestures as slow and cumbersome as his nose. His skull and waxy face are held up by a body which seems to be at a tilt. His most frequent gesture is to raise both forearms while keeping his elbows at his side. At the end of his arms, his hands, attached to frail wrists, seem very pale and a bit feminine, with palms extended, they appear to be holding up a whole world of abstract burdens … He is not fond of other men but admires their history, especially that of France, which he is apparently writing as he goes along, like an impassioned Michelet.[13]

During this first conversation, the general asked his new recruit if he would go to Washington to try to win over official American opinion to the Fighting French cause. D'Astier agreed and managed to see Roosevelt's confidant Harry Hopkins, but to no effect, no doubt because the Americans were still angry about the Gaullist intervention on St. Pierre and Miquelon. After returning empty-handed to London, d'Astier was dropped into France near Lyon, where he was greeted by two representatives of Combat, the Catholic Yvon Morandat and the Protestant Bertie Albrecht. In August 1943, he sojourned briefly in Paris, then in November was summoned to Algiers to replace Philip.

The prospective commissioner found the man he was to supplant reviewing lists of *commissaries* and prefects to be appointed throughout France following Liberation. He describes Philip as "a professor, virtuoso orator and thinker but as scatterbrained in his actions as a sphinx would be eating out of a flower-bed." He adds, rather cattily, that Philip appeared to be bloated with the bourgeois pleasures that his earlier experience as an austere Protestant had kept him from enjoying.[14]

During a lengthy conversation with de Gaulle, d'Astier demurred before agreeing to take over from Philip, insisting that he must receive absolute assurance beforehand that arms and supplies would be dropped to the beleaguered Resistance. De Gaulle's somewhat offhanded consent did not satisfy the left-leaning aristocrat, who only agreed to take on the job following intense pressure from Morandat and Philip's *directeur du cabinet,* Georges Boris, who became in time his own deputy and counsellor.

D'Astier's second condition for accepting his new post was a guarantee that, following the Liberation, France would be governed by men of the Resistance rather than by the personalities he encountered in Algiers. He describes the North African city as "an operetta capital out of touch both with France and with all that is taking place in the world around us."[15] D'Astier was just as disparaging about his new colleagues on the CFLN who, as he saw it, functioned in isolation from the real world in a land about which they knew or understood very little. All major decisions, he concluded, were taken at *Les Glycines,* de Gaulle's sumptuous villa, to which access was made all but impossible by the urbane Palewski. Seen as a restive and undesirable element in the CFLN by Capitant and François de Menthon, d'Astier insisted that his aim was not to promote revolution inside France but simply to arm the partisans and carry out a necessary purge of the reactionary forces still in place thanks to Pétain.

Frustrated in his efforts to obtain satisfaction in the policy matters that concerned him most, d'Astier persuaded *Le Connétable* to let him talk directly with Churchill about aid for the Resistance during January 1944. The British prime minister, who was at Marrakesh in mid-January recuperating from a bout of pneumonia, began their encounter with a diatribe against de Gaulle, charging the general with xenophobia. Then, in answer to one of d'Astiers concerns, Churchill indicated his firm opposition to any radical purge of *vichyssois* being contemplated by the CFLN. He was, however, more forthcoming concerning the commissioner's second concern, promising that arms and supplies would be dropped to French partisans by British planes.[16]

Back in Algiers, d'Astier sought Jacques Soustelle's support in a continuing effort to get arms delivered to the Resistance as well as to shore up the leftist strength on the CFLN. Soon after his arrival in Algiers in May 1943, Soustelle had been assigned to de Gaulle's cabinet and charged with evaluating the orientation of the disparate political groups that existed throughout North Africa and developing, as a result, a coherent Gaullist policy for the area. Over the next several weeks, he held meetings with those who sympathized with Fighting France, with Communists, with

Muslims, and with the Jews who had taken part in the 7 November rising. Massigli disapproved of these exploratory talks, some of them with known leftists, out of a concern that they might in time pose a threat to the pragmatic course of domestic as well as foreign policy he was trying to steer. Soustelle countered these criticisms by suggesting that his colleague was unable to function effectively outside the salon set with whom diplomats spent most of their time.[17]

On 27 November, de Gaulle named Soustelle to head a new agency, the Direction générale des Services spéciaux (DGSS), whose function was to integrate the diverse intelligence services which had separately served Fighting France and their *giraudiste* equivalent. The new appointee describes the extensive responsibilities involved in this new assignment as follows:

> To create, sustain and finance our information networks and our armed action groups; to prepare for intervention on D-Day against the Wehrmacht in line with plans drawn up by the Allies; to facilitate the dispatch of telegrams, courier service and agents in and out of France through the use of clandestine radios, airplanes, patrol boats and submarines; to supply our underground fighters with arms and ammunition and to keep the Provisional Government and the Allied military apprised of all information reaching us in London from inside France as well as Algiers; finally, to subvert all efforts to penetrate and dismantle our organization.[18]

In his new capacity, Soustelle had daily meetings with de Gaulle to discuss and analyze the financial and military implications of the actions being undertaken by the Resistance. By the end of 1943, he estimated that some 270,000 members of the Armée secrète were ready for action inside France apart from the 30,000 who had taken to the *maquis*. The increased presence of the Communists in the ranks of the Resistance was a matter of concern, but Soustelle applauded de Gaulle's decision to seek their cooperation rather that reject them as potentially subversive.

Part of de Gaulle's aim in putting Soustelle in charge of all intelligence services was to alter the image of the BCRA which, under "Passy," had been seen as a hotbed of reaction, governed by men intent on curbing the revolutionary elements in the Resistance. Despite Soustelle's nominal control, however, "Passy" remained executive director of the BCRA, continuing to exercise a dominant influence on its outlook. The result was an undeclared conflict between the head of the DGSS and his subordinate, which was exacerbated as radical elements of the Resistance showed up in Algiers. In these circumstances, Soustelle seemed a logical person to whom d'Astier might turn for sympathy in support of the Resistance.

In the end, having discovered that the director of the DGSS was either unwilling or unable to act, the interior commissioner tried to help his friends in the Resistance by securing the appointment of his fellow leftist Raymond Aubrac as "Passy"'s deputy. This effort was blocked, ironically, by René Mayer on the ground that there were already too many Jews in the Commissariat à l'Intérieur. "Thus," d'Astier notes bitterly, "even in the Algiers Committee, a shameful form of racism made its appearance, creating a *numerus clausus* whose most influential advocate was Jewish and whose victim is a hero of the Resistance!"[19]

The intervention of Mayer (who was, it should be remembered, fundamentally *giraudiste* in outlook), provoked a considerable stir. Georges Boris was sufficiently outraged to pen a letter of resignation as well as a note to the commissioner. Mayer did not deign to reply to Boris, but revealed his own racial complexes as well as his inherent conservatism in a letter to d'Astier:

> I consider that I have no lesson in patriotism or in my conduct as a Frenchman of Jewish confession from this personage (Boris). I can only remark that, after eight years, M. Boris has not yet understood the damage which he and his like have caused their compatriots through their indiscreet pursuit of political power in association with Léon Blum … damage which sowed the seed without which Hitler's anti-Semitism would never have had the effect that, sadly, as you well know, it had.[20]

Emmanuel d'Astier's efforts during the winter of 1943–44 on behalf of the increasingly vulnerable underground army inside France were deployed not only on the CFLN, where Mayer and others were unsympathetic,[21] but also in the Assemblée consultative provisoire, a body which had been meeting in Algiers since November 1943.

De Gaulle's arrival on sovereign French soil in the spring of 1943, his unilateral proclamation of the CFLN soon afterward, and his subsequent outmanœuvring of Giraud, established *Le Connétable* as the undisputed (if still not formally recognized) champion of the republican cause. However, his encounter in Algiers with men who now opposed fascism but who, for a variety of reasons, had stayed inside France after June 1940, posed a number of problems to de Gaulle and his supporters. Some of the newcomers were sympathetic to Giraud, whose socially reactionary views they shared; others were doughty republicans who were skeptical of de Gaulle's devotion to democracy. For that matter, many *gaullistes de la première heure* were doubtful that the new arrivals shared the general's view that victory must bring with it a radical transformation of French society. The introduction into this already charged political atmosphere of a crypto-parliament, the Assemblée consultative provisoire, which included members of the internal resistance in its ranks, would give new hope and vigour to de Gaulle's core supporters.

CHAPTER SIXTEEN

Legislating for La France Nouvelle: The Provisional Consultative Assembly

The demand for the creation of an assembly which would reflect the democratic aspirations of Fighting France had been growing since the early days of La France libre in London. Dedicated republicans including Henry Hauck, Pierre-Olivier Lapie and, most persistently, René Cassin, had been pressing de Gaulle to create such a body as had Félix Gouin, Blum's emissary in London, who chaired a group of French parliamentary exiles in the British capital. Anxious to see some restraints placed on the authoritarian side of the general whose cause he had endorsed from the beginning, Churchill gave the idea his full support.

Yielding to this cumulative pressure in the summer of 1943, de Gaulle asked André Philip to organize the convening of an Assemblée consultative provisoire. After much deliberation, Philip and his advisors selected eighty-four delegates to this Assembly which would meet in the elegant Palais Carnot on the Algiers shoreline between November 1943 and July 1944.

Formally sanctioned by a 17 September 1943 ordonnance, the Assembly represented a broad cross-section of the internal and external resistance. Twenty of its members came from the pre-war Chamber of Deputies and Senate, including Pierre Cot (who had been banned from Free France in 1940 on the ground that he was too leftist) and the Gaullists Pierre-Olivier Lapie and Pierre-Bloch. Twelve came from the *conseils généraux,* consultative bodies which had been in existence even before the war in various parts of the Empire. Another dozen came from the external resistance, most of them devout Gaullists such as René Cassin and René Capitant. A full forty of the delegates – or almost half – came from the internal resistance, including two key Communists, Fernand Grenier and François Billoux.

Among the more remarkable delegates chosen to reflect the views of the resistance inside France were the "ecumenical" husband-and-wife team of Raymond and Lucie Aubrac. Born in 1914 to a middle-class Jewish couple whose religious practice was limited to respect for the Jewish high holy days, Raymond Aubrac read the anti-militarist literature of Romain Rolland and Henri Barbusse as a youth and joined Marxist discussion groups while earning an engineering as well as a law degree in Paris. It was during his association with Communist intellectuals that Aubrac met his future wife, the Protestant Lucie Bertrand, a student of the philosopher of science Jean Cavaillès, her co-religionist, who would be a leading figure (and ultimately martyr) in the wartime resistance. The Aubracs married in December 1939. Captured during the Battle of France, Raymond would escape through his wife's cunning.[1]

The flight of the Aubracs to London in February 1944 was to have been the prelude to Mme Aubrac's travelling to Algiers as a delegate to the Consultative Assembly. Her advanced pregnancy, however, obliged Lucie Aubrac to stay in London; she was replaced by Emmanuel d'Astier. Raymond Aubrac became a delegate in his own right in March.

As its name indicates, the Provisional Consultative Assembly had limited powers. It could only discuss issues which the CFLN submitted to it for deliberation except in two instances: its opinion had to be sought when the overall budget was being drawn up, or when two-thirds of its members decided to place what they considered to be a matter of national interest on its agenda. More dramatically, in major policy areas, the Committee often issued *décrets-lois* or *ordonnances*, thereby bypassing the Assembly altogether.

The passive aspect of the Assembly's role galled delegates, who refused to regard themselves as "robots or yes-men" and soon began to contest decisions made without their knowledge or consent.[2] The most restive among them made their frustrations known to the man they had chosen to preside over their deliberations, the veteran Socialist Félix Gouin, who had been Blum's delegate to de Gaulle in London. Whatever its limitations, however, the Consultative Assembly was significant in a number of ways. It confirmed the resurrection of France's traditional political parties, which de Gaulle had come to see as a countervailing force against the tightly structured PCF. The militant republicans who sat in the Assembly made it their business to urge a restoration of *gouvernement d'assemblée,* a system in which the legislative branch is all but sovereign.

On 9 November 1943, Philip was made *commissaire d'État* in charge of relations between the CFLN and the Assembly. From the beginning, this proved to be a difficult if not impossible responsibility. Philip would inevitably be seen by members of the Assembly as their advocate inside the Committee, while his colleagues on the CFLN wanted him to act as their agent and orchestrator in dealing with the eighty-four increasingly restive delegates in the Palais Carnot. Although the veteran Socialist politician would in time despair of his role as political intermediary, his inaugural speech to the Consultative Assembly was an earnest republican as well as Gaullist profession of faith.

Addressing the Assembly on 10 November, Philip insisted that the Republic that the CFLN was fighting to restore must have no traffic with Vichy, nor should any indulgence be shown those who had collaborated. Welcoming delegates from France's vast empire, including Senegal and Guyana, he pointed out that the Jacobin principle of France's total, indissoluble, and incontrovertible unity was a guiding principle of the CFLN. On the following day, 11 November, recalling the Armistice of 1918, Philip analyzed the way in which that victory had been thrown away by military weakness and domestic treason. As a result, the French in 1940 had been resigned to their defeat until the great rallying cry of 18 June. "That day," Philip declared, in one of his most categorical professions of Gaullist fidelity, "would remain in French history as the moment when, through the faith of one of her sons, who took the risk and responsibility of continuing the struggle, our country rediscovered her true self and thereby saved her soul." The Resistance that followed is described by Philip as "the reaction of men and women of faith, whatever that faith might be, producing a new and regenerate France, thoroughly reconciled with herself. The two great spiritual families into which France has been divided – the France of the Christian tradition and the France which finds inspiration in the Revolution – have discovered, under the boot of the enemy, that their faith was one and the same."[3]

Inevitably, one of the central issues underlying the Assembly debate was the constitutional question. The case for the paramountcy of the legislative branch was (not surprisingly) made with great vigour by veteran parliamentarians sitting in the Assembly, including Vincent Auriol, P.-O. Lapie, Jules Moch, André Philip, and Henri Queuille.

De Gaulle, who had (like Brossolette) made clear his hope that France, after Liberation, would not return to the multi-party regime which had weakened the national will, had modified this view after 1942 in order to counter the hegemonic pretension of the Communists in the internal resistance. However, he soon revived his old antipathy as a result of tensions with the Assembly in Algiers. For their part, those sitting in the Assembly revived skills which would allow them to play key roles during the Fourth Republic.

There was a general consensus both on the CFLN and among delegates to the Assembly on the socio-economic front. At the opening session on 3 November, Georges Buisson, a delegate from the internal resistance, condemned "the feudal money lords who are responsible for our current tragedy." De Gaulle followed suit, attacking a system "in which the conduct of businesses has excluded any participation by the organizations of workers or technicians on which they depend."[4]

In the ensuing months, a verbal consensus emerged that a regenerate Republic should foster *la démocratie sociale,* a rather vague concept which the strong contingent of Socialists in the Assembly joined Catholic disciples of *Rerum novarum* in endorsing. During a debate on 18 March 1944, delegates reiterated this commitment to social democracy, defined to include the right to work, a principle inherited from the 1848 revolution and later enshrined in the constitution of the Fourth Republic.

The challenge of articulating the message of social democracy in concrete terms was eagerly taken up by André Philip who, in addition to his role as intermediary between the CFLN and the Assembly, had been handed responsibility for coordinating plans for post-war French society. As *commissaire d'État aux études de reconstruction après-guerre,* Philip published a number of articles and gave a series of speeches before the Assembly. What emerged was a vision for post-Liberation France that would find a broad consensus in Algiers before being transformed into reality during the twelve years of the Fourth Republic. Philip's agenda included broad-ranging health reform, financial support for family welfare, an intensive increase in industrialization, the introduction of the cooperative principle in production, and the replacement of the *grandes écoles* by a less elitist system of higher education.[5]

As is turned out, both the CFLN and the Assembly agreed with Philip that France's economy be radically restructured following liberation. On 21–22 July 1944, a resolution was passed by the Assembly declaring that post-war France be subject to a program of overall economic planning. This radical resolve would be transformed into reality during the Fourth Republic by a team of economic experts led by Jean Monnet. And, in a remarkable display of working-class solidarity, the commitment to work toward a non-revolutionary modification of laissez-faire capitalism was endorsed by Marcel Poimbeuf, representing the Catholic trade-union movement, as well as by delegates from the Communist-inspired CGT.[6]

Among other issues on which a clear majority in the Assembly agreed was female enfranchisement. Support for the measure proved overwhelming, despite the fact that only two of the proposed delegates were women and only one of these managed to reach Algiers. The Protestant Lucie Aubrac, having just given birth to a new baby in London, was unable to travel. Her husband Raymond, however, made the trip in time to add his voice to the case being made for women's rights. Ironically, it remains true that there was only one woman, Marthe Simard, in the Assembly as this historic debate proceeded.

Clear evidence of the heroic role played by French women in the internal as well as external resistance was cited in support of female emancipation. The exploits of Soviet and British women were also generously cited in defence of realizing an old aim of the French Left which, acting symbolically, had, under the Blum government, named three women to junior cabinet posts. The Jew René Cerf-Ferrière, who had been a Young Turk among pre-war Radicals and then helped organize the resistance group Combat before escaping to Algiers, insisted that granting the vote to women must be seen as just the beginning of female emancipation in a nation which still required (among other things) that women obtain their husbands' consent before acting autonomously in financial transactions.[7]

The final vote in favour of female suffrage (51 to 16) came on 24 March 1944. As Raymond Aubrac sees it, representatives of the internal resistance voted unanimously in support of the measure while a number of old-style Radicals and others, who feared that the female vote would be susceptible to clerical influence, voted against the motion in the belief they were warding off reaction.[8] In any event, de Gaulle had no hesitation in transforming the will of the Assembly into legislative fiat, thereby helping to transform the demographic base (if not the direction) of French civic life.

To meet the challenges posed by Vichy's counter-revolutionary educational agenda, the nominally Catholic René Capitant, put in charge of the education portfolio, created a Commission pour la Réforme de l'Enseignement on 21 January 1944, and shortly afterward appeared before the Consultative Assembly to indicate what he felt should be the Commission's priorities.

The discussion which followed was vigorous, exposing fault lines which would re-open during the Fourth Republic. Marcel Poimbeuf of the CFTC argued that *laïcité* was an outmoded fetish; the battle to achieve this goal of nineteenth-century Republicans had been won as a result of the laws separating church and state, which granted full freedom of conscience and thus of choice in one's schooling. What was vital in 1944 was to avoid reviving such anachronistic battles and to work for harmony in battling fascist ideology. Pierre-Olivier Lapie was unconvinced, insisting that, since Vichy had not only restored clerical influence in France's schools but had allowed the conditioning of young minds to fascism, *laïcité* was of the essence. Capitant agreed, insisting that "the Republic must be reintroduced to the school" and that French youth, misled by Vichy, must be reminded that the source of the nation's greatness came, not from counter-revolutionary ideologues, but from the 1789 Declaration of the Rights of Man. The broad outline of what he hoped from the Education Commission was wholeheartedly endorsed by the Assembly.[9]

In August 1944, the *rapporteur* for the Education commission, Professor Marcel Durry of the University of Paris, submitted his findings to the Assembly. France's pre-war elites, he concluded, had, with few exceptions, shown a lamentable lack of moral character in 1940: "Our defeat and the tyranny which accompanied it were as overwhelming as they were only because of the weakness, incompetence and treason of the governing classes whether in the army, navy, politics, finance, industry or commerce. Those who graduated from the summit of our educational system were those whose cowardice was the most striking."[10]

What was needed to renovate this sclerotic system, Durry pursued, was to be found in the educational reforms begun by Jean Zay, born to a Jewish father and Protestant mother, who had been education minister during the Popular Front. In this regard, all education should be compulsory and pursued in common until children were fifteen, then prolonged for three more years in three separate streams (classical, modern, and technical), providing France with the basis for three differently qualified elites.

At the university level, the report recommended a substantial broadening of access and the creation of what would become after the war the École nationale d'administration (ENA), designed to prepare men and women of solid republican background to serve as upper-echelon civil servants.

Between November 1944 and February 1945, André Philip presided over a parliamentary commission charged with examining the historically vexed issue of the relationship between France's public and Catholic schools. Paul Ricœur, the distinguished philosopher (and a co-religionist of Philip), wrote later that, in the year during which the war was winding down (1944–45), there existed the political will to deal with this question, thanks to the shared experience of Christians and Freethinkers in battling fascism, adding that only a grand vision clearly presented would prevent

France from falling back into familiar discord over the school issue. Jacques Poujol adds that Philip, as a Protestant who was at the same time a veteran of the Resistance, was admirably placed to seek consensus among the thirty personalities coming from all ideological backgrounds who sat on the commission.[11]

Philip ended up guiding his colleagues toward the inclusion in a single state school curriculum of a "common moral inheritance," urging that this not be identified as the agnostic, scientistic credo dear to militant proponents of *laïcité de combat* in the Third Republic but rather as the shared values derived from the Two Frances which the men and women of the Resistance, whatever their spiritual background, had defended.

While the atmosphere of reciprocal respect developed between Christians and Freethinkers in Philip's commission offered the promise of reconciliation in what had been one of the most divisive sectors of French public life since the Revolution, the promise would remain unfulfilled and old tensions would soon enough surface in the early years of the Fourth Republic.

Among the most critical discussions on the CFLN and the Consultative Assembly were those related to the restoration of Republican law and justice and the prosecution of those seen to have betrayed the national interest through collaboration or other treasonous activities. The logical person to whom to entrust these dossiers, René Cassin, had been left behind in London in the spring of 1943 to handle much of Fighting France's day-to-day affairs; on 6 August, he was charged with presiding over a newly created Comité juridique, which was being organized in Algiers. After moving to the North African city late in August, he assumed his new responsibilities on 1 September.[12] In the end, the Comité juridique came to play the role normally assumed by the Conseil d'État, supreme custodian of the Republic's laws and arbiter of all prospective legislation.

One of the highest priorities for Cassin as for delegates to the Assembly, especially among those who had suffered at the hands of the *milice*, Vichy's special police, was *l'épuration*, the weeding out of civil and military collaborators and traitors. On 8 August 1943, de Gaulle had made clear that national unity could not be achieved without taking measures against those who had betrayed the national interest; and, ten days later, the CFLN created a commission of enquiry to investigate and then charge suspected collaborators. This was followed in September by a decision to bring before a duly constituted high court all those who had exercised executive authority at Vichy or in territories under its control.

André Philip joined a majority in the Assembly in urging a purge, not only of those who had served L'État français, but also of all 569 deputies and senators who had voted to transfer power to Pétain on 19 July 1940. He joined the Catholic Justice Commissioner François de Menthon in proposing that special courts to try the accused be presided over by magistrates of good repute, assisted by jurors chosen from lists submitted by local comités de libération.

On 20 December 1943, several key figures compromised by their association with Vichy, including General Boisson, former governor of French Equatorial Africa who had committed troops to repel de Gaulle's attack on Dakar in 1940; Admiral Derrien, former naval prefect at Bizerta, who had helped the Germans move into Tunisia following Operation "Torch"; and General Bergeret, who had been Darlan's close advisor, were arrested. Pierre Pucheu, ex-minister of the interior at Vichy, who had ordered the shooting of forty-seven Communist hostages at Chateaubriant in October 1941, had been apprehended on 15 August 1943.[13] What to do with the four detainees became an issue of some urgency on 12 January 1944 when Jacques Médéric, a delegate to the Assembly from the Resistance, demanded swift justice for all of them, implicitly criticizing the slower, more formal procedures proposed by the CFLN. Under pressure from the Assembly, on the one hand and, on the other, by Churchill, who urged that Boisson, Peyrouton and Flandin be spared, de Gaulle and his colleagues on the CFLN ended up focusing on the case of Pucheu, by far the most compromised of the four.

Tried by a special court made up of two civil magistrates and three generals in front of a state procurator who was deeply prejudiced against him, Pucheu had to face testimony from the Communist Fernand Grenier, who had narrowly escaped the October 1941 massacre of partisans for which he held the ex-minister responsible. Found guilty on 17 March and denied a pardon by de Gaulle, Pucheu was shot three days later. The procedures followed at the trial, and the less than absolutely convincing evidence of Pucheu's personal responsibility for the crimes alleged against him, seriously clouded the image of the Gaullist administration of justice in the months preceding Liberation.[14]

Apart from the restoration of Republican legality and the prosecution of those who had subverted it, no challenge deserved greater attention from the CFLN and the Assembly than the post-war disposition of France's vast colonial holdings. It is all the more ironic, given that these bodies were meeting in Algeria, one of the most prized parts of the empire, that so little time was given to dealing with the colonial question and that no clear policy in the area emerged.

The wartime struggle between Free France and the État français was, of course, bound to weaken loyalty to and respect for the motherland, especially in areas where nationalist elites had already expressed their grievances before the war. However, even greater challenges were posed to French authority during the war by other world powers, two of them at least nominally friendly. In the spring of 1941, Great Britain played the leading role in liberating Syria and Lebanon, French mandates under the League of Nations, from an imminent Nazi assault abetted by Arab nationalists. Operation "Torch" had introduced into the Mahgreb the anticolonialist message which Roosevelt's America saw as an integral part of the combat against fascism. Finally, the intensifying pressure of Japan on French Indo-China beginning in 1942 and the inability of Vichy to resist ceding effective control of the area to Tokyo by the war's end, made the choice of maintaining, reforming, or relinquishing France's vast imperial possessions a matter of real urgency.

At the end of May 1943, just as de Gaulle and most of his colleagues were moving to Algiers from London, Félix Eboué, France's first black governor, who had been among the few colonial personalities to offer the general his support in June 1940, wrote an admonitory letter to Commissioner of Colonies Pleven:

> [The Americans] are about to "discover Africa." They are subjecting our native policy to intense scrutiny. You are no doubt aware that the idea of imposing an international control of our colonies is not only being thought about but is being actively promoted by certain Anglo-Saxon personalities. Under the circumstances, is it not our national obligation to meet what we must consider a threat to French sovereignty by bringing ourselves to apply new concepts so that we may make our own position in this area clearer?[15]

The Brazzaville conference, which opened on 30 January 1944, offered just such an opportunity. Following an opening address by Pleven, de Gaulle offered a celebratory review of France's colonial history before pledging that the Republic would take up again its role as promoter of the moral as well as material amelioration of all the African peoples committed to its care.

The preamble to the recommendations which were issued at the end of the Brazzaville meeting seemed to reinforce the traditional Jacobin view of the empire as an indissoluble entity within which progress toward civilization would be achieved so long as *self-government* (English in the text) was never to be the objective. The same view of an indivisible imperial system within which various ethnic groups could find cultural and material emancipation through assimilation prevailed in debates in the Assembly in January 1944. One of the few dissenting voices during these debates was that of the Jewish leftist Aubrac who deplored the reluctance to empower the colonized.[16]

While the Jacobin vision of a united empire within which progress would be promoted from Paris emerged as the prevailing view in Brazzaville, Pleven and Eboué proposed an approach more parallel to that of the British Commonwealth. The two experts in colonial administration urged their colleagues to commit new responsibilities into the hands of local notables and to institute a federal assembly representing all of France's black African colonies, in which fifty per cent of delegates would be indigenous. The Socialist Jules Moch, speaking for the Left, countered that such an arrangement would be regressive because native delegates, clearly less sophisticated politically, would be at a disadvantage confronted by representatives of the well-entrenched white settler community.

Whatever the philosophical divisions at Brazzaville and in the Constituent Assembly, the debate in both bodies reflected a recognition that the old imperial system of direct government from Paris must be replaced. Native elites must be given a role either in the national parliament in Paris or in their own territory. It had also become clear that, whatever the future political structure of the empire, the central government must assume the major financial responsibility for transforming the socio-economic life of the millions of Africans living in a regime pledged to offer liberty, equality, and fraternity to all those living under its protection.

However limited their sovereign authority and their recognition by the Allies and however awkward their mutual relationship, the CFLN and the Provisional Consultative Assembly had managed by the late winter of 1944 to provide what amounted to an agenda for the prosecution of the war and the restoration of the Republic. By March 1944, however, both bodies were beginning to feel considerable frustration.

Philip had become thoroughly fed up with his role as intermediary between the CFLN and the Consultative Assembly. Delegates to the Assembly, especially representatives of the Resistance and militant Socialists, saw him as limiting them to a purely passive political role vis-à-vis the Committee, while de Gaulle resented what he considered Philip's tendency to encourage rather than restrain the more turbulent spirits in the consultative body. After being taken to task for his alleged bias by the general, Philip replied on 7 March 1944 with a long letter in which he expressed his distress both at the overall political atmosphere in Algiers and at *Le Connétable*'s role as leader of Fighting France.[17]

Philip's letter clearly signals his intention to resign from his thankless middleman role. It reflects an exalted idealism which made the Protestant in him always judge politics and politicians by rigorous spiritual standards. There were few natural leaders in the Consultative Assembly, Philip began; they had no party organization to guide them; they talked mindlessly and there was, as a result, a daily loss of the kind of mystical faith in Fighting France which had brought the best of them to Algiers. New recruits to the cause from the internal Resistance, after a few intoxicating days of life in a free country, tended to experience serious disillusionment. They had brought a mystical fervour with them, expecting to find in Gaullism the pure incarnation of the ideal for which they had been fighting, the moral force which would guarantee the nation's redemption. Instead, they were ordinary men with all their weaknesses, their egoism, their petty vanity, men who were worn down with administrative tasks, some of whom were themselves fully disenchanted.

Philip added that new arrivals were bound to be alienated by the class tensions, secret deliberations, a disproportionate preoccupation with purely personal concerns, and a government given over to compromise in a society where the enthusiasm and revolutionary ardour they had known in France were every day less evident. Philip went on to note that the Assembly was particularly angered at de Gaulle's arrogation of full political responsibility to himself at a time when those who were fighting for their freedom insisted on sharing in the process of national renewal.

The commissioner even went so far as to cite a letter from his eighteen-year-old son Olivier who was about to graduate from officers' training school in England and who had written of his willingness to die to defend the right of the next generation to live in a true republic "where the working masses will be finally liberated and where equality for all will be achieved." The commissioner added that he shared this feeling personally, not only through his son but through his party, his union, his church, and perhaps, above all, through the young students whom he had taught and who had placed their confidence in him.

Moving from the bluntly political to the more intimately psychological mode, Philip suggested that the heart of de Gaulle's problem was clearly his deep reserve, his cold solitary style which was designed to evoke respect but which was unfortunately rooted in an utter contempt for other human beings. The tragedy in all this, Philip observed, was that "your intelligence is republican but your instincts are not." To avoid a total political impasse, de Gaulle must agree to share responsibility with the Assembly as well as with the CFLN. In any event, the commissioner made clear, he was through with playing go-between: "I cannot accept being either the slave driver of the Assembly or the warden who simply gives it your orders."

Looking ahead past the immediate political deadlock in Algiers, Philip warned that the difficulties which would face the nation following Liberation would bring inevitable discontent and, in facing this, the general would need to have behind him the combined resources of the Resistance, including the Communists. Dealing effectively with the heterogeneous elements in the Consultative Assembly offered the ideal dress rehearsal for this later challenge and a good test of the general's willingness to accept democratic control. Rejecting this challenge would clearly alienate republican and socialist forces and turn de Gaulle into a symbol of anti-democratic and anti-proletarian politics.[18]

On 31 August 1944, a week after the triumphant entry of de Gaulle into liberated Paris, the CFLN, which had been transformed into the Gouvernement provisoire de la République française (GPRF) on the eve of D-Day, left Algiers for the French capital. A little more than a week later, a "Government of National Unanimity" was formed under de Gaulle. The "political ecumenism" which had sustained Free France and its successor organizations for four years would now be put to its most severe test.

CHAPTER SEVENTEEN

Liberation: The Triumph of Political Ecumenism

Having established the CFLN and the Provisional Consultative Assembly to help him debate both wartime strategy and post-war planning, Charles de Gaulle waited through the winter of 1943–44 in Algiers to be invited to London to join in devising Allied strategy for the liberation of France. Much time was spent during these months in vain efforts to secure formal recognition of the CFLN by the Allies. Thanks to the unbudging antipathy of Roosevelt to de Gaulle and to the growing bitterness of Churchill toward what he saw to be the general's increasingly perfidious behaviour, this diplomatic acceptance would not be forthcoming until well after the Normandy landings.

What *Le Connétable* and his colleagues were able to achieve, however, while still in Algiers, was the setting in place of an effective political infrastructure to administer the regions of France as they were liberated. When, on the eve of D-Day, de Gaulle was invited to London to join in detailed discussions concerning the Normandy invasion, he would be ably seconded in a last-minute diplomatic effort to ensure that this infrastructure would function and that France's national integrity, financial as well as political, was respected by Anglo-American forces operating on French soil.

Two months after the Normandy landings, the liberation of Paris in August 1944 would offer de Gaulle a splendid opportunity not only to assert his domination of the French national stage but also to establish his credentials as a champion of the Republic and his insistence that the Catholic hierarchy, deeply compromised by its support of Vichy, be brought at last to accept the Ralliement urged on its predecessors by Leo XIII.

De Gaulle and his colleagues in Algiers had every reason to suspect that London and Washington would at best allow them to play a marginal role in the liberation of their homeland. Anglo-American plans to take over the civil administration of those parts of Europe they liberated had already become clear in July 1943 with the establishment of the Allied Military Government of Occupied Territories (AMGOT) in Sicily. In anticipation of the problems that might arise from the application of AMGOT to France, Henri Queuille, then André Philip, chaired a Commission française de débarquement for the CFLN. Then, in July 1943, General Henri d'Astier, commander of French forces in the United Kingdom, taking for granted the need for close liaison between Anglo-American liberation and their Gaullist allies, created a Service militaire d'études administratives and handed its direction to Pierre Laroque, a member of the French Conseil d'État who had escaped to London in April 1943.

Born on 2 November 1907, Laroque was the child of a mixed marriage.[1] His father was descended from a Jewish family that had lived in the Comtat-Venaissin for generations. His mother, English by birth and Anglican in faith, counted among her ancestors a Catholic bishop and a Jesuit general; her maternal grandparents, on the other hand, bore the name Montefiore and were thus linked, if only remotely, to the Haute société israélite. His parents left the young Pierre to find his own way spiritually, which led him to become a Freethinker with a general belief in human goodness.

A lawyer by training as well as a graduate of Sciences po, Laroque ended up serving on the Conseil d'État during the 1930s. With the coming of war in 1939, he was made an inspector of the clothing trade in the Paris area. While he did not hear de Gaulle's 18 June radio broadcast, Laroque soon learned about it from subordinates. During the Occupation, he worked for a while for Vichy. Then, although he had never been a Jew in the religious sense, he was inevitably excluded from public office by the Vichy government's racist laws. In these grim circumstances, he was (like René Mayer) helped by friends to find work in the silk trade in Lyon, where he soon made contact with key members of the local resistance, including P.-H Teitgen, Alexandre Parodi, René Courtin, Paul Bastid, and François de Menthon. When he met de Gaulle's delegate-general Jean Moulin, who was on a mission to the southern city, Laroque was persuaded to go to London where, after a number of botched attempts, he arrived in April 1943. *Le Connétable* was sufficiently impressed to put Laroque in charge of liaison work between different commissioners in what was soon to become the CFLN.

From the very beginning of his stay in London, Laroque was dismayed by what he saw to be the mediocre quality of most of de Gaulle's subordinates and by their failure to cooperate with their British counterparts. As though to respond to this latter concern, Laroque was on 14 July named to head the Service des Affaires civiles of the Fighting French forces in the United Kingdom, with a special mandate to prepare for the post-Liberation administration of France. A team of advisers was seconded to him including the Radicals Mendès France and Jacques Kayser.

The mandate of the Service included an analysis of the political attitude of the population in the areas of France likely to be liberated, the training of military personnel to deal with civilians following Allied landings, and the establishment of liaison with equivalent bodies in the Allied camp. Laroque made a point of establishing a link with his British counterpart, Brigadier Lee, and set up a training camp for French liaison troops at Camberley. By early June, some 160 officers and 50 female volunteers had graduated from this camp and were prepared to act during and after the D-Day landings, some of them with special skills in terms of police operations, food distribution, justice, and transportation. Their integration had, however, not been fully worked out by D-Day despite an agreement between Eisenhower and General Koenig.

When de Gaulle arrived in London on 3 June, "more intransigent than ever," and without instructing Laroque to participate in last-minute deliberations about cooperation during and after D-Day, the head of the Service des Affaires civiles felt close to despair. Of his feelings after a year in London, he would later write, "I must confess that, despite all my admiration for de Gaulle, everything about him shocked me."[2] In the end, but only at the very last minute, Laroque was accepted as a member of the team which served as liaison between the GPRF and the Allied armies in Normandy.

Even more important than the presence during the Normandy landings of the liaison team created by Laroque was the planned despatch of a corps of civil administrators groomed to take over from Vichy officials and to establish their authority in advance of any effort by the Anglo-Americans to apply the AMGOT formula.

Chosen in March 1944 to be de Gaulle's delegate-general inside France, Alexandre Parodi managed during the ensuing five months to put in place a shadow administration for each area of the nation as it was liberated. The plan was to put three levels of Gaullist administrators in place in the immediate aftermath of Liberation before the Anglo-Americans filled the political vacuum created by the flight or removal of Vichy appointees, and in advance of any revolutionary attempt by the Communists. *Commissaires de la République* were chosen to take charge of the eighteen regions into which Vichy had divided France and, at a lower level, prefects and departmental liberation committees were selected and given well-defined roles.

Although resistance groups were given the right to nominate members of this administrative structure, the final choice of those who were to serve as top cadres was left to two key men. The Protestant mining engineer and lawyer Émile Laffon (code-named "Guizot" after the celebrated Protestant prime minister of Louis-Philippe) was chosen by his co-religionist Philip to take charge of this critical mission; he made every effort to ensure that prospective commissioners and prefects would be reliable state functionaries rather than ideological partisans. He was joined in the critical selection process by Michel Debré, a *juif d'origine* (his grandfather had been a rabbi) converted to Catholicism, who had been named by the CFLN as president of its Commission clandestine de désignations.

Despite their title, with its throwback to the revolutionary ethos of 1848, all of the men chosen to be *commissaires de la République* were solid Gaullists. Three of them reflected in symbolic fashion the political ecumenism which had characterized Free France from the beginning. François Coulet, the Protestant aide-de-camp and confidant of de Gaulle, was charged with establishing the authority of the GPRF in Normandy even as it was being liberated. Raymond Aubrac, the Jewish leftist, was to take control of Marseille and a large zone in southern France following Allied landings on the Mediterranean coast. The Catholic Louis Closon, who had been on a number of missions inside France, would be given responsibility for much of northeastern France centred on the city of Lille.

To finalize plans for the effective use of the liaison team created by Laroque, as well as to ensure the defence of French sovereign interests in the wake of Allied landings, de Gaulle selected a devoutly Catholic patriot, Pierre Viénot, to serve as "Ambassador" of the still unrecognized CFLN in London.

Born three years before the turn of the century, Viénot had a rigorously Christian upbringing (cold showers at 6:30 a.m., bedside prayers at night) in the provincial city of Clermont-Ferrand.[3] His grandfather nurtured the young Pierre's patriotism with stories of battle against the invading Germans in 1870. Sent to Paris for higher education, Viénot combined Catholic instruction at the École Gerson with the secular curriculum of one of the city's lycées. The declaration of war in 1914 brought precocious army enlistment at age seventeen and, four years later, a serious wound which permanently undermined Viénot's health and contributed to his death as World War II was ending.

Dreams of a career in the diplomatic corps led to a post-war trip to Morocco, where Viénot met the remarkable proconsul Marshal Hubert Lyautey, a passionate Catholic like himself who had come to admire Muslim culture. The two men, separated by a generation but sharing an austere Catholic faith and practice, developed something of a father-and-son relationship. At the end of his four years with Lyautey, Viénot noted, as though in anticipation of his later devotion to de Gaulle, "Morocco has at last provided the contemporary world with a lesson which democracy has failed to come up with, that of the efficacy of one man who in truth belonged neither to the Left nor to the Right."[4]

Back in France after his Moroccan apprenticeship, Viénot prepared for the diplomatic career that had always been his ambition. Disturbed by the ruthless germanophobia of the Poincaré government, he formed a Comité franco-allemand in what turned out to be a vain effort to bring together the intellectual elite of the two nations.

In 1932, Viénot was elected deputy for Rocroi in the Chamber of Deputies. Sitting with the Left, he broke off relations with his brother André over the significance of the 6 February 1934 riots. Elected as a Socialist in 1936, he served as undersecretary for foreign affairs in the Blum government, helping to achieve the September 1936 accord that would have granted Lebanon and Syria their independence had it not been sabotaged by right-wing elements in the Senate as well as in the settler community in the Levant.

With the coming of World War II, Lieutenant Viénot served as an interpreter at the headquarters of France's Fourth Army. Then, in April 1940, he accepted Premier Reynaud's request that he return to Paris to direct the Ministry of Information's German section. In this new function, ironically, Viénot still believed that he might succeed in changing the mind-set of the new generation of Germans. On 20 June 1940, Viénot was among those who embarked on the *Massilia*, hoping that they might be able to continue the battle from Casablanca. As a result, on 27 July, he was charged with desertion by the Vichy government, arrested, and sentenced to six years in prison.

After escaping late in 1942, Viénot, although in poor health, made his way to London in April 1943. Delighted to welcome such a gifted recruit, de Gaulle (who was about to depart for Algiers) named Viénot "Ambassador" of the CFLN to the United Kingdom. Two Jews, Olivier Wormser and Jacques Kayser, would act as his deputies in this critical diplomatic exercise.[5]

With his British counterpart Alfred Duff Cooper, whom Churchill had named ambassador to the CFLN, Viénot did his firm but tactful best to renew the Entente Cordiale which de Gaulle had done nothing to advance. In similar vein, he explained to the francophile Anthony Eden that the French people, soon to be released from the German grip by their Anglo-American allies, would find it hard to live under what might seem like another foreign occupation. Despite the British foreign secretary's reassurances, the prospect of the application of AMGOT to France clouded the discussions between the two diplomats.

On 23 May 1944, roughly two weeks before D-Day, Churchill invited de Gaulle to come to London to discuss plans for the Allied landings in Normandy. Three days later, the general made clear to his colleagues that, if he accepted the invitation, it would be on condition that three key aspects of French sovereignty were respected. He would not surrender control of the internal resistance; he would not accept American assumption of civil administration in areas liberated from Vichy and the Nazis; and he rejected out of hand the use on French soil of currency printed in the United States which did not recognize the authority of the CFLN.

On 2 June, after a long and hectic debate, a majority on the CFLN (Philip and Pleven dissenting) sanctioned de Gaulle's trip to London but not, however, before throwing down the gauntlet to the Anglo-Americans by transforming the Comité français de libération nationale into the Gouvernement provisoire de la République française (GPRF).

De Gaulle and a modest military retinue, which included General Émile Bethouart (a classmate from St-Cyr who had been part of the French expedition to Narvik, then a partisan of Giraud, before siding with *Le Connétable*) and General Pierre Billotte, secretary of the CFLN defence committee, arrived in London on 3 June. They were joined the next day for discussions with the British by General Koenig, chief of Fighting French Forces in the United Kingdom.

Given the absence of the veteran diplomat René Massigli, left behind in Algiers, and the tense relationship which had developed between de Gaulle and Churchill since the transfer of Gaullist headquarters to Algiers a year earlier, it is not surprising that the tenuous diplomatic link between His Majesty's government and Free France worked out by Cassin in 1940 and sustained through many intervening crises by francophiles on the one hand (notably Eden), and anglophiles on the other (Pleven and Palewski), almost collapsed in the two days of dialogue which followed.

On 4 June, de Gaulle and his entourage were invited to lunch by Churchill, who had set up temporary headquarters in a railway coach near Portsmouth on the Channel coast. Pierre Viénot was added to the party at the very last minute. When the plans for 6 June were laid before the French delegation, de Gaulle was understandably outraged at being kept in the dark until the very last moment. In the immediate circumstances, he demanded a clarification of the relationship between the Allied military command and the civilian authority which would administer the areas about to be liberated. Churchill replied that he would have to take this up with Roosevelt. When de Gaulle responded to this comment with bitter sarcasm, Churchill made his subsequently notorious remark that, if and when he had to choose between the Continent and America, he would always follow the transatlantic option ("le grand large").[6]

Following this bitter exchange, Churchill and de Gaulle started shouting angrily at each other while Eden and Viénot continued to discuss the matter at hand. Then, for a moment when it looked as though the two leaders were about to battle each other physically, Viénot intervened. He recounted the incident later to Jacques Kayser, perhaps overdramatizing a bit: "If I had not been present, they would have struck each other. I was obliged to restrain the general … [It had been] a combat between giants!"[7]

After this stormy session, the high-level quartet adjourned to the nearby railway coach which served as Eisenhower's headquarters, where de Gaulle was in for a new shock. For the first time, the leader of the Free French discovered that the commander-in-chief of the Allied invasion force was to broadcast a proclamation to the French people which he, de Gaulle, would not be allowed to see in advance. (The broadcast had in fact been recorded a fortnight earlier). To make matters worse, de Gaulle learned that the American general's address was to be preceded by speeches from representatives of the Dutch, Belgian, and Luxemburg governments-in-exile! His own speech, coming after Eisenhower's, would surely lose much of its potential impact.

Over lunch the following day (5 June) with Viénot, Soustelle, and other intimates, de Gaulle relayed his continuing cold fury over the dialogue with Churchill and reiterated his determination that the Provisional Government should prevail over any obstacles the Allies might put in its way. That evening, Viénot was summoned to the Foreign Office, where Eden informed him that the crisis between the Allies and de Gaulle had, if anything, deepened. There was renewed distress that the general had now threatened to withdraw the services of the Mission militaire de liaison administrative put together by Pierre Laroque.

Just before midnight, Viénot left Eden to discuss the matter with de Gaulle who insisted that, before giving way on the liaison issue, he must be granted the right to address the French people with whatever text he felt was appropriate. At 1 a.m., Viénot returned to the Foreign Office, where he faced not only the usually conciliatory Eden but a furious British prime minister whose tone of voice so outraged him that Viénot felt obliged to cut matters short. "Mr. Prime Minister," he admonished, "if you continue to address me in that tone of voice, I will not cross this threshold again!"[8] When the ambassador of Free France left the room after this sally, Churchill issued an order to American General Walter Bedell Smith that de Gaulle be placed aboard a plane for Algiers (in chains if necessary) and kept at all costs from returning to France! Happily, Eden was later able to persuade the prime minister to have this order countermanded.

At 11 a.m. on the morning of 6 June, de Gaulle arrived at BBC headquarters, read his prepared text and then boasted afterward about its contents: "I have just told Eisenhower to go fuck himself!" ("Je viens d'envoyer faire foutre Eisenhower").[9]

Toward dawn on 6 June, détente ended this terrifying battle of pride and precedence. De Gaulle agreed to address the people of France at 6 p.m. that day, and Duff Cooper was able to persuade him to release some of the liaison officers Laroque had prepared.

De Gaulle's speech can be seen as vindication of his petulance and obduracy. The general urged the people of France to follow orders given them by qualified French authorities (namely those mandated by the GPRF). In this way, he did his best to ensure that France would not be treated like Sicily.

The ultimate fate of the Gaullist enterprise would of course be decided, not in London or Portsmouth, but by the people of France. More immediately, it would be influenced by the network of devoted Gaullists chosen to assume civil authority in the wake of the Allied armies. In many ways the most remarkable of these was the Protestant François Coulet, chosen to be *commissaire de la République* in Normandy following the Anglo-American landings.

Invited to dinner on the morrow of D-Day, Coulet found the general "in very good health, keen, serene, light-hearted and sure of personal victory." Five days later, de Gaulle had truly exciting news: Coulet was to join him on 14 June on a trip to Normandy where he would remain as "Commissaire de la République pour les Territoires libérés."

Crossing the Channel with de Gaulle on the Free French warship *La Combattante,* Coulet felt a sense of high excitement. After landing, he moved to set up headquarters at Bayeux, which would serve as the temporary capital of an area covering five French departments and where he watched as the crowd gave the general a warm (although not rapturous) reception. The transfer of power from the local representatives of Vichy was made easier for Coulet when he discovered that the sub-prefect in Bayeux, Rochat, was a fellow Protestant. Rochat, who would go on to pursue a career as a Reformed pastor, had (as it turned out) already put himself at the disposal of the first British troops he had seen nine days earlier and was only too pleased to provide de Gaulle, General Koenig, and Coulet with all the information they asked of him.

Coulet began what was to be a three-month career as Gaullist proconsul with a flourish. He dictated a series of proclamations; he helped launch *La Renaissance du Bessin,* the first French-language newspaper to appear following the Normandy landings; and he appealed to the Bishop of Bayeux and Lisieux to arrange for a special Te Deum mass to be sung on 18 June to commemorate de Gaulle's appeal from London four years earlier, as well as to celebrate the triumphal arrival of Allied troops. The bishop reacted rather coolly to this ecumenical gesture, expressing surprise that de Gaulle had chosen a Protestant to represent him in such a clearly Catholic part of the nation and adding rather caustically that he was aware that Coulet's father, the first French rector appointed to Strasbourg when it reverted to France in 1918, had restored lay schools throughout the newly recovered provinces of Alsace and Lorraine. When, in the end, rather grudgingly, the bishop agreed to have the Te Deum sung, Coulet took the cleric's procrastination quite philosophically. "The French are like that!" he reflected, concluding that his fellow-citizens were still given to defining one another in terms of different religious denominations rather than as part of the same spiritual community.[10]

Far more important for the success of Coulet's mission than the attitude of a narrow-minded Catholic prelate was the reaction of the Allied military command, which had no instructions about how to deal with a representative of de Gaulle. The *commissaire* decided against presenting himself at General Montgomery's headquarters in order to preclude what might be seen as suggesting a dependent relationship. Instead, on 16 June, Coulet faced a group of British and American reporters, responding in English (and in kind) to their forthright, if not insolent, questions about the legitimacy of his authority, his relationship to AMGOT, and his policy regarding the French banknotes which the Allies were planning to circulate. In the end, after being asked what he would do if the Allies were to dismiss him from office, he remarked that this was quite hypothetical and then asked the reporters in equally provocative fashion what they thought would happen if he were to slap Eisenhower across the face!

Coulet's sally ended the exchange. Three days later, he was visited by a contingent of Allied officers led by General Lewis, who declared, red-faced with anger, that the invading armies intended to deal directly with the local population rather than through intermediaries such as Coulet. The *commissaire* again stood his ground and the general allowed that, pending consultation with Washington and London, Coulet's presence would be conditionally accepted. De Gaulle's proconsul replied rather tartly that his presence did not in fact depend on the Allied military. His mandate was from France's Provisional Government; he would remain in his function until he heard otherwise from that source.

Coulet's firmness paid off. Cordiality replaced contempt, and on 9 July he was introduced to Montgomery by Koenig. The hero of El Alamein opened the conversation rather bluntly, asking why the commissioner and his people had not accepted the currency printed for use in liberated France. Coulet replied that Normandy's farmers would not take these notes seriously; he added pointedly that even the Nazis had not imposed their own money during the Occupation!

Worried that the conversation was taking a disastrous turn, Koenig turned to the British general, observing, "Ah! You don't know Coulet. He is very hard! He is a very hard man! Ah! Ah! He is a Protestant!" These remarks brought an instant change in attitude on the part of Montgomery, the son of an Anglican bishop, who had ordered his troops to pray together in the Libyan Desert. Turning to Coulet with a smile, he observed, "Oh! Really? So you are a Protestant, eh? A Protestant, indeed! Very interesting! How many Protestants are there in France? What part of France do you come from?" The conversation continued in similarly amiable fashion. When it was over, Montgomery saluted Coulet as "Mr. High Commissioner" and offered him unconditional support.[11]

Coulet's power, henceforth uncontested, suited him admirably. He saw himself not as a classic prefect of the ill-fated Third Republic but as a reincarnation of the Protestant member of the revolutionary government of 1793, the former reformed pastor Jeanbon-Saint-André, using his authority to advance a just cause against reaction, freed from parliamentary intrigue. Like so many others who had joined de Gaulle, he hoped that the inspired leadership of the few that had so ably served Free France, together with the fundamental virtue of the nation's peasants and workers, might purge the republic of the ills which had led to 1940. He would return to the Quai d'Orsay after the war, determined to turn this aspiration into reality.

Coulet's reference to the effort by the Anglo-Americans to impose their own version of French currency in Normandy touched on a major concern of the Gaullist commissioner. In Washington in the fall of 1943, Jean Monnet (in close collaboration with Mendès France in Algiers) persuaded the Americans that francs rather than dollars or pounds should be used by Allied troops. After a great deal of tense negotiation, the Americans decided to produce their own francs stamped on one side with the simple word "France" or the phrase "Émis en France" and on the obverse the tricolour and the motto "Liberté, Égalité, Fraternité," with no reference anywhere to the CFLN. Predictably, de Gaulle regarded these notes as counterfeit from the beginning. This attitude was shared by Interior Commissioner d'Astier, who arrived in the area in the company of Boris and Schumann. On the eve of D-Day, d'Astier and General Koenig had requested that 2,000,000,000 francs be made available for the parts of France still under German control and 5,000,000,000 for the areas about to be freed. Unfortunately, Mendès France had been able to provide only 3,000,000,000 francs.

In the end, the problem of an inadequate supply of notes was resolved in large measure because banknotes found in key branches of the Bank of France open to the Gaullist administration were far more numerous than had been anticipated. Meanwhile, the money printed by AMGOT had not been welcomed by the local population which saw it as spurious – not, however, d'Astier adds, before paying off personal debts with it! Meanwhile, Normandy's *caisses publiques* had, on Coulet's orders, rejected these notes which the Allies had been, as a result, forced to exchange for Bank of France currency.

D'Astier returned from his brief sojourn in Normandy convinced that the entire AMGOT operation, financial as well as political, had quickly gone up in smoke. Representatives of the Provisional Government were firmly installed in the newly liberated areas. In fact if not yet in law, the political horizon was serene.[12]

Commissioner Coulet's success in establishing the Gaullist claim to administer the first area of France to be liberated set what would prove to be a decisive precedent. However, the political disposition of the area surrounding Marseille, which was the object of a massive American military assault in mid-August, provided what was in some ways an equal challenge to the GPRF.

The Jewish leftist Raymond Aubrac was sitting in the Consultative Assembly in Algiers as a representative of the resistance group Libération-Sud while the preparations for the Allied landing on the French Mediterranean coast were being made.[13] On 6 July, he was informed that he had been chosen to serve as *commissaire de la République* for a substantial part of southern France, centred on Marseille. The following day, he saw de Gaulle, who made clear that one of his chief responsibilities would be to frustrate any American attempt to impose the AMGOT system within his jurisdiction. Aubrac got further details about his mission from d'Astier who told him that, following a nine-day partisan insurrection inside the city, a wave of arrests had decapitated the resistance in and around Marseille, a politically and socially turbulent area at the best of times. D'Astier also gave the *commissaire* the names of those who would be serving under him as prefects or presidents of local liberation committees and handed him 10,000,000 freshly minted francs in case the Germans, in their retreat, had destroyed existing French bank notes.

Flown first to Naples, then to Ajaccio in Corsica, Aubrac was brought on 18 August to the landing beach at St-Tropez, part of the Allied bridgehead. He met the local comité de libération and, the next day, was assured by labour unions from Marseille that they and their comrades had forced German troops there to retrench. Battles still raged along the French coast, and on 24 August War Minister Diethelm and General de Lattre de Tassigny urged Aubrac to stay away from Marseille until it was cleared of German troops. A Jeep arrived during this conversation carrying "Lionel," the code name of Francis Leenhardt, the Protestant and Socialist resistance leader, whom Closon had put in charge of resistance in southern France and who was now acting as president of the liberation committee in the Bouches-du-Rhône. Aubrac was delighted that "Lionel" appeared to have shifted so easily from his role as military leader of an anti-fascist insurrection to willing counsellor of the new civil authority.

Aubrac began what would be a five-month stint as *commissaire* with what he saw as two distinct handicaps: he was just thirty, with very little administrative experience, and he was ideologically very far to the left, facing a multiplicity of challenges. First of all, there was the question of restoring public order in a period of virtual anarchy under the critically watchful gaze of the American military. To cope with this problem, Aubrac created special new units, the Forces républicaines de sécurité (FRS), a 3,000-man body recruited from the leftist FFI, charged with general police responsibilities, including the guarding of vital factories and the arrest of suspected collaborators. While he had been mandated to restore republican legality, Aubrac admits that there was a fair amount of arbitrary jailing and summary justice during the early weeks of his administration, excusing it on the ground that the repressive acts of Vichy and the Gestapo had led to a forgivable yearning for expeditious justice.

An ordinance issued by the GPRF on 26 June 1944 had established ad hoc courts to try those charged with collaboration and for a while there was no appeal from these tribunals except to Aubrac himself. Happily, de Gaulle soon relieved Aubrac of this burdensome responsibility, and a more formal court was established for the region. By 15 January 1945, this tribunal had met some 400 times, charging seventy-three citizens with capital offences, forty-one of whom were put to death. Aubrac was understandably relieved that the period of *justice sauvage* over which he had presided was behind him.

Even more controversial than Aubrac's role in the supervision of rough-and-ready justice was his decision to requisition the factories and businesses of suspected collaborators. The process began on 10 September with the seizure of the *Aciéries du Nord* and the appointment of a "patriotic engineer" to direct this substantial enterprise under the supervision of a consultative committee made up of workers, technicians and engineers as well as representatives of the company's board of governors. Later, businesses employing some 15,000 workers were similarly taken over in what Aubrac describes as a bold prelude to the extensive nationalizations proposed by the Resistance.

Not surprisingly, moderates in the GPRF were deeply troubled by this frontal assault on the workings of the capitalist system. On a visit of enquiry, René Mayer urged Aubrac to go slow, and others in Algiers charged the commissioner with playing the Communists' game. In his defence, Aubrac, who rationalized his interventions as promoting the *participation* to which de Gaulle himself was pledged, later argued that big business in the south of France, as elsewhere, managed not only to deflect challenges such as his but consciously bided its time waiting to plot revenge.

As was the case with his fellow-commissioners Coulet and Closon, Aubrac was charged with receiving de Gaulle at Marseille during the general's grand tour of liberated France in the fall and winter of 1944–45. One of the chief challenges in terms of protocol for this visit was the place to be given to the local prelate, Mgr Delay, during the reception for the general. As Aubrac notes, while the archbishop had taken a clear position against the persecution of the Jews, he had not explicitly repudiated his pledge to

Pétain. As a result, Aubrac had not paid him a courtesy visit; nor had the prelate taken a similar initiative. On his arrival, de Gaulle proposed that he receive Mgr Delay at the prefecture, the citadel of republican authority, rather than at the episcopal palace.

To deal with any untoward manifestation of popular wrath at the presence of the politically ambivalent archbishop at the reception, Aubrac kept a pistol at his side and, with a mischievous sense of political scheming, arranged to have the local prefect, an ex-seminarian, speak before the archbishop. Lucie Aubrac, meanwhile, added to the politically charged feeling at the reception by seating de Gaulle between two celebrities of the local leftist resistance. Despite this provocation, which led the general to keep a stony silence during the dinner, de Gaulle commented on the proceedings at the end by remarking to the commissioner, "Aubrac, you've got the message! We must restore the Republic!"[14]

From the beginning of his mandate, Aubrac was confronted with rising demands for a salary hike in a situation of runaway inflation. Closely related to the frustrations engendered by this problem was the desperate shortage of basic food supplies in the region and the resultant flourishing black market. In the continuing crisis, Aubrac saw himself as the victim of a plot to oust him by the region's well-organized Socialists, including Leenhardt and Gaston Defferre (also Protestant and future mayor of Marseille) who helped encourage the rumour that the commissaire was wilfully neglecting the distribution of vital supplies to the civilian population. In any event, summoned to Paris early in 1945, Aubrac was replaced in his absence. A week later, Aubrac notes bitterly, the Socialist Supply Minister Paul Ramadier ordered the release of much needed food and other necessities to the region. Aubrac's departure convinced him that, from the point of view of the Gaullist majority, the Republic was to be restored, not transformed.

While Aubrac was doing his best to cope with the complex political and socio-economic problems in the Marseille area, de Gaulle had established his personal power and the authority of the GPRF in the nation's capital. On 20 August 1944, having learned that most of Paris was already in the hands of the Resistance, de Gaulle urged Eisenhower to move at once on the capital to forestall any attempt to create a de facto revolutionary power which might challenge his own political ascendancy. There the result was a swift and successful operation, in which the Second French Armoured Division led by General Leclerc played a key role.

The general had already made up his mind that when he entered Paris he would not proceed first to the Hôtel de Ville, where the Conseil national de la Résistance and the Comité parisien de la libération were already sitting. Instead, he would go to what he called *le centre,* the nucleus of state power, the War Ministry (where he had had an office in June 1940) and the Paris Prefecture of Police.[15]

Quite apart from this calculated snub of those in control at the Hôtel de Ville, de Gaulle had historic precedents to guide him in this decision to dramatize the continuity as well as the paramountcy of the central state rather than recognize the often ephemeral and sometimes turbulent role played by the city government, most dramatically in recent history though the establishment of the revolutionary Paris commune of 1871.

De Gaulle was driven first to the War Ministry where elements of the leftist FFI, already installed, yielded to him grumblingly. He then dropped in at the Prefecture of Police, where he saluted the officers of the law who had played a key role in the liberation of the city from the Germans. Finally, pressed by Parodi, *Le Connétable* showed up at the Hôtel de Ville at 7:15, long after he was expected. He was greeted by his fellow-Catholic Georges Bidault on behalf of the CNR and the CPL but, the general argues in his memoirs, the presence of these intermediary organizations mattered far less than his own arrival as far as the huge crowd was concerned. "It sufficed," he wrote, "that the masses and I came together for our unity to carry the day against all others."[16]

When Bidault, speaking in the name of the CNR and CPL, turned to de Gaulle, who was standing beside him on the City Hall balcony, and asked him to proclaim the Republic in front of the assembled people, the general's reply was swift and devastating. The Republic had never ceased to be, he declared: it had found expression in La France libre, La France combattante, the CFLN and the GPRF, while Vichy from the beginning had been a political nonentity. After all, I am the president of the Republic, de Gaulle asserted. Why then should I proclaim its existence?[17] In any event, the rapturous celebration of his arrival by the crowd below was taken to be sufficient endorsement of his claim to represent republican continuity.

The republican accolade which de Gaulle had been given at the Hôtel de Ville was complemented the next day, Saturday, 26 August, by the triumphal procession which he led down the Champs-Élysées to attend a Te Deum mass at Notre Dame Cathedral. This procession was preceded by a huge rally at the Arc de Triomphe, where the general placed a Cross of Lorraine on the Tomb of the Unknown Soldier and intoned the Marseillaise, the first time the anthem had been publicly sung there since France's defeat. Then, at the head of a huge parade accompanied by two prominent Catholic members of the Resistance, Bidault and General

Leclerc (both of whom, he made sure, marched a few steps behind him), de Gaulle strode down the broad boulevard under occasional fire from rooftop snipers, convinced that the wild enthusiasm of the crowd that had gathered signalled the forging of a new, all-embracing national unity, the kind of *rassemblement* he had dreamed about in exile. The Catholic historian René Rémond agrees, arguing that 26 August 1944, is, with February 1848, 2 August 1914, and 11 November 1914, one of those rare moments of spontaneous national unanimity which the French have experienced in the modern era.[18]

When de Gaulle reached the square in front of Notre Dame, the normal protocol would have been for the cardinal-archbishop of Paris, Emmanuel Suhard, to greet him there. Pressure from militant Christian Democrats, including Bidault and Closon – what de Gaulle calls "the new authority" (the Resistance) – was such, however, that the prelate had been told that he would be persona non grata at the service.

The reason for this extraordinary banishment from his own cathedral was not the cardinal's overall record during the Occupation. Although, like most of the French ecclesiastical establishment, Suhard had been *pétainiste* in sympathy, he had not supported the Marshal's policy of collaboration, and he had joined the Assembly of Cardinals and Archbishops in condemning the deportation of foreign-born Jews by Vichy. What brought the wrath of the Resistance (including its Catholic component) down on Suhard was the willingness he had shown in June 1944 to officiate at the funeral mass for Philippe Henriot, the onetime minister of propaganda at Vichy, who had called for collaboration with Nazi Germany over the national radio network before being killed by the Resistance.

De Gaulle's consent to the cardinal's exclusion led to Suhard being confined to the archiepiscopal palace during the ceremony. While acquiescing in this temporary banishment, de Gaulle insists in his memoirs, he was fully aware of the Church's traditional policy of respecting the powers that be (*l'ordre établi*), whatever their ideology. He knew, too, that Suhard was renowned for his piety and charity and for his innocence in matters political. His own willingness to go along with the ban, he later insisted, was based primarily on his determination that Suhard be spared any public manifestation of hostility during the Te Deum.[19]

Inside the cathedral, the cardinal's representative, Mgr Brot, offered his greeting to the general, together with Suhard's protest at being kept a prisoner inside the cathedral palace. De Gaulle replied by expressing his regret at the "incident," together with his desire for national reconciliation and his intention to receive the cardinal as soon as possible.

The 26 August ceremony in Notre Dame Cathedral has been described as the consecration (*le sacre*) of Charles de Gaulle, the anointing by Catholic France of a man who had the day before been acclaimed leader of the Republic by the sovereign people.[20] It would be hard to imagine a greater contrast in this regard between the craven invocation of the Almighty made by the clutch of non-believers (many of them soon to become *capitulards*) in the Reynaud cabinet who attended high mass on 19 May 1940, and the Gaullist participation in the Te Deum on 26 August four years later, during which Republicans and Catholics shared their jubilation at the restoration of French liberty.

The two-day secular and spiritual investiture of de Gaulle had in fact begun the process of bringing the Two Frances together. The Catholic hierarchy, which had by and large supported Vichy and condemned de Gaulle, now offered the general its blessing and, in so doing, took the first steps toward repudiating the fascist ideology with which it had become associated. But while the Te Deum in Notre Dame was a positive act of healing, Bidault and his Catholic colleagues Justice Minister de Menthon and Information Minister Teitgen were determined that the Church be purged of those members of the hierarchy who had compromised themselves during the Vichy period. In the end, seven bishops would either leave office of their own accord (as was the case with Mgr Florent du Bois de la Villerabel of Aix-en-Provence) or put their fate in the hands of the papacy and withdraw from public view, as did Mgr Felix Auvity of Mende.

De Gaulle made no efforts to save the careers of the seven bishops, but he was determined that Mgr Valerio Valeri, the papal nuncio who had not only represented the Vatican in Vichy but had expressed public deference to Pétain (and thus covered the French episcopate's similar behaviour), be recalled. Pius XII stalled, unwilling to abandon formal recognition of Vichy until its appointed ambassador, Léon Bérard,[21] departed. The pope, it might be added, was also concerned that his yielding to the new French government might invite further demands, including consent to a massive *épuration* of the nation's clergy.

In November 1944, Bidault sent a mission to Rome which negotiated papal consent to Valeri being categorized as persona non grata in Paris. Suhard followed this up by sending the abbé Jean Rodhain, chaplain-general of France's war prisoners, to the Vatican. Rodhain's forceful intervention brought Pius XII to name Mgr Roncalli as Valeri's successor. On 1 January 1945, Roncalli, the future Pope John XXIII, presented his credentials to de Gaulle at the Élysée Palace, then, in his first diplomatic act, offered his best wishes for the New Year to the president of the GPRF. The formal reception by the new French government of the man who was soon to become the most ecumenical pontiff in history symbolized what may be called the start of the third and definitive Ralliement, the completion of the process Cardinal Lavigerie had tried to inaugurate in 1890.

The rebuke given Cardinal Suhard, the modest purge of the French episcopate, and the recall of Valeri helped remove the stigma attached to members of the Church hierarchy as a result of their sympathy for l'État français. To complete the process of ecclesiastical purification, Interior Minister Tixier in December 1944 charged the Catholic historian André Latreille with investigating the wartime attitude and behaviour of the lower clergy. The result, prepared with the collaboration of *commissaires de la République* and submitted in 1945, indicated that, with few exceptions, members of the clergy, regular as well as secular, had not compromised themselves and were now responding favourably to the leadership of de Gaulle and to the presence of Catholics in the GPRF. Among other noteworthy conclusions in Latreille's report was the observation with reference to the Jewish minority "that the sympathy aroused for them by the appalling injustices committed against them has brought representatives of the different faiths closer together and would seem to create among them a bond which would not otherwise have been formed."[22]

In the aftermath of the remarkable forty-eight hour secular as well as spiritual consecration of de Gaulle, representatives of the Two Frances paid their respects to the general, in effect further reinforcing his legitimacy as the nation's leader. Henri d'Orléans, comte de Paris, heir to both the Orleanist and Bourbon claims to the throne, and Prince Jerôme Napoléon, who had played a minor role in the Resistance, offered the general their support. *Le Connétable*, meanwhile, did not deign to reply to a letter from Pétain who, insisting on his own legitimacy, offered to negotiate a transfer of power to avoid civil war. Nor was he much impressed when the man who had been head of state in June 1940, Albert Lebrun, came to pay him tribute. In his memoirs, de Gaulle notes with contempt that Lebrun had lacked only two things in the summer of 1940: he was no leader and there was no longer a French state to govern![23]

The seemingly universal acclamation of the Catholic Charles de Gaulle as champion of the Republic by the people of Paris was in itself remarkable. The spiritual divisions which had plagued the Third Republic seemed a thing of the past. The Catholics, Jews, and Protestants who had joined *Le Connétable* in London and Algiers were still at his side, symbolizing what appeared to be a new era of political ecumenism. On 1 January 1945, for instance, on his return from a visit to the Soviet Union, de Gaulle was greeted by France's Grand Rabbi Weill and Pastor Boegner, each of whom he received in private, following which he was welcomed by Nuncio Roncalli. This and other reciprocal gestures of recognition and respect reflected the new relationship between the Republic and the nation's spiritual communities, which the internal and external Resistance had generated and which Free France had so effectively incarnated.

In the meanwhile, the battle to liberate Europe would continue for another nine months and, with it, the effort to establish the authority of the GPRF throughout those parts of France which had not yet been liberated. Nowhere did this effort prove more critical than in the strategic northeast, the historic invasion route of attackers from across the Rhine. The challenge of defending the Provisional Government there was taken up by the Catholic Louis Closon, who had been chosen by the GPRF to act as *commissaire de la République* for the Nord and Pas-de-Calais departments.

In Paris following the city's liberation, Closon had been waiting for a signal from Delegate-General Alexandre Parodi before travelling to Lille, the headquarters of his designated jurisdiction.[24] Arriving at the Lille prefecture on 3 September, he ran into a man who had been *directeur du cabinet* to Roger Salengro, the Socialist minister of the interior during the Popular Front, who had committed suicide in November 1936 following a false charge in the right-wing press that he had deserted during World War I. A huge crowd had attended Salengro's funeral, at which Cardinal Liénart had condemned journalists for violating basic principles by engaging in unsubstantiated defamation.

Closon was invited by Cardinal Liénart to attend a special 8 September Te Deum mass in celebration of the Liberation. Since Liénart, who had earned a reputation as a friend of the working class, had also been (like most of his ecclesiastical colleagues) sympathetic to Vichy, Closon imposed two conditions before accepting: the prelate must come to the prefecture and publicly profess his acceptance of the Republic; and the newly arrived commissioner should be seated in the cathedral choir so that the congregation might witness the consecration of the new political order by the Church.

On 30 September, Closon welcomed de Gaulle to Lille. In an address to the local citizenry, the general outlined his vision of the radical changes which would come in the wake of Liberation: much of the economy would be nationalized and made subject to an overall plan; no tolerance would be shown to France's financial and industrial trusts which were responsible for much of the nation's pre-war weakness; and the working class would become an active participant in the governance of France's industrial enterprises.

Like de Gaulle, Closon was clearly committed to radical social and economic reform, but he was equally determined to prevent the overthrow of the republican order. Nevertheless, some local businessmen whose behaviour during the war he questioned saw the commissioner as "a red-heeled Robespierre"[25] (*Robespierre à talon rouge*). Ironically, while trying to calm the nervous bourgeoisie, Closon was challenged on the left by elements of the FFI and FTP, some of them still heavily armed, who frequently engaged in vengeful settling of accounts outside the courts or who engaged in acts of pillage (no doubt understandable given the grim winter of 1944–45 when the black market flourished). More alarming for Closon than this generalized turbulence was the slow dissipation of the popular enthusiasm with which de Gaulle had originally been welcomed. "Teetering on the verge of anarchy," Closon wrote, "France, after expressing an ephemeral gratitude, acted as though she owed him nothing."[26]

As winter gave way to spring, the sense of imminent crisis gave way in Lille and elsewhere to more mundane political concerns centred on the debates in the Constituent Assembly. When a year later, on 31 March 1946, the *commissaires de la République* ended their mandate, Closon noted bitterly that they were let go with no expression of gratitude from those they had tried to serve except from *Le Connétable*, in internal exile at Colombey-les-deux-Églises since his surprise resignation two months earlier.

The triumph of Charles de Gaulle and his ecumenical team of *commissaires* over Anglo-American (and Communist) plans to control the administration of France after D-Day was in itself a remarkable achievement. The double consecration in August 1944 of the Catholic general at the Paris City Hall and in Notre Dame Cathedral opened a new chapter in modern French history, signalling (among other things) the effective integration of the Catholic majority into the republican family. The subsequent purge of obviously reactionary members of the upper clergy helped end the virulent anticlericalism of the left.

As we shall see, the political ecumenism of Free France, which reflected the unity-in-diversity of the Second Republic, would prevail throughout the Fourth Republic and flourish under the Fifth.

EPILOGUE

Political Ecumenism, 1945–2005

Within the Free French camp, there had been a lively debate about whether the close communion among the men and women who had joined de Gaulle in London or Algiers should be transformed after victory into a permanent political *rassemblement*. Such a regrouping, it was argued, would perhaps even replace the pre-war parties whose sectarianism was seen as partly responsible for the catastrophe of 1940. The case for such a radical shift was put most passionately by Pierre Brossolette, who foresaw the emergence under de Gaulle's leadership of a vast political communion beyond old divisions of class and confession, citing Britain's Labour Party as evidence of its feasibility.

The commitment of the French Communist Party to the Resistance after Hitler's invasion of the Soviet Union in 1941, followed by what was seen as an effort by the PCF to establish its hegemony over all other anti fascist groups inside France and even to assume its dominance during Liberation, brought de Gaulle, despite his personal feelings in the matter, to encourage the revival of traditional parties as a counterweight. The vision of a post-war order in which new political formations would replace parties remained alive, however. Abjuring the label "party" and resorting to more "ecumenical" names such as "Mouvement," "Rassemblement," or "Union," a new generation of leaders, shaped by the political ecumenism of the Resistance, tried to aim at a national electorate above and beyond old fault-lines of faith and fortune, some on the left, others on the right.

Ironically, the first of these efforts at transcending old party labels was made by a group of progressive Catholics who had been an integral element in the internal as well as the external resistance. Men such as Georges Bidault, Louis Closon, and Maurice Schumann had clearly established their democratic and republican credentials, their *droit de cité* in post-war France. They possessed self-confidence and a capacity to govern; they had worked "ecumenically" with colleagues of other faiths and cultures; they had repudiated Vichy and all its works; and they had even insisted on the purging from the ecclesiastical as well as the political establishment of co-religionists who had collaborated with Vichy and the Nazis.[1]

Early in 1943, representatives of the Parti démocrate populaire, Jeune République, and other progressive Catholic groups decided to create a "Mouvement" based on their shared convictions and to do so without seeking episcopal sanction. The result was the Mouvement républicain populaire (MRP) which held its founding convention in late November 1944, presided over by Maurice Schumann, with Marc Sangnier as honorary president.

The MRP got more than one-quarter of the vote in 1946, in part because of its undeclared but obvious confessional (and thus *not* ecumenical) outlook, in part because of the absence in the immediate post-war situation of a structured conservative party which might defend Catholic interests in face of the militantly *laïque* SFIO and PCF. Many Catholic moderates who had "parked their votes" with the MRP would, however, shift to de Gaulle's more broadly based Rassemblement du peuple français (RPF) by 1951.[2]

Paradoxically, at a time when the MRP was still in its heyday, its leaders in the National Assembly made what amounted to a revolutionary reversal of philosophy by agreeing that *laïcité* be included as one of the founding principles of the Fourth Republic's constitution. *Laïcité* had been a watchword of republican devotion, binding Communists, Socialist, and Radicals in electoral alliances (in 1924 and 1936, for example) which otherwise made little sense, and forcing progressive Catholics to choose between endorsing anticlericalism or opting for Marc Sangnier's principled but marginal PDP or JR. Maurice Schumann and his colleagues having supported the motion, the National Assembly on 27 October 1946 voted that Article I of the new constitution read "La France est une République indivisible, laïque, démocratique et sociale."[3]

Tensions inside as well as outside the National Assembly between Catholics and non-Catholics over issues such as the public funding of *écoles libres* or laws dealing with human sexuality (abortion, contraception, and homosexuality, for instance) would remain; but, in accepting the principle of *laïcité,* Catholics helped open the way to their post-war participation in broad-based parties of the Left as well as the Right.

Unlike the MRP, the Union démocratique et socialiste de la Résistance (UDSR) derived both its membership and its doctrine directly from the Resistance and aimed from the beginning to produce the French equivalent of the Labour Party, bringing together secular and Christian socialists.[4] Its first president, the ex-Gaullist René Pleven, saw the UDSR as opening the way toward a third and definitive *Ralliement,* a hope reinforced by the substantial presence of Catholics (as well as Protestants) in its ranks. Its second president, the *catholique d'origine* François Mitterrand, would use the UDSR as a stepping-stone on his way to assuming the leadership of the new Parti socialiste in 1971.

Spurning both the MRP and the UDSR, either of which would have welcomed his endorsement (and even more his leadership), de Gaulle resisted appeals made to him by intimates that he take the lead right after the war in organizing a *rassemblement* across and beyond old party lines. Instead, he urged some of his chief lieutenants to join parties he had once reviled so that they might disseminate the unitary Gaullist gospel (including its anti-Communist component) across the political spectrum. In response to this advice, Alain Savary, the twenty-three-year-old Free French navy ensign who had been involved in the liberation of St. Pierre and Miquelon and had stayed on afterward as the islands' chief administrator, joined the SFIO; Michel Debré and Jacques Chaban-Delmas, de Gaulle's *délégé national militaire* at the time of the Normandy landings, joined the Radical Party; René Capitant and Jacques Baumel, a Protestant doctor who had joined Combat, acted as secretary-general of the MUR, and served as a member of the Consultative Assembly,[5] became members of the UDSR; and Edmond Michelet, a disciple of Péguy who had written for *Sept* and *L'Aube* in the 1930s, one of the first to defy Vichy on 20 June 1940 when he organized a Catholic resistance in his local town, (for which he was sent to Dachau), and Louis Terrenoire, joined the MRP. However, by the end of 1945, on the eve of his resignation from the presidency, it was clear to the general that the tactic of infiltrating France's conventional parties was not converting them to what he deemed to be a truly national vision.

On 16 June 1946, at Bayeux in Normandy, a town liberated by the Allies two years earlier, de Gaulle delivered a blistering indictment of the fledgling Fourth Republic. The speech ended with a call for a major constitutional reform to give France a powerful executive independent of political parties and thus able to represent and execute the national will. Then, throughout the early months of 1947, accompanied by a number of wartime comrades (including Admiral Thierry d'Argenlieu, Maurice Schumann, and Jacques Soustelle), the general made a series of speeches, climaxed by an appearance on 6 April at Strasbourg, where he celebrated the city's liberation and participated in a special commemorative mass.

The following day, surrounded by what amounted to a cabinet of personal advisors, (the Protestants Jacques Baumel and Jacques Soustelle, the Catholic René Capitant, and André Malraux[6]), de Gaulle appealed to a huge crowd to join him in launching the Rassemblement du peuple français, whose chief aim would be a radical reform of the state and the emergence of *La France nouvelle.* That same evening, Soustelle was named general secretary of the new formation and Malraux chosen to be its chief propaganda agent. The executive committee of the new formation included the Catholics Christian Fouchet and Gaston Palewski,[7] the Protestants Baumel (a veteran of the internal resistance), André Diethelm, and Louis Vallon, and the Jewish media baron Marcel Bleustein-Blanchet.

Throughout these months of hectic activity, de Gaulle had declared over and over again to his aide-de-camp Claude Guy, "We must recreate Free France!" adding on at least one occasion, as though echoing Brossolette, "After tearing one another apart, the old parties will give way, yes! To a single party!"[8]

France's three religious families were as well represented among new recruits to the RPF as they had been in Free France. Among Protestants, apart from Baumel, there was Pierre Lefranc, born in 1922, who had organized his fellow-students from the University of Paris law faculty to join him on 11 November 1940 in the first public demonstration inside France in favour of Free France at the Tomb of the Unknown Soldier. He would serve the RPF in a variety of capacities: as national secretary for youth, as party organizer in close electoral battles, as close advisor during the general's twelve-year exile, and as confidant during the 1958 crisis which brought *Le Connétable* back to power. After de Gaulle's death, Lefranc helped found the Institut Charles de Gaulle in Paris.[9]

The RPF found a third prominent Protestant recruit in Jacques Debû-Bridel, another veteran of the internal resistance, who was named under-secretary of the Navy following the Liberation. In 1948, a year after the founding of the *Rassemblement,* Debû-Bridel published *Les partis contre de Gaulle,* a powerful indictment of all the old-line parties. The neophyte Gaullist began by celebrating the remarkable legislative achievements of de Gaulle's administration during 1944–46 when it was not hobbled by partisan opposition. He followed this up by contending that, following the general's resignation, France found herself, much like early fifth-century

Athens, driven apart by factional quarrels from which only the RPF could rescue her.[10]

A less public but just as influential Protestant presence in the early days of the RPF was the banker Jean Richemont, who used the pseudonym "Alain Rozel." As a member of the Haute société Protestante, Richemont was in a position to offer financial aid as well as political counsel to the new organization.

No fewer than four veteran Protestant Gaullists – Jean-Marc Boegner, François Coulet, Pierre Denis, and Maurice Couve de Murville, who were neophyte diplomats when they joined Free France – maintained close links to de Gaulle after the war. By contrast, René Massigli, who never shared the general's long-term goals, parted company with de Gaulle before the end of the conflict.[11]

The Catholic contingent in the RPF was substantial. Claude Hettier de Boislambert was a successful candidate for the Rassemblement in the 1951 elections to the National Assembly, as was Christian Fouchet, who later served the Mendès France government as minister for Moroccan and Tunisian affairs. Gaston Palewski, a founding member of RPF's executive committee, was also elected in 1951 and was chosen vice-president of the National Assembly two years later. He was ambassador to Italy between 1957 and 1962, minister in charge of research in Premier Pompidou's administration and, finally, president of the Conseil constitutionnel as of 1965.

There were two major "converts" to the RPF from Christian democracy. After returning from a German prison camp, Edmond Michelet was named deputy minister of the Army in the de Gaulle government in 1945–46, became an RPF senator in 1952, served in de Gaulle's 1958 government and, later, in the administration of Prime Minister Debré in 1959. Louis Terrenoire, a journalist by profession, became director of news broadcasting for the national radio and television network after the war, belonging to the MRP until 1951, when de Gaulle selected him to replace Soustelle as secretary-general of the Rassemblement.

Yvon Morandat, the trade-union leader who had served as de Gaulle's emissary to the internal resistance, was another early Catholic recruit to the RPF. So, too, was Louis Joxe, France's ambassador to Moscow, then Bonn, before rejoining de Gaulle after 1958 as education minister, then as minister in charge of Algerian affairs, in which role he played a major part in negotiating the peace between France and Algeria in 1962. As justice minister in 1968, he faced the student insurrection in May of that year.[12]

Among the early Jewish adherents to the RPF was the political philosopher Raymond Aron, who explained years later that he decided to back de

Gaulle in 1947 for a variety of reasons. He felt guilty about not having participated in the Free French movement in wartime London, acknowledging that his judgment of de Gaulle's authoritarian personality had been unduly severe; he had become convinced that the only way to solve France's constitutional problems (which, he insisted, the Fourth Republic had worsened) was to back the general, who was now showing a proper respect for the parliamentary system; finally, he believed that the RPF offered the only effective guarantee against a Communist takeover.[13] Fear of social and political upheaval clearly played a role in the support given the Rassemblement in the late 1940s by Jewish industrialists and financiers. As Lacouture notes, Marcel Dassault, the brilliant Jewish aeronautical designer and manufacturer; Bleustein-Blanchet, the media baron; and Guy de Rothschild, the banker, were in all probability generous donors to the Rassemblement beginning in the late 1940s.[14]

The presence of RPF deputies in the National Assembly as of 1951 and the return to power of de Gaulle seven years later produced a major shift in the French political and social landscape. Despite the general's desire to gather all the elements of the population into the RPF and the presence of *gaullistes de gauche* in his inner circle, the Rassemblement turned more and more to the right, a process which would be accelerated with the arrival of Georges Pompidou as president in 1969. Paradoxically, this shift would help set the stage for the emergence of a broad, equally ecumenical, coalition on the left.

To begin with, through a tactical alliance with the MRP, moderates, and Radicals, RPF deputies helped pass a number of laws providing funding for the *écoles libres*. This legislation ended the attempts at a secular monopoly of the primary school system insisted on by partisans of *laïcité*, thereby effecting a compromise solution to the vexed school question.[15]

Second, the return of de Gaulle to power in 1958 provided the general with an opportunity to fashion a new constitution for what became the Fifth Republic. The result was the granting of vastly enhanced executive power to the president and prime minister and an effective end to *gouvernement d'assemblée*. When, following his near-assassination in 1962, de Gaulle succeeded in winning a referendum allowing for the election of the president by popular vote, the left was again opposed. Although most leftists began by denouncing the new constitution as Bonapartist in design, this view changed following the nearly successful run for the presidency by the Socialist (and Catholic) François Mitterrand in 1965, and ultimately brought the left to triumph by rallying around a single candidate and common program in 1981.

Third, the failure of *gaullistes de gauche,* led by Capitant and Vallon, to lobby successfully within the RPF for the radical socio-economic program they advocated through the 1950s and 1960s also, if indirectly, helped the left. Following principles de Gaulle had himself enunciated, left-wing Gaullists, as of 1951, pushed the case for an Association Capital-Travail, the replacement of laissez-faire capitalism by a free contract between workers and employers which would bring both working-class participation in management and its logical corollary, profit-sharing.[16] This lobbying effort, together with the conviction in a large part of the French proletariat that de Gaulle favoured their moral as well as economic emancipation, undoubtedly helps explain the strong support given the general by the working class. The defeat of *participation* (the code-name for the Capitant-Vallon reform) by business interests, despite its legislative enactment in 1965, and the lack of sympathy shown for it by de Gaulle's successor Georges Pompidou, gave the left a chance to recover its "natural" clientele among blue-collar workers.[17] It is worth noting here that Vallon, who denounced Pompidou for distorting the Gaullist ideal by pulling Gaullism to the right, supported the Socialist Mitterrand for the presidency in 1976.

A fourth element in this paradoxical contribution of Gaullism to its leftist counterpart came as a result of the resolution of the Algerian conflict by de Gaulle in 1962 and the subsequent transformation of almost all of France's vast empire into independent states linked by association to the former mother country. French imperialism in the modern age had been essentially the creation of stalwart republicans, most notably Jules Ferry in the 1880s, who justified colonization as an expression of France's "civilizing mission" in the world. And in post-war France it had been equally militant republicans (Prime Minister Guy Mollet, Interior Minister Mitterrand, and Jacques Soustelle, governor general of Algeria in 1955–56) who fought most ardently to retain the territory as an integral part of France. Gaullist policies of decolonization would thus liberate the left to focus more effectively on domestic affairs.

Finally, the overwhelming June 1968 electoral victory of the Gaullists following the student-worker insurrections of the previous month confirmed the conservative, not to say reactionary, nature of what had begun as an ideologically ambiguous *rassemblement.* It also offered the parliamentary left a chance to absorb the significance of the May 1968 "Revolution," to dismiss its Troyskyist and anarchist exuberance, and to evolve a program which would have broad-based appeal.

No one learned or profited more from the crises of the Fourth Republic than François Mitterrand, who would be the chief orchestrator of the all encompassing left-wing rally which gathered momentum in the 1970s.[18] Born in 1916, Mitterrand, like Charles de Gaulle, came from a deeply pious Catholic family; in his youth he had even thought of becoming a priest.[19] In the end, however, the young François chose to study law and political science in Paris before being called up for military service in 1939. Escaping after a brief experience as a German captive, Mitterrand served the État français as an administrator of prisoner-of-war affairs for which he was awarded Vichy's highest honour, the *Franciscque*. In terms of his post-war career, he at least partially redeemed himself by working in the internal resistance and then fled to London in November 1943 with a view to joining the Gaullist cause. Mitterrand refused, however, to pledge himself personally to the general; and a later interview with de Gaulle in Algiers proved unpleasant for both parties.[20]

Back in Paris in time for the city's liberation in August 1944, when he helped storm the War Prisoners' commissariat, Mitterrand joined de Gaulle's provisional government in a minor post. There followed cabinet positions in successive governments of the Fourth Republic. As interior minister in 1954, he declaimed "L'Algérie, c'est la France!" and justified the ruthless repression of the nationalist rising across the Mediterranean as an internal police operation. In June 1958, Mitterrand denounced the return to power of de Gaulle as "an act of insurrection and sedition." Later that year, he condemned the constitution of the Fifth Republic, and, in 1962, he expressed outrage at the passage of a referendum mandating the direct election of the president.

Three years after his protest at this constitutional revision, however, Mitterrand shifted course, running for the presidency on behalf of a newly formed leftist coalition, the Fédération de la gauche démocratique et socialiste (FGDS). Throughout the fall of 1965, he conducted a brilliant campaign – much of it on television – against a visibly aging de Gaulle, ending up a close second (45 to 54 per cent of the vote) behind the general in the December run-off. At the height of the May 1968 revolt, Mitterrand called for the creation of a provisional government under Pierre Mendès France and offered himself as candidate for the presidency in a prospective July election. Not surprisingly, given the electoral triumph of conservative forces in June, Mitterrand resigned as president of the FGDS in November. The grand rally of the left would have to be relaunched from scratch. A dozen years later Mitterrand won a decisive election as the socialist president of France.

That François Mitterrand, a socialist of Catholic background, had become president of the Republic was remarkable enough in itself. That his political ascendancy was paralleled by that of other prominent politicians who shared his faith reflects the fundamental shift toward Catholic support not only for the Republic but for the left in post-war France. It is evident that this shift was related to the Church's review of its place in the world at the Second Vatican Council.

Vatican II, convened by John XXIII in 1962 and concluded by Paul VI three years later, would have a transformative impact on French Catholics. Especially significant in this regard was the Council's *Declaration on Religious Liberty*, which repudiated traditional Church teaching that the rulers of Catholic states were bound to act as custodians, even enforcers, of the faith. While the text did not declare freedom of conscience to be an absolute right, it made clear that no power, secular or ecclesiastical, was justified in imposing spiritual conformity, thereby, indirectly at least, endorsing religious pluralism. Meanwhile, the ecumenical outlook of the papacy in matters theological was reflected by the presence at the Council of non-Catholic Christian observers, including the leader and chief representative of French Protestantism, Marc Boegner.

Even more relevant to Catholic voters than the new tolerance toward non-Catholics shown at Vatican II was the public declaration *For a Christian Political Practice* issued by the French episcopate in 1972, a year after the founding convention of the Parti socialiste (PS). The French ecclesiastical hierarchy made clear in this text their commitment to political pluralism and encouraged the faithful to involve themselves in all political parties except the PCF, thereby lifting what had been a proscription directed against Socialists and Radicals, whose leadership had usually been agnostic (and often Masonic) and who had championed the cause of integral *laïcité*.[21]

In many ways the most striking Catholic presence in the ministries over which Mitterrand and his prime ministers would preside during the 1980s was Laurent Fabius. Laurent was born in 1946.[22] His parents were Jewish, but they decided early in his childhood that he should be raised in the Catholic faith; his first communion took place in Notre Dame Cathedral. Although Fabius made almost no reference to his origins later in life, he was identified as a Jew by most of his fellow-citizens (and, with obvious racist overtones, by the extreme Right). His marriage in April 1981 to Françoise Castro, a practicing Jew, confused the public's perception of Fabius's ethnic and religious identity, making him even more vulnerable to anti-Semitic attacks.

Fabius *père* being a wealthy antique dealer and an indulgent father, the young and ambitious Laurent lived a rather sybaritic lifestyle while pursuing political studies at "Sciences-Po" and modern literature at the École normale. After becoming an *énarque,* Fabius served on the prestigious conseil d'État and engaged in municipal politics before being elected as a Socialist deputy in 1978. Re-elected in the Socialist sweep in 1981, he was named deputy to the minister of energy and finance, charged with preparing the budget. Two years later, he would be chosen prime minister.[23]

The presence of Jacques Delors in the winning coalition put together by Mitterrand substantially reinforced its Catholic component. Born in Paris in 1925 to devout parents, Delors (in many ways the heir to Marc Sangnier) conducted a lengthy search for a political party that would allow him to translate his religious faith into social action.[24] At age fourteen, he became a member of the JOC. Following the Liberation, at the beginning of a seventeen-year-long career with the Bank of France, he joined the MRP. Less than a year later, in February 1946, he quit the Mouvement because of the conflict between its radical rhetoric and its conservative policies, most notably (in his view) its overt exploitation of religious references for electoral purposes. Not embarrassed to be thought of as an "anticlerical believer," Delors endorsed the principle of *laïcité* as the indispensable prelude to a fruitful dialogue among Catholics, Jews, Protestants, and Muslims, without which social progress was impossible.[25]

Two related problems haunted Delors during these years of political searching: the failure of France's Christian democrats and democratic socialists to come together; and the absence of a powerful personality to unite the non-Communist left and lead it to power.[26] The founding convention of the new Parti socialiste in 1971, dominated by Mitterrand, set the stage for the all-inclusive coalition Delors had been waiting for. The PS named him national delegate for international relations in 1976, a post he held until 1981 when, following the victory of the left, he was named minister of the economy and of finance. By the 1990s, Delors's daughter Martine Aubry was a prominent figure in the PS.

The prominence of Jews in the PS is due in large measure to Mitterrand's pronounced philo-Semitism.[27] One of his most durable friendships was with Georges Dayan, a secular Jew from Oran whom he met while both were studying law and whom he cherished until Dayan's death in 1979. As an experienced politician, Mitterrand counted among his intimates his brother-in-law, the actor Roger Hanin, the brilliant economist Jacques Attali, born in Algiers in 1943, who became his special advisor in 1981, and the jurist Robert Badinter, whom he would name justice minister. His philo-Semitism led Mitterrand to encourage these and other Jewish friends to express their ethnic inheritance openly and abandon the excessive discretion which had not, in any event, saved their co-religionists from prejudice and discrimination.

Unlike most gentile politicians of his generation, Mitterrand had a sophisticated understanding of the Old Testament. Ten years before coming to power, he had visited Israel and met with its leading politicians, angering the substantial pro-Palestinian elements in the PS in the process.[28]

As Maurice Szafran has noted, Mitterrand's favourable disposition toward the Jews contrasted radically with what they had experienced with French heads of state since de Gaulle's description of the Jews as elitist, arrogant, and domineering at a November 1967 press conference following the Six Day war.[29] Georges Pompidou had further undermined good relations by opening a diplomatic dialogue with Libya; by pardoning Paul Touvier, head of the Vichy Milice at Lyon during the Occupation and thus ultimately responsible for the death of many Jews; by suggesting that Jews felt a divided loyalty to Israel as well as France; and by delaying the screening of the documentary *Le Chagrin et la Pitié*, which offered a candid glimpse of collaborationist attitudes in wartime Clermont-Ferrand. Finally, Valery Giscard d'Estaing had continued the pro-Arab tilt of French foreign policy and had neglected to attend the religious service which commemorated those killed in the terrorist bombing of a Paris synagogue on October 1980; and he had mandated the Jewish health minister Simone Veil to pilot legislation through the National Assembly sanctioning abortion, exposing her to right-wing charges that she was thereby abetting genocide!

The deepening antipathy felt by Jews toward Mitterrand's predecessors clearly helps explain the massive Jewish vote (150,000–200,000) the Socialist leader obtained in May 1981, especially when it is seen in the context of his public display of confidence in, and affection for, Jews. This spontaneous sympathy, together with the president's keen awareness of French Jewish life and culture led, naturally enough, to close links between the *Élysée* and the Jewish minority during the 1980s and to the appointment of a number of Jews to high-level political and administrative positions, including Jack Lang and Dominique Strauss-Kahn.[30]

Protestants were, not surprisingly given their traditional support for the left, well represented in the PS. Lionel Jospin, who was perhaps as responsible for the party's victory in 1981 as Mitterrand himself, came from a solidly Protestant background. His father Robert, an austere *Réformé*, presided over regular family Bible-reading and studied for the pastorate before committing himself to the pacifist cause in the 1930s. The young Lionel attended temple regularly enough but apparently without much conviction. In this regard, his biographers conclude, "If it is perhaps excessive to speak of an education stamped with the seal of religion, there is no question that Protestant culture, with its strong moral concern for justice, its focus on individual responsibility and its rejection of hypocrisy, profoundly affected the Jospin children ... The young Lionel laid proud claim to this inheritance."[31]

Following military service, a stint at "Sciences-Po," and training as an *énarque*, Jospin joined the diplomatic service for a five-year period, beginning in 1965. During these youthful years, Jospin belonged to a Trotskyist group although, unlike so many others of his generation, he played no role in the student insurrection of May 1968. In 1969, he began what would be a brief academic career.

In the summer of 1971, Jospin phoned his co-religionist Pierre Joxe,[32] son of the wartime Gaullist (and Catholic) Louis Joxe, with a view to meeting Mitterrand. In short order, he became part of the future president's inner circle, commissioned, among other things, to organize the newly created PS in the Paris region. In late 1970, no doubt because of Jospin's exposure to ideological debate during his Troyskyist phase, Mitterrand charged his brilliant lieutenant with working out an entente with the Communists. The result was an agreement by both parties, if elected, to engage in a comprehensive program of nationalization, something social democrats in the PS viewed with considerable alarm. In 1980, Jospin was made first secretary of the party, a role which he exploited to the fullest by orchestrating both Mitterrand's successful campaign for the presidency in 1981 and the subsequent triumph of the PS in securing an absolute majority in the National Assembly.[33]

Another of Mitterrand's close, if not intimate, Protestant collaborators was Michel Rocard.[34] Born in 1930 to a physicist of Catholic background turned agnostic and a mother who had been baptized in the Roman communion before converting to the Reformed faith, the young Rocard's outlook would be greatly influenced by his experience in two key Protestant institutions. His primary education was at the École alsacienne, founded to educate the children of Protestants who had fled Alsace following its transfer to Germany in 1871; and he spent years in France's Protestant scout organization, the Éclaireurs. Higher education included "Sciences-Po" and the Paris law faculty, where Rocard battled (with the help of the Jeunesse étudiante catholique) for the autonomy of the leading student union against right-wing militants, led by Jean-Marie Le Pen, as well as against the Communist-led student syndicate.

In 1949, Rocard joined the SFIO. Eight years later, he bitterly criticized his party's Algerian policy, condemning Prime Minister Mollet's sanctioning of torture and incarceration of Muslim rebels and arguing that national liberation movements in the Third World were irreversible and should be accommodated. In 1958, unlike most of his colleagues, Rocard insisted that de Gaulle's return to power did not pose a fascist threat and even went so far as to suggest, in terms Gaullists would not challenge, that France's incapacity to resolve the Algeria dilemma derived in large part from the fractious and sectarian nature of her multi-party system. Rocard observed the student and working-class insurrection of May 1968 from a critical distance, deploring the ideological excesses of *gauchisme* while finding much to admire in the grass-roots search for more autonomy at the local level in French institutions. After running unsuccessfully for the presidency in the 1969 campaign, he joined the PS in 1974 and was seconded to the Jewish economist Jacques Attali to negotiate a common program with the PCF.

As Mitterrand's grand coalition took form in the late 1970s, Rocard situated himself clearly as a social democrat, favouring decentralization and experimentation in contrast to the "Jacobin" tendencies in the PS, which supported increase of state control and massive nationalization of banking and industry. Following the PS triumph of 1981, he was put in charge of national economic planning and regional development. He was prime minister between 1988 and 1991.

One can only speculate about the role André Philip, the leading Protestant Socialist of his generation, might have played in a PS led by Mitterrand. In any event, Philip died in July 1970, a few months before de Gaulle and a year before the PS was born. His generation was represented in the new party by an engaging figure, Gaston Defferre, who managed to accommodate himself well enough to the new leader.

Defferre was born in 1910. His father, a lawyer, took his family to Senegal ten years later. In 1922, Defferre returned to France with his mother.[35] He studied law at the university in Aix-la-Chapelle and opened up a practice in Marseille.[36] In September 1935, the young lawyer married Andrée Aboulker, daughter of a prominent Jewish doctor in Algiers (and sister to the José Aboulker who played a key role in the November 1942 Gaullist uprising in support of Operation "Torch").

Unable to enter military service in 1939 on health grounds, Defferre played a decisive role in the underground network "Brutus" which, by the fall of 1942, was solidly implanted throughout southern France. A face-to-face meeting with de Gaulle in Algiers in 1943 created what would be a durable feeling of animosity between the two men. Disdaining a role in the Consultative Assembly, Defferre returned to France in October 1943 where, with the help of his co-religionist Francis Leenhardt, he established a solid political base.

Defferre served in a number of post-war governments, most notably as minister of overseas affairs under Guy Mollet, beginning in January 1956. The law of 19 June 1956, which he piloted through the National Assembly and which granted substantial autonomy to France's African and Asian colonies, turned out to be a decisive step toward the mutually arranged independence of much of France's empire.

Defferre opposed de Gaulle's return to power following the May 1958 uprising in Algiers but urged support for the constitution of the Fifth Republic on the grounds that only a strong executive could impose the kind of liberal policies in Algeria and elsewhere that he favoured. Following de Gaulle's resignation in 1969, he stood as a candidate for the presidency, ending up with a lamentable 5 per cent of the popular vote in the first round. Two years later, he was involved in the launching of the PS and, subsequently, in the hammering out of a common program with the Communists. Following Mitterrand's triumph in May 1981, he was named interior minister.[37]

Quite apart from Defferre, Jospin, Joxe, and Rocard, France's Protestants (who were beginning to be described as a "micro-minority" by sociologists) held a number of political offices far out of proportion to their population.[38] This obvious over-representation aroused old prejudices and fueled a lively public debate.[39]

The triumph of the PS in 1981 and its subsequent electoral successes were achieved by a politically ecumenical team reflecting *La France plurielle* and led by a *catholique d'origine.* There is an obvious symmetry and complementarity between this left wing *rassemblement* and that which came together under the Catholic Charles de Gaulle in Free France and again in the RPF. Both *rassemblements* were led by men who represented what is still a culturally and sociologically Catholic nation, what Maurras called *La France réelle* and is now described, in politically correct terms, as *La France profonde.* Thus, a decade after the death of Charles de Gaulle, the Two Frances, Catholic and republican, which had experienced reconciliation and reunion in the hectic atmosphere of wartime London and Algiers, had found a way to live out this new-found political ecumenism in peacetime and to express it on both sides of the National Assembly as well as in the democratic contest for the presidency of the Republic.

Notes

INTRODUCTION

1 V. M. Boegner, *L'exigence oecuménique. Souvenirs perspectives,* for a French Protestant's view of the ecumenical movement since the end of World War II, when Catholics became committed to it. For an account of the Catholic interest (and ultimate participation) in the cause of Christian unity, v. E. Fouilloux, *Les catholiques et l'unité chrétienne du XIXe au XXe siècle.*

2 Public opinion polls in which the French are asked to declare their religious affiliation give us at least an approximate sense of the proportion of the Catholic majority, broadly defined. In 1952, for instance, some 79 per cent of those polled defined themselves as Catholic. V. Sutter, *La vie religieuse des Français à travers les sondages d'opinion,* I, 623.

For a comprehensive survey of Catholic, Jewish, and Protestant history in the modern period, see Le Goff and Rémond, *Histoire de la France religieuse,* Vol. 4. Cholvy and Hilaire, *Histoire religieuse de la France contemporaine,* focuses on the modern period. Both multi-volume studies give special attention to French Catholicism.

3 The Jewish population, broadly defined, made up at most 1 per cent of the population during the period which concerns us. A useful survey of Franco-Jewish history is offered in Philippe, *Être juif dans la société française.* The most comprehensive scholarly account is to be found in Blumenkranz, *Histoire des juifs en France.* Malino and Wasserstein, *The Jews in Modem France* includes a lively debate among Jewish scholars with differing perspectives.

4 Michael Marrus, *The Politics of Assimilation*, offers a highly critical assessment of the impact of France's assimilationist policy on the Jewish minority. At the same time, Marrus points to the persistent efforts of secular Jews to assert their links to their ancestral faith, citing, among others, the Jewish writer Pierre Abraham who recalled that his secular father, during the late nineteenth century, went to synagogue for Rosh Hashanah, celebrated Passover at home, fasted strictly on Yom Kippur, and arranged for a religious education for his sons until their bar mitzvah (62–3).

5 In *Essai sur la régénération physique, morale et politique des juifs* (1787). Léon Bloy, in *Le Salut par les juifs* (1892), and through his personal proselytizing, encouraged a number of conversions in the early twentieth century.

6 Excellent surveys of modern and contemporary French Protestant history can be found in Baubérot, *Le Retour des Huguenots*; Cabanel, *Les Protestants et la République*; and A. Encrevé, *Les Protestants en France de 1800 à nos jours.* Indispensable for this research were two works by Poujol, *Protestants dans la France en 1939–1945* and, in collaboration with A. Encrevé, *Les protestants français pendant la deuxième guerre mondiale.*

7 Latreille and Siegfried, *Les forces religieuses et la vie politique. Le catholicisme et le protestantisme*, 167, 206.

8 Cabanel, *Les Protestants et la République*, 117.

9 In chapter 14, devoted to the 1942 Allied invasion of French North Africa, an explanation will be offered as to why France's "fourth religious family," the Muslims, were not, in the end, included in de Gaulle's ecumenical alliance during the war.

10 One of the key organizations of anti-fascist action inside France was Combat, co-founded in the fall of 1941 by the Catholic Captain Henri Frenay, future leader of the underground Armée secrète, and the Protestant Bertie Albrecht, born to Swiss-Lutheran parents, who, after joining in the struggle against Vichy and the Nazis, was captured by the Gestapo in June 1943 and died three days later in a Paris prison. A number of Christian Democrats, including Georges Bidault, Claude Bourdet, François de Menthon, and Pierre-Henri Teitgen, were also active participants in Combat.

Further to the left and more secular in outlook was Libération whose leadership included the Protestant philosophy professor Jean Cavaillès, the Catholic trade-unionist Yvon Morandat, and the nominally Catholic aristocrat Emmanuel d'Astier de la Vigerie. Also on the left was the organization Franc-Tireur, which included in its ranks a few members of the Catholic Jeune République party, as well as a number of secular Jews such as Jean-Pierre Lévy and the eminent historian Marc Bloch.

One of the most defiant and therefore most celebrated underground newspapers during the war, *Témoignage chrétien*, was produced at Lyon by two Jesuits, Pierre Chaillet and Gaston Fessard, together with the Protestant pastor Roland de Pury. Originally calling itself *Témoignage catholique*, the clandestine paper renamed itself after absorbing its much smaller Reformed equivalent, *La Feuille*. Articles from *Témoignage chrétien* were reprinted in wartime London by two Catholic *Français libres*, Louis Closon and Maurice Schumann, editors of *Volontaire pour la cité chrétienne*. V. Bédarida, *Les armes de l'Esprit. Témoignage chrétien 1941–1944*.

Finally, it should be noted that the training school established with the support of Pétain at Uriage near Grenoble in the fall of 1940 was dominated by conservative Catholics including its leader, Pierre Dunoyer de Segonzac, Hubert Beuve-Méry (post-war editor of *Le Monde*), and the ideologically versatile Emmanuel Mounier. The Protestants René Gillouin, Georges Casalis, and André Dumas were part of the group whose aim was to promote a new "State culture" that was authoritarian, anti-liberal and, at least to some degree, racialist (no Jews were to be found either among the cadres or students at Uriage). V. Hellman, *The Knight-Monks of Uriage*.

11 Pétain, a World War I hero, had been a cabinet minister and ambassador to Spain; he assumed the premiership following Paul Reynaud's resignation in June 1940 and was voted plenipotentiary power as head of a new entity, L'État français, on 10 July. De Gaulle, who had been made under-secretary of war on the eve of the disaster, used this second-tier link to the Reynaud government to justify the creation in London, not of a government-in-exile, but of an ad hoc organization he called La France libre, to which Winston Churchill extended his personal support.

12 This position is consistently taken by the abbé Georges de Nantes, editor of the ultra-orthodox periodical *La Contre-Réforme au XXe siècle*.

13 To evaluate the status of the Catholic faith in the generation which concerns us here, two pioneers in the sociology of religion, Gabriel Le Bras, a professor of law at the University of Paris, and Canon Fernand Boulard undertook, beginning in the 1930s, a comprehensive study of Catholic France, parish by parish, throughout France. The result, published in 1947, was "a religious map of France," which, with subsequent refinements, is regularly cited by students of recent French history. Le Bras and Boulard identify the East and West of France, together with the Massif central and the western Pyrenees, as centres of abiding faith, while the Centre, the South-West and the Mediterranean Midi, together with several major urban areas (Paris and Marseilles among them), are characterized as lost to the faith or, at best, indifferent. Boulard, *Premiers itinéraires en sociologie religieuse*.

Challenging these conclusions, the English historian Theodore Zeldin has asked what results such a survey would have uncovered centuries before 1947 when mass illiteracy, the confusion of Christianity with earlier pagan beliefs, and the pressure by priests and monarchs to conform at least outwardly to Catholic practice all influenced religious belief. As Zeldin puts it,

> The myth that France was pious and Catholic before the Revolution was invented by modern conservatives idealizing the middle ages. In the eighteenth century there was little militant abstention from religion, but only a small and unorganized minority was fervently devout. Most people went to church, but by no means every Sunday; nearly everybody took Easter communion, but though faith was sincere it was frequently passive, induced by social pressure or combined with appalling ignorance of the doctrines of the Church and with much superstition … The study of the different varieties of Catholicism in France is still in its infancy; but it is clear that in certain regions the marriage between them was not successful, so that once the pressure for religious conformity was lifted by the revolution of 1789 and then again by that of 1830, the divorce, often latent, became public. Zeldin. *France 1845–1945*, II, 984.

14 *Le Monde*, 19 January 1996. A month earlier, it should be noted, during a visit to Paris by Pope John Paul II to commemorate the 1500th anniversary of Clovis's conversion, a crowd of some 10,000 Parisians gathered to celebrate the separation of Church and state ninety years earlier. Demonstrators in this militantly secularist crowd denounced His Holiness as "l'assassin par opium du peuple," updating the old Marxist maxim that religion was the opiate of the masses. Reference to these two events and to their symbolic meaning for the Two Frances is made in Chadwick, *Catholicism, Politics and Society in Twentieth-Century France*, 5– 6.

15 Members of the Reformed, or Calvinist, communion, popularly known as Huguenots, numbered about 500,000 in 1789. The rights of the roughly 200,000 Lutherans living in Alsace had been guaranteed by the Treaty of Westphalia (1648).

16 France's Jews were not only few in number but were also geographically dispersed and ethnically diverse. The Ashkenazi in Alsace, Lorraine, and Paris were essentially ghettoized; their Sephardic cousins in Bordeaux, Bayonne, Avignon, and the Comtat-Venaissin were often already being integrated, albeit at a slow pace and with varying degrees of acceptance.

17 The long-term significance of the Declaration is reflected in the creation of the Ligue pour la défense des Droits de l'Homme in February 1898, at the height of the Dreyfus Affair. Membership in the Ligue became a symbol of fidelity to the Republic and a prime target for Vichy and the Nazis after 1940.

18 J. Bild, *L'abbé Grégoire*, offers a full account of the abbé's life, together with letters and speeches attesting to Grégoire's loyalty to both Church and Republic.

19 Some 225 priests were murdered during the September 1792 massacres in Paris. Louis XVI, guillotined in January 1793, is often seen as a saintly victim, as are some of those who suffered during the brutal de-Christianization campaign which raged between October 1793 and March 1794. The "Trinity" of revolutionary martyrs – Joseph Cambon, Le Peletier de Saint-Fargeau, and Jean-Paul Marat – left a much less impressive mark on the popular mentality.

20 V. Roberts, "The Origins of a Mythology: Freemasons, Protestants, and the French Revolution." Poland, *French Protestantism and The French Revolution*, effectively demonstrates the ideological rifts within the Protestant communion in the 1790s and thus puts to rest any remaining belief in a coherent Protestant plot against the ancien régime.

V. Glaudes, *Images de la Réforme au XIXe siècle*. Baubérot, "La vision de la Réforme chez les publicistes antiprotestants (fin XIX–début XXe siècle)," in Joutard, *Historiographie de la Réforme*, 216–38, analyzes the continuing presence of anti-Protestant prejudice throughout the nineteenth century.

21 C. Maurras, *L'Enquête sur la Monarchie* (1900).

22 Fears of an authoritarian military figure of Catholic background presuming to guide France's destiny led many republicans to condemn de Gaulle as well as Pétain in 1940.

23 The atheist Cult of Reason (1793), the deist Worship of the Supreme Being (1794), Philanthropy (1797), and the *Culte décadaire* had an equally ephemeral impact.

24 A more thoroughly researched attack on the Protestant moneyed interests and their influence on political life is to be found in Beau de Lomenie, *Les responsabilités des dynasties bourgeoises*. It is worth noting that this indictment of France's financial oligarchy was launched during the Vichy period.

25 Catholic bankers were also a part of the nineteenth-century banking scene. But their boldest venture, the Union générale, launched in 1878 by Paul-Eugène Bontoux and supported by members of the aristocracy and lower clergy, collapsed in January 1882, in part because Protestant and Jewish competitors flooded the market with Union générale stock and thereby depreciated its value. The crash of the Union générale helps explain the virulence of popular anti-Semitism at the time of the Dreyfus Affair.

26 V. Christophe, *Les choix du clergé dans les révolutions de 1789, 1830 et 1848*, II, 113–223.

27 Anticlerical in outlook, the emperor nevertheless came to see the Catholic Church as a key element in his authoritarian rule. Although Protestants were suspected of harbouring Orleanist or republican sentiments during these

decades, the banker Achille Fould, a convert from Judaism to the Reformed faith, was the emperor's finance minister between 1849 and 1852. Jews not only participated actively in the economic and political life of the regime; in 1860 some of their most prominent leaders launched the Alliance israëlite universelle which spread the gospel of French civilization among Jewish communities throughout the Mediterranean basin. Finally, Napoleon III saw himself as patron and protector of France's fourth religious family, Algeria's Muslims, an attitude which was reversed during the Third Republic when the European settlers established a powerful lobby in Paris.

28 There are usually exceptions to any such sweeping generalization. The role of the Protestant Louis Rossel during the Commune is analyzed in Encrevé, "Les protestants et la Commune de Paris en 1871."

29 V. Encrevé and Richard, *Les Protestants dans les débuts de la Troisième République*, for an analysis of the role played by Protestants in the formative years of the Third Republic.

30 V. Larkin, *Religion, Politics and Preferment in France since 1890*. For a polemical point of view on this issue, v. Michelon, *La République contre les libertés*, where a case is made that freedom for monastic orders, anarchists, civil servants, prostitutes, and France's royal families was radically reduced or eliminated during these years.

31 V. Baubérot, *Vers un nouveau pacte laïque*, for a discussion of the idea of *laïcité* as it has evolved in modern France.

32 It was Gambetta who, in May 1877, uttered the phrase, "Le cléricalisme, voilà l'ennemi!" Émile Combes, an ex-seminarian, Freemason, spiritualist, and intransigent anticlerical, was prime minister from June 1902 to January 1904, during which time he vigorously applied laws against Catholic teaching orders but hesitated about total church-state separation on the ground that the Concordat of 1802 had given successive French governments adequate control over the ecclesiastical hierarchy.

33 Nicolet, *L'idée républicaine en France*.

34 *Égalité*, in Poulat's view, was bound to engender (especially in its Marxist formulation), an impossible vision of a worldwide classless society.

35 Poulat, *Liberté, Laïcité*.

36 Much of the inspiration for this reform came from intellectual reactions to France's defeat at the hands of Protestant Prussia. The historian Ernest Renan, in *La Réforme intellectuelle et morale* (1871), argued that Prussia's schoolmasters, steeped in Protestant culture, had inculcated in their nation's youth a self-reliance, critical intelligence, and sense of social responsibility which French soldiers, many of whom had been trained by priests, were unable to match.

37 In his memoirs, the Protestant novelist André Chamson gives an amusing account of real-life street battles between students at public school such as

himself and Catholic boys fighting for the honour of the *école libre* in the town of Le Vigan. Chamson, *Le chiffre de nos jours*, 313–25.

38 A succinct historiography of the scholarly debate over whether the cardinal or His Holiness was the prime initiator in the process leading toward the Ralliement is offered in de Montclos, *Le Toast d'Alger*, 1–47.

39 Delbeil, *Marc Sangnier*, offers a collection of portraits of Sangnier by sympathetic devotees and supporters.

40 A full account of this socially radical protestant group is offered in Crespin, *Des protestants engagés*.

41 In fact, France's Jewish community by and large believed Dreyfus to be guilty and in any event was convinced that anti-Semitism was a German pestilence, which had temporarily infected French society.

42 The literature on the Dreyfus Affair is enormous. A comprehensive analysis of all aspects of the Affair, including a study of *dreyfusard* and *antidreyfusard* opinion is offered in J.-D. Bredin, *L'Affaire*.

43 V. A. Leroy-Beaulieu, *Les doctrines de haine. L'antisémitisme, l'antiprotesantisme, l'anticléricalisme* (1902). There is an abundant literature in the case of all three prejudices. Mellor, *Histoire de l'anticléricalisme français* and Rémond, *L'anticléricalisme en France de 1815 à nos jours* deal with the origins and historic variations in French anticlericalism. Byrnes, *Anti-Semitism in Modern France*, Vol. 1 covers the nineteenth century evolution of this prejudice thoroughly. Isaac, *Genèse de l'antisémitisme*, insists on the Christian origins of anti-Jewish feeling, and exercised a key role in reshaping official Catholic attitudes toward Jews before and during Vatican II.

The foremost propagator of anti-Semitism in the last decades of the nineteenth century was Edouard Drumont whose two-volume *La France Juive*, published in 1886, went through 127 editions in two years. Drumont portrayed for his readers an idealized version of medieval France held together until the French Revolution by shared Catholic faith and values. Anticlericalism and the appetite of a ruthless bourgeoisie had undermined this ideal society. The Revolution, by subverting Church, monarchy, and family, had released a rapacious capitalist class whose most destructive elements were the Jews with their all-powerful banking interests. In contrast to those scholars who have seen anti-Semitism as primarily a product of Christian and, more particularly Catholic, teaching, Pierrard, *Juifs et catholiques français*, points to the dedicated efforts by a succession of Catholic thinkers, including Charles Péguy, Stanislas Fumet, and François Mauriac, to promote Judeo-Christian rapprochement. It might be noted here that Judeo-Protestant amity throughout modern French history has been based on a common stress on scripture, parallel memories of persecution by the clergy and monarchy and, often, by intermarriage.

Steven C. Hause, "Anti-Protestant Rhetoric in the Early Third Republic," offers a useful update of a theme dealt with by earlier scholars. Ernest Renauld, *Le Péril Protestant. Essai d'Histoire Contemporaine* (Tolba, 1899) expresses the virulence of late nineteenth-century anti-Protestant propaganda.

44 The literature dealing with the Separation law is substantial. Key analyses include the following: A.-M. and J. Maudit, *La France contre la France. La Séparation de l'Église et de l'État, 1902–1906*; and Méjan, *La Séparation des Églises et de l'État.*

45 Among its chief functions, the Conseil d'État advises on legal disputes between citizens and the state.

CHAPTER ONE

1 It is worth noting, because it reflects the continuing deep rift in the national mentality, that the president of the Republic, Raymond Poincaré, as well as Prime Minister Clemenceau and the entire cabinet, boycotted the Te Deum mass held in Notre Dame Cathedral in 1919 to celebrate the nation's victory over the Central Powers. By contrast, in August 1944, de Gaulle headed the procession to the cathedral for the same Catholic ceremony.

2 It was Barrès who, in this text, relayed to the French public a remarkable anecdotal case of ecumenical brotherhood in the heat of battle on 19 August 1914. A friend of the novelist, Père Janin, serving as an army chaplain, had been present when the Grand Rabbi of Lyon, Abraham Bloch, offered a crucifix to a mortally wounded Catholic soldier, practicing a compassionate spiritual deception before in turn dying in Janin's arms. Barrès rightly saw in this sublime gesture a signal both of reciprocal spiritual respect and exalted patriotism. Barrès, *Les Diverses Familles spirituelles de la France* in *L'Œuvre de Maurice Barrès*, vol. 8, 364. In one long passage at the core of the text, Barrès delivers a passionate tribute to all the spiritual families of modern France, urging them to harness their faith to universal as well as purely national aims:

> "For God and France!" was the universal cry of our ancestors when they marched against the foe. Today, we give voice to the same thought in a dozen different ways. Our soldiers tell themselves that, as they devote themselves to France, they are defending the Catholic Church or the Protestant churches, or the social Republic, or Free thought. Each one associates his religion or his philosophy with France. And, miraculously, they are all right!

3 "La France, pays de mission ou 'Le Grand Retour.'" V. Cholvy and Hilaire, *Histoire religieuse de la France*, Vol. 3, 121–5, offers a succinct analysis of this revival as do Le Goff and Rémond, *Histoire de la France religieuse*, Vol. 4, 215–58. Rémond gives a more detailed account of Catholic political life in *Les Catholiques dans la France des années 30* as does Christophe, *Les catholiques et le Front populaire.*

4 In March 1943, a pilgrimage characterized as *Le Grand Retour* set out from Boulogne on the Channel to travel all over France, preceded by a statue of the Virgin Mary, in an ambitious effort to encourage the reconsecration of the nation (now identified as *un pays de mission*) to the Church.

5 Fouilloux, *Les chrétiens français entre crise et Libération.*

6 Chief among these new associations were: the Confédération française des travailleurs chrétiens (CFTC) founded in 1919; the Jeunesse ouvrière chrétienne (JOC), created in 1926; and the Jeunesse agricole chrétienne (JAC) and Jeunesse étudiante chrétienne (JEC), both dating from 1929.

7 The injunction of Pius XI to stop reading Maurras, issued in 1926, had some effect (de Gaulle's father ended his subscription): but it was lifted in July 1939, just two months before the opening of World War II and the seeming triumph of Maurrassian thought.

8 Amouroux, *Quarante millions de pétainistes.*

9 Kevin Passmore, "Catholicism and Nationalism: the *Fédération républicaine*, 1927–1939," in Chadwick, *Catholicism, Politics and Society in Twentieth-Century France*, 47–72.

10 Jean-Claude Delbreil, "Les formes politiques de la démocratie chrétienne en France au vingtième siècle," in ibid., 119–41.

11 In 1938, the PDP supported the moderate right government of Édouard Daladier and worked with the premier for a new church-state accommodation with representatives of Pius XI, an initiative aborted by the death of the pontiff and the beginning of the war. Three PDP deputies voted plenipotentiary powers to Pétain in July 1940; others supported the internal resistance and Free France.

12 Rémond, *Les catholiques dans la France des années 30*, 208–41. Rémond notes with interest the existence on the far left of an ecumenically Christian group including André Philip and Paul Ricœur, calling themselves "Christian revolutionaries" and committing themselves to a total transformation of the capitalist system.

13 Hellman, *Emmanuel Mounier and the New Catholic Left*, provides a comprehensive study of Mounier's ideological itinerary.

14 For an overall view of the internal resistance, v. Kedward, *Resistance in Vichy France* or the more concise Muracciole, *Historie de la Résistance en France.*

How France's Catholics reacted to the crisis of 1940 has been a matter of substantial scholarly debate. In the immediate aftermath of World War II, when the Left enjoyed a quasi-monopoly on French cultural as well as political life, the Occupation and Vichy were put inside a historical parenthesis and replaced by the myth of an all but unanimous resistance. In *The Vichy Syndrome*, Henry Rousso examines this blotting out of *les années noires* ("The Dark Years, 1940–1944") and its implication for historians and for the French sense of their own recent past. A quarter-century after the Liberation, two works by outsiders did much to demolish the "resistentialist" myth and to expose the reality of Vichy France. In *Le Chagrin et la Pitié* (1970), the Swiss filmaker Marcel Ophuls presented what purported to be a documentary enquete on life in Clermont-Ferrand during the Vichy period. The result was a depressing view of political passivity or worse still, collaboration with the Nazis. Happily for their reputation, among historians at least, the American John Sweets spent many months among the men and women of Clermont-Ferrand and concluded that the townsfolk soon rejected Pétain's "New Order," and often joined the resistance. V. Sweets, *Choices in Vichy France.*

More broadly influential than the Ophuls film in debunking the "resistential" myth was the examination of Vichy France by the American historian Robert Paxton, published in 1972 and translated into French the following year. Paxton reveals the extent to which the Catholic Church as well as Vichy disenfranchised intellectual and religious minorities, collaborated in the dispatch of forced labour to work in the Third Reich, and facilitated Hitler's plan to liquidate European Jews. V. Paxton, *Vichy France. Old Guard and New Order, 1940–1944.*

Writing in 1995, fifty years after the Liberation, the British historian W.D. Halls reintroduced Paxton's bill of attainder against Vichy with damning new evidence. Halls excoriates those Catholics who tried to expunge 150 years of French history and effect a full-blown counter-revolution; he cites the August 1940 declaration by France's Assembly of Cardinals and Archbishops that France has a sacred duty to obey the new *pouvoir légitime* and Cardinal Gerlier's cry, "Pétain, c'est la France! Et la France, c'est Pétain!" as clear evidence of the hierarchy's eager subservience to a man whose authority depended in the last analysis on Hitler's good will. *Politics, Society and Christianity in Vichy France.*

Halls might well have added to his list of culpable Catholics François Mitterrand, whose service as a Vichy functionary is described in Jackson, *France: The Dark Years, 1940–1944.* In 1942, Jackson notes, Mitterrand wrote a number of pro-Vichy newspaper articles, including a piece condemning France for "150 years of mistakes," the phrase regularly used by Vichyites to describe the period 1789–1939. For these and like-minded articles, the Catholic Mitterrand received Vichy's highest honour, the *francisque*, in the spring of 1943.

In yet another critical review comparing Vichyites and members of the resistance, Nicholas Atkin notes that, even among Christian Democrats and Social Christians, there was support for Pétain in the first few months of the État français. Vichy's Labour Charter won favour among Catholics who felt it derived from Leo XIII's *Rerum Novarum.* "*Ralliés* and *résistants*: Catholics in Vichy France, 1940–44", in Chadwick, *Catholicism, Politics and Society in Twentieth-Century France*, 97–117. As John Hellman has pointed out, Catholics were prominent in the direction of the leadership school founded at Uriage near Grenoble with Pétain's blessing. V. *The Knight-Monks of Vichy France.*

Writing from a very different perspective, the Catholic scholar Étienne Fouilloux makes a persuasive defence of his co-religionists' spiritual as well as political action during World War II. The Church was as dynamic in 1940 as it had been in 1914, Fouilloux contends. Opposition to Vichy by a small group of Dominicans and Jesuits gave the internal resistance a sturdy theological base; and, while millions of French citizens were undoubtedly *pétainiste*, almost none were collaborators. Fouilloux adds that, if two-thirds of French Jews escaped death during the "Dark Years," it was thanks in large part to the intervention of Catholic individuals or institutions. All told, what Fouilloux presents is the spiritual and political preparation of *le grand retour*, the return in force of Catholic leadership to the national stage from which it had been excluded for two generations. V. *Les chrétiens français entre crise et libération.*

15 In 1919, with the return to France of Alsace, the substantial Lutheran minority there (as well as the Reformed) joined the FPF. In April 1938, after much deliberation, all but a few of the diverse elements within the Reformed communion, as well as other smaller sects which had not been included in Napoleon's religious settlement, came together as the Église reformée de France (ERF), again under the magisterial direction of Boegner.

16 Apart from pacifist opposition by partisans of the leftist *Christianisme social*, the Protestants demonstrated their patriotism as heroically as the overall population. V. Robert, "Les protestants français et la guerre de 1914–1918."

17 A concise scholarly analysis of French Protestantism during this period is found in Cabanel, *Les Protestants et la République.*

18 Davie, "Right-wing Politics among French Protestants (1900–1944)." The foundation in 1920 of La Cause, an expression of evangelical Calvinism with an assertively nationalist outlook, led by elements of the Protestant bourgeoisie, signaled a radical change of course. This theological and moral shift to the Right was complemented in 1930 by the creation of the *Association Sully*, a more explicitly political organization named after the Protestant duc de Sully, chief counselor to Henry IV, the Huguenot prince who had converted from the Reformed to the Catholic communion to win the throne. The Association was closely (if not formally) linked to Maurras's Action française.

19 For a succinct review of the early years of *Christianisme social*, v. Crespin, *Des protestants engagés*, 17–28.

20 Zay was born to a Jewish father and Protestant mother. The latter ensured that Jean was baptized in the Reformed communion. Zay's refusal to repudiate his Jewish heritage or to escape persecution by claiming to be a Protestant led to his assassination during the Occupation.

21 Outside parliament, a number of left-leaning Protestants tried to mobilize public opinion against the fascist threat following the 6 February crisis. In November 1935, the Protestant novelist André Chamson, together with progressive Catholic colleagues, including the future Gaullist Pierre Viénot, launched *Vendredi*, a weekly paper designed to confront the vitriolic right-wing mass circulation press. Contributors to *Vendredi* included André Gide, a recently disabused Communist sympathizer, and Jacques Soustelle, a militant leftist who joined Free France in wartime London.

André Philip, all but omnipresent in the democratic left during the 1930s, was one of several Protestants to support the Front uni des chrétiens révolutionnaires and its newspaper *Terre Nouvelle*, both of which sought to reconcile Marxist and Christian approaches to the challenge of producing a regenerate world. The presence of the brilliant young Protestant Paul Ricœur as well as a number of gifted Catholic thinkers in the Front uni has led Jean Baubérot to describe this collaboration among leftist Christians as illustrative of a precocious political ecumenism. V. *Réforme*, 3 May, 1986.

22 Fabre, *Les Protestants en France depuis 1789*, 69. Protestant scholars concede that, during the first phase of the Vichy regime, their co-religionists were overwhelmingly sympathetic to Pétain's call for national redemption at the personal as well as at the national level. Pastor Boegner encouraged this respectful attitude by remaining in the capital of the État français both to shield his flock and to exercise what moderating influence he could on his friend Pétain.

A number of prominent Protestants served in the Vichy administration, none more dramatically than Admiral Charles Platon, secretary of state for colonies, who by 1943 moved toward open collaboration with the Third Reich; he was summarily executed by the internal resistance in August 1944. Pastor Noël Nougat ("Vesper"), who had been a member of the Association Sully before the war, displayed both anti-Semitic and monarchist sympathies during the Occupation for which he was shot after the Liberation.

Protestant resistance to Vichy and the Germans took several forms. Pastor Roland de Pury, even in the summer of 1940, preached against both German fascism and its Vichy counterpart. Pastor Boegner, often acting in concert with his Catholic colleague Cardinal Gerlier, spoke out against the regime's anti-Semitic policy and the dispatch of forced labour to German war plants. Madeleine Barot, a history student with an archivist's degree, became in June 1940 secretary-general of Cimade, a Protestant relief organization which helped German-speaking refugees from Alsace settle in southern France and later turned its attention to rescuing Jews from arrest and deportation. In September 1942, Mlle Barot helped plan a secret meeting of Protestant lay people and pastors in the tiny village of Pomeyrol. The result was the formulation of the *Thèses de Pomeyrol*, eight arguments justifying resistance to tyrannous governments and in favour of battling to free consciences from oppression. Protestants became part of the editorial team with Catholics who had launched the underground resistance newspaper *Témoignage chrétien*.

Armed resistance to tyranny by Protestants has a glorious history. Toward the end of the reign of Louis XIV, who had proscribed the Reformed faith in 1685, armed bands of peasants, led by exalted lay preachers, engaged in the Camisard revolt in the Cévennes area, fighting for freedom of conscience and against royal tyranny. Memories of their heroic combat inspired many of the Protestant *maquisards* who rose up against Vichy and the Nazis.

The Socialist André Philip, having joined Free France in London, helped organize the internal resistance and orchestrate the appointment of key figures (many of them Protestant) to replace Vichy officials both at the local and regional level as Liberation approached. Protestants also made a significant contribution to the study-groups (which came together as the Comité général d'études) which met secretly inside France to formulate post-war policy recommendations that were forwarded to London for the consideration of the Free French administration. At the conclusion of a colloquium held in 1992 to review the role of French Protestants during the war, the eminent Catholic scholar René Rémond declared, "The Protestants behaved as a vanguard, as precursors, demonstrating a capacity to liberate themselves from slogans and propaganda, a greater disposition to criticize and a superior discernment."

Rémond added that "the Protestant minority tended to be more world oriented, more outward-looking, as well as more conditioned by their past to disobey and to resist authority and, instead, to follow God and their conscience first, a lesson which my fellow-Catholics would benefit from learning." René Rémond, Conférence de clôture, 615–16, in Encrevé and Poujol, *Les protestants français pendant la seconde guerre mondiale*. V. also Poujol, *Protestants dans la France en guerre, 1939–1945*.

23 A full account of the Jewish minority's political, social, and religious life in this period can be found in Hyman, *From Dreyfus to Vichy. The Remaking of French Jewry, 1906–1939* and Phillipe, *Être juif dans la société française*, 253–88. Birnbaum, *Un mythe politique: la "République juive,"* deals with the right-wing charge that the Jewish minority effectively assumed power during the Popular Front. Weinberg, *A Community on Trial. The Jews of Paris in the 1930s*, deals, as its title suggests, with the Jewish experience in the capital as World War II approached.

24 Membership in the Ligue became one of the touchstones of republican fidelity in the generations which followed. Victor Baesch, president of the Ligue when World War II began, was murdered by the Vichy *milice* in 1944 while the

Provisional Government led by de Gaulle (and including Baesch's close friend René Cassin) was still in Algiers.

25 In *Scènes et doctrines du nationalisme* (F. Juven, 1902), I, 68, Barrès had written,

> The Jews have no fatherland in the sense in which we use the term. For us, the fatherland means the soil and our ancestry, the earth and the dead. For them, it is the place where their interest lies while the fatherland is only an idea. And what idea? That which is the most useful to them – for example, the notion that all men are brothers and that nationality is simply a prejudice.

26 Phillipe, *Être français*, 265.

27 Writing about this sad phase of Franco-Jewish experience, Laura Hyman concludes that, as during the Dreyfus affair, most French Jews concluded that "cowardly neutrality" would be the most effective policy in the face of the rising fascist threat. Hyman adds, in this same vein, that, during the interwar years, a number of politically conservative Jews converted, with great fanfare, to Catholicism, convinced that only as Catholics could they be "truly and completely French." Hyman, *From Dreyfus to Vichy*, 228, 239.

28 Birnbaum, *Un mythe*, 99.

29 Weinberg, *A Community on Trial*, 98.

30 Following the assassination in Paris of the legal counsel to the German ambassador by a teenage Jewish refugee from Eastern Europe on 7 November 1938, a Nazi-inspired assault on synagogues and Jewish businesses took place throughout the Third Reich.

31 The Jews living in France after June 1940 adopted radically different strategies to cope with what became an increasing threat to their security and, ultimately, to their survival. The immigrant communities knew what was in store from their own experience across the Rhine and were, as a result, prepared to resist anti-Semitic legislation, often by joining the Resistance. By contrast, the Central Consistory, presided over by Jacques Heilbronner, a close friend of Pétain, assumed that an understanding could be reached with Vichy that would save the Franco-Jewish community even if this meant the sacrifice of their immigrant cousins.

Until November 1942, when German troops occupied the territory which Pétain had governed since the Armistice, this calculation worked, and many prominent Jews were thereby spared. A month later, Vichy passed a law requiring all Jews living in France, whatever their status, to register at the local commissariat of police. The Consistory, again ready to conciliate, whatever the cost, urged compliance, despite the plea of one of its few tough-minded members, the Communist Georges Wormser. Compliance led to the creation of the Union générale des Israëlites de France (UGIF). A nation-wide registration of arrests and deportations ensued, beginning early in 1943, German authorities confidently entrusting this shameful task to their French counterparts.

The arrest of Heilbronner in October 1943 ended the self-delusion of many of his colleagues, including his successor Léon Meiss, who was open to dialogue with other Jewish groups, including the Communists, none of whom he had ever met! The result was the creation in May 1944 of the Conseil représentatif des Juifs de France (CRIF), the first secular organization to bring together the multi-faceted Jewish minority. The CRIF was able to act as a lobby with Conseil national de la Résistance (CNR), the united resistance organization linked to the Provisional Government led by de Gaulle which moved from Algiers to Paris in the late summer of 1944.

In the end, thanks in large part to the calculated bargain made by the Central Consistory, three out of four French Jews survived the war. While the behaviour of the Franco-Jewish establishment toward their vulnerable immigrant cousins may be seen as deplorable, it must be weighed against the role played by those fully assimilated Jews of leftist persuasion who found their way to London to continue the battle against fascism under the Free French banner – or who, like Léon Blum, stayed behind to defend the Republic (and his own role as leader of the Popular Front) and who, from the internal exile into which Vichy had forced him, offered his support to de Gaulle as a worthy champion of the republican cause.

32 For a critical analysis of the attitudes of Jews living in France during the war, v. Adler, *The Jews of Paris and the Final Solution. Communal Responses and Internal Conflicts, 1940–1944*; Marrus and Paxton, *Vichy, France and the Jews*, and Lazare, *La résistance juive en France.*

33 Chastenet, *Histoire de la Troisième République*, VII, 179.

34 A series of essays brought together in Blatt, *The French Defeat of 1940*, offers an update on the lengthy debate about the causes of France's sudden collapse. May, *Strange Victory*, argues provocatively that the French might have won the Battle of France.

CHAPTER TWO

1 The bibliography dealing with the life and career of Charles de Gaulle, already enormous, continues to grow apace. Three studies in particular have helped establish the context for this and some later chapters. Volume I of Jean Lacouture, *De Gaulle*, provides a basically sympathetic portrait of the general and a balanced view of his relationships with both associates and adversaries. Recently released archives, including de Gaulle's personal papers, have added new shading to our understanding of his personality and motivation. Barré, *Devenir de Gaulle*, traces the intuitive sense which led de Gaulle to see himself as a national redeemer as early as the 1930s and to use all his psychological

resources to realize this vision in Algeria by the fall of 1943. Roussel, *Charles de Gaulle*, portrays a figure from another age, inspired by heroes, warriors, and saints, disdainful of most of his colleagues and cynical about the moral worth of his compatriots.

2 V. Jeanneney, *Georges Mandel*, for an account of the interior minister's action during June 1940. For a comprehensive study of Mandel's pre-war career, v. Irvine, *French Conservatism in Crisis.*

3 In the end, after being tried for acts of subversion at Riom in 1942, Mandel was shot by the Vichy militia on 7 July 1944, a month after D-Day.

4 Cited, in Irvine, *French Conservatism in Crisis*, 28.

5 Charles de Gaulle, "Discours prononcé à la radio de Londres," *Discours et messages*, I, 3–4.

6 Monographs and articles on the subject abound. A succinct account of de Gaulle's religious outlook is offered in Lacouture, "De Gaulle entre Dieu et César," 13–16.

7 This term had been used during the reign of François 1er to characterize the traitorous *Connétable de Bourbon*, an agent of the Valois interest at court. It was taken up out of spite by de Gaulle's jealous fellow-recruits and irritated military instructors, then, in more positive vein, by Winston Churchill when he learned of the general's arrival in London in 1940.

8 One of the most striking manifestations of de Gaulle's deep piety came after the war when he greeted his nephew, a Père Blanc about to set off on a mission to Africa, by kneeling to ask the younger man's blessing. V. interview between Catherine Trouiller and Christine Clerc, in *Espoir* 126 (March 2001), 145.

9 Moll, *Yvonne de Gaulle*, 202.

10 Letter of de Gaulle to Cardinal Saliège, 27 May 1942. De Gaulle, *Lettres, notes et carnets*, 277–8.

11 It might also be noted that, on 25 August 1944, shortly after the Liberation of Paris, the city's archbishop, Cardinal Suhard, was informed that he would not be allowed to join in the celebratory Te Deum being arranged in Notre Dame. The reason, left implicit, was that the prelate had received Pétain in his cathedral four months earlier, a clear indication of his sympathy for the Vichy regime V. Lacouture, *De Gaulle*, I, 835.

12 De Gaulle admired the philosopher Henri Bergson, of Jewish background but drawn toward Catholicism, who saw faith as derived in purer form from intuition than from reasoned reflection. Charles Péguy satisfied his feeling that faith in God and in nation could be found fused together in one mystical rapture. The mature de Gaulle read the leading-edge philosophy of Teilhard de Chardin, who brought Darwinian science and Christian faith to meet in a vision of human progress that alarmed the orthodox. Jean Guitton, a *pétainiste* during the

war, brought consoling meditations on the Christian approach to death. The poet and playwright Paul Claudel, much admired by the general, dedicated an ode to him after the Liberation although he had been *vichyssois* just before. De Gaulle was also familiar with the works of the Catholic philosophers Étienne Gilson and Jacques Maritain. The latter, who became a Free France sympathizer from safe exile in New York, refused to cross the Atlantic to sit on the Gaullist Comité national, but accepted an ambassadorship to the Vatican when peace came. Among the favourite authors of *Le Connétable* were two Catholic novelists who had already established their reputations in the 1930s. De Gaulle regarded the *Journal d'un curé de campagne* of Georges Bernanos as one of the great twentieth-century works of fiction, and during the war reinforced his admiration for François Mauriac whose son Claude became his personal secretary in 1943. A comprehensive analysis of these influences is offered in Larcan, *Charles de Gaulle. Itinéraires intellectuels et spirituels.* V. also Serroy, *De Gaulle et les écrivains.*

13 For a full discussion of the influence of "Social Catholicism" on de Gaulle's thought, v. Philippe Levillain, "La pensée sociale du général de Gaulle face à héritage du catholicisme social," *De Gaulle en son siècle,* I, 448 as well as François-Georges Dreyfus, "La lecture gaullienne du catholicisme social: actualité d'une synthèse," ibid., I, 164.

14 Philippe de Gaulle, *Mémoires accessoires,* 126.

15 Marin, *Petit bois pour un grand feu,* 333.

16 Mauriac, *De Gaulle,* 94.

17 When the then President de Gaulle and his wife attended mass at the church inside the French consulate in Leningrad on 26 June that year, Yvonne de Gaulle rose to take communion. De Gaulle realized that protocol required him to follow suit. When he returned from the altar-rail, he gave his wife a furious stare, outraged that she had trapped him into making a public display of his faith, violating his own resolve never to do this in circumstances where it would cause a stir and raise the old question of church-state relations. Afterward, Yvonne de Gaulle discussed the incident with her aide-de camp, asking why her husband should hide his Christian faith, especially in a country where such practices were mocked. She was reassured. Her little plan had worked! Moll, *Yvonne de Gaulle,* 306.

18 Cited in Lacouture, "De Gaulle entre Dieu et César," 13.

19 De Gaulle, *Discours et messages,* I, 20.

20 De Gaulle, *La France et son armée,* 244.

21 Péguy's visionary recreation of Joan of Arc appears most dramatically in *Le mystère de la charité de Jeanne d'Arc* (1910).

22 Lacouture, *De Gaulle,* I, 291. Challenging Lacouture's view, François Delpha sees the young officer at that stage in his career ideologically ambivalent, even

Maurrassian, ready to put the case for the takeover of the state by a strong man as France's parliamentary system staggered from crisis to crisis. In support of his contention, Delpha cites a key paragraph in *Vers l'armée de métier,* the manuscript of which de Gaulle submitted to his publisher just a few weeks after the 6 February disturbances:

> There is no group, party or council which is not now calling for a fundamental national renewal, a "New Order," a reassertion of authority. Nor is there any doubt but that very soon, depending on the shifting circumstances of the day, the fate of our institutions will present an opportunity to the resolute. If such a recasting of our national life were to begin with the army, this would be in conformity with the natural order of things ... Not only because force remains more necessary than ever in those nations that have a will to survive but because the military corps is the most complete expression of a society's spirit ... In the difficult struggle to rejuvenate France, the new army can serve as both instrument and ferment.

Delpha reinforces his case by citing a letter from de Gaulle to Reynaud at the end of 1935 in which the officer argues that the creation of a special tank corps might serve not only to prepare France against external aggressions but also to repress violent civil disobedience, adding that it was regrettable that such a force was not available in February 1936. *L'appel du 18 juin 1940,* 53.

Less surprisingly, the right-wing ideologue Gilbert Comte insists that, like most of his intellectually alert contemporaries, de Gaulle not only read but admired Maurras, at least until the mid 1930s. What the future leader of Free France took from Maurras, Comte concludes, is the conviction that France needed a powerful executive authority, together with a horror of money and the political influence it bought, and an emphasis on the individual will as a motivating force in history. V. G. Comte, "De Gaulle et Maurras," in Serroy, *De Gaulle et les écrivains,* 99–110.

23 De Gaulle, *La France et son armée.*

24 It is perhaps worth noting that Gambetta, charged by the Provisional Government of 1870 with seeking foreign support for the fledgling Third Republic, was lifted out of Paris by balloon very much as Charles de Gaulle, a member of the last government of the same regime, was air-lifted out of France in June 1940.

25 Details of this wartime discussion were relayed to the author during an interview with Senator Schumann on 8 September 1996.

26 De Gaulle, *Articles et écrits,* 52.

27 It might be noted that de Gaulle's attitude toward the Jews of eastern Europe in 1920 parallels the nervous distance which France's assimilated Jews kept between themselves and victims of Russian and Rumanian pogroms at the time

of the Dreyfus Affair. V. Philippe, *Être juif dans la société français du moyen âge à nos jours*, 239–40.

28 For a fuller view of the relationship between Émile Mayer and de Gaulle, v. Lerner, "Le colonel Mayer et son cercle d'amis," 75–94.

29 What follows concerning de Gaulle's relations with the Jewish Agency for Palestine is taken from Catherine Nicault, "De Gaulle et l'Agence Juive pour la Palestine pendant la Seconde Guerre Mondiale," Espoir 74 (May 1991), 25–44. Information concerning Free French links to the World Jewish Congress comes from *Unity in Dispersion. A History of the World Jewish Congress.*

30 Cassin, *Les hommes partis de rien*, 120.

31 Cited in *A History of the World Jewish Congress*, 211.

32 Lacouture, *De Gaulle*, I, 472.

33 Cited in Nicault, "De Gaulle et l'Agence juive," 38.

34 Cited in *A History of the World Jewish Congress*, 211.

35 Ibid.

36 V. Chapter 14, 324–9, 333–5, 337–43.

37 Mendès, who became France's premier in 1954 and later joined the reorganized Socialist party, had openly challenged de Gaulle during the student/worker insurrection of May 1968, putting an end to nearly three decades of mutual respect. Twelve years later, his memory perhaps enhanced by a new-found animosity toward the general who had become president in 1958, he recalled for Lacouture the verbal exchange he had had with de Gaulle on 10 July 1944 while both men rode with New York mayor Fiorello La Guardia in a victory motorcade through Manhattan. Gazing out at the huge crowds which lined the streets to greet those in the lead car, the general observed to Mendès,

> "So that's it! My supporters turn out to be niggers and Porto-Ricans, the ill-formed and the cuckolds, émigrés and Jews!" "Yes, as a matter of fact," Mendès remembers adding: "And you'll have to make the best of it! You've become the leader of a kind of Popular Front!" (Lacouture, *De Gaulle*, I, 796).

While de Gaulle's contempt for many in his entourage was sometimes expressed quite openly to intimates, the crudity of the language cited here makes the text suspect; but Lacouture left it unedited in his biography, so it remains to give tenuous legitimacy to the charge of racism against *Le Connétable*.

The second bit of evidence upon which the charge of anti-Jewish prejudice has been laid against de Gaulle comes more convincingly from a press conference given by the president on 28 November 1967, more than five months after Israel's triumph in the Six Day War against its Arab neighbours. Among other comments, the head of state observed,

Some are even concerned that the Jews, until recently dispersed, remain as they have always been – an elitist people, sure of themselves and domineering. Now, gathered together, they have transformed into a burning and conquering ambition the ancient and very moving wish they expressed during nineteen centuries: "Next year in Jerusalem!" (Philippe, *Être juif dans la société française*, 389).

This seemingly spontaneous sally created an enormous stir among French Jews. Among others, Raymond Aron, who had been a generally sympathetic observer of Free France during the 1940s, issued a stinging rebuke, accusing de Gaulle of providing a new rationalization of anti-Semitism. V. *De Gaulle, Israël et les Juifs*.

38 Jacques Robert, "Le général de Gaulle et les protestants," *De Gaulle en son siècle*, I-A025.

39 De Gaulle, *Discours et messages*, I, 207–9.

40 Ibid., 232.

41 De Gaulle, *Lettres, notes et carnets*, V, 407.

CHAPTER THREE

1 The June 1993 (92) issue of the Gaullist periodical *Espoir* contains an *Hommage à Geoffroy de Courcel* which is the source of much of the information concerning Courcel in this chapter.

2 Bouchinet-Serreulles, "Du collège Stanislas à Carlton Gardens," ibid., 7

3 Text of Françoise Parturier, ibid., 99.

4 Geoffroy de Courcel to Elisabeth de Miribel, 17 August 1940, E. de Miribel, "Le premier jour de La France libre," *Espoir* 92, 26.

5 In *La liberté souffre violence*, Elisabeth de Miribel gives an account of her contribution to Free France. The young aristocrat's efforts to win over Canadians to the Gaullist cause are analyzed in detail in a series of articles ("La France libre et le Canada, 1940–1944") in *Espoir* 72, September 1990, 65–90.

6 Elisabeth de Miribel, *La liberté*, 49. Fortunately, there were a few dissenters from this overwhelmingly pro-Vichy sentiment. Among the Gaulle's partisans in francophone Canada were two Radio-Canada journalists, Jean-Louis Gagnon and Guy Jasmin; General Georges Vanier, commander of the Quebec City garrison and his wife; Father Georges Henri Levesque of Laval University; Pierre-François Casgrain, secretary of state of the federal government; and Professor Henri Laugier, a physiologist at the University of Montreal (who had helped members of the Joliot-Curie physics team escape from France).

7 The source for much of what follows is Claude Hettier de Boislambert, *Les fers de l'espoir*.

8 Born in Cognac in 1888, Monnet was the son of a prominent local distiller, J.-G. Monnet. As he puts it in his *Mémoires*, the outlook of his parents in matters religious prepared him to be tolerant:

> My mother was at once very pious and very tolerant. Catholic, but respectful of our (Protestant) friend M. Barrault, who on Sundays put down his plough to attend services at the *temple* in Segonzac. "He's a man of the Bible," she would declare solemnly (39).

His father, Monnet goes on to say, was a non-believer who spent his Sundays in philanthropic activity, helping to organize mutual-aid societies, the foundation of France's later social security system.

Trained to take over his father's business, Monnet helped Allied economic mobilization during World War I. Two of his collaborators on the World War I committee, Pierre Denis as well as Pleven, became Gaullists.

When the radical proposal to merge the British and French empires fell through and de Gaulle decided to found La France libre, Monnet had Denis transmit a letter to the general criticizing the decision. Then, on 2 July 1940, he resigned from the Comité de coordination franco-britannique and headed to Washington where he lobbied on behalf of the Allied cause until February 1943 when he went to Algiers as an advisor to de Gaulle's rival, General Henri Giraud. In the Algerian capital, as earlier in London, Monnet concluded that de Gaulle's "impatience and intolerance seemed to predispose him to certain forms of personal power" (229) which would end up dividing rather than uniting France.

9 Details concerning René Pleven's early life and his role in La France libre are taken from Bougeard, *René Pleven. Un Français libre en politique.*

10 Monnet, *Mémoires*, 23–4.

11 General Edgar de Larminat, "Le général de Gaulle et le catholicisme," Fonds René Pleven, AN, 560 AP 25.

12 Ibid.

13 "Témoignage de M. Claude Bouchinet-Serreulles," 12 December 1948 and 12 February 1950, AN 72 AJ 200.

14 Cited in Bourgeaud, *René Pleven*, 100.

15 Claude Bouchinet-Serreulles, *Nous étions faits pour être libres*, offers a detailed account of Bouchinet's wartime activities.

16 Ibid., 24.

17 Ibid., 57.

18 His closeness to de Gaulle allowed Bouchinet to make what is perhaps the fullest first-hand analysis of the general's political weaknesses. He notes that, while *Le Connétable* admired the British parliamentary system and the civic virtue that underpinned it, he only reluctantly yielded to pressure from Churchill and Eden

to make his own administration more transparent and responsible. He added that de Gaulle paid little attention to notes submitted by subordinates; he intimidated his colleagues, preventing the brighter ones from offering candid advice; he made little effort to cultivate the francophile elements in the British government and in Labour Party ranks; he let relations between Free France and Westminster depend almost exclusively on his highly unstable personal relationship with Churchill; and he disparaged as mediocre most of those who had risked everything to join him in exile.

19 Ibid., 194.

20 Ibid., 197.

21 Ibid., 198.

22 Gaston Palewski, *Mémoires d'action, 1924–1974*, is the source of much that follows.

23 "Témoignage de M. Claude Bouchinet-Serreulles ," 12 February 1950, AN 72 AJ 220.

24 Palewski, *Mémoires*, 23.

25 Palewski arrived in Aden on 18 May 1941 wearing the uniform of a lieutenant in the Free French Air Force. He faced and surmounted two immediate challenges – the relief of the beleaguered port of Djibouti and the rallying of some 8,000 Somalis to the Gaullist cause. Later, settling in at the French embassy in Addis Ababa, which Allied troops had liberated from the Italians in April, he looked after France's considerable interests in Ethiopia. While still based in the Ethiopian capital, Palewski even managed to arrange for the raising of a battalion of Free French troops in the Comores Islands and to recruit volunteers for the cause in Kenya.

26 In *Vertu des temps difficiles*, Coulet recounts his diplomatic and political career, with chapters devoted not only to his role in La France libre but also to his post-war association with de Gaulle.

27 Once his replacement by Coulet was arranged, Courcel in August 1941 joined a Free French army group being formed in Lebanon. Then, in December, he moved to Egypt where the Gaullist General Pierre-Marie Koenig was putting together an army brigade to join the British in repulsing Italian troops who were threatening Suez from Libya. Courcel ended up with the First Regiment of Spahis, in whose ranks he finally saw the action he longed for in November 1942 in the victorious battle of El Alamein against General Erwin Rommel. This triumph, in which Free French troops played a signal part, boosted Gaullist morale enormously. While still in uniform, Courcel received in 1944 the bitter news from France, that his father had been taken away by the Gestapo for harbouring a Polish Jew since 1939.

28 Bouchinet-Serreulles, *Nous étions faits pour être libres*, 161.

29 Coulet, *Vertu*, 73.

30 Ibid., 108.

31 Ibid., 166.

32 Ibid., 178

CHAPTER FOUR

1 "Fragments autobiographiques," in Cassin, *La pensée et l'action*, 181.

2 Ibid., 182.

3 Ibid.

4 Cassin was among those who applauded Mandel's involvement in the *Massilia* venture in 1940, hoping that the Jewish interior minister might become the leader of a republican government which would pursue the war from North Africa.

5 Cassin, "Avertissements Salutaires," in *Cahiers de l'UFAC*, October 1938.

6 Cited in Agi, *René Cassin*, 83.

7 Cassin, Journal de 1940, AN 382 AP27 as well as Cassin, *Les hommes partis de rien*, 75 8, offer the jurist's impressions of his first meeting with de Gaulle.

8 V. Cassin, *Les hommes partis de rien*, 79–104, for a full account of the negotiations leading to this agreement.

9 As Eric Roussel has discovered from Churchill's secret wartime correspondence, His Majesty's government, contrary to the wording of the 7 August accord, was not in fact absolutely committed to guaranteeing the territorial integrity of France and her empire but simply to work toward that end; nor was it ready to guarantee that Free French soldiers would not fight those loyal to Vichy; nor, finally, was Britain ready to acknowledge the automatic jurisdiction of La France libre over all French citizens then in the United Kingdom. V. Roussel, *Charles de Gaulle*, 162.

10 Cassin, *La France libre*, vol. I, December 1940 – January 1941, 1–48.

11 Cassin, Notes for a broadcast over Radio-Brazzaville, 16 November 1940, AN Fonds René Cassin, 382 AP31.

12 Barré, *Devenir de Gaulle*, 83–4.

13 Cassin, "Doctrine et politique de La France libre," Fonds René Cassin, 382 AP31.

14 Agi, *René Cassin*, 138.

15 Jean Lacouture, de Gaulle's most sympathetic biographer, writes convincingly that the general had emancipated himself from his parents' monarchist sympathies and that he was a republican in outlook who, in 1940, muted his political beliefs to conciliate the many reactionaries in his entourage. V. Lacouture, *De Gaulle*, I, 661.

16 Paradoxically, the apparent ideological ambiguity of de Gaulle during this period paralleled that of his one-time mentor Pétain, whom he now excoriated. In orchestrating the 20 July 1940 coup d'état which made him "Chef de l'État français," the hero of Verdun suspended the republican form of government and produced a constitutional hiatus, which left open either a republican restoration (something much talked about in August 1944) or its permanent replacement by a crypto-monarchy.

17 Cassin, *Les hommes partis*, 406.

18 V. Lacouture, *De Gaulle*, I, 377.

19 *New York Herald Tribune*, 8 January 1943.

20 Note pour le général de Gaulle, 20 March 1943, AN 382 AP71.

21 Lacouture, *De Gaulle*, I, 677.

22 Cassin, *Les hommes partis*, 78.

23 Ibid., 141.

24 De Gaulle, *Mémoires*, 87.

25 Entretien de M.R.C. au Conseil constitutionnel avec M. Michel, 14 décembre 1961, AN 72 AJ220.

26 "Antisémitisme au Quartier général, le 30 décembre 1941," AN Fonds Cassin, 382 AP27.

27 Cassin, *Les hommes partis de rien*, 138.

28 Cassin, Journal de 1940, AN, 382 AP27.

29 Cassin, Journal de 1940, 30 octobre 1940, ibid.

30 "Israëlites de France," in ibid., 480–1.

31 *Volontaire pour la cité chrétienne*, 20 April 1942.

32 Cassin, *Les hommes partis*, 403–4.

33 Journal du 2 novembre 1940, AN 382 AP27.

34 Ibid.

35 Entretien de M.R.C., AN 72 AJ220.

36 Journal du 25 septembre 1943, AN 382 AP27.

CHAPTER FIVE

1 Much of what follows concerning Schumann's life and career comes from Rimbaud, *Maurice Schumann*. Additional information about his religious and political experience was obtained during an interview given the author by then Senator Schumann in Paris on 8 September, 1997

2 Schumann, *Bergson ou le retour de Dieu*, 75.

3 Péguy died on the battlefield early in World War I. During his spiritually formative years, Schumann made a point of attending the salon on the rue de Rennes where the poet had been a regular visitor and where his devotee met an

ecumenical assemblage of personalities, including the Protestant Geneviève Favre, daughter of former premier Jules Favre and mother to Jacques Maritain, who became in 1906 one of the most celebrated converts to Catholicism of his generation, in large part thanks to Bergson and the polemical novelist Léon Bloy.

4 Christiane Rimbaud, "Les années de formation," *Espoir* 108 (October, 2001), 9. This issue of *Espoir* is entirely devoted to Schumann's life and career.

5 On a more spiritual level, close contact with the Dominicans prompted Schumann to ask himself whether he might opt for the celibate life himself, a dilemma he did not finally resolve until he met his future wife at Gaullist headquarters in London.

6 The right-wing riots of 6 February in Paris, which took on the appearance of a putsch against the republican regime, reproduced the kind of dialectical exchange of petition and counter-petition which had occurred during the Dreyfus Affair. In October 1935, Catholic conservatives mobilized to stop the application of sanctions against Italy for attacking Ethiopia. This intervention was met by a counter-petition signed by a number of progressive Catholics including Emmanuel Mounier and Jacques Madaule. For a comprehensive analysis of this exchange of tracts and petitions, see Sirinelli, *Intellectuels et passions françaises.*

7 *Sept*, 19 February 1937. For a comprehensive examination of the efforts at collaboration between French Communists and Catholics, v. Murphy, *Communists and Catholics in France, 1936–1939*.

8 Sirinelli, *Intellectuels*, 103–6.

9 Ibid., 110–11. In a subsequent article, published in *Le Figaro* on 30 June 1938, Mauriac expressed his outrage at the contention of Franco's generals that they were leading a holy war, acting as soldiers of Christ, trying to make millions of Spaniards believe that Christianity and fascism were synonymous. Georges Bernanos, meanwhile, who lived on Majorca between 1934 and 1938, published a clear indictment of the Franco regime in *Les grands cimetières sous la lune* (Plon, 1938).

10 As his eminent biographer Jean Lacouture remarks, "Here we discover a Colonel de Gaulle very different from the earlier partisan of Maurras and the extreme right, against whom the only man who had any influence on his thinking after the death of his father, Colonel Mayer, had for a long time been warning him."

11 Using his pen name "André Sidobre," Schumann expressed this thesis more fully in a forty-eight-page brochure *Le germanisme en marche* (Cerf, 1938), prefaced by his friend François Mauriac. The following year, the same publisher brought out a recapitulation of his views on Italian fascism in an essay simply titled "Mussolini."

12 *Temps présent*, 17 June 1938.

13 Ibid., 15 September 1939.

14 Entretien avec Maurice Schumann, le 5 juillet, 1994, in Delbeil, *Marc Sangnier,* 255.

15 Schumann, "Propos sur la victoire, 1945–1985," *Revue des deux mondes* (June 1985), 659.

16 L'âme commune 31, November 1980.

17 AN 72 AJ220, "Texte de Maurice Schumann, le 26 octobre, 1948," part of a series of interviews in preparation for Pilleul, *L'Entourage et de Gaulle.*

18 Schumann made more than 1,000 broadcasts to the people of France over the BBC. Those, cited on 192–204 are taken from three sources: Crémieux-Brilhac, *Ici Londres*; and two volumes edited by Schumann himself: *Honneur et Patrie* and *La voix du couvre-feu.*

19 Cerf-Ferrière, *L'assemblée consultative vue de mon banc,* 29–30.

20 Crémieux-Brilhac, "Maurice Schumann à Londres," *Espoir* 108, 17.

21 *L'âme commune* 15, July 1961.

CHAPTER SIX

1 Denis, *Les métiers et les jours,* 31.

2 Denis, *Souvenirs de* La France libre, 31.

3 Ibid., 18.

4 Crémieux-Brilhac, *La France libre,* 80.

5 Delpha, *L'appel du 18 juin 1940,* 74–5.

6 Denis, *Souvenirs,* 212.

7 Ibid., 94. Throughout his wartime career with Free France, Denis was a loyal servant of the Gaullist cause but, as he points out in his memoirs, he never wore the Cross of Lorraine, partly because he lacked the requisite esprit de corps, partly because he felt that France's unity transcended any such insignia; de Gaulle and his followers, in Denis's view, had no monopoly on patriotic faith or sacrifice. The Caisse manager adds that he might have worn the cross *inside* France where such a public display of patriotism would have involved the assumption of a risk.

8 Ibid., 96.

9 This outline of Diethelm's career is derived from Roxane Philippe, "André Diethelm: un itinéraire politique."

10 Letter of André Postel-Vinay to the author, 21 May 2001.

11 Postel-Vinay offers a full account of his dramatic experiences in the French underground in his *Un fou s'évade.*

12 Ibid., 199.

13 Postel-Vinay, "Souvenirs de la Caisse centrale de La France libre," *Bulletin de l'Amicale des Anciens de la Caisse centrale 3* (April 1996), 13–14.

14 Ibid., 13.

15 Ibid., 73. Although Denis felt an urge to broach this non-Gaullist heresy to *Le Connétable*, he thought better of it, no doubt anticipating the hostile reception it would be given. Among other factors that discouraged the Caisse director from promoting this pan-European view was the intense anglophobia he encountered in de Gaulle's entourage, something he tells us in his memoirs he was precluded from sharing by his education as a citizen of the world. Ibid., 91.

16 Denis, *Souvenirs*, 133.

17 The details concerning Couve de Murville's life and career are in large part derived from Bertrand Fessard de Foucault, "Un secret Français," *Espoir* 126 (March 2000), 7–36, a radically abbreviated version of a biography of Couve de Murville published in 2002.

18 Seydoux, *Mémoires d'outre-Rhin*, 15–16.

19 Testimony of André Fontaine concerning Couve de Murville, *Espoir* 126, 89.

20 Fessard de Foucault's sympathetic treatment of Couve's dealings with the Germans can be contrasted with the less charitable analysis in Tristan Mage, *Maurice Couve de Murville-François Mitterrand.*

21 Denis, *Souvenirs*, 135.

22 Ibid., 151.

23 Ibid., 156.

24 Daniel Desmarquest, "Entretiens avec Maurice Couve de Murville," *Espoir* 126, 79.

25 Pierre Mendès France, "Financement de La France libre," a pre-budget speech before the Assemblée consultative provisoire, 4 January 1944, in Mendès France, *Œuvres complètes*, II, 29–32.

26 Between 7 August 1940 and 30 June 1943, when British aid ceased, the commissioner noted, only a tiny proportion of the credit held by French interests in Britain had been released to the Gaullist cause. Finally, the finance commissioner stressed that the overall Free French wartime bill amounted to some 25,000,000 pounds (or 5,000,000,000 francs), less than the cost of the Paris exposition of 1937 or, for that matter, of ten days' worth of the payment extracted from Vichy by Berlin for the cost of the German occupation! In a February 1984 letter to de Gaulle's biographer Jean Lacouture, Postel-Vinay puts the Free French debt to the British Treasury at 30,000,000 pounds but adds that inflation beginning in 1943 helped reduce its real value by the spring of 1945 when *Le Connétable* insisted that it be fully repaid.

CHAPTER SEVEN

1 Soustelle, *Envers et contre tout*, I, 203.

2 Soustelle, *Vingt-huit ans de gaullisme*, 249.
3 Soustelle, *Mexique terre indienne.*
4 Soustelle, "Musées vivants. Pour une culture populaire," *Vendredi*, 26 June 1936
5 Stopping off in New York on his way back to England, Soustelle ran into Geneviève Tabouis, a passionately anti-Munich French journalist who had chosen exile in the United States over combat with de Gaulle in London. She could only commiserate with the ethnologist turned political activist: "My poor old friend! What in earth are you going to do over there?" *Envers et contre tout*, I, 24.
6 Ibid., 30.
7 "Honneur et patrie," BBC, 14 December 1941, Crémieux-Brilhac, *Les Voix de la liberté*, I, 158.
8 Soustelle describes the conditions under which the improvised equivalent of the Quai d'Orsay had to function at Carlton Gardens:

> Our entire external affairs personnel with their flimsy dossiers fit into two or three rooms on the third floor where we had only cheap wooden tables to work on. The central heating apparatus having failed, we used small oil lamps instead which fouled the air without giving off much heat. Long black curtains on the windows added a funereal note to our already somber, cold and poorly furnished rooms. *Envers et contre tout*, I, 203–204.

9 *Vingt-huit ans de gaullisme*, 12.
10 *Envers et contre tout*, I, 214.
11 Ibid., 238.
12 Ibid., 268.
13 Marin, *Petit bois pour un grand feu*, 309.
14 Ibid., 280.
15 Ibid., 278.
16 Envers et contre tout, 278–80.
17 Ibid., 284.
18 Ibid., 286.
19 Ibid., 38–9.
20 Ibid., 312.
21 A full account of Cavaillès' heroic role in the Resistance is given in Ferrières, *Jean Cavaillès. Un philosophe dans la guerre, 1903–1944.*
22 *Envers et contre tout*, I, 402–3.
23 V. Chapter 14 for discussion of Operation "Torch."
24 Ibid., 468.
25 Ibid., II, 77.
26 Ibid., 187.
27 Ibid., 184–5.
28 Ibid., 228.

29 Ibid., 241.
30 Ibid., 257.

CHAPTER EIGHT

1 A critical review of French Socialist activity during the war is given in Guidoni and Verdier, *Les socialistes en Résistance 1940–1944*.
2 Georges Boris left no memoirs. The best account of his life and work is to be found in Mendès France, *Georges Boris. Servir la République.* and Toinet, "Georges Boris 1888–1960, un socialiste humaniste," typewritten doctoral dissertation.
3 Toinet, "Georges Boris," 184. This enthusiasm led to the publication *of La révolution Roosevelt* (Gallimard, 1934).
4 V. Interview with Boris on the BBC, 19 June 1943, Archives du Comité d'Histoire de la 2e guerre mondiale, Paris.
5 The biographical details which follow are taken from Weil-Curiel, *Le temps de la honte.*
6 Ibid., I, 202.
7 Ibid., 223.
8 Boris, *Servir*, 286.
9 V. André Wurmser, *De Gaulle et les siens* (Éditions "Raisons d'être," 1947) and Weil-Curiel, I, 318.
10 *Servir*, 299.
11 Weil-Curiel, *Le temps*, I, 238.
12 Ibid., 269.
13 Boris's letter to Blum is reproduced in its entirety in *Servir*, 289–303.
14 Weil Curiel, *Le temps*, I, 234.
15 Ibid., 331.
16 Ibid., 9.
17 Pierre-Bloch, *Londres, capitale de* La France libre, 83.
18 Aron, *Mémoires*, 266.
19 Bret was head of the London branch of the Havas Agency in 1940 and thus a colleague of Maurice Schumann. He had covered the diplomatic crises of the 1930s and been nauseated both by the appeasement policy of the democracies and the venality of French domestic politics. As soon as the war opened, Bret was appalled at the prospect that all journalists would now turn into propagandists. At the time of the Armistice, he wrote,

> Between the *don de ma personne* of Marshal Pétain which seemed like one of yesterday's third-rate theatrics and the *Moi* of the general which fifteen years of life in Britain had taught me to pass over in silence, I feel equally frustrated.

In the end, as Bret puts it, "My conscience instructed me against blind submission to either of these Frances." Summoned to submit by Vichy, the Protestant journalist stood his ground. Reflecting back on this defiance years later, Bret wrote, "My Calvinist inheritance made the decision for me without hiding from me the difficulties it would bring."[19] In Algiers in 1943, Bret created the *Agence France-Afrique* in which he established his journalistic autonomy by condemning what he saw to be the national-socialist tendencies developing in de Gaulle.

Pierre Maillaud, Bret's deputy, who took the nom de plume Pierre Bourdan after the name of his native village, had been diplomatic editor at Havas in London. He met de Gaulle on 19 June and, finding him unbearably arrogant, accepted instead an offer by Michel Saint-Denis to take charge of a daily half-hour BBC broadcast beamed at France. "Ici Londres. Les Français parlent aux Français" would become the most popular of the British network's programs aimed at boosting French morale. There was respectful attention to de Gaulle in these talks, but no blind support. In the summer of 1945, however, Maillaud/Bourdan relinquished the microphone to serve under the Gaullist General Leclerc in the battle to liberate France.

Bret, *Au feu des événements*, 157.

20 The gravest of these crises occurred in November 1942, when de Gaulle and his colleagues were deliberately excluded from the plans for Operation "Torch," the Allied invasion of French North Africa. The general and his porte-parole Schumann, backed by Boris, retaliated for this wilful exclusion by cancelling the nightly "Honneur et Patrie" broadcast until the crisis was resolved.

21 Interview of Crémieux-Brilhac by Jean Lacouture, July 1983, in Lacouture, *De Gaulle*, I, 728. The Gaullist's own account of his career as a soldier is given in Jean Brilhac, *Retour par l'Urss.*

22 The gist of Boris's articles in *La Marseillaise* is given in Crémieux-Brilhac, *La France libre*, 381.

23 The account of Pierre-Bloch's wartime activities which follows is taken mainly from his four-volume wartime memoir, *De Gaulle ou le temps des méprises*; *Le temps d'y penser encore*; *Le vent souffle sur l'histoire. Témoignages et documents inédits*; and *Londres, capitale de* La France libre.

24 Pierre-Bloch, *Londres*, 19.

25 Pierre-Bloch, *Le temps d'y penser*, 208.

26 Ibid., 208–9.

27 For a full account of the role of "Passy" during the war, see André Dewavrin, *Souvenirs*.

28 Pierre-Bloch, *Londres*, 40.

29 Ibid., 73.

30 Among other documents which reached Pierre-Bloch during this new assignment was a manuscript which was to become the leading work of fiction produced by the Resistance. Two copies of *Le Silence de la Mer*, written by Vercors, were brought to London by the Catholic Resistance leader Yvon Morandat, including one for de Gaulle. Given the rather sympathetic portrait of a German officer which is essential to the plot, there was some discussion at Hill Street about whether the text ought to be published. In the end, *Le Connétable* agreed with Pierre-Bloch's decision that the novel should see the light of day. With a preface by Maurice Druon (future member of the Académie française who co-authored the Résistance anthem *Le chant des partisans*), the book appeared as part of a collection of texts in French published by a press funded by the banker Philippe de Rothschild.

After the war, *Le Silence de la Mer* became a successful film directed by Jean-Pierre Melville, pseudonym of Jean-Pierre Grumbach, a fellow-Jew whom Pierre-Bloch had interrogated when he showed up at Hill Street to pass the standard filtering process that faced all new arrivals from the Continent.

31 The material which follows dealing with Bingen is taken from the Gaullist review *Espoir* 48 (October 1984) which includes a special *Cahiers Jacques Bingen. Compagnon de la Libération, 1908–1944*, 25–56.

32 On 14 August 1943, two days before being parachuted into France, Bingen had penned what he believed might be a final message to his comrades, a kind of testament. Among other things, he wrote,

> I hope someone will tell General de Gaulle the overwhelming admiration which bit by bit I have come to feel for him. During these grim years, he has been the incarnation of France. I beg him to keep his nobility and his purity but not to forget, following our radiant victory, that, if France is a grand lady, her children are utterly exhausted. He must have not only great ambition for them but also a great deal of indulgent tenderness.

Letter of Bingen, London, 14 August 1944, ibid., 56.

33 Crémieux-Brilhac, *La France libre*, 761.

34 Boris and his wife Germaine offered their hospitality to Pierre Mendès France on his arrival in the British capital in 1942. He later welcomed his old friend, fellow-Jew and Socialist comrade Jules Moch, whom he had come to know years earlier when they were both students at the École polytechnique in Paris.

35 Crémieux-Brilhac, *La France libre*, 720.

36 Lacouture, *Léon Blum*, 481.

37 Letter of Boris to Blum, 22 June, 1942, in *Servir la République*, 298–303.

38 V. Pierre-Bloch, *De Gaulle*, 72–81.

39 Letter of Blum to Gouin, 21 October 1942, Lacouture, *Blum*, 484–5.

40 Letter of Blum to de Gaulle, November 1942, ibid., 485–6.

41 Ibid., 486–7.
42 Blum's abduction might well have led to a death-sentence. Instead, housed in the next room to his fellow-Jew Georges Mandel, he deepened his friendship with the Radical leader, whom Churchill would gladly have welcomed to London in de Gaulle's place, and who was assassinated on 7 July 1944 by members of the notorious French special police, *La Milice*, in the forest of Fontainebleau. Blum spent much of his time at Buchenwald writing notes for what became *À l'échelle humaine*, a secular humanist's uplifting tribute to the human spirit.
43 To back up Blum's letter of unconditional support for de Gaulle, one of the Socialist leader's chief lieutenants, Daniel Mayer, who shared his Jewish and agnostic background, managed to travel to London in April 1943, bringing with him the formal endorsement of the general by the resurrected Socialist party.
44 Letter of de Gaulle to Blum, February 1943, ibid., 279–80.
45 Letter of de Gaulle to the parliamentary group, Pierre-Bloch, *De Gaulle*, 144–5.
46 Letter of Blum to de Gaulle, 15 March 1943.
47 Pierre-Bloch, *Le vent souffle*, 100–1.
48 "Les émigrés," signed by "Un de juin 1940," in *La Marseillaise*, 2 June 1943.
49 Pierre-Bloch, *De Gaulle*, 157.

CHAPTER NINE

1 Pierre Mendès France, "Carnet de notes," in *Œuvres complètes*, I, 699.
2 Mendès France, "Lettre ouverte à mes amis," 13 April 1932, ibid., 177.
3 Mendès offers a full account of his experiences in the first two years of the war in *The Pursuit of Freedom*, which was then translated as *Liberté, liberté chérie* by the same publisher. Mendès contributed minor revisions to this French version when it was republished by Fayard in 1977. The citations below are taken from the 1984 edition of the *Œuvres completes*.
4 Mendès, *Liberté*, I, 365.
5 Ibid., 421.
6 Lacouture, *De Gaulle*, I, 548–9.
7 Mendès, *Liberté*, I, 363.
8 Mendès, "Carnet de notes," in *Œuvres*, I, 611–753.
9 Ibid., 688.
10 Ibid., 693.
11 Ibid., 730.
12 Ibid., 660.
13 V. Pierre-Bloch, *Le vent souffle sur l'histoire*, 84.
14 "Carnet de notes," I, 700.
15 Ibid., 704.

16 *Le Monde*, 12 November 1970.
17 "Carnet de Notes," I, 729.
18 Ibid., 730.
19 Ibid., 739.
20 Ibid., 615–16.
21 Ibid., 687.

CHAPTER TEN

1 The biographical details which follow are taken from Closon, *Le temps des passions. De Jean Moulin à la libération, 1943–1944.*
2 Closon, *La politique financière du président Roosevelt* .
3 When, a few weeks later, Closon was invited to dinner at the Hotel Connaught, the general's wartime residence, and ventured to describe the atmosphere at Carlton Gardens as "sanctimonious (*saint-sulpicienne*)," de Gaulle took no offence, even remarking sympathetically, "Je comprends Closon." *Le temps des passions*, 24.
4 Bédarida, "Un journal de La France libre," 227.
5 *Volontaire pour la cité chrétienne* 2, 15 November 1941.
6 Ibid.
7 *Volontaire* 2, 15 November 1941.
8 *Volontaire* 8, 20 May 1942.
9 Maurice Schumann to Père Chaillet, *Témoignage chrétien* 16, 16 September 1944.
10 *Volontaire* 8, 20 May 1942.
11 *Volontaire* 10, 25 July 1942.
12 Ibid.
13 *Volontaire* 7, 20 April 1942.
14 *Volontaire* 11, 4 September 1942.
15 *Volontaire* 17, 29 March 1943.
16 *Volontaire* 3, 25 December 1941.
17 *Volontaire* 9, 24 June 1942.
18 *Volontaire* 11, 4 September 1942.
19 *Volontaire* 12, 30 September 1942.
20 Ibid.
21 Ibid.
22 *Volontaire* 15, 20 January 1943.
23 *Volontaire* 16, 24 February 1943.
24 *Le temps des passions*, 30
25 Alain Clinton, *Jean Moulin, 1899–1943. The French Resistance and the Republic* summarizes the work of earlier scholars. An exhaustive examination of Moulin's

life and career is offered by his wartime secretary Daniel Cordier in *Jean Moulin. L'Inconnu du Panthéon.* Other scholarly studies include: Bédarida and Azéma, *Jean Moulin et le Conseil national de la Résistance.* and Michel, *Jean Moulin. L'unificateur.*

26 In September 1926, Moulin married Marguerite Cerruti, a devout Catholic, in a religious ceremony. Their separation soon followed.

27 Clinton, *Jean Moulin,* 100.

28 As a prefect, Moulin occupied a higher rung in the public service than de Gaulle, who had been named *général de régiment à titre temporaire* in the spring of 1940.

29 Cordier, *Jean Moulin,* I, 56.

30 Emmanuel d'Astier de la Vigerie, Henri Frenay, and Jean-Pierre Lévy represented, respectively, Libération, Combat, and Franc-Tireur.

31 Ibid., 275. By implication and clearly without irony, Cordier is thus bestowing regal status on de Gaulle!

32 Bidault, *Resistance. The Political Biography of Georges Bidault,* is a bitter personal memoir of Bidault's collaboration with de Gaulle in 1943–44, followed by a justification of his break with the general over the issue of Algerian independence in 1962. More detached analyses of Bidault's role can be found in Dalloz, *Georges Bidault: Biographie politique*; Demory, *Georges Bidault, 1899–1983*; and Ott, *Georges Bidault, l'indomptable.*

33 Bidault, *Resistance,* 13.

34 Ibid, 22.

35 Lacouture, *De Gaulle,* I, 721.

36 Dalloz, *Georges Bidault,* 70.

37 Ibid., 71.

38 Bidault, *Resistance,* 37

39 Closon, *Le temps des passions,* 60.

40 In the course of this second mission, Closon dispatched four major reports as well as a number of personal memos to Philip. All four reports (10 September 1943; 10 October 1943; 11 November 1943; and 1 April 1944) are to be found in manuscript form at the Institut pour l'Histoire du Temps présent (IHTP), Fonds Closon, Vol. I.

41 "Rapport #4 de Fouché, 1 avril 1944," Fonds Closon, I; *Le temps des passions,* 155.

42 Letter of Closon to Philip, 6 October 1943, Fonds Closon, I.

43 Crémieux-Brilhac, *La France libre,* 748.

44 Note, Paris, 5 December 1943, Fonds Closon I, CDD/EP.

45 Liste d'évêques non-résistants, Fonds Closon, I.

46 Jules-Géraud Saliège, archevêque de Toulouse, "Lettre pastorale. Mandement pour le Carême de l'an de grâce 1944," Fonds Closon, I.

47 Closon, "Les catholiques et notre temps," ibid.

48 Closon, "Réflexions sur la constitution future de la France." ibid.

CHAPTER ELEVEN

1 An extensive literature has been devoted to the life and career of Simone Weil. The most comprehensive of these studies is by Weil's close friend Simone Pétrement who manages to provide her readers with a mix of compassionate sympathy and critical analysis; much of the biographical material in this chapter is taken from Pétrement's *Vie de Simone Weil.* Coles, *Simone Weil. A Modern Pilgrimage*, combines deep spiritual sympathy for Weil with total repugnance for her anti-Judaism. Philippe Dujardin, *Simone Weil. Idéologie et politique*, examines with high disdain Weil's ideological drift from far left to seeming sympathy for Pétain's "Moral Order." Hellman, *Simone Weil*, provides a succinct synthesis of Weil's central ideas. Saint-Sernin, *L'action politique selon Simone Weil*, offers a sympathetic study of Weil's efforts to link her empathy with the suffering masses to a critical analysis of the forces which led to such suffering in the first place. Thomas, *Simone Weil et Edith Stein. Malheur et sacrifice*, compares the parallel but in the end very different ways in which the German-Jewish woman who became a Carmelite nun ended up at Auschwitz while the Franco-Jewish woman who lived as a vicarious Catholic and strove to sacrifice herself in a noble cause died pointlessly in what the English press concluded was a suicide.

2 At one point, Weil wrote, "The Hebrews took as their idol, not something made of metal or wood, but a race, a nation, something just as earthly. Their religion is essentially inseparable from idolatry, because of the notion of the 'chosen people.'" Weil here seems to have succumbed to the early second-century heresy propagated by the philosopher Marcion who saw the wrathful Yahveh as spiritually inferior to the merciful God revealed in Jesus.

3 In the course of these services at Solesmes, Weil felt Christ's Passion enter her head and lodge there forever. Earlier experiences had already moved Weil toward the Church. In 1935, while witnessing a procession of Portuguese fishermen bearing the image of their patron saint, she felt the spiritual power faith transmitted to the poor and humble. In 1937, during a visit to Assisi, she felt impelled by a kind of rapture to kneel and pray.

4 V. Schumann, *La mort née de leur propre vie. Trois essais sur Péguy, Simone Weil, Gandhi*, 73.

5 Weil preferred the term *déracinement* ("uprooting") to express what is conventionally called alienation in English.

6 Cited in Pétrement, *Simone Weil*, II, 290.

7 Robert Coles, a clinical psychologist as well as writer of biographies, discussed Weil's attitude toward her Jewish heritage with Freud's daughter Anna before finishing his study. His own conclusion was that Weil's feelings were not unlike those he had encountered while talking to southern blacks about their racial

background. In any event, his verdict concerning Weil's anti-Judaism is categorical: "Her thrusts against Jewry demean her and have made many of us who admire her cringe." Coles, *Simone Weil*, 57.

8 The first of these schemes, a "Projet d'une formation d'infirmières de première ligne," submitted to Roosevelt in 1942, then to Philip when Weil arrived in London, was relayed to de Gaulle who exclaimed, "C'est de la folie!" and made clear he had no desire to meet its author. Cabaud, *Simone Weil à New York et à Londres*, 53. Weil may well have been inspired to hatch her improbable plan by reading in Tacitus about the custom among primitive German tribes of placing a young maiden surrounded by warriors in the line of combat. Coles, *Simone Weil*, 33.

9 V. Pétrement, *Simone Weil*, II, 438.

10 Weil, *L'enracinement. Prélude à une déclaration des devoirs envers l'être humain.*

11 Ibid., 83.

12 Ibid., 106.

13 Ibid., 116.

14 Ibid., 61.

15 Ibid., 87.

16 "By overpraising the courage and boldness required for a nine-month stint in a factory or a few weeks' stay with the International Brigades, one fails to analyze the real significance of those experiences while obscuring the radically reactionary contents of Weil's final writing." Dujardin, *Simone Weil. Idéologie et politique*, 185.

17 Weil, "Note sur la suppression générale des partis politiques," in *Écrits de Londres et dernières lettres*, 126–48.

18 Born in 1903, Brosselette had grown up in the wealthy 16th arrondissement of Paris. A devoted follower of Léon Blum, he had become a member of the editorial board of the socialist newspaper *Le Populaire*. Outraged at the Munich settlement and even more scandalized by the acceptance of defeat by Pétain, he had organized a clandestine meeting place where the Protestants André Philip, Jean Cavaillès, and Louis Vallon, among others, foregathered in the bookshop he owned on the rue de la Pompe. For a full account of Brossolette's career, see Piketty, *Pierre Brossolette. Un héros de la Résistance.*

19 This hostile reaction is reflected in Soustelle, *Envers et contre tout*, I, 312.

20 *La Marseillaise*, 27 September 1942. In a January 1943 article in the same paper, responding to charges that he was intent on establishing a single-party system under de Gaulle, Brosselette modified his view but still argued against the artificial revival of moribund parties left over from the Third Republic. "If there are parties that are now dead, let them not be reawakened," he wrote. "If there are others on their deathbeds, let us not give them oxygen! If they do reconstitute

themselves, let them be rational and fraternal organizations, less like battle-formations than like strong currents in the midst of a vast movement of national revival."

21 La France libre became la France combattante ("Fighting France") on 14 July 1942.

22 De Gaulle, *Discours et messages*, I, 233–40.

23 Weil, "Réflexions sur la révolte," in *Écrits de Londres*, 109–25.

24 Cabaud, *Simone Weil*, 53.

25 Weil, "Légitimité du gouvernement provisoire," in *Écrits de Londres*, 58–73.

26 Ibid., 73.

27 Félix Gouin, "Nouveau projet de constitution," in Michel and Mirkine-Guetzévitch, *Les idées politiques et sociales de la Résistance*, 299–301.

28 Weil, "Remarque sur le nouveau projet de constitution," in *Écrits de Londres*, 84–97.

29 Weil, "Déclaration des obligations envers l'être humain," ibid., 74–84.

30 Weil, "Cette guerre est une guerre de religions," ibid., 105.

31 V. Pétrement, *Vie de Simone Weil*, 477.

32 *Table ronde* 46 (October 1951), 9–25.

33 Not too long after returning to France, the Protestant academic turned resistance hero was arrested by the Gestapo in August 1943. He was shot by the Germans in January 1944.

34 Robert Coles, again after discussing Weil's situation at this last stage with Anna Freud, concludes that she was neither anorexic nor suicidal but that she refused food out of an "embittered helplessness" at being unable to help the cause. At age five, Coles points out, Weil had refused to take sugar because it was not part of the French soldiers' rations. *Simone Weil*, 33

35 "Elle est morte croyante et non chrétienne." V. Cabaud, *Simone Weil*, 76.

36 Cited in Pétrement, *Simone Weil*, 49.

37 Ibid., 500.

38 Crémieux-Brilhac, *La France libre*, 615, n.4.3.

CHAPTER TWELVE

1 Following France's collapse and the creation of the État français, Pastor Marc Boegner felt duty-bound to stay with his flock. Quite apart from this decision, the leading figure in French Protestantism felt a general affection for Pétain, who was aided by a number of political and military advisors of Reformed background, most notably Admiral Platon. The new regime's expressed desire to launch a "National Revolution" based on "Travail, Famille et Patrie" seemed attractive to some conventional Calvinists. Like the majority of their fellow-citizens, many Protestants became *pétainistes* at least in the passive sense; a few

were members of the monarchist Sully Association, the Protestant complement to Maurras's *Action française;* others were drawn to the conservative policies of Vichy out of reaction against what they saw as the abandonment of the sober view of human nature presented by Calvin in favour of the liberal illusions favoured by a number of Protestant politicians and intellectuals. By contrast, the Protestant rebels against Vichy who drew up the *Thèses de Pomeyrol* in September 1941 took their inspiration from radical sixteenth-century critics of ecclesiastical and political tyranny.

2 Details about the wartime career of André Philip are largely drawn from Loïc Philip, *André Philip* and *André Philip par lui-même ou Les voies de la liberté,* and Poujol, "André Philip. Les années de guerre, 1939–1945."

3 Letter of Philip to a friend, 13 July 1920, cited in *André Philip par lui-même,* 8–9.

4 Philip, "Réponse à Jean-Paul Sartre," *Le Nouvel Observateur,* 17 July 1965.

5 "André Sidobre" (Maurice Schumann), "André Philip – l'envoyé de La France combattante du dedans," *Volontaire pour la cité chrétienne* 11, 4 September 1942.

6 Journal officiel de la République française. Débats parlementaires. Chambre des Députés, 12 June 1936.

7 Philip's concern for bettering working-class life was matched by a campaign in print and on the floor of the Chamber of Deputies for the nationalization of France's banking system and the democratization of credit. Like his fellow socialists, the Protestant deputy had to settle for a modification of the statutes of the Bank of France. V. Philip, *La toute-puissance bancaire et la nationalisation du crédit.*

8 *Les parlementaires du Rhône. À Vichy 10 juillet 1940. Manifeste des 8 Résistants* (Librairies-Imprimeries Réunies, 1944), 7–8.

9 Dewavrin ("Passy"), *Souvenirs,* 231.

10 Pineau, *Histoire vécue de la Résistance,* I, 12

11 Ibid., 130.

12 Ibid., 159

13 Ibid., 184.

14 Closon, *Le temps des passions,* 30

15 Jean Fleury, "Louis Vallon, mon ami," *Espoir* 39 (June 1982), 7. This entire issue of *Espoir* is devoted to Vallon.

16 This reflection anticipates the thesis set forth by the Catholic Alain Peyrefitte in *Le mal français,* esp. chapters 11 and 18, in which Protestant economies are seen to be based on trust and Catholic cultures on mistrust.

17 Cited in Fleury, "Louis Vallon," 12.

18 Bouchinet-Serreulles, *Nous étions faits pour être libres,* 213.

19 Poujol, "André Philip," 196.

20 Letter of Pierre Brossolette to André Philip, London, 30 May 1942, cited in Dewavrin, *Souvenirs,* 219–28.

21 Crémieux-Brilhac, *Les voix de la liberté*, III, 176.
22 Poujol, "André Philip," 199–200.
23 V. Chap. 13, 424–31. (*page subject to change)
24 Christol, "Quelques souvenirs de guerre, 1939–1946," 132–47.
25 Poujol, "André Philip," 206.
26 "Un syndicaliste chrétien. L'apport ouvrier dans la lutte libératrice," 18, 29 April 1943.
27 Crémieux-Brilhac, *Les voix de la liberté*, III, 121.
28 Ibid., 132.

CHAPTER THIRTEEN

1 For a thorough discussion of de Gaulle's wartime relations with the British, v. Kersaudy, *De Gaulle et Churchill. La mésentente cordiale.* A concise survey of the same theme is offered in Martin Thomas, "Le Royaume-Uni et La France libre," *Relations internationales* 108 (Winter 2001), 575–93.
2 Aglion, *De Gaulle et Roosevelt.* La France libre *aux États-Unis*, offers a Gaullist perspective on *Le Connétable*'s unhappy efforts to achieve an understanding with the American president. A more recent scholarly overview is offered in Charles Cogan, "Les États-Unis et la France combattante: des relations instables et souvent conflictuelles," *Relations internationales* 108 (Winter 2001), 595–612.
3 François Broche, *L'épopée de La France libre, 1940–1946*, 58.
4 Soustelle, *Envers et contre tout*, I, 203–4, describes the conditions under which the improvised equivalent of the Quai d'Orsay had to function at Carlton Gardens.
5 Bouchinet-Serreulles, *Nous étions faits pour être libres*, 154.
6 De Gaulle, *Mémoires de guerre*, I, 193.
7 Broche, *L'épopée*, 192. For a discussion of Soviet policy toward Fighting France during the later stages of war, v. M. Narinsky, "Moscou et le Gouvernement provisoire du général de Gaulle," *Relations internationales* 108 (Winter 2001), 561–73.
8 Direct Lend-Lease assistance to Free France would be accorded in 1942.
9 Aglion, *De Gaulle et Roosevelt*, 43.
10 De Gaulle, *Mémoires de guerre*, I, 482.
11 Aglion, *De Gaulle et Roosevelt*, 67–8.
12 Jean-Paul Cointet, "Les relations entre de Gaulle et le problème mondiale," *Revue historique* 268 (1982), 436.
13 Bouchinet-Serreulles, *Nous étions faits pour être libres*, 176.
14 Brossolette, *Souvenirs*, II, 129.
15 Aglion, *De Gaulle et Roosevelt*, 158.

16 Letter of General de Gaulle to President Roosevelt, 26 October 1942, *Espoir* 119 (June 1999), 57–60.

17 Aglion, *De Gaulle et Roosevelt,* 161–2.

18 What follows is a composite record of the Roosevelt-Philip exchange based on a series of sources, including Raoul Aglion and Philip himself as he recounted the story of his conversation with the president to Crémieux-Brilhac.

19 Aglion, *De Gaulle et Roosevelt,* 167.

20 Soustelle, *Envers et contre tout,* II, 32.

21 Ibid., 61.

22 Ibid., 33.

23 Ibid., 169. Bouchinet-Serreulles relays to the reader the following cruel assessment of Dejean he gave to de Gaulle in September 1941:

> He is like a cook who has been in the habit of preparing decent meals in his kitchen and has as a result sometimes been invited to sit at the dining room table where he is so lost that his head spins. But quite apart from this, the man is unstable. He imagines himself to be a diplomat because he has spent a few years in an embassy; but a true diplomat is presumed to possess some sang-froid and to be able to negotiate, qualities Dejean lacks. Clearly, he should not be entrusted with a key post.

24 Much of what follows concerning Massigli's wartime career in London and Algiers comes from René Massigli, *Une comédie des erreurs, 1943–1956. Souvenirs et réflexions sur une étape de la construction européenne,* 1–59. The title itself reveals the diplomat's ultimately non-Gaullist perspective.

25 Ibid., 16.

26 Bouchinet-Serreulles, *Nous étions tous faits pour être libres,* 269.

27 Ibid., 19.

28 "Instructions à la presse et à la BBC en cas de rupture avec le général de Gaulle."

29 Soustelle, *Envers et contre tout,* II, 186.

30 Ibid., 184.

31 Massigli, *Une comédie des erreurs,* 31–3.

32 Kersaudy, *De Gaulle et Churchill,* 275.

33 Massigli, *Une comédie des erreurs,* 20.

34 The reorganization of Fighting France's foreign affairs department in Algiers is analyzed in depth in Raphaële Ulrich-Pier, "René Massigli et la réorganisation des Affaires étrangères à Londres et à Alger (1943–1944)," *Relations internationales* 108 (Winter 2001), 471–85.

35 Massigli, *Une comédie des erreurs,* 35.

36 Chief among the issues that Massigli was anxious to raise were the recognition in advance of the CFLN as sole civilian authority in territory liberated from Vichy and the Nazis, the Committee's right to issue francs in such territory, and the

right to have separate Fighting French units take part in the Allied invasion of the Continent.

37 Pierre Viénot to René Massigli, 29 September 1943, Archives du ministère des Affaires étrangères. Guerre 1939–1945. Alger CFLN-GPRF, #1455, fol. 84.

38 Massigli, *Une comédie des erreurs*, 37–42.

39 Roussel, *Charles de Gaulle*, 391–2.

40 The legitimization of the CFLN brought Stalin to shift course and invite de Gaulle to Moscow, where the general signed a treaty of alliance and mutual aid with the Soviet Union on 10 December 1944. Although, on the surface, this pact constituted a diplomatic coup for de Gaulle, Moscow continued to prioritize its alliance with the English-speaking powers and to expand its control in eastern Europe, an area of traditional French influence, and did its best to prevent France from joining a west European anti-Soviet bloc. The Yalta conference of February 1945 (from which Stalin agreed France should be excluded) confirmed Moscow's decision not to give special weight to relations with de Gaulle. As Bogomolov noted in a 12 March 1945 memo to Molotov, "The Yalta conference finally convinced de Gaulle of the unwillingness of the USSR either to pull France's German chestnuts out of the fire or to seek out quarrels with the Allies on her account." For a close scrutiny of Soviet relations with Fighting France toward the end of the war, v. M. Narinsky, "Moscou et le Governement provisoire du général de Gaulle," *Relations internationales* 108, 561–73.

41 This documentation included an analysis of the Arab reaction to the growth of Zionism; a study of the radical differences between archaic Arab societies such as Yemen and more evolved cultures such as Syria; an examination of the efforts to create a pan-Arab federation; a critical analysis of British and American attempts to establish hegemonic influence in the area; and a study of the encouragement given to Arab independence movements by Roosevelt's special envoy in the eastern Mediterranean, General Hurley. V. "Politique extérieure du CNF. Questions arabes 1939–1945." Archives du ministère des Affaires étrangères, II A2, AIC, Londres CNF.

42 Viénot to Massigli, 16 November 1943, Archives du ministère des Affaires étrangères. Guerre 1939–1945. Alger. CFLN-GPRF, #1455, fol. 97.

43 Memo of General Catroux to de Gaulle, 22 November 1943, cited by Crémieux-Brilhac, *La France libre*, 658.

44 Record of interview at 3 PM on 4 April 1944 between the Prime Minister and Mr. Ambassador Viénot at 10 Downing Street (in English), Archives du ministère des Affaires étrangères, Guerre 1939–1945. Alger CFLN-GPRF, #1455, fol. 180.

45 Martin Thomas, "Le Royaume-Uni et La France libre," *Relations internationales* 108 (Winter 2001), 593.

CHAPTER FOURTEEN

1 Atkinson, *An Army at Dawn: The War in North Africa, 1942–1943*, examines Operation "Torch" as a testing-time for the untried US Army in World War II.

2 Among the most prominent of these were the poet Saint John Perse and the journalists Henri de Kérillis and Geneviève Tabouis.

3 American policy in North Africa in 1940–42 is closely examined in Pierre-Gosset, *Expédients provisoires*. The best and most up-to-date history of French North Africa during the war is Levisse-Touzé, *L'Afrique du Nord dans la guerre, 1939–1945*. Rondeau and Stéphane, *Des hommes libres*. La France libre *par ceux qui l'ont faite*, 289–379, offers a detailed recapitulation of the 8 November 1942 plot by many of those involved in it. The most complete study in English is Amipaz-Silber, *The Role of the Jewish Underground in the American Landings in Algiers, 1940–1942*. For a comprehensive and authoritative history of French Algeria in the modern era, see Ageron, *Histoire de l'Algérie contemporaine*.

4 Colonel Jousse offers a first-hand account of the collaboration between the Americans and anti-Vichy French officers during these months in ACDJC 84, 70, "Mémoire du colonel Jousse."

5 Precise figures about the size of Algeria's Jewish population in 1940 vary. Amipaz-Silber (30) offers the figure 130,000, but quotes the American Jewish Distribution Committee which helped wartime Jews in distress as estimating the total to be about 125,000, while also quoting the British historian Martin Gilbert as putting the number at 117,000.

6 V. Amipaz-Silber, 16–19 for a description of Jewish-Muslim relations in the interwar years.

7 Ibid., 30.

8 Steinberg, *La révolte des Justes. Les Juifs contre Hitler, 1933–1945*, 232–3.

9 Among the many first-hand accounts of Jewish resistance to the anti-Semitism of Vichy and the new Algerian administration, one of the earliest is Marcel Aboulker, *Alger et ses complots*.

10 Jean Daniel, *Le temps qui reste*, 27.

11 ACDJC 84, 69, "Témoignage du professeur Henri Aboulker sur les événements du 8 novembre 1942."

12 Décout-Paolini, "René Capitant, homme de gauche et gaulliste. Un juriste sous la Ve République, 1958–1970."

13 Joxe, *Victoires sur la nuit, 1940–1946*, 34.

14 Ibid., 35.

15 A decade later, during the Algerian war, when Boumenjel "committed suicide" following his arrest under suspicious circumstances, Capitant resigned from the Paris Law Faculty in protest.

16 Joxe, *Victoires sur la nuit, 1940–1946*, 18.
17 Ibid., 65.
18 José Aboulker gave a full account of the conspiracy to de Gaulle in London, in June 1943. This account was reproduced in the August 1943 issue of *Les cahiers français*, published in London. The general was so impressed by Aboulker's story that he sent the young conspirator on a medical mission to the internal resistance. Aboulker went on a second mission in July 1944, this time to help prepare the way for the arrival of Gaullist *commissaires de la République* from Algiers and to assist in overseeing the military activity of the Forces françaises de l'intérieur in and around Paris.
19 The short-term success of the conspirators' coup in Algiers was not matched in Oran, where an overwhelmingly Jewish band of insurgents led by Roger Carcassonne had been waiting to act. Colonel Toustain of the regular French army, who was in on the plot, had ill-advisedly informed one of his superiors who had him arrested. Some of those involved in the plan did, however, manage to act as guides for an American commando unit in what turned into a bloody three-day battle. In Morocco, meanwhile, a similar lack of coordination meant that the resistance played an insignificant role in the liberation of the western part of the Maghreb.
20 Soustelle, *Envers et contre tout*, II, 426.
21 The comte de Paris had enlisted in the foreign legion in 1939, then, following France's collapse in 1940, had moved to Spanish Morocco. Following Operation "Torch," he traveled to Algiers at the invitation of conservative groups who saw him as a replacement for the fascistic Darlan who might reconcile *gaullistes* and *pétainistes* and promote the restoration of the Third Republic.
22 Levisse-Touzé, *L'Afrique du Nord*, 277.
23 Pierre-Gosset, *Expédients provisoires*, 427.
24 Lacouture, *De Gaulle*, I, 607–8. During this conversation, de Gaulle noted that he had just received a letter of support from Georges Mandel, then under house arrest inside Vichy France. Churchill, always an admirer of Mandel, asked the general if he would consider offering the former Jewish interior minister a post in any future provisional government in North Africa, to which he received a rapid and very positive response.
25 De Gaulle, *Mémoires de guerre*, cited by Lacouture, 609.
26 The fullest account of this dinner party and the political repression which followed it is given in the testimony offered by Dr. Henri Aboulker, ACDJC 84, 69.
27 Cited in Julien, *L'Afrique du Nord en marche*, 238–9.
28 V. Lacouture, *De Gaulle*, I, 652.
29 V. *Unity in Dispersion*, 214–16.

30 Cassin, Note documentaire sur le décret Crémieux, n.d., AN 382 AP60.
31 Cassin, Note pour le général de Gaulle, 20 mars 1943, AN 382 AP71.
32 André Philip, "Rapport du commissaire à l'intérieur André Philip sur la caducité de l'ordonnance Giraud du 14 mars 1943," cited in Agi, *René Cassin*, 172.
33 Letter of de Gaulle to Dr. Wise, 27 September 1943.
34 Letter of Sergeant Zaquer to Cassin, 4 February 1944, AN 382 AP60.
35 AN 382 AP71.
36 The account of African Muslim soldiers in the French army is taken from Recham, *Les musulmans algériens dans l'armée française*.
37 Ibid., 179.
38 Cited in Ageron, *Histoire de l'Algérie contemporaine*, 89.
39 Recham, *Les musulmans*, 278.
40 Ferhat Abbas, *Message aux autorités responsables, 20 décembre 1942*, in Ageron, *Histoire*, 90.
41 Ferhat Abbas, "Le manifeste du peuple algérien" in Jauffret, *La guerre d'Algérie par les documents*, 38.
42 Cited in Guy Pervillé, "La commission des réformes musulmanes de 1944," *Les chemins de la décolonisation de l'empire colonial français*, 361.
43 By an ordonnance of 7 March 1944, the CFLN proclaimed the equality of all Algerians in terms of rights and obligations and sanctioned the access to citizenship of some sixteen categories of Muslims, essentially those who had received a certain degree of education or who occupied certain posts. This selective group (about 65,000) would henceforth join the European minority in elections for a single Algerian assembly. The ordonnance further decreed that all Algeria's Muslims might in time acquire French citizenship, subject to provisions, which a future constitutional assembly would establish. At the same time, the 7 March decree precluded the Muslim majority from gaining representation by population in the national parliament in Paris on the ground that, given the demographic explosion under way in Algeria, the territory's Muslims would have a disproportionate say in French political debates, a decision which deeply troubled Catroux. Ibid., 363.

CHAPTER FIFTEEN

1 De Gaulle, *Mémoires de guerre*, II, 432.
2 Giraud, *Un seul but: la victoire*, 98.
3 The "Testament" exposes and condemns what *Le Connétable* saw as a concerted plot by the Americans to use Giraud as a foil to establish their dominance in French North Africa before pursuing the same end in France itself. De Gaulle

urged Tochon to make sure that the letter reached René Capitant so that his own efforts to defend France's sovereignty, even if in the end fruitless, would be made known.

4 Lacouture, *De Gaulle*, I, 669.

5 AN 72 AJ/1923, Memorandum of Soustelle to CNF, early February 1943.

6 Memorandum of Soustelle to de Gaulle, 17 February, 1943, ibid.

7 Monnet, *Mémoires*, 229.

8 Mayer, *Études, témoignages, documents*, ed. Denise Mayer, 1–120, offers a full account of Mayer's career up to the end of World War II.

9 Letter of Philip to de Gaulle, 27 June 1943, carbon copy given the author by Olivier Philip.

10 Soustelle, *Envers et contre tout*, II, 269.

11 Lacouture, *De Gaulle*, I, 677.

12 Queuille, *Journal de guerre*, 132.

13 D'Astier, *Sept fois sept jours*, 60.

14 Ibid., 100.

15 D'Astier, *Les dieux et les hommes*, 6.

16 Although d'Astier pursued his lobbying with Churchill in London later in the month, he made no further headway. The prime minister insisted that bombing missions in aid of Tito in Yugoslavia had a higher priority in Allied plans. AN 72 AJ/1903. Dossier Churchill.

17 Soustelle, *Envers et contre tout*, II, 184–5.

18 Soustelle, *Vingt-huit ans de gaullisme*, 24.

19 D'Astier, *Les dieux*, II, 184–5.

20 Letter of René Mayer to Emmanuel d'Astier, Algiers, 26 April 1944, cited in ibid., 115.

21 The presence on the CFLN as of 4 April 1944 of the Communist Fernand Grenier as *commissaire à l'Air*, and of his comrade François Billoux as *commissaire d'État*, no doubt strengthened the minority on the Committee eager to come to the aid of the Resistance. However, by the time of their appointment, the partisan units d'Astier had been anxious to help had already been vanquished.

CHAPTER SIXTEEN

1 The extraordinary adventures of Raymond and Lucie Aubrac in the Resistance, when they joined Cavaillès and Emmanuel d'Astier in Libération-Sud and slowly overcame their diffidence about accepting de Gaulle's leadership; Raymond's arrest at the secret meeting in Lyon on 21 June 1943 called by Jean Moulin to plan the future of underground operations following the arrest of General

Delestraint in Paris; his subsequent escape, thanks again to his inventive and courageous wife, form an epic tale and have been the inspiration for a film, *Lucie Aubrac.* (1997), directed by Claude Berri.

2 René Cerf-Ferrière, *L'assemblée consultative provisoire vue de mon banc, novembre 1943–juillet 1944* (Les Éditeurs français réunis, 1974), 265.

3 Supplément au Journal officiel de la République française. Débuts de l'assemblée consultative provisoire. Séance du 11 Novembre 1943.

4 Cerf-Ferrière, *L'assemblée,* 55.

5 As a devotee of Christian socialism, Philip also urged a vigorous campaign against alcoholism, which he saw to be a moral scourge as well as an economic problem. Ironically, his wartime Jewish colleague Pierre Mendès France, as prime minister in the mid-1950s, campaigned against the excessive consumption of alcohol and in favour of the drinking of milk (although, as wags would have it, this may well have had less to do with puritanical enthusiasm than with the interests of dairy farmers in his electoral district!).

6 Ibid., 118.

7 Ibid., 240.

8 Raymond Aubrac, *Où la mémoire s'attarde,* 120.

9 Cerf-Ferrière, *L'assemblée,* 116.

10 AN 71/AJ 63, Réformes de l'enseignement. Commission Capitant.

11 Poujol, "André Philip. Les années de guerre, 1939–1945," 240.

12 Cassin's first preoccupation in this new function, as we have noted, was to work toward the full restoration of the Crémieux decree and thus to restore their full citizenship to some 140,000 Algerian Jews.

13 Philip protested on the eve of Pucheu's arrest that the ex-*pétainiste* had escaped to North Africa with a safe-conduct from Giraud and that, since the general had been a member of the CFLN, the man he had protected should be exempt from prosecution, ibid., 227.

14 The Assembly's concern about the meting out of justice to collaborators apprehended in North Africa was paralleled by the interest shown by René Cassin and the Comité juridique in the punishment of war crimes. Cassin directed his colleagues' attention to the need to punish French citizens who had violated the Republican creed which guaranteed equal justice to all or who had subverted France's national integrity. Although French law did not normally accept the principle of retroactive application of justice, the Comité juridique sanctioned in advance a verdict of *indignité nationale* against persons found guilty of such violations following the Armistice. The punishment in question could involve the loss of civil rights or a substantial increase in income tax levy, a far less severe punishment, Cassin remarked, than the death penalty, which might well be thought of as appropriate in such cases.

15 AN 72/AJ535. Letter of Félix Eboué to Pleven, 30 May 1943.

16 R. Aubrac, *Où la mémoire s'attarde*, 118.

17 Letter of André Philip to de Gaulle, 7 March 1944, carbon copy given the author by Olivier Philip.

18 The feeling of spiritual letdown reported by Philip was shared as soon as she arrived in Algiers by Elisabeth de Miribel, who had spent many months propagating the Free French gospel in North America. Writing to her Canadian journalist friend Gladys Arnold, Mlle de Miribel describes the unexpected "shock" and "despair" she felt during her first few weeks in the North African city, where Vichy appointees were more often than not still in power, doing their best to subvert de Gaulle, confident in the backing they had in Washington, which persisted in seeing them as representing France's true interests. Politicians and office-seekers in Algiers, whatever their ideology, all seemed intent on the pursuit of power and privilege. Gone was the heroic, selfless atmosphere she and her colleagues had known in London. Arnold, *One Woman's War*, 147.

CHAPTER SEVENTEEN

1 Laroque, *Au service de l'homme et du droit.*

2 Ibid., 181.

3 Viénot's story is told by his brother in André Viénot, *Pierre Viénot 1897–1944, sous-secrétaire d'État aux Affaires étrangères, ambassadeur à Londres du comité d'Alger.*

4 Ibid., 12.

5 Viénot had brought with him to London a letter from Édouard Herriot, the veteran Radical politician who had been president of the Chamber of Deputies before the war. In this note, Herriot expressed his willingness to join a government led by Charles de Gaulle, whom he described as "the only man able to bring about the union of the vast majority of the French in the restoration of France." Viénot transmitted the letter to the American ambassador in London, John Winant. Like earlier such missives, it would do nothing to modify Roosevelt's antipathy to de Gaulle. Cited in Crémieux-Brilhac, *La France libre*, 473.

6 De Gaulle, *Mémoires de guerre*. I. *L'Unité*, 488.

7 Viénot recounted the events of the night of 5–6 June 1944 to his secretary Miriam Cendrars, daughter of the poet Blaise Cendrars. His own textual notes of that night's discussions were bequeathed to his widow. After André Gillois, the historian of Free France, convinced her that he had essentially the same story from British sources, Mme Viénot had the notes published in the 6 July 1957 issue of *Le Monde*.

8 André Viénot, *Pierre Viénot*, 37.

9 V. Crémieux-Brilhac, *La France libre*, 841 and n.1.

10 Coulet, *Vertu des temps difficiles*, 235.

11 Ibid., 250.

12 The Interior Commissioner's reflections on his visit to Normandy are summed up in d'Astier, *Les dieux et les hommes*, 86–91.

13 Aubrac's account of his role as *commissaire* is included in his autobiography *Où la mémoire s'attarde*, 124–63.

14 Ibid., 146.

15 De Gaulle, *Mémoires de guerre*. I. *L'unité*, 551–84, offers the general's own version of his triumphal entry into Paris in August 1944.

16 Ibid., 569.

17 Ibid., 570.

18 Rémond, *Notre siècle, 1918–1988*, 344.

19 De Gaulle, *Mémoires de guerre*, 576.

20 Jean Lacouture uses the words *le sacre* to describe de Gaulle's reception in Paris in his *De Gaulle*, I, chap. 40; J.-L. Crémieux-Brilhac in *La France libre*, 903, follows suit.

21 A conservative intellectual, Bérard had been education minister in the early 1920s and a senator in the 1930s.

22 Michel Brisacier, "De Gaulle et les Églises," *Espoir* 103 (July 1995), 51–2. Brisacier notes that, rather naively, Latreille hoped that the successful handling of his mandate might have prepared the way for the negotiation of a new concordat between Paris and the Vatican, which would settle all outstanding issues between them (the school question, Catholic missionary activity, and left-over property issues from the Separation laws). As Brisacier has pointed out, Latreille, who had been among those anxious to have Valeri recalled, should have realized that any further concessions from Pius XII were bound to be problematic.

23 De Gaulle, *Mémoires de guerre*, 609.

24 Francis-Louis Closon gives a detailed account of his experiences as commissioner in *Commissaire de la République du général de Gaulle*.

25 Ibid., 113.

26 Ibid., 155.

EPILOGUE

1 Running into him after mass during the days which followed the liberation of Paris, the Christian Democrat Charles d'Aragon shared with Georges Bidault his reflections about the prospects for the newly formed MRP in France's first post-war election. Bidault was confident that the party would win a minimum of 100 seats, signing himself with feigned solemnity and murmuring, "In the name of the Father, Son, and Holy Spirit." Cited in Dalloz, *Georges Bidault*, 83–4.

2 By 1951, de Gaulle's initial enthusiasm for the MRP had given way to disillusionment, even contempt. The proper role of the Mouvement, he confided to Pierre-Henri Teitgen, should have been to act as "a large and intelligent conservative party" which would face and then defeat the anti-statism of the left. Instead, the MRP had participated "in a corrupt parliamentary system in which the national will was being subverted." Cited in Lacouture, *De Gaulle*, II, 208–9.

3 Twelve years later, when the constitution of the Fifth Republic was ratified, the same clause was included in the text, together with an addendum proposed by the Catholic Pierre Pflimlin to the effect that "Elle [la République] respecte toutes les croyances."

The path toward acceptance of the cardinal principle of republicanism had been made easier because of a ruling arrived at during a meeting of France's cardinals and archbishops in the fall of 1945. In a 13 November Declaration which signified a major strategic reorientation, the Catholic hierarchy defined for the faithful the forms of *laïcité* which were or were not acceptable. A militant secularizing policy, *laïcité de combat*, which was posited on a materialist or atheist view of human nature, was clearly anathema, as was any refusal by the State to acknowledge a higher power than itself and leave only raw self-interest as a moral compass. On the other hand, the upper clergy noted, a *laïcité* which simply affirmed the sovereign authority of the State in the temporal arena while guaranteeing freedom of conscience in a multi-confessional society (*laïcité de tolérance)* posed no threat to Catholic consciences.

4 A comprehensive study of the UDSR is offered in Eric Duhamel, "L'Union Démocratique et Socialiste de la Résistance, 1945–1965," a doctoral thesis supervised by J-M Mayeur and successfully defended at the Sorbonne in 1993. The manuscript is deposited at the FNSP in Paris.

5 The title of Jacques Baumel's account of his role in the wartime underground against fascism – *Résister. Histoire secrète des années d'Occupation* – is clearly inspired by the mythic memory of the heroic resistance of Marie Durand, a Protestant made prisoner in the medieval Tour de Constance for worshipping publicly in the proscribed Reformed faith following the Revocation of the Edict of Nantes. Durand inscribed the single word *Résister* on the fortress wall to signal her determination to reject conversion to Catholicism in exchange for her freedom.

6 Born in 1901, Malraux was a banker's son who developed an interest in Oriental art early in life and, in the 1920s, committed himself to the Communist camp in the Chinese Civil War, then served as an air squadron commander on the Republican side during the Spanish Civil War. Mobilized in 1939, Malraux was captured, then escaped to join the internal resistance and to share in the liberation of Alsace. After the war, he joined the UDSR. De Gaulle made him minister of information in November 1945. His philosophical outlook was atheist.

7 De Gaulle had hoped that the Catholic René Pleven would join the new organization. Pleven's refusal was something the general never forgave.

8 Guy made notes of his private conversations with de Gaulle during the years 1946–49, when *Le Connétable* made clear the utter contempt in which he held most politicians of the Fourth Republic. The general considered only three of them (René Mayer, René Pleven, and Jacques Soustelle) worthy of holding cabinet positions. Guy, *En écoutant de Gaulle.*

9 Lefrance, *25 ans avec le général de Gaulle.*

10 Debû-Bridel, *Les partis contre de Gaulle.*

11 Boegner served the Quai d'Orsay in a number of capacities before being named technical advisor to Prime Minister de Gaulle in 1958, and retained the same post when the general became president of the Republic the following January. Later, he again served in various diplomatic roles before acting as special counselor to Prime Minister Jacques Chirac in 1986. François Coulet was put in charge of the European desk at the Quai d'Orsay in 1946, then acted as ambassador in a number of countries, interrupting his career to serve as a paratroop commander in the Algerian war. Pierre Denis took up a number of diplomatic appointments in Latin America after the war. Maurice Couve de Murville pursued his diplomatic career until he was summoned by de Gaulle in 1958 to become foreign minister, a post he held for a decade before de Gaulle named him prime minister.

12 Other Catholic veterans of Free France avoided committing themselves to partisan politics. Claude Bouchinet-Serreulles was a member of France's delegation to the founding meeting of the United Nations in San Francisco and later acted as secretary-general of the European committee administering the Marshall Plan. Geoffroy de Courcel served with distinction as ambassador to Britain. Louis Closon was director-general of the Institut national de la statistique et des études économiques between 1946 and 1961 while maintaining a number of business interests. Among the more fascinating post-war careers of Free France veterans is that of Elisabeth de Miribel. After serving as part of de Gaulle's immediate staff when the general was president of the Provisional Government, Mlle de Miribel joined the Carmelite Order in 1949. When ill-health forced her to give up her religious vocation, she joined the diplomatic staff of the Mendès France government in 1954, then completed a number of missions in France's diplomatic service, acting as advisor to her friend Alexandre Parodi when he was named ambassador to newly independent Morocco in 1957.

13 Raymond Aron, *Le spectateur engagé*, 167–71. Aron broke definitively with de Gaulle in 1967 following the Six Day War between Israel and the Arab states when the general, during a 28 November 1967 press conference, characterized

Jews as "this elitist people, sure of itself and tending to dominate." V. Aron, *De Gaulle, Israël et les Juifs.*

14 Like other Jewish members of the Radical party who had joined La France libre, Pierre Mendès France returned to the fold after the war. Chosen premier in 1954, he brought into his administration two close associates from his days in wartime London – Georges Boris and Jean-Louis Crémieux-Brilhac. Mendès managed in his short term of office to negotiate peace in Indo-China and to prepare the way toward independence for Morocco and Tunisia. René Mayer, who represented the conservative wing of the Radical party, was elected deputy for Constantine in Algeria and lobbied on behalf of the settler community. In 1953, he served briefly as French premier.

René Cassin, whose ideological sympathies lay with the Radical party, became honorary president of the Conseil d'État after the war. He also presided over the newly created École nationale d'administration, represented France at the United Nations and in UNESCO, became a member of the Conseil constitutionnel in 1960 and helped draft the UN Declaration of Human Rights. He was awarded the Nobel Peace Prize in 1968.

15 Although the triumph of the left in the 1981 election resulted in a proposal three years later to restore state control of all primary schools, the public protest was such that the bill was withdrawn and the compromise still stands.

16 In *Le changement de régime*, Capitant describes the changes in labour-management he proposes as a *révolution*, the completion of work begun in 1789, through a total transformation of France's socio-economic order.

17 When a referendum asking public support for the implementation of *participation* in its political form through the devolution of substantial power to the regions was defeated in 1969, de Gaulle saw the result as a disavowal of his overall leadership and almost immediately resigned. Pierre Lefranc, "Le geste de 1962," *Espoir* 39 (June 1982), 37–8, goes so far as to suggest that, had the basic changes proposed by *gaullistes de gauche* been implemented, the student and working-class revolt of 1968 might never have occurred.

18 A good account of Mitterrand's life and political career up to 1981 is offered in Denis MacShane, *François Mitterrand – A Political Odyssey.*

Péan, *Une jeunesse française. François Mitterrand 1934–1947* is a remarkably detailed study of Mitterrand's spiritual and political evolution from his student days in Paris to his full commitment to the leadership of the UDRS in 1947. Péan not only consulted all the available primary sources but interviewed his subject on several occasions. He concludes that the right-wing involvement with student protests against a leftist Jewish professor while he was a student; the support of Mussolini in Ethiopia; the contact he made with the comte de Paris; and the open contempt he felt for the Third Republic stem largely from his Catholic and conservative upbringing. Péan adds that, while Mitterrand was clearly devoted to Pétain, he never became an anti-Semite and never collaborated with the Germans. His defining moment, as Péan sees it, was the sense of innate leadership ability he felt while living among a socially heterogeneous group of fellow prisoners of war in Germany. His active participation in the Resistance began in the late spring of 1943 and helped condition Mitterrand to assume the presidency of the UDSR after the war.

19 Mitterrand's father, Joseph, a native of Cognac, was president of the Vinegar-Makers of France, served as a stretcher-bearer at Lourdes, and was prominent in the St. Vincent-de-Paul Society; his mother, Yvonne, was known for her piety; his uncle was active in Sangnier's Sillon.

20 In fact, when, during this meeting, Mitterrand boasted of his work on behalf of war prisoners, the general, who took an instant and durable dislike to his visitor, suggested that the organization of France's hairdressers might be of equal interest to the cause! Not surprisingly, Mitterrand was deeply wounded by this sarcasm.

21 While it is difficult to quantify the impact of the Church's embrace of theological tolerance and political pluralism, it is worth noting that, in the 1973 legislative elections, only 17 per cent of Catholics backed candidates of the left while in the presidential election of 1994, Mitterrand attracted some 24 per cent of the votes of Catholics who defined themselves as *pratiquants*.

22 V. Szafran, *Les juifs dans la politique française*, 293–307 for an analysis of Fabius's career.

23 According to rumour, Fabius has dreamed of becoming president of France since childhood. Whatever truth there may be in this rumour, Fabius's close friends know that he is haunted by what he has heard of Léon Blum's ordeal in the face of race-baiting reactionaries during the Popular Front; and the putative candidate for the highest office is intimately aware of the torments endured by Mendès France in the face of the same xenophobic opposition during his term as premier in 1954–55.

24 V. Delors, *L'Unité d'un homme*, for a study of the career of Delors.

25 A welcome development in this respect, as far as Delors was concerned, was the de-confessionalization of the CFTC and its transformation in November 1974 into the Confédération française des travailleurs démocratiques (CFTD).

26 There were exceptions: Delors respected Mendès France; he supported the presidential campaign of the Protestant mayor of Marseille, Gaston Defferre, in 1965; and he advised the Gaullist minister Jacques Chaban-Delmas four years later.

27 In the French Catholic community in general, substantial parts of which had been complicit in the anti-Semitic activities of the Vichy regime, many were no

doubt brought to abandon their anti-Jewish prejudice as a result of the reflections on the Jewish question issuing from Vatican II. Influenced in part by the lobbying of the French Jewish scholar Jules Isaac, the Council affirmed the Jewish origins of Christianity, denounced anti-Semitism in all its forms, and condemned as aberrational the Church's earlier allegations that the Jews had been responsible for the Crucifixion and that their subsequent Diaspora was God's punishment for a crime for which all humanity must share responsibility.

28 As head of state, Mitterrand paid another visit to the Jewish state, bringing with him two prominent Jews – the leftist politician Jean Poperen, and the film maker Claude Lanzmann, director of *Shoah*, a movie devoted to the Holocaust, accompanying both men to Yad Vashem, the museum which focuses on the same genocidal tragedy.

29 V. Szafran, *Les Juifs*, 164–233.

30 Lang was born in September 1939 in the Vosges department and educated at the Lycée Henri-Poincaré in Nancy before studying law at the University of Paris. He began his career as theatre director at the University of Nancy before taking over the direction of the Palais de Chaillot Theatre in Paris. He was thus a logical (and, as it turned out, highly successful) choice as minister of culture throughout the decade following the victory of the left. Strauss-Kahn, born in 1949 in the Paris suburb of Neuilly, studied at lycées in Monaco and Paris before completing university degrees in commerce, law, and politics. His career included teaching at the University of Nancy and serving as a high-level national research adviser. In 1981, he was a professor at the Nanterre campus of the University of Paris. A year later, he was chosen to head the Commissariat du Plan.

31 Leclerc and Muracciole, *Lionel Jospin. L'héritier rebelle*, 22. His friend and fellow Protestant Claude Allègre, whom Jospin as premier would select to be education minister, is convinced that Jospin's Protestant education "with all that that connotates in terms of rigour, personal autonomy, free will and even rebelliousness," played a decisive role in the Socialist politician's development. *L'Express*, 7 March 2002.

32 While Joxe's father was Catholic, his mother, Françoise-Hélène Halévy, was Jewish in background. Joxe *fils* was a graduate of the Lycée Henri-IV, the Paris law faculty and the École nationale d'administration. After serving as counselor to the Cour des Comptes, he joined the executive committee of the PS in 1971 and was made minister of industry and administration in 1981.

33 Jospin would be elected in 1984 and 1988 to the European Parliament and serve as France's minister of education, youth and sports (1988–91) before becoming prime minister between 1997 and 2002, when he ran unsuccessfully for the presidency against Jacques Chirac.

34 V. Rocard, *Le cœur à l'ouvrage*, for Rocard's reflections on his political career.

35 At primary school in Nîmes, he was discouraged by his teachers from mixing with Catholic children (much as Mitterrand was urged against associating with the few Protestants in his town).

36 A good account of Defferre's career is given in Marion, *Gaston Defferre*.

37 One of his first public acts was to join the Socialist president in attending memorial services for the Jews murdered during a terrorist attack on the Goldenberg restaurant in Paris in August 1982.

38 Among other Protestants occupying key ministries during the decade were Georgina Dufoix, Catherine Lalumière, Louis Mexandeau, and Nicole Questiaux. Louis Mermaz presided over the National Assembly for part of this period.

39 In 1976, half a decade before the formation of the Mauroy government which included so many of their number, the Catholic Robert Beauvais in *Nous sommes tous des protestants* (Plon, 1976) assailed the Protestants for trying to establish "a subtle hegemonic power which is far from proportionate to their demographic importance." This would-be update of a polemical assault, which pre-dated Bossuet and had found its most effective twentieth-century champion in Maurras, amounted to several rounds of indiscriminate buckshot. Beauvais identified as targets the banker William Baumgartner, the conservative politician Couve de Murville and his radical counterparts Louis Vallon and Jacques Soustelle, the film personalities Delphine Seyrig and Jean-Luc Godard, the homosexual André Gide, and the political scientist François Goguel, all part of a "plot" to subvert France's basic values and institutions.

That same year, as though in response, the Catholic (and Gaullist) Alain Peyrefitte produced *Le Mal français* (Plon), a large part of which was devoted to a condemnation of Louis XIV for having tried to rid France of the Huguenot minority which, like its counterparts elsewhere in the world, was (in the author's view) largely responsible for developing the values of self-reliance, self-discipline, entrepreneurship, civic spirit, religious tolerance, and political democracy which it had taken far longer for France to adopt.

The debate over the creative or subversive role of the Protestants in modern France continued into the 1980s. Responding to a rhetorical question posed on the front page of the 26 November 1987 issue of the weekly *L'Événement* ("La France conquise par les Protestants?"), Alain Duhamel suggested that the roughly 900,000 member Protestant minority (out of 55 million) had in fact to a large extent "protestantized" France. Recent evidence, he argued, could be found in the legalization of abortion, divorce, and contraception, and in the provocative presence of female pastors. Would Protestants now simply disappear, Duhamel asked, half in jest, because, through their triumphant influence, they had lost their own raison d'être? The Protestant sociologist and historian Jean Baubérot took up this issue in *Le protestantisme doit-il mourir?*, suggesting that their very success in transforming French society might imply that the historic mission of the Reformed was finished. Baubérot's answer to this dilemma was to urge his fellow-believers to revive their essential spiritual and moral integrity and to avoid the trap of theological and cultural dissipation introduced by Vatican II and other phases of the ecumenical movement.

Bibliography

Unless otherwise indicated, all sources listed below were published in Paris.

PRIMARY SOURCES

Archives

ARCHIVES NATIONALES, PARIS

72 AJ/567 Papiers André Philip

72 AJ/1923 Papiers Jacques Soustelle

72 AJ/1901–1903 Dossiers Boris/d'Astier

363 AP Fonds René Mayer

382 AP Fonds René Cassin

ARCHIVES DU MINISTÈRE DES AFFAIRES ÉTRANGÈRES

Guerre 1939–1945: Londres, Alger

Dossiers Massigli

BIBLIOTHÈQUE NATIONALE: PÉRIODIQUES

Espoir

La Marseillaise

Volontaire pour la cité chrétienne

BIBLIOTHÈQUE DE LA SOCIÉTÉ DE L'HISTOIRE DU PROTESTANTISME FRANÇAIS

Papiers Pastor Frank Christol

FONDATION NATIONALE DES SCIENCES POLITIQUES

Décout-Paolini, R. "René Capitant, homme de gauche et gaulliste. Un juriste sous la Ve République, 1958–1970." Typescript *mémoire de maîtrise*, University of Paris I (Sorbonne), 1994.

Duhamel, Eric. "L'Union Démocratique et Socialiste de la Résistance, 1945–1965." Thèse de doctorat directed by J.-M. Mayeur, University of Paris I (Sorbonne), 1993.

Philippe, R. "André Diethelm: un itinéraire politique." *Mémoire de maîtrise.* University of Paris X (Nanterre), 1999.

Toinet, M.-F. "Georges Boris 1888–1960, un socialiste humaniste." Thèse de doctorat directed by René Rémond. University of Paris I (Sorbonne), 1969.

Actors or Witnesses

Aboulker, José, "La part de la Résistance française dans les événements d'Afrique du Nord." London: Les cahiers français, August 1943.

Aboulker, Marcel, *Alger et ses complots.* Fournier: Les Documents Nuit et Jour, 1945.

Aglion, Raoul, *De Gaulle et Roosevelt. La France Libre aux États Unis.* Plon, 1984.

Arnold, Gladys. *One Woman's War. A Canadian Reporter with the Free French.* Toronto: James Lorimer, 1987.

Aron, Raymond. *Mémoires. 50 ans de réflexions politiques.* Julliard, 1983.

– *Le spectateur engagé. Entretien avec Jean-Louis Missika et Dominique Wolton.* Juillard, 1981.

Astier de la Vigerie, Emmanuel d'. *Les Dieux et les Hommes 1943–1944.* Julliard, 1952.

– *Sept fois sept jours.* Éditions de Minuit, 1947.

Aubrac, Lucie. *Ils partirent dans l'ivresse.* Éditions du Seuil, 1984.

Aubrac, Raymond. *Où la mémoire s'attarde.* Odile Jacob, 1996.

Baumel, Jacques. *Résister. Histoire secrète des années d'Occupation.* Albin Michel, 1999.

Bidault, G. *Resistance. The Political Biography of Georges Bidault.* Translated by M. Sinclair. New York and Washington: F.A. Praeger, 1967.

Boegner, M. *L'exigence œcuménique. Souvenirs perspectives.* Albin Michel, 1968.

Boris, Georges. *Servir la République.* Julliard, 1963.

Bouchinet-Serreulles, Claude. *Nous étions faits pour être libres.* Grasset, 2002.

Bourdan, Pierre. *Carnets des jours d'attente.* Pierre Trémois 1945.

Bret, Paul-Louis. *Au feu des événements. Mémoires d'un journaliste. Londres-Alger, 1929–1944.* Plon, 1959.

Brilhac, Jean-Louis. *Retour par l'Urss.* Calmann-Lévy, 1945.

Capitant, René. *Le changement de régime.* Imprimerie générale du RPF, 1952.

Cassin, René. *Les hommes partis de rien. Le réveil de la France abattue, 1940–1941.* Plon, 1975.

– *La pensée et l'action.* Éditions Lalou, 1972.

Catroux, General Georges. *Dans la bataille de la Méditerranée.* Julliard, 1949.

Cerf-Ferrières. *L'assemblée consultative vue de mon banc, novembre 1943–juillet 1944.* Les Editeurs français réunis, 1974.

Chamson, André. *Le chiffre de nos jours.* Gallimard, 1954.

Christol, Frank. "Quelques souvenirs de guerre, 1939–1946." *Bulletin de la Société de l'Histoire du Protestantisme français* (BSHPF) (1977): 132–47.

Closon, Francis-Louis. *Commissaire de la République du général de Gaulle. Lille, septembre 1944–mars 1946.* Julliard, 1980.

– *Le Temps des passions. De Jean Moulin à la Libération.* Presses de la Cité, 1974.

– *La politique française du président Roosevelt.* Paris, 1937.

Cooper, Duff. *Old Men Forget.* London: Rupert Hart-Davis, 1953.

Coulet, François. *Vertu des temps difficiles.* Plon, 1967.

Crémieux-Brilhac, Jean-Louis, ed. *Ici Londres … Les voix de la Liberté, 1940–1944.* 5 vols. La Documentation française et Club français des bibliophiles, 1975–77.

– *Souvenirs de la France libre.* Berger-Levrault, 1947.

Daniel, Jean. *Le temps qui reste. Essai d'autobiographie professionnelle.* Stock, 1973.

Debû-Bridel, Jacques. *Les partis contre de Gaulle.* Aiméry-Somogy, 1948.

de Gaulle, Charles. *Mémoires.* Edited by M.-F. Guyard. Gallimard, 2000.

– *Lettres, notes et carnets.* Vols. III–V. Plon, 1981–84.

– *Discours et messages.* Vol. I. *Pendant la guerre, juin 1940–janvier 1946.* Plon, 1970.

– *La France et son armée.* Plon, 1938.

De Gaulle en son siècle. Actes du colloque de Paris, 1990. 6 vols. Plon et La Documentation française, 1990–92.

De Gaulle, Ph. *Mémoires accessoires, 1921–1946.* Plon, 1997.

Delors, Jacques. *L'Unité d'un homme. Entretiens avec Dominique Wolton.* Odile Jacob, 1994.

Denis, Pierre ("Rauzan"). *Les métiers et les jours.* Juillard, 1951.

Dewavrin, André: see Passy.

Eden, Anthony. *The Reckoning.* London: Cassell, 1965

Giraud, General Henri. *Un seul but: la victoire.* Julliard, 1949.

Guy, Claude. *En écoutant de Gaulle, Journal 1946–1949.* Grasset, 1996.

Hettier de Boislambert, Claude. *Les Feux de l'espoir.* Plon, 1978.

Jacob, François. *La Statue intérieure.* Odile Jacob, 1987.

Jousse, Germain. "Mémoire du colonel Jousse sur la Résistance et le Débarquement en Afrique du Nord." L'Archives du centre de documentation juive contemporaine. (ACDJC) 84, p. 70.

Joxe, Louis. *Victoire sur la nuit.* Flammarion, 1981.

Lapie, Pierre-Olivier. *Les Déserts de l'action.* Flammarion, 1946.

Laroque, Pierre. *Au service de l'homme et du droit. Souvenirs et réflexions.* Association pour l'étude de l'histoire de la Sécurité sociale, 1993.

Lefranc, Pierre. *Avec De Gaulle. 25 ans avec le général De Gaulle*. Plon, 1979.

Marin, Jean. *Petit bois pour un grand feu: la naissance de la France libre*. Fayard, 1994.

Massigli, René. *Une comédie des erreurs, 1943–1956. Souvenirs et réflexions sur une étape de la construction européenne*. Plon, 1978.

Mayer, René. *Études, témoignages, documentation*. Edited by Denise Mayer. Presses universitaires de France, 1983.

Mendès France, Pierre. *La vérité guidait leurs pas*. Gallimard, 1976.

– ed. *Georges Boris. Servir la République. Textes et témoignages*. René Juillard, 1963.

– *Liberté, liberté chérie* New York: Éditions Didier, 1943.

Miribel, Elisabeth de. *La liberté souffre violence*. Plon, 1981.

Monnet, Jean. *Mémoires*. Fayard, 1976.

Palewski, Gaston. *Mémoires d'action, 1924–1974*. Plon, 1988.

Passy, Colonel (André Dewavrin). *Souvenirs*, 2 vols. Monte-Carlo: Raoul Solar, 1947–48.

Philip, André. *La toute-puissance bancaire et la nationalisation du crédit*. Éditions SFIO, 1936.

Philip, Loïc. *André Philip par lui-même ou Les voies de la liberté*. Aubier-Montaigne, 1971.

Pierre-Bloch, Jean. *Londres, capitale de la France libre*. Carrère/Michel Lafon, 1986.

– *Le temps d'y penser encore*. Jean-Claude Simoën, 1977.

– *De Gaulle ou le temps des méprises*. La Table ronde, 1969.

– *Le vent souffle sur l'histoire. Témoignages et documents inédits*. Éditions SIPEP, 1956.

Pierre-Brossolette, Gilberte. *Il s'appelait Pierre Brossolette*. Albin-Michel, 1976.

Pineau, Christian. *Histoire vécue de la Résistance*. Vol. 1, *La Simple vérité 1940–1945*. Geneva: Éditions de Crémille, 1972.

Postel-Vinay, André. *Un fou s'évade. Souvenir de 1941–1942*. Éditions du Félin, 1997.

Queuille, Henri. *Journal de guerre. Londres-Alger, avril 1943–juillet 1944*. Plon/Fondation Charles de Gaulle 1995.

Rocard, Michel. *Le cœur à l'ouvrage*. Odile Jacob, 1987.

Rondeau, Daniel et Roger Stéphane. *Des hommes libres. La France libre par ceux qui l'ont faite*. Grasset, 1997.

Schumann, Maurice. *Bergson ou le retour de Dieu*. Flammarion, 1999.

– *La mort née de leur propre vie. Trois essais sur Péguy, Simone Weil, Gandhi*. Fayard, 1994.

– *La Voix du couvre-feu. Cent allocutions 1940–1944*. Plon, 1969.

– *Honneur et Patrie*. Éditions du livre, 1946.

Seydoux, François. *Mémoires d'outre-Rhin*. Bernard Grasset, 1975.

Soustelle, Jacques. *Vingt-huit ans de gaullisme*. La Table ronde, 1968.

– *Envers et contre tout*. 2 vols. Laffont, 1947–50.

– *Mexique terre indienne*. Grasset, 1935.

Weil, Simone. *Ecrits de Londres et dernières lettres*. Gallimard, 1957.

– *L'enracinement. Prélude à une déclaration des devoirs envers l'être humain.* Gallimard, 1949.

Weil-Curiel, André. *Le temps de la honte.* 2 vols. Éditions du Myrte, 1945–46.

SECONDARY SOURCES

Adler, J. *The Jews of Paris and the Final Solution. Communal Responses and Internal Conflicts, 1940–1944.* New York and Oxford: Oxford University Press, 1985.

Ageron, Charles. *Histoire de l'Algérie contemporaine. De l'insurrection de 1871 au déclenchement de la guerre de libération, 1954.* Presses universitaires de France, 1979.

Agi, M. *René Cassin, fantassin des Droits de l'Homme.* Plon, 1979.

Amipaz-Silber, G. *The Role of the Jewish Underground in the American Landings in Algiers, 1940–1942.* Jerusalem and New York: Gefar Books, 1992.

Amouroux, H. *Quarante millions de pétainistes.* Robert Laffont, 1988.

Anderson, Malcolm. *Conservative Politics in France.* London: George Allen and Unwin, 1974.

Anon. *Unity in Dispersion. A History of the World Jewish Congres.* New York: World Jewish Congres, 1948.

Aron, R. *De Gaulle, Israël et les Juifs.* Plon, 1968.

Atkinson, R. *An Army at Dawn: The War in North America 1942–1943.* New York: Henry Holt, 2002.

Azéma, J.-P. and Fr. Bédarida. *La France des années noires.* 2 vols. Seuil, 1993.

Barré, J.-L. *Devenir de Gaulle, 1939–1943.* Perrin, 2003.

Barrès, Maurice. *Les Diverses Familles spirituelles de la France.* In *Œuvres de Maurice Barrès,* Philippe Barrès, ed. Plon, Club de l'homme, 1966.

Baubérot, J. *Vers un nouveau pacte laïque?* Seuil, 1990.

– *Le protestantisme doit-il mourir?* Seuil, 1988.

– *Le Retour des Huguenots. La vitalité protestante, XIXe–XXe siècle.* Paris and Geneva: Labor et Fides and Cerf, 1985.

Beau de Lomenie, E. *Les responsabilités des dynasties bourgeoises.* 4 vols. Denoël, 1943–63.

Bédarida, Fr. and J.P. Azéma, eds. *Jean Moulin et le Conseil national de la Résistance. Étude et témoignages.* CNRS, 1983.

Bédarida, Renée. *Les armes de l'Esprit. Témoignage chrétienne 1941–1944.* Les éditions ouvrières, 1977.

– "Un journal de La France libre: 'Volontaire pour la cité chrétienne.'" *Revue historique* 268 (1968).

Bild, J. *L'abbé Grégoire.* Nouvelles éditions latines, 1946.

Birnbaum, B. *Un mythe politique: la "République juive."* Fayard, 1988.

Blatt, J., ed., *The French Defeat of 1940. Reassessments.* Providence, RI: Berghahn Books, 1998.

Blumenkranz, B., ed. *Histoire des juifs en France.* Toulouse 1972.

Bougeard, C. *René Pleven. Un Français libre en politique.* Rennes: Presses universitaires de Rennes, 1994.

Boulard, F. *Premiers itinéraires en sociologie religieuse.* Les éditions ouvrières, 1966.

Bredin, J.-D. *L'Affaire.* Juillard, 1983.

Broche, Fr. *L'épopée de la France Libre, 1940–1946.* Pygmalion, 2002.

Byrnes, R.F. *Anti-Semitism in Modem France.* Vol. I: *The Prologue to the Dreyfus Affair.* New Brunswick, NJ: Rutgers University Press, 1950.

Cabanel, P. *Les Protestants et la République de 1870 à nos jours.* Éditions Complexes, 2000.

Cabaud, J. *Simone Weil à New York et à Londres: les quinze derniers mois (1942–1943).* Plon, 1967.

Chadwick, K., ed. *Catholicism, Politics and Society in Twentieth-Century France.* Liverpool University Press, 2000.

Chastenet, J. *Histoire de la Troisième République.* 7 vols. Hachette, 1952–63.

Cholvy, G. et Y.-M. Hilaire. *Histoire religieuse de la France contemporaine.* 3 vols. Privat, 1985–88.

Christophe, P. *1939–1940. Les Catholiques devant la guerre.* Éditions ouvrières, 1989.

– *Les catholiques et le Front populaire.* Éditions ouvrières, 1986.

– *Les choix du clergé dans les révolutions de 1789, 1830 et 1830.* 2 vols. Lille: chez l'auteur, 1975–76.

Clinton, Alain. *Jean Moulin, 1899–1943. The French Resistance and the Republic.* New York: Palgrave, 2002.

Cointet, M. et J.-P. *La France à Londres, 1940–1943.* Complexe, 1990.

Coles, Robert. *Simone Weil. A Modern Pilgrimage.* Reading, MA: Addison-Wesley, 1987.

Cordier, D. *Jean Moulin. L'inconnu du Panthéon.* 3 vols. J.-C. Lattès, 1989.

Crémieux-Brilhac, Jean-Louis. *La France Libre. De l'Appel du 18 juin à la Libération.* Gallimard, 1996.

– *Les Français de l'an 40.* 2 vols. Gallimard, 1990.

Crespin, R. *Des protestants engagés. Le christianisme social 1945–1970.* Genève et Paris: Les Bergers et les Mages, 1992.

Dalloz, J. *Georges Bidault. Biographie politique.* L'Harmattan, 1992.

Davie, G. "Right-wing Politics among French Protestants (1900–1944), with Special Reference to the Association Sully." PhD diss., University of London, 1975.

Delbeil, J.-C., ed. *Marc Sangnier, Témoignages.* Beauchesne, 1997.

Delpha, F. *L'appel du 18 juin 1940.* Grasset et Fasquelle, 2000.

De Montclos, X. *Le Toast d'Alger. Documents 1890–1891.* Éditions Broccard, 1966.

Demory, J.-C. *Georges Bidault, 1899–1983.* Juillard, 1995.

Dujardin, Philippe. *Simone Weil. Idéologie et politique.* Grenoble: Presses universitaires de Grenoble, 1975.

Duroselle, J.-B. *L'abîme, 1939–1945.* Imprimerie nationale, 1982.

Edelstein, A. *An Unacknowledged Harmony. Philo-Semitism and The Survival of European Jewry.* Westport, CN and London: Greenwood Press, 1982.

Encrevé, A. "Les protestants et la Commune de Paris en 1871." *Christianisme social* (1971): 368–471.

Encrevé, A. and M. Richard, eds. *Les Protestants dans les débuts de la Troisième République, 1871–1885.* Société de l'Histoire du Protestantisme français, 1979.

Fabre, R. *Protestants en France depuis 1789.* Éditions La Découverte, 1999.

Ferrières, G. *Jean Cavaillès. Un philosophe dans la guerre 1903–1944.* Seuil, 1982.

Fouilloux, E. *Les chrétiens français entre crise et Libération.* Seuil, 1997.

– *Les catholiques et l'unité chrétienne du XIXe au XXe siècle.* Centurion, 1992.

La France Libre. Actes du colloque international tenu à l'Assemblée nationale les 15 et 16 juin 2004. Edited by Philippe Oulmont. Panazol: Lavauzelle, 2005.

Galtier, J. *Protestants en révolution.* Labor et Fides, 1989.

Gillois, A. *Histoire secrète des Français libres à Londres de 1940 à 1944.* Hachette, 1972.

Glaudes, P., ed. *Images de la Réforme au XIXe siècle. Actes du colloque de Clermont-Ferrand, 9–10 novembre 1990.* Diffusion des Belles Lettres, 1992.

Guidoni, P. and R. Verdier. *Les socialistes en Résistance (1940–1944).* Seli Anslam, 1999.

Halls, W.D. *Politics, Society and Christianity in Vichy France.* Oxford and Providence, RI: Berg, 1995.

Hause, Steven C. "Anti-Protestant Rhetoric in the Early Third Republic." *French Historical Studies* 6, no. 1 (Spring 1989): 183–201.

Hellman, J. *The Knight-Monks of Vichy France. Uriage, 1940–1945.* Montreal and Kingston: McGill-Queen's University Press, 1993.

– *Emmanuel Mounier and the New Catholic Left 1930–1950.* Toronto: University of Toronto Press, 1981.

– *Simone Weil. An Introduction to Her Thought.* Philadelphia: Fortress, 1984.

Hyman, L. *From Dreyfus to Vichy. The Remaking of French Jewry, 1909–1939.* New York: Columbia University Press, 1979.

Irvine, W.D. *French conservatism in crisis: the Republican Federation in France in the 1930s.* Baton Rouge: Louisiana State University Press, 1979.

Isaac, J. *Genèse de l'antisémitisme. Essai historique.* Calmann-Lévy, 1956.

Jackson, J. *France: The Dark Years, 1940–1944.* Oxford: Oxford University Press, 2001.

Jauffret, Jean-Charles, ed. *La guerre d'Algérie par les documents.* Vincennes: Société de l'histoire de l'armée de terre (SHAT), 1990.

Jeanneney, J.-N. *Georges Mandel. L'homme qu'on attendait.* Seuil, 1991.

Joutard, Ph., ed. *Historiographie de la Réforme.* Paris, 1977.

Julien, C.-A. *Histoire de l'Algérie contemporaine.* Presses universitaires de France, 1990.

– *L'Afrique du Nord en marche. Nationalisme musulman et souveraineté française.* Juillard, 1972.

Kedward, H.R. *Resistance in Vichy France.* Oxford: Oxford University Press, 1978. 2001.

Kersaudy, Fr. *De Gaulle et Churchill. La mésentente cordiale.* Perrin, 2001.

Lacouture, Jean. "De Gaulle entre Dieu et César." *Notre Histoire. La mémoire de l'humanité* 71 (October 1990): 13–16.

– *De Gaulle.* 3 vols. Seuil, 1984–86.

– *Léon Blum.* Seuil, 1977.

Larcan, A. *Charles de Gaulle. Itinéraires intellectuels et spirituels.* Nancy: Presses universitaires de Nancy, 1993.

Larkin, M. *Religion, Politics and Preferment in France since 1890. La Belle Époque and its Legacy.* Cambridge: Cambridge University Press, 1995.

Latreille, A. and A. Siegfried. *Les forces religieuses et la vie politique. Le catholicisme et le protestantisme.* Cahiers de la Fondation nationale de sciences politiques 23. Armand Collin, 1951.

Lazare, I. *La résistance juive en France.* Stock, 1987.

Leclerc, G. and F. Muracciole. *Lionel Jospin. L'héritier rebelle.* Jean-Claude Lattès, 1996.

Lecœur, E. *Un néo-populisme à la française. Trente ans de Front national.* La Découverte, 2003.

Le Goff, J. and R. Rémond. *Histoire de la France religieuse.* 4 vols. Seuil, 1991–92.

Lerner, Henri. "Le colonel Mayer et son cercle d'amis." *Revue hisorique* 266 (1981): 75–94.

Lévisse-Touzé, C. *L'Afrique du Nord dans la guerre, 1939–1945.* Albin Michel, 1998.

MacShane, D. *François Mitterrand. A Political Odyssey.* London: Quartet Books, 1982.

Mage, T. *Maurice Couve de Murville-François Mitterrand: de la rupture avec le régime de Vichy à la Résistance et à l'ascension vers les sommets de la V*ième *République.* 2 vols. T. Mage, 1994.

Malion, F. and B. Wasserstein, eds. *The Jews in Modern France.* Hanover, NH: University Press of New England, 1985.

Mandrou, R. et al.. *Histoire des Protestants en France.* Privat, 1977.

Marion, G. *Gaston Defferre.* Albin Michel, 1989.

Marrus, Michael. *The Politics of Assimilation. The French Jewish Community at the Time of the Dreyfus Affair.* Oxford: Clarendon Press, 1971.

Marrus, Michael and R. Paxton. *Vichy et les juifs.* Calmann-Lévy, 1981.

Maudit, A.-M. and J. Maudit. *La France contre la France. La Séparation de l'Église et de l'État, 1902–1906.* Plon, 1984.

Mauriac, Fr. *De Gaulle.* Grasset, 1964.

May, E.R. *Strange Victory, Hitler's Conquest of France.* New York: Hill and Wang, 2000.

Mayer, N. *Ces Français qui votent Le Pen.* Flammarion, 2002.

Méjan, L.V. *La Séparation des Églises et de l'État. L'œuvre de Louis Méjan.* Presses universitaires de France, 1959.

Mellor, A. *Histoire de l'anticléricalisme français.* Henri Veyrier, 1978.

Michel, H. *Histoire de la France Libre.* Presses universitaires de France (Que sais-je?), 1972.

– *Jean Moulin. L'unificateur.* Hachette, 1964.

Michel, H. and Mirkine-Guetzevitch, eds. *Les idées politiques et sociales de la Résistance. Documents clandestins, 1940–1944.* Presses universitaires de France, 1954.

Michelon, J.P. *La République contre les libertés: les restrictions aux libertés publiques de 1879 à 1914.* Presses de la fondation nationale des Sciences publiques, 1976.

Moll, Geneviève. *Yvonne de Gaulle. L'Inattendu.* Éditions Ramsay, 1999.

Murphy, F.J. *Communists and Catholics in France, 1936–1939: The politics of the outstretched hand.* Gainseville: University of Florida Press, 1989.

Muracciole, J.-F. *Histoire de la France Libre.* Presses universitaires de France (Que sais-je?), 1996.

Nicolet, C. *L'idée républicaine en France (1789–1924). Essai d'histoire critique.* Gallimard, 1982.

Ott, B. *Georges Bidault, l'indomptable.* Annonay: Éditions du Vivarais, 1975.

Paxton, R.O. *Vichy France. Old Guard and New Order, 1940–1944.* New York: A.A. Knopf, 1972.

Péan, P. *Une jeunesse française. François Mitterrand, 1934–1947.* Fayard, 1994.

Pervillé, Guy. "La commission des réformes musulmanes de 1944 et l'élaboration d'une nouvelle politique algérienne de la France." In *Les chemins de la décolonisation de l'empire colonial français.* Éditions du CNRS, 1986.

Pétrement, S. *La vie de Simone Weil.* 2 vols. Fayard, 1973 75.

Peyrefritte, Alain. *Le mal français.* Plon, 1976.

Philip, Loïc, ed. *André Philip par lui-même ou Les voies de la liberté.* Aubier Montaigne, 1971.

Philippe, B. *Être juif dans la société française du Moyen Age à nos jours.* Éditions Montalba, 1979.

Pierrard, P. *L'Église et la Révolution, 1789–1889.* Nouvelle cité, 1988.

Juifs et catholiques français. De Drumont à Jules Isaac, 1886–1945. Fayard, 1970

Pierre-Gosset, R. *Expédients provisoires.* Fasquelle, 1945.

Piketty, G. *Pierre Brossolette. Un héros de la Résistance.* Odile Jacob, 1998.

Pilleul, G., ed. *"L'Entourage" et de Gaulle.* Plon, 1979.

Poland, B. *French Protestantism and the French Revolution.* Princeton: NJ: Princeton University Press, 1957.

Poujol, J. "André Philip. Les années de guerre, 1939–1945," *BSHPF* 138 (April–June 1992), 181–241.

– *Les Protestants français pendant la seconde guerre mondiale, en collaboration avec André Encrevé.* Société de l'Histoire du Protestantisme français, 1994.

– *Protestants dans la France en guerre, 1939–1945. Dictionnaire thématique et biographique.* Éditions de Paris, 2000.

Poulat, E. *Liberté, laïcité. La guerre des deux France et le principe de la modernité.* Cerf, 2004.

Recham, B. *Les musulmans algériens dans l'armée française.* L'Harmattan, 1996.

Rémond, René. *Notre siècle, 1918–1988.* Fayard, 1988.

– *Les catholiques dans la France des années 30.* Éditions CANA, 1979.

– *L'anticléricalisme en France de 1815 à nos jours.* Fayard, 1976.

Rimbaud, C. *Maurice Schumann. Sa voix, son visage.* Odile Jacob, 2000.

Robert, D. "Les protestants français et la guerre de 1814–1918." *Francia* 2 (1974): 415–30.

Robert, J.M. "The Origins of a Mythology: Freemasons, Protestants, and the French Revolution." *Bulletin of the Institute of Historical Research* (May 1971): 78–97.

Rondeau, Daniel and Roger Stéphane. *Des hommes libres. La France libre par ceux qui l'ont fait.* Grasset, 1997.

Roussel, E. *Charles de Gaulle.* Gallimard, 2002.

Rousso, H. *The Vichy Syndrome. History and Memory in France since 1944.* Translated by A. Goldhammer. Cambridge, MA, London, UK: Harvard University Press, 1991.

Saint-Sernin, Bertrand. *L'action politique selon Simone Weil.* Cerf, 1988.

Serroy, J. *De Gaulle et les écrivains.* Grenoble: Presses Universitaires de Grenoble, 1991.

Sirinelli, Jean-François. *Intellectuels et passions françaises. Manifestes et pétitions au XXe siècle.* Fayard, 1900.

Steinberg, Lucien. *La révolte des justes. Les Juifs contre Hitler, 1933–1945.* Fayard, 1970.

Sutter, J. *La vie religieuse des Français à travers les sondages d'opinion.* 2 vols. Centre national de recherche scientifique (CNRS), 1984.

Sweets, J.F. *Choices in Vichy France. The French under Nazi Occupation.* New York and Oxford: Oxford University Press, 1986.

Szafran, M. *Les juifs dans la politique française. De 1945 à nos jours.* Flammarion, 1990.

Thomas, Jean-François. *Simone Weil et Edith Stein. Malheur et sacrifice.* Namur: Culture et vérité, 1992.

Viénot, A. *Pierre Viénot 1897–1944, sous-secrétaire d'État aux Affaires étrangères et ambassadeur à Londres du comité d'Alger.* Lahure, 1950.

Weinberg, D. *A Community on Trial. The Jews of Paris in the 1930s.* Chicago: University of Chicago Press, 1977.

Zeldin, T. *France 1845–1945.* 2 vols. Oxford: Clarendon Press, 1977.

Index